Primitive Christianity
In Crisis

The World
of Primitive Christianity

(WPC Series)

WPC Series
(The World of Primitive Christianity)

Volume 1

PRIMITIVE CHRISTIANITY IN CRISIS

Alan Knight

The 'Mystery of Lawlessness' Prophecies, Gnostic Christianity for Our Time

Third Edition, Revised
2006

A.R.K. RESEARCH
ANTIOCH, CALIFORNIA

Published by A.R.K. Research, 1917 Mt. Hamilton Dr.,
Antioch, California 94531
aknight1d@earthlink.net

ISBN 0-9679332-0-X

Printed in the United States of America

CONTENTS

Abbreviations key:

CO   *The Chaldean Oracles of Zoroaster*, edited and revised by Sapere Aude, Edmonds, Wash., Sure Fire Press, 1984.

EB   *Encyclopedia Britannica*, 1966 Edition.

GH   *Gnosis and Hermeticism, From Antiquity to Modern Times*, editors Roelof van den Broek and Wouter J. Hanegraaff. Albany, NY, State University of New York Press, 1998.

KJV   *King James Version* translation of the Bible.

NHLE *The Nag Hammadi Library in English*, general editor James M. Robinson. San Francisco, Harper and Row, 1988.

NIV   *New International Version* translation of the Bible.

NKJV *New King James Version* translation of the Bible.

NRSV *New Revised Standard Version* translation of the Bible.

PSL   *The Pythagorean Sourcebook and Library*, editor David Fideler. Grand Rapids, Phanes Press, 1988.

REB   *Revised English Bible Version* translation of the Bible.

RSV   *Revised Standard Version* translation of the Bible.

INTRODUCTION

Primitive Christianity In Crisis

Why can't Christians just get along? Over the past two thousand years millions of Christians have been slaughtered by supposedly fellow Christians in the name of God. Most Christians today find that embarrassing and shameful, and rightly so. Fueled partly by reaction to this sad history, most Christians now embrace some form of ecumenical tolerance and mutual acceptance.

Today this touches nearly all parts of the Christian world. One of the last holdouts resisting this global change is a comparatively small but stubborn segment of Christianity known as 'Primitive Christianity,' with some 16 million followers worldwide. The name comes from the fact these Christians claim to practice the earliest (primitive) Christianity from the first century A.D. This is sometimes called 'Jewish Christianity' because in that early time Christianity had not yet broken away from its Hebrew roots and continued to observe the seventh-day Sabbath and other Jewish practices.

Now that has begun to change. In the past several decades the trend towards ecumenical unity finally has begun to register significant success within the world of Primitive Christianity.

Many Primitive Christians now argue that the basic teaching of faith and grace alone, the hallmark of Protestantism, is a common bond between all Christians. Therefore Primitive Christians should consider themselves part of Protestantism and accept all Protestants as Christian brothers. Some argue for treating observance of the seventh-day Sabbath as optional. Many encourage ecumenism and joint worship with traditional Protestant believers. This has led to a genuine sense of crisis, causing many to fear the very existence of their religious tradition is at stake.

Not surprisingly there is a conservative faction within Primitive Christianity that vigorously opposes all compromise with mainstream Christianity. They generally rely on the same arguments that have kept Primitive Christianity separate throughout history. This is the belief that Christians must continue to follow what they consider the original revelation of Christianity, the unique Jewish Christianity that characterized the church in the first century A.D., including observance of the seventh-day Sabbath.

All serious scholars accept the fact that Christianity today is substantially changed from what it was in the first century. The question is whether that change is valid. In other words, was it ordained by God? Much heated argument has centered on the simple question of whether the New Testament sanctions on-going theological change after the New Testament itself was completed. Mainstream Christianity, of course, says it does. Primitive Christianity generally denies that is so.

Whom should we believe? It is difficult even to decide how to debate the issue. Many of those who argue for change base their claim on the private inspiration of the Spirit. Since that is both intangible and private, how can it be evaluated? It is one person's word against another. Indeed, is there any concrete basis for deciding who is right?

In fact there is one approach that rises from a genuinely rational and tangible foundation. As we look into the historical sources from the early centuries after Christ, we find a way out of this impasse. If the historical process of change and the groups that promoted it appeared early enough so they are mentioned in the New Testament, then we may have something solid on which to base a conclusion. Did the process of change begin as early as the first century? Does the New Testament mention it? If so, does the New Testament specifically embrace or reject those changes and the groups behind them?

In just recent years much new historical information has become available that has a direct bearing on these questions. We now know there were two major movements that changed Christianity into what it is today. Volume one of our series, *Primitive Christianity in Crisis,* is the story of the first of those two religious movements. Significantly, this first movement did arise in the first century at the same time the New Testament was being written.

Recent research demonstrates that this first religious movement is in fact repeatedly mentioned in the New Testament. Therefore, when we consider the question of whether the evolution of Christianity into its present form is sanctioned by God, we need not argue hypothetically.

The purpose of this volume is to factually review the latest historical evidence in light of Primitive Christianity's traditional rejection of the evolutionary process that produced modern, mainstream Christianity. Is there a valid, substantive basis for adhering to an earlier standard of the Christian faith? Should we reject and keep separate from later forms of Christianity that evolved after the first century? Or are Primitive Christians perpetuating a shameful heritage of intolerance? Is Primitive Christianity's traditional rejection of mainstream Christianity an anachronism, an embarrassment that has outlived its time and should be cast aside? Is Primitive Christianity truly *primitive* in the negative sense of the word, and is it time to join the modern world?

This volume is written both for Primitive Christians, embroiled in spiritual crisis and pondering a proper course for the future, as well as for those among mainstream Christianity who would like to better understand the basis for Primitive Christian beliefs and their radically different worldview.

For those not accustomed to theological terminology, please note the meaning of the word *antinomian.* That term is used liberally throughout this volume. *Antinomian* literally means 'against the law.' Scholars often use this word in a general sense to describe many teachings and doctrines that claim man is liberated from the principle of obedience to biblical law. The reader should note that *immorality* is a completely separate concept. Though immorality sometimes is the result of antinomian beliefs, the term *antinomian* merely signifies the absence of any specific 'obligation' to obey biblical law.

– 1 –

Hellenism

Christianity Then and Now

Religion today is filled with so much controversy and confusion. Wouldn't it be easier to have lived in the first century A.D.? In that time, so-called Primitive Christianity was the only choice. Religious truth, freshly delivered to man, would have been free from the confusion and contention of our day. No arguments about which day of the week to observe. No hassle about what grace really means. No competing groups condemning each other and claiming only they practice genuine Christianity. What an appealing idea! Unfortunately, it also would be completely untrue. Historical research in just recent decades reveals a Christian community, as early as the second half of the first century that was strikingly similar to our world today.

Just decades after the founding of the New Testament church, most of the basic teachings from today's world were present in Christianity in some form. And just as today they fought over it. A diverse array of independent groups competed for leadership of the Christian movement, frequently condemning each other, each claiming to represent the genuine, more spiritual or most advanced form of Christianity. Also not widely known is that the New Testament very openly talks about it.

The Apostle Paul regularly complained about the preaching of new, deviant versions of the gospel, already in the first century (for example Galatians 1:6-9). Are some of those alternate versions of Christianity still being preached today? Is it possible the Christianity you and I practice today is one of those alternate versions condemned in the New Testament?

Recognizing the historical connection between the first century and today presents us with an unusual and unique opportunity. If today we are struggling with many of the same problems and issues that prevailed in the first century, then what the New Testament says about the first century directly applies to our situation today. What would be helpful is to have historical information about the first century that helps illuminate what the New Testament says about these matters.

Supplying that historical background is one of the major functions of this book. Here is one poignant example:

In the first century there was a religious teacher named Nicolas who founded his own independent Christian movement. Its followers were known as Nicolaitans, and they are mentioned in the New Testament in Revelation chapter 2, where they are strongly condemned. The New Testament only says that the Nicolaitans were immoral. By looking at other historical sources, however, we find a much more detailed and fascinating story that clarifies what was involved.

The early church fathers record a strange tale about Nicolas. He is said to have married a young and particularly beautiful wife. Shortly after the founding of the church in the 30s A.D., he called the apostles together, to whom he presented his wife. Before them all, he publicly offered her to anyone who wanted to possess her sexually. What kind of Christian was Nicolas?! How could he even call himself a Christian?

The church fathers, however, also record that Nicolas and his entire family, including his children, led very pure and saintly lives. What was going on? How could a supposedly righteous man do such an apparently evil thing?

Fast-forward nearly 1,500 years to Martin Luther, father of the Protestant Reformation. In the year 1521 Luther wrote a letter in which he advised the reader *"Be a sinner, and let your sins be strong, but let your faith in Christ be stronger.... No sin can separate us from Him, even if we were to kill or commit adultery a thousand times each day."* [1]

---

[1] Martin Luther, Saemmtliche Schriften, Letter number 99, 1 August 1521, translated by Erika Flores in "The Wittenberg Project, The Wartburg Segment", as published in Grace and Knowledge, Issue 8, Sept. 2000, Article "Ecclesiasticus: The Wisdom of Ben-Sirach", page 27.

Luther sounds a little like Nicolas. What were they really talking about? Were they actually, openly advising Christians to practice evil? When we look deeper into the historical sources, we find that neither man actually was suggesting we should sin. As we will see, it was all part of a very sophisticated teaching about a new and more advanced Christian spirituality. And the New Testament repeatedly talks about the appearance of that new teaching in the first century.

The book of Revelation roundly condemned the Nicolaitans. If the New Testament condemned Nicolas and his followers in the first century, might it condemn us too? Should we be concerned about this?

We now begin a journey through a little known and only recently illuminated history of the first years after the founding of Christianity. The religious turmoil of the first century and how it relates to the practice of Christianity in our day, is a story you will find truly amazing.

The Historical Background

Before we get into direct evidence from early Christianity we need to cover additional background. One cannot fully comprehend what was happening in the first-century church without first understanding the cultural and religious environment of the world in which Christianity was born. When the New Testament talks about the "world" or about pagan or popular practices, generally it is talking about 'Hellenistic' culture and 'Hellenistic' religion. This was the dominant cultural tradition throughout the Mediterranean world during the New Testament era.

The term **Hellenistic** technically refers to that period of Greek culture after Alexander the Great defeated the Persians and briefly united the Near East and eastern Mediterranean in a single empire. In their conquests, the Greeks spread a distinctive culture and religion throughout the Near East and Mediterranean, which became known as 'Hellenistic.' Generally this is dated as beginning around the year 332 B.C.

When Alexander the Great died, his conquests quickly broke up into four regional empires. Most of their territory in turn was conquered by Rome, but Hellenistic culture and religion continued seamlessly through the rise of Roman power into the first century A.D., the birth of Christianity, and on till Christianity became the dominant religion in the fourth and fifth centuries A.D.

The importance of Hellenistic culture and religion is illustrated by a passage in John's letters to the church. Over several chapters in 1 John, the Apostle talks about a great apostasy in the primitive church, concluding with this thought:

> They are from the world; therefore what they say is from the world, and the world listens to them. We are from God. Whoever knows God listens to us.... From this we know the spirit of truth and the spirit of error. (1 John 4:5–6)

John in effect is setting up the religious teachings of the Hellenistic world of his time as an identifying mark of religious apostasy. As he says, the religious message of Hellenistic culture in the first century *(what they say is from the world)*, and its wide popularity *(the world listens to them)*, are identifying marks of religious error *(from this we know the spirit of truth and the spirit of error)*. It would seem, then, that understanding what Hellenistic culture was teaching in the first century A.D. could be very important.

What is it in Hellenistic culture that drew the criticism of the Apostle John in the passage cited above? To answer that, we go back even further in time. In the seventh and sixth centuries B.C., long before the Hellenistic age officially began, there occurred an extraordinary event of truly historic proportions. At that time a complex of changes in religious belief appeared simultaneously throughout the Indo-European world, from Europe through India. This was a true reformation that radically ***transformed*** pagan religion and laid the foundation for what later became Hellenistic religion. It was perhaps the greatest reformation of religion in all of human history, and this unique event explains much about why most of the world's population practices religion today in the way they do.

Early Greek Religion

Before the religious reformation in the seventh and sixth centuries B.C., Greek religion was similar to many other Near Eastern traditions. Most importantly it was highly materialistic. Man worshipped the gods through animal sacrifice and performance of rituals. In return the gods gave man success in his endeavors. Specifically they guaranteed the flow of fertility in nature that brings good harvests and prosperity.

There were "mystery" cults whose rituals were based on the ebb and flow of fertility in the world. Many of these had savior deities who died and were reborn annually. This depicted the annual seasons. The captivity of the savior in the underworld portrayed the disappearance of fertility in winter (death). His release each spring (rebirth) represented the restoration of fertility that sustains material human life. The focus was on material success and salvation in this life, not the hereafter. (The 'mysterious' forces of nature, and 'mysterious' religious rituals by which man sought to influence those forces to obtain prosperity, are the "mystery" in the term mystery cults.)

The Reformation

Beginning in the seventh and sixth centuries B.C. something happened that radically transformed the purpose and meaning of religion, both in Greece and ultimately throughout the entire world. The first indication was the appearance of a new mystery religion in Greece called Orphism. Its founder, Orpheus, claimed to be a great religious reformer who reinterpreted the earlier mysteries in a new spiritual fashion. In Orphism the mysteries now focused on the human soul and the fate of the soul after death.[2]

Another religious reformer followed soon after. In the late sixth century a philosopher and religious teacher, Pythagoras, adopted the same new religious themes introduced by Orphism. He established his own cult, Pythagoreanism, in southern Italy. From there it spread through Greece, to Egypt and ultimately Rome.

Pythagoreans and Orphics saw the material world and religion in a radically new light. For them the purpose of religion was not so much to gain material blessings in this world. They believed in the immortality of the human soul and its repeated reincarnation in the human body. Spirituality no longer centered on material issues. Instead, man should suppress his material passions in order to focus on the spiritual development of the inner spirit. Thereby the soul will escape from the cycle of rebirth and ascend to eternal rest in the heavens.[3] Typical of this is the description of Pythagoras' ministry by the Greek author Iamblichus:

---

[2]   For Orphism as a reformation, see Guthrie, *Orpheus and Greek Religion,* p 194–5.

[3]   For a general discussion of Pythagorean and Orphic belief, see Kingsley, *Ancient Philosophy, Mystery and Magic,* and Guthrie, *Orpheus and Greek Religion.*

Hence also he ordered them to abstain from wine, to be sparing in their food, to sleep little, and to cultivate...contempt of...fame, wealth, and the like....

In short, Pythagoras procured his disciples the most appropriate [relationship] with the Gods ...something that never occurs in a soul disturbed by anger, pain, or pleasure, and surely all the more by any base desire.... By all these inventions, therefore, he divinely purified and healed the soul, resuscitating and saving its divine part....[4]

As part of this general change in religious focus, both Pythagoreans and Orphics taught that man should turn away from the materialism of animal sacrifice. This is a theme that appears over and over in many parts of the Indo-European world at this time.[5] Henceforth, religious worship must be spiritual, from the heart, an expression of the inner man.

A New Cosmology

What brought about the great religious reformation in ancient Greece? There were many causes. However, unlikely as it might seem, one very important factor was not religion itself, but science. Early Greece was a hotbed of scientific advance, especially in the field of astronomy. The Greeks, for example, were the first to discover that the earth is round. (This scientific truth was subsequently lost for more than a thousand years, eventually declared a heresy by the Roman church but rediscovered in medieval Europe by Columbus and his contemporaries.)

This was a truly revolutionary development, not only for science but for religion as well. In the end, it played an important role in the adoption of radically new religious beliefs, such as the immortality of the soul and other beliefs that centuries later impacted Christianity.

The way science influenced religion is through cosmology. *Cosmology* is a term used to signify the theoretical structure and arrangement of the universe. What does that have to do with religion? As unlikely as it may seem, it is at the very heart of the matter, because this was believed to

---

[4]   Iamblichus, *On the Pythagorean Life,* Number 16 Pythagorean Asceticism, from **PSL**, p 73–74.

[5]   See Laertius, *Life of Pythagoras,* (12) Diet and Sacrifices; Guthrie, *Orpheus and Greek Religion,* p 196 ff. For rest of Indo-European world, see Appendix C.

explain the existence of the immortal soul in man. Eventually it even defined the day of the week on which most Christians today worship.

The ancient Babylonians believed the earth is a solid flat disk floating in a vast expanse of water. This was the earliest cosmology, generally taught throughout the Near East and in Greece before the seventh century B.C. According to this view, the sun is a great ball of fire passing overhead during the day. At night it enters the underworld through a great opening in the earth somewhere in the distant west, returns invisibly beneath the earth, to rise again in the east each day. No one had ever seen the huge gates through which the sun sank into the earth nor those from which it arose. But it was obvious to men in that time that is what must be happening.

The Greek discovery that the earth is round was truly revolutionary. This produced a more accurate concept of outer space. Now they understood the earth as only a single ball of matter floating within a vast cosmic system. However, some scientific error persisted under the new Greek cosmology. Greek astronomers retained the Babylonian concept of earth as the center of the universe. So they thought the sun orbits around the earth. For them this was the only obvious explanation for the daily rising and setting of the sun.

This new Greek cosmology is known as the Ptolemaic system.[6] It was named after Ptolemy, a Hellenistic scientist and astronomer at the famous library of Alexandria, Egypt. Ptolemy lived in the second century A.D., but the ideas behind the Ptolemaic system date from much earlier and were only systematically organized and expanded by the person after whom it was named.

From its beginning in ancient Greece, the Ptolemaic system prevailed for more than 1,500 years until replaced by the modern Copernican model in the late Middle Ages. Copernican cosmology finally correctly identified the sun as the center, and today we understand the earth as only one of many planets orbiting in space around the sun.

---

[6] For Ptolemaic cosmology, see Martin, *Hellenistic Religions,* p 6 ff, and Taub, *Ptolemy's Universe.*

From Cosmology to Religion

How did all this get involved with religion? The Greeks now understood that earth along with the planets and stars comprise millions of balls of matter hanging in space. The question naturally arose – What ties the whole system together? Do they float about in disordered chaos? If not, how do they relate to each other and what are the forces that maintain order? The answers to those questions were religious in nature and explain the close ties between science and religion in Hellenistic society.

As stated above, one key to the influence of Greek science on religion was the Ptolemaic error in thinking that the earth is the center of the universe. Ptolemaic cosmology claims that everything orbits around the earth. The sun and moon were counted as two of the planets circling the earth, and since the planets beyond Saturn could not be seen with the naked eye, early Greek astronomers came up with a total of only seven planets.

Between the earth and stars, then, the planets were believed to be arranged in the following order:

--- stars ---

Saturn

Jupiter

Mars

Sun

Venus

Mercury

Moon

--- earth ---

Planets and stars were believed to revolve around the earth in concentric orbits. Those orbits mark off layers of space, or spheres, that separate the outermost realm of the stars from earth.

The realm of the stars is the outermost and eighth sphere, frequently symbolized by the number eight. The number seven symbolized the realm of the seven planets, which mark the descent from heaven to earth. As we shall see, the symbolism of the numbers seven and eight assumed a particularly important role in Hellenistic religion. Seven came to represent evil because it symbolized descent into the world of matter. In contrast, eight symbolized the peaceful order and goodness of the heavens, and the immortal soul within man that comes from heaven.

Observation of the movement of the heavenly bodies through the night sky naturally suggested these ideas. The heavens are a place of stability and harmony. That was only too obvious to the first Greek astronomers as they observed the orderly and stable movement of the stars. Therefore, from a religious point of view, the heavens were assumed to be the origin and source of unchanging stability, in other words immortality.

As they looked below the stars, however, the Greek astronomers noticed a gradual degradation of the perfection they saw in the highest heavens. As you go downward from the stars towards the earth, order begins to break down. Below the stars are the planets, which follow more erratic orbits than the stars. Finally, when you reach earth you find a place of constant change, instability, conflict and chaos. The pattern of increasing instability is fully realized on the surface of the earth in the chaos and misery of human existence.

Religion assigned many supernatural beings to rule over each layer of space descending from the stars to earth. The large inner cavity below the orbit of the moon, in which the earth floats, is the realm of demonic and elemental powers that influence and control the lives of men. At the other end of the spectrum, in the realm of the stars, there is total peace, tranquility, immortality, and the purity and goodness of God.

This is one of the basic principles of Hellenistic religion. At one extreme is the beauty and purity of the heavens, at the other the chaos and misery of earth. In Hellenistic thought, the human soul originates in the heavenly sphere of the stars. From there it descends and becomes incarnate in human bodies. Here on earth it remains trapped in a place sometimes considered merely inferior, other times outright evil. In ancient Greece, entrapment in the material world frequently involved the idea of reincarnation. Hellenistic salvation is the breaking of the soul's bondage to human existence, ending the chain of reincarnation, allowing the soul to escape back to its original home in the heavens.

The human problem, then, is defined primarily as bondage versus freedom. On earth we are in bondage to material lust. This is imposed on us by the demonic forces associated with planets and earth. If we can become free from material lust by which the demonic forces keep us in bondage to this world, then at death we will ascend and return to our original home in heaven.

As we saw above, all this religious content was tightly integrated with scientific observation of the heavens. The gradual change in orderly movement of the heavenly bodies as it proceeds from extreme stability among the stars to increasingly disordered movement of the planets, and the chaos of nature and life on earth, naturally suggested this new theology.

Greek Science and Atheism

Religious interpretation of the new breakthroughs in astronomy was not at first universally accepted. In fact there was a major struggle over this. Some of the early Greek philosophers favored a more scientific explanation based on evolution. For them, the world came into being through the random action of natural forces. It was as though Greece was on the verge of leaping directly into the 20th century and its scientific theories of evolutionary progress. But it was not to be.

In ancient Greece just as today, evolutionary theory sparked a huge religious controversy. The evolutionary camp was split among many different schools, who frequently agreed on little more than the fact everyone but themselves were wrong. The end result was a huge religious scandal and backlash against the purely scientific interpretation. In the end, evolution was discredited on the basis it leads to both social discord and atheism.

The affair finally was settled by one of the most famous individuals from ancient history – Plato, the great Greek philosopher. Plato was converted to the religious reformation pioneered by Orphism and Pythagoreanism, and he used its new teachings about astronomy and the cosmos to harmoniously blend science and religion. Plato argued that the regularity and intelligence in the movement of the stars is proof that the orderly processes of nature do not operate alone nor by chance. Rather, he said, they reflect divine intelligence radiating from the heavens. So Plato validated and preserved the new religious ideas which centuries later would transform Christianity. The existence of God and immortality in heaven, the fall and descent of Spirit into the material world, the immortal soul in man and its destiny to return to heaven, thus became the primary explanation for the structure of the cosmos and how it came to be.

Many Greeks insisted the basic principles of the great pagan religious reformation lay hidden within their older traditions. Though hidden, they could be drawn out by allegorical interpretation. Plato wholeheartedly embraced that idea. Therefore, he argued, all Greek citizens should be educated in the movements of the sun, moon and other planets. By understanding the intelligence of their movement and the divine nature of the heavens, Greeks would better understand their own ancestral religion.

Plato also endorsed propagating the ideas of the new religion by force. In his work *The Laws*, Plato sets out his views on the ideal society. According to Plato, society should be based on the divine order of the cosmos. This included a chilling solution for dealing with non-believers. For those who defy the religious interpretation of astronomy, he said, they should be instructed in the truth, but if they continue in their error they must be executed. One of the naturalist astronomers, Anaxagoras, a noted Greek scientist and one of the first to discover the earth is round, at one time was put on trial for "offences against piety." Fortunately he was not executed.

Socrates, Plato's teacher and one of the great pioneers of Greek philosophy, was less fortunate. The death of Socrates, one of the most famous stories from ancient Greece, occurred partly because of this same controversy over science and religion. Socrates was accused of atheism (apparently wrongly so), in part because of his association with other philosophers who believed in an evolutionary explanation of the new astronomic data.

As Greece extended its empire through much of the Mediterranean and Near East, it carried with it Plato's idea of reinterpreting native religions to draw out the truths taught by their new reformation, and imposing that reinterpretation by force. Their record in ancient Israel, preserved in part in the book of Daniel, was particularly abusive. The resulting mixture of Hellenistic religious beliefs with Jewish religion in Palestine was an important historical event. As we will see later, this played a key role in the subsequent infiltration of Hellenistic religion into Christianity.

Greek Philosophy

Orphics and Pythagoreans were organized as secret societies. They met as small groups in which a teacher would impart the new doctrines of Hellenistic religion to a select group of initiates. It was taught as the revelation of a secret truth hidden until now within traditional Greek religion. Orphism and Pythagoreanism were transmitted orally and never systematically recorded in writing. The evidence for its existence and content comes from later writers, oblique references in early, often esoteric texts and poetry, and early inscriptions, especially inscriptions deposited with the dead.

From this humble beginning the new religion grew to dominate the Greek world. The key to its acceptance and wide popularity is Plato, who incorporated Orphic and Pythagorean teachings in his own philosophy. By this means, in the fourth century B.C., the new religious tradition jumps into the mainstream of Greek society and achieves near universal acceptance.

Today we tend to think of philosophy as a system of pure reason, separate and distinct from religion. In classical times, however, this was viewed quite differently. Religion, physical science, political science, sociology – virtually all learning – was wrapped up together under the heading of philosophy. In fact, much of the pure reasoning employed in classical philosophy was expended on creating and justifying what we would consider religious doctrine. Most importantly, the religious beliefs we find in classical Greek philosophy are the same ideas first taught by Orphism and Pythagoreanism, including the new Ptolemaic cosmology. Also, now for the first time we find texts that systematically record the new religious tradition.

Plato

Plato lived and taught in Athens (428–348 B.C.). He traveled widely, however, especially among the Pythagorean communities in southern Italy and Sicily. At Athens he founded a university-style institution for the study of philosophy and science, known as the Academy, which survived after his death. He became the dominant force in Greek philosophy and is still studied as one of the greatest names in the Greek tradition. In the early centuries of the Christian era it survived under the name Neoplatonism, still the dominant philosophic tradition at Rome and in the Hellenistic world at large.

In Plato's writings,[7] especially in the *Phaedrus*, we find the key idea that the existence of intelligence in man is the effect of an inner soul. And what is the origin of soul? When you look at the heavens and observe the

---

[7] For Platonic philosophy and its religious component, see Scott, *Origen and the Life of the Stars,* chapter 1. For the Orphic and Pythagorean influence in Platonic philosophy, see Kingsley, *Ancient Philosophy Mystery, and Magic,* especially chapter 10.

regularity and apparently purposeful movement of the stars, then the inescapable conclusion is this heavenly 'intelligence' is the same intelligence found in man. Further, as you observe the limitation of order and intelligence on earth (human chaos and suffering), compared to the perfect and unlimited order in the heavens, then it is not difficult to conclude that soul originates from a perfect state in the heavens and in its manifestation in humans has fallen into an imperfect state that limits its true nature.

At the two extremes are the perfect regularity and intelligence of the stars, and the debased state of intelligence as seen in human chaos and suffering on earth. In between you find the planets. These display some of the order and stability of the stars, but their movements are less regular, sometimes stopping and even moving backwards.[8] They also appear to move opposite to the stars, from west to east, against the background of stars moving east to west.[9] Thus the very conduct of the planets as well as their physical location suggests they represent an intermediate state between the perfection in the heavens and the relative disorder on earth.

In Platonic philosophy, God, like the soul itself, is ethereal and invisible. God would never deal directly with man and the disordered worlds beneath the starry realm. Instead he works through angelic intermediaries.

Material creation is carried out by one of these intermediate beings, known as the 'demiurge.' In Plato's time the creator of the material world was not considered outright evil, though the final outcome of his work was clearly deficient. Plato, for example, believed the demiurge was responsible for the force that caused the planets to move in the opposite direction to that of the stars. Anything that operates contrary to the divine patterns of the heavens must be deficient.

In the *Timaeus*, Plato portrays the demiurge as producing a world based on patterns and forms that exist in the heavens. Everything that is beautiful and good in the world is due to its resemblance to those eternal and perfect patterns in heaven, though the world is an imperfect reflection of God's heavenly perfection.

---

[8]   Though planets never actually stop and move backwards, because of their relative orbital speed compared to the earth they sometimes appear to do so, based on the phenomenon known as paralax.

[9]   The starry background appears to move from east to west because of the earth's rotation in the opposite direction. Because the planets orbit in the same direction as the earth's rotation, they appear to move in the opposite direction against the backdrop of the stars.

How did human souls get to where they are today? According to Plato each star is the home of one human soul created specifically for it. While it is still living in its assigned star, the soul is informed of its impending descent into the material world and the plan of salvation that will bring it back. The essence of that plan is to gain mastery over the human emotions and passions that become attached to it when it enters a human body. The human soul thus begins life as a much less perfect and impure mixture than the perfect divinity of the heavens. If it can overcome passion and lust, however, it will become totally pure again and thus return to its native star.

If the soul lives badly in its human incarnation it may be reborn as a (gasp) woman. (Political correctness still had a long ways to go in ancient Greece.) Further failure to reform could drop it into the realm of animal life. If it lives well, however, the soul will escape after death and ascend to the heavens. Here again we meet the belief in reincarnation Plato inherited from the Orphics and Pythagoreans, with return of the soul to heaven as the ultimate goal of religion.

The idea of evil in the planets, or the idea the material world is inherently evil or that creation is an evil act, is generally missing from early Platonic philosophy. Though the world of man is imperfect, the creator is well intentioned. All of creation is designed for man to succeed in realizing the goal of return to the heavens. The action of the planets ranges from very positive to no worse than neutral. In much of Platonic reasoning, the planets were viewed as helping purify the soul as it ascends back to the heavens.

A radically negative interpretation of the planets and the material world appears only much later, in the early centuries A.D. when it reached a climax in a deviant form of Christianity called Gnosticism. We will encounter the topic of Gnostic Christianity many times in the remaining chapters of this volume.

After Plato there was an explosion of speculation about the heavens and the soul. Heraclitus, another Greek philosopher, made an important addition to Plato's thought. He introduced the idea that the human soul is identical to the substance found in the heavens, called *ether*. This is the substance of outer space in the realm of the stars. It is the substance of which the stars themselves are composed. Thus the soul by its very essence is heavenly, divine, and immortal.

Historical Dispersion of the New Religion

How did a religious reformation in ancient Greece come to have such a huge impact on our world today? To answer that question let's briefly review the historical background for its appearance and dispersion around the Mediterranean, which uniquely positioned it to influence our practice of religion today.

Before the great reformation, Greece was mired in a cultural dark age produced by the fall of an earlier civilization known as Mycenaean. The Greek dark ages were so profound that even the art of writing disappeared for several centuries. Orphism and Pythagoreanism appeared just as Greece was emerging from that dark age. The cultural rebound in Greece was swift and powerful. Writing reappeared and Greece became the dominant force over a wide area, from what today is Russia in the east to as far as France in the west. Greek colonies were established around the Mediterranean, including northern Africa, and in parts of the Black Sea. Sicily and southern Italy became dotted with Greek colonial cities, so much so it became known as Magna Graecia (Greater Greece).

What followed was the classical age of Greek culture, the time of independent city-states of which Athens is the most famous. There were Sparta and Thebes, and also Corinth and Thessalonica that later became home to Christian churches addressed in books of the Bible. This was the age of the philosophers Plato, Aristotle and many other great names in various disciplines, including politics and science, who are counted as founders of the traditions under which we live today. Thus the new religion that appeared first in Greece was spread around the Mediterranean world.

In the fourth century B.C., soon after Plato first recorded in writing and popularized the traditions of Orphism and Pythagoreanism, what had been fomenting in Greece spilled over onto the world stage, engulfing the entire Near East, and most importantly the land of Israel. The ambition and greed of one man, Alexander the Great, launched Greece on a campaign of conquest that overthrew Persian control of the Near East. Alexander was the first man to establish a professional full-time standing army. Before that time, battles were fought in effect by part-time armies. Farmers and noblemen alike became experienced at war because of its frequency, but generally they followed their various professions and engaged in war only when called up. Alexander's fresh approach produced a war machine virtually unbeatable in its time. In just a few years beginning in 332 B.C., the entire Near East including Egypt and Persia were unified in a single empire dominated by Greece, Greek culture and, most importantly, its new religion.

Hellenistic is the term used to refer to the stage of Greek culture and religion that flourished in the Mediterranean and Near East beginning with the empire created by Alexander the Great. When Alexander died, the empire was divided among his generals. Persia eventually regained its independence. After only a few centuries more, Rome rose to power and replaced Greece as the dominant force in the Hellenistic world. Alexander's primary focus had been the Near East, but now Rome turned in the opposite direction. By expanding to the west and north, it extended the reach of Hellenistic culture through Europe as far as the British Isles.

Historians talk about the end of the Hellenistic age and beginning of the Roman era with Rome's victory over the Hellenistic government of Egypt. This was decided by the great naval battle of Actium in 31 B.C. when Rome defeated the last great Hellenistic ruler of Egypt, the famous queen Cleopatra. Despite the change from Greek to Roman control, however, it was the same Hellenistic culture and religion that continued seamlessly right up to the triumph of Roman Christianity in the fourth and fifth centuries A.D.

Promotion of the Orphic and Pythagorean religious reformation, first by Plato and later by other classical Greek philosophers, secured the initial dominance of the new religious tradition in Greece. Alexander the Great's conquests in the fourth century B.C. extended the new religion's dominance to the entire Near East. Finally, the shift of power to Rome moved the focus of Hellenistic religion further westward to the European theater, from which all of modern Western culture has sprung.

The Stoics

Returning to earlier times, in Greece we find the new religion spreading throughout the philosophic world as Platonism is picked up and developed by other schools. Foremost among these were the Stoics, one of the largest philosophic schools that developed out of Platonism and which embodied much of its religious philosophy.[10]

---

[10] For a description of the religious content of Stoic philosophy, see Scott, *Origen and the Life of the Stars,* especially chapter 3.

Stoicism was founded in 301 B.C. by a man named Zeno. We use the word *stoic* today, according to Webster, to mean *'not affected by passion; able completely to repress feeling.'* The reason we use the word in that sense today stems from the stoics' belief in the Greek religious reformation. It is an expression of the idea that man can achieve salvation, meaning release from material existence and ascent to heaven, by modeling his personality and conduct after the order and stability of the starry heavens. Uncontrolled emotion and passion are what binds man to this world. If you can retreat into a calm and placid (stoic) state in which you are unaffected by material passions, and nurture the inner life of the soul, then you will both escape much suffering in this life, and upon death your soul will escape the material world and return to the heavens. Thus the Stoics were 'stoic' precisely because they saw it as an expression of the peaceful stability and orderliness of the heavens. This is what they viewed as the spirituality of the heavens.

For Zeno, reason and intelligence come from pure *ether,* the hot gaseous substance of which the starry realm is composed. Soul, however, is composed of *pneuma*, a mixture of *ether* and air. So the human soul is a less pure form of the same substance of which heaven is composed. Some Stoics explained differences in human intelligence, personality and character as the result of the differing purity of the *ether* and the ratio of its mixture with air in the souls of individual people.

Greeks in general thought all material things are a mixture of four basic elements – fire, air, water and earth. These tend to separate into strata depending on their weight. Fire is the lightest and is associated with the heavens. Below come air, then water and finally earth. The ratio of the elements in any substance therefore causes it to sink or rise to the level corresponding to the relative weight of its components.

Stoicism used this as a scientific explanation for the descent and ascent of the soul between heaven and earth. Souls are less pure and cooler than *ether*. That is what makes them descend from the heights of heaven. On earth, however, they are always lighter and hotter than the body in which they reside. The human body is composed primarily of cooler, more dense components, so it remains on earth after death. Once released from the body, the soul naturally tends to rise. But since it is less pure than the *ether* in heaven, it only rises to the level of the moon.

There is a continuous grading of the purity of *ether* as you leave the surface of the earth and ascend into the heavens where it exists in totally pure form. The conditions prevailing in the sphere of the moon correspond to the purity of righteous souls. For those whose soul is corrupted through evil and therefore much less pure, their souls become trapped in the thick, dense air just above the earth, which the Stoics called Hades (Hell). This was their original teaching. However, under the influence of Platonism, Stoics later taught that the soul both originates from and returns fully to the heavens.

For Stoics an important source of the knowledge of God was the older beliefs and mythology of Greek religion. Like Orphism and Pythagoreanism before it, and like many other religious movements of the time, Stoicism claimed its new theology of the stars and the heavens was a hidden tradition within ancient Greek religion, which they could draw out by allegorical interpretation.[11] So they too promoted the new religion as a reformation of existing Greek religion.

Popular Hellenistic Religion and Astral Fatalism

By the time Christ appeared on earth the great pagan reformation had impacted virtually all religious movements within the Hellenistic world. This was especially true of popular superstitions, such as astrology. The new religion taught that planets play an important role in the descent and ascent of the soul, sometimes helping, sometimes hindering. This gave a new credibility and relevance to astrology, which became increasingly popular.

A basic idea of astrology, still very popular in our time, is that your birth date identifies spiritual and cosmic forces that shape your personality and affect what happens to you throughout life. This also is called "astral fatalism," which means that stars (including the planets) determine your fate in life.

How does your birth date affect what happens to you? According to Hellenistic religion, the condition of the soul when it appears on the earth is in part the effect of the stars from which it came and the planets through whose realms it passes as it descends. Many early philosophers believed the planets play a role in creating and forming portions of the soul as it descends to earth. Therefore the heavenly bodies that dominated the sky on the date you were born have a substantial effect on the condition of your soul. That in turn determines your personality type and spiritual tendencies, and will continue to affect you in special ways throughout

---

[11] See Scott, *Origen and the Life of the Stars,* p 47.

life. For example, if Saturn dominated the sky during the time you were born, it might cause you to develop a listless and unfocussed personality, because Saturn was the slowest moving of the seven planets.

Astrology was only a baser, more superstitious expression of the new religion and its focus on the heavens. Though it thrived most among the common populace, astrological beliefs were nearly universally accepted in Hellenistic culture under the Romans, including the educated upper class.[12] Recall from the preceding section the reasoning of Stoic philosophers, who believed that subtle differences in the composition of the soul account for the different personality and spiritual traits of individuals. Today millions of people still consult newspapers and other media to see what events are likely to occur in their lives, based on the heavenly bodies that ruled the skies on the date they were born.

Astrology played an important role in another development within Hellenistic religion. That is the tendency to see the planets and the world of man on earth as evil.

In the beginning, Greek religion did not view the world as terribly evil. Entrapped in the material world, the soul leads a life inferior to what it will find when it escapes back to heaven. How soul got mixed up with matter, and how the world came to be created, was viewed at worst as morally neutral. The important thing about the physical creation is its expression of God's beauty, order and intelligence. The mixture of soul and matter explains the presence of evil among men, but it also points the way to salvation. By turning away from obsession with material possessions and passion, and by developing one's inner, heavenly nature – the soul – man can assure the return of his soul to heaven after death. The important lesson to be learned from human existence is the need to develop inner spiritually.

On the other hand, the very nature of the beliefs surrounding man's condition on earth left the new religion open to a more negative interpretation. If human misery stems from the human tendency to misuse the material world, then couldn't you say the material world itself is evil? Why did it have to happen in the first place? Why didn't soul just stay in a state of perfection in the heavens? Therefore, isn't creation of the material world and the soul's descent into creation essentially evil?

Astrology provided additional motivation to interpret the material world as a place of bondage and entrapment. If all your experiences are

---

[12]   Ibid, p 145.

fatalistically determined by influences of the stars and planets when you were born, then doesn't that apply to the bad things that happen to you as well as the good? Gradually this evolved into an obsession with Fate and Fortune. Human existence now was understood as bondage to the fate determined by the planets. Or, as it was conceived in that time, man is in bondage to the spiritual powers of the planets.

This is reflected in the ancient worship of the gods Fate and Fortune. These two became major deities in the Hellenistic world. Romans worshipped Fortuna (fortune) and Tyche (fate) in hope they could get them to provide good fortune and good fate. By the third century B.C. nearly all large cities in Greece had temples devoted to the goddess Fortuna. Pliny, writing in the first century B.C. testifies to her universal acceptance and popularity:

> Everywhere in the whole world at every hour by all men's voices Fortune alone is invoked and named...and we are so much at the mercy of chance that Chance herself, by whom God is proved uncertain, takes the place of God.[13]

Over time there was an increasing tendency to hope to be freed from the oppressive control of the planets. Life then, as now, was not easy. Simple practical experience demonstrated that on average, over time, it really didn't pay off that well. Otherwise Fortune and Fate would produce much better results.

Fortune came to be regarded in a negative light, as well, because what happens to you is completely disconnected from your conduct. Hence Fortune often was described as blind and unfair. Her capricious, untrustworthy nature was her most prominent trait. Once again Pliny testifies:

> Fortune...is...alone applauded, alone rebuked and visited with reproaches; deemed volatile and indeed by most men blind as well, ...fickle in her favors and favoring the unworthy.[14]

Another example of the negative view of Fortune comes from an ancient work of fiction known popularly under the title *The Golden Ass*. It gained considerable fame for its author, Lucius Apuleius. Essentially *The Golden Ass* is a morality tale associated with the mysteries of Isis. This is, an originally Egyptian mystery cult that had spread throughout the Hellenis-

---

[13] Natural History II,5,22
[14] Ibid.

tic world. It presents the world as an ugly, disordered place in which man is buffeted by fear and uncertainty, without the support of the gods. In the end the main character Lucius is saved by the goddess Isis and finds security in this world and the next through initiation into her mysteries. The story remarkably reflects the change in the Hellenistic mind-set in which the material world has come to be seen as essentially evil.

In *The Golden Ass*, the travails of Lucius begin with a business trip to Thessaly. This is a region of east central Greece famous for magic and witchcraft. Here he stays in the home of a friend, where he is enticed into exotic adventures by the wife of his host and her servant girl. First he becomes sexually involved with the servant girl. From that involvement he becomes curious about the magic and sorcery practiced by her and her mistress.

Lucius observes the mistress use a potion to transform herself into an owl so she can fly off as part of an erotic adventure. Lucius decides to try it for himself. Unfortunately, the servant girl gets the bottles mixed up. Poor Lucius is transformed into an ass. The rest of the story recounts his long and tragic quest for the antidote. The story winds its way through a series of misadventures, all of which depict the evil and depravity of the world, which it presents as lawless, dangerous, and full of magic, degradation, abuse and exploitation. This is vividly expressed in one passage where it talks of:

> ...the slippery changes, the shifting forces, and constant reversals of Fortune. [15]

In the end, the goddess Isis appears to Lucius in a dream and he is transformed back into human form. A priest of Isis then delivers a speech that states in part:

> Dear Lucius, after enduring so many labors and being driven by so many storms of Fortune, finally you have arrived at a peaceful port and the altar of mercy. ... Let Fortune rage and fume in some other place, for Fortune has no power over those who have been liberated for the service of our goddess. [16]

The importance of astral fatalism in Hellenistic culture is its nurture of a negative view of material creation. Man came to be seen as subject to the

---

[15] Met. I,6.
[16] Met. XI,15.

bondage of the spirits that control the material world, from the planets on down to earth. In the end it fostered the rejection of material creation. And here we come to the most important conclusion. If creation is evil, then the spirits and gods involved in creation must be evil as well. In the end, as we will see in following chapters, this led to radical beliefs within radical, heretical Christian sects, who preached that the key to salvation and return of the soul to heaven is rejecting the Hebrew God of creation and his religion.

By the time Christianity came on the scene, Hellenistic culture was already equipped with a mindset that saw man as in bondage to the creator God and the angelic spirits surrounding him that control the material world. Salvation depends on rejecting both the material world and the God that created it. True spirituality is found only in the heavens. In following chapters we will see this amply and repeatedly demonstrated by religious movements that directly affected Christianity.

The Mystery Cults

In the aftermath of the Greek reformation of the seventh and sixth centuries B.C., virtually all religious traditions in Greece were affected, including even the mystery cults. That is not surprising. After all, the first manifestation of the Greek religious reformation, Orphism itself, claimed to be a reformation of an earlier mystery religion.

Mystery cults were ancient religious traditions founded on the idea of human interaction with spirit. This does not mean spirituality in the modern sense, however. Before the great reformation, spirit generally meant the life force within nature, specifically the power of fertility. In the Near East for example, fertility was closely associated with water. One ancient Babylonian mystery tradition taught that moisture retreats to a great underground abyss during the dry season. This abyss, known as the Deep, is the source of life-giving energy that sustains the world. It is from here the life-giving waters return at the start of the wet season each year.

In the mystery cult tradition the essence of fertility also was identified with a hero figure. The hero was usually but not always male. The seasonal disappearance of fertility was depicted as the death and captivity of the hero in the Deep, and its return signified the hero's resurrection or rebirth. The primary purpose of the cult was to secure material blessings and the continuation of human life through the annual renewal of fertility.

In the aftermath of the great pagan reformation of the seventh to sixth centuries B.C., the mystery cult tradition was spiritualized along modern lines. In a dramatic turnaround, they now downplayed their former concern with fertility and material prosperity. Many of the mysteries now incorporated the negative view of the material world that we saw in the preceding section on astral mysticism. Now the goal became nurturing the immortal soul to prepare for its ultimate escape from the world. The primary focus now is the soul, the spirit within man rather than the spirit in nature.

This also led to a reversal in the concept of the captivity of spirit. Before the reformation, the problem was seen as spirit getting trapped in the other world, what the Babylonians called the Deep. The problem was to make sure it was released back into our world each year to renew the fertility of nature. After the reformation, man's problem is reversed. Because the material world has been recast as evil, now spirit tends to get trapped on our side rather than in the otherworld. Spirit flows into our world in the form of human souls. Now the problem is to free human souls to get spirit flowing outward, back to its place of origin in the heavens.

The role of the hero figure likewise has been reinterpreted. Previously he represented material fertility. Now he is the savior of human souls. His function is to reveal the truth to man about the cosmic process, where the immortal soul came from, the fact that it is in bondage in this world, and how to escape back to heaven.

The mystery cults also taught a mystical identification of the worshipper with the hero figure. By linking oneself mystically to the hero, the worshipper now could claim for himself the same promise of rebirth to life after death that the hero experiences in the annual cycle of nature. In Egypt, for example, as time went on, more and more people opted for burial with rituals designed to identify themselves with the hero-saviors Osiris and Horus. These rituals explicitly invoked the promise that the dead will be granted the same resurrection to life as that of the heroes.

As explained, after the great pagan reformation the focus is on the liberation and flow of spirit back to heaven, in the form of human souls. Before that the hero had been identified with the flow of spirit power into this world, and that has not totally disappeared. There still is a positive belief in the inward flow of spirit for the purpose of nourishing and restoring human souls. The soul is awakened and healed by putting man in touch with the same heavenly spirit of which the soul itself is composed. Remember how the idea of the immortal soul originated in the Greek belief that the soul is composed of the same substance, the *ether*, that exists in the heavens. The hero's primary function now is to awaken and restore the soul by reconnecting it to the power of the heavens. Thus the hero restores the souls of his followers to their original purity and shows them the way back to their true home in the heavens.

We now turn to a brief review of two mystery cults, as well as a surprising passage in the Bible that speaks directly about the exotic religious ideas they promoted.

The Mysteries of Isis [17]

Worship of the goddess Isis and her mate Osiris is an ancient mystery cult from the land of Egypt. The Hellenistic version, however, was created after Alexander the Great conquered Egypt. Throughout the Near East, Alexander's conquests produced new Hellenistic versions of local cults and religions, including Hellenistic Jewish sects in Israel.

The Hellenistic version of the mysteries of Isis spread throughout the Mediterranean world and attracted a wide popular following right up to the final suppression of the pagan cults in the 400s A.D.

The basic 'mystery' is the death and resurrection of Osiris. Osiris is murdered by Set, the evil one. His body is cast into the sea. Faithful Isis wanders through the world searching for him. Finally she locates and brings his body back to Egypt, but once again Set intervenes, cuts up the body and scatters the parts. Ever-faithful Isis gathers the parts, restores the body and resurrects her husband.

In ancient Egypt a similar myth and associated rituals depicted the annual disappearance and restoration of fertility. In the Hellenistic cult, however, it represents man's hope of salvation for the afterlife. It demonstrated the goddess' power to restore and give life, and was proof to her followers she would do the same for them.[18]

The worship of Isis was carried out daily in the hundreds of her temples scattered throughout the Mediterranean world. There was organized prayer in the morning and afternoon. At midday the temples were open to individuals for private prayer and meditation. A joyful chanting accompanied the closing of the temple at the end of the day. Annual festivals

---

[17] For background on the Isis mystery cult, see Witt, *Isis in the Ancient World.*

[18] Martin, *Hellenistic Religions,* p 73 ff.

depicted the suffering of Isis and the passion of Osiris and his restoration to life.

In front of each temple was a sacred pillar, prominently displayed as a symbol of the hope of salvation for the goddess' followers. In the myth, Osiris' body was cast into the Nile in a chest. It floated out into the Mediterranean and finally came to rest at Byblos (modern-day Lebanon). Cast up on the shore, the chest became entangled in a bush, which grew up around it into a tree. In time it was cut down and fashioned into a pillar for the palace of the local king. It was here Isis first recovered Osiris' body hidden inside the pillar. The sacred pillar became the symbol of his suffering, death and resurrection, and the hope of salvation for the faithful.[19] The life-giving waters of the Nile as they flowed into the Mediterranean were interpreted as a missionary commission for the cult to go beyond Egypt and bring the message of salvation to all mankind.

Initiation into the cult is described by Lucius in his novel *The Golden Ass*, which we first encountered in the preceding section. To be initiated one must receive a supernatural invitation from Isis. To make it happen, one rented a room at the temple and spent some days worshipping and receiving instruction from temple officials while waiting for the call. This would come after a time in the form of a dream. The initiation process then began with baptism and 10 days of fasting. Finally, clothed in a new linen robe, the initiate was led into the most sacred inner rooms of the temple. This depicted descent into hell, a ritual death and resurrection, in imitation of the death and resurrection of their hero-savior Osiris.

For the devotees of Isis, initiation replaces the emotional suffering of this chaotic world with internal peace and comfort, and secures the promise of being in paradise with the goddess in the world to come. From that time on the initiate looked to the priest of Isis as his spiritual father and the goddess herself as his spiritual mother.[20]

Paul and the Mystery Cults

The mystery cult tradition was widespread throughout the Near East. There was a long-standing trend, especially in Egypt, towards viewing the seasonal renewal of nature as the basis for the hope of resurrection and

---

[19]   Ibid., p 80.
[20]   Ibid., p 80 ff.

life after death. This process came to a head in Greece, where Orphism was the first mystery cult to make a sharp break with its materialistic past and convert to a primary focus on the soul and the afterlife. Over time, and certainly by the time Christ appeared on earth, most mystery cults had similarly converted to the new religious format.

Thus Hellenistic religion reinterpreted the symbolism previously attached to the seasonal departure and return of fertility. Now it was seen as an allegorical presentation of a deeper truth about bondage to material existence, death, rebirth to the life of the spirit, and how to secure the promise of entry into the heavens after death.

Just as we saw in the mysteries of Isis, many mystery cults practiced an initiation ritual in which a person descends into and re-emerges from an underground chamber.[21] The similarity of this to biblical Christianity can be disconcerting. For those who feel uncomfortable, it may be helpful to begin to explain some of the profound differences between pagan and biblical salvation, a topic that will appear repeatedly in this volume. It is surprising, indeed, how superficially similar they are – the teaching of death and rebirth to the life of the spirit. This was so common in Hellenistic culture that Paul refers to it in his letter to the Romans:

> But the righteousness that comes by faith says, 'Do not say to yourself, "Who can go up to heaven?" ' (that is to bring Christ down) 'or, "Who can go down to the <u>abyss</u>?" ' (to bring Christ up from the dead). And what does it say next? 'The word is near you: it is on your lips and in your heart' (that is, the word of faith that we proclaim).... (Romans 10:6–8)

The point Paul is making is that New Testament spirituality is a very simple and practical thing, open and accessible to all. Specifically he is saying it is **not** otherworldly. It is not something obtained by mystically ascending to heaven or descending into the underworld. One does not have to go out of this world to make contact with Christ (to 'bring Christ down' or 'bring Christ up').

In saying this, Paul is paraphrasing a passage from the Old Testament, namely Deuteronomy 30:11–14. The original passage in Deuteronomy is making essentially the same point as Paul, rejecting the idea of placing exotic, otherworldly conditions on man's relationship to God. Instead, it

---

[21]   See Vermaseren, *Cybele and Attis,* p 117f for similar rites in the mysteries of Orphism, Cybele and Attis, and Mithra.

says, it is a simple and practical application of God's Word in our daily conduct in this world. Here is the Old Testament version:

> Surely, this commandment that I am commanding you today is not too hard for you, nor is it too far away. It is not in heaven, that you should say, 'Who will go up to heaven for us, and get it for us so that we may hear it and observe it?' Neither is it beyond the sea, that you should say, 'Who will cross to the other side of the sea for us, and get it for us so that we may hear it and observe it?' No, the word is very near to you; it is in your mouth and in your heart for you to observe. (Deut 30:11–14)

Yahweh's demands are fulfilled by belief manifested in words and the orientation of the heart. That is why Paul sees the simplicity of New Testament salvation as the fulfillment of this Old Testament passage. It is transformation of the heart of man by belief and faith to become obedient to God.

At first glance Deuteronomy seems to differ from Paul in its description of the otherworldly activities it rejects. Both Paul and Deuteronomy mention ascending to heaven, but Deuteronomy talks about travelling over the sea, while Paul refers to descending into the 'abyss.' Is there a difference?

Both of Deuteronomy's otherworldly allusions reference Near Eastern pagan beliefs in vogue at the time Deuteronomy was composed. The idea of ascending to heaven was a major Babylonian religious theme involving contact between man and the gods. The ancient Babylonian stepped pyramid *(ziggurat)* was believed symbolically to reach into heaven. This is the model on which the tower of Babel was based, described in Genesis 11:4 as *"a tower with its top in the heavens"* (compare NRSV). Various rituals were performed atop the Babylonian pyramids in which the gods were believed to directly interact with man. Babylonian priestesses sometimes spent the night atop a pyramid to engage the gods sexually.

Travelling over the seas is a reference to the ancient Babylonian tradition of seeking immortality from the gods by returning to the Garden of Eden and partaking of the Tree of Life. In ancient Babylonian myth this was depicted as an arduous expedition over the sea to a distant land.[22] There the plant of life was believed to be growing at the bottom of a profoundly deep spring. In Babylonian tradition this signified the abyss or Deep, the great underworld storehouse of life-giving waters.

---

[22] For example as depicted in the Epic of Gilgamesh.

This is the same thing Paul is talking about in Romans when he paraphrases from Deuteronomy. Here Paul uses a Greek term variously translated into English as 'abyss' (NRSV) or the 'Deep' (KJV) – *"Who can go down to the abyss?"* In fact, Paul and Deuteronomy are referring to the same ancient Babylonian mystery tradition known as 'the Deep.'

If Deuteronomy was warning against the otherworldly mystery traditions of its time, what was Paul referring to when he reused the same symbolism? Was he only making a passing reference to ancient history, or was he talking about something unsavory in his day that we should try to avoid? Just look around the Hellenistic religious landscape of Paul's day. Immediately one finds startling matches to what Paul was describing – both mystical ascent and mystical descent.

For example, there was a highly developed system of Hellenistic Jewish mysticism in Paul's day. This tradition taught that spiritual revelation is obtained by mystical ascent into the heavens to make direct contact with God and his angels. Other religions, especially the mystery cults, equally emphasized mystical descent into the underworld. In the cult of Isis the initiate was believed to experience mystical visions of the sun god during his symbolic descent into the underworld.

Paul is mentioning, almost in passing, two important mystical religious movements of his time, both of which played major roles in the downfall of the first-century Primitive Christian church. The Hellenistic Jewish tradition associated with ascent to the heavens was a major problem in the church at Corinth, for example. (This is covered in more detail in *Spirit of Antichrist,* volume two of our series The World of Primitive Christianity.) The other, the mystery tradition of the Deep, evolved into a major antinomian religious movement that we will examine in more detail in a later chapter.

For now, the important thing is to understand Paul's general position regarding otherworldly mystical contact with divinity. The essential question is, How does one acquire religious knowledge and spirituality? Is it primarily by a mystical, otherworldly process of private revelation?

Not so, says Paul. According to him, our primary source of religious knowledge is the gospel message preached by the apostles to the first-century church, recorded for us today in writing as the New Testament. Paul refers to it as *'the word of faith **that we proclaim'*** (vs 8). For Paul, the revelation of truth is the message the apostles proclaimed openly to the New Testament churches. Its effect is confession of belief (conversion) and a transformation of the heart (*it is on your lips and in your heart*). One of Paul's key points, however, is that it proceeds from the open teaching of the apostles, recorded for us in the New Testament. It is *not* a private revelation of truth obtained by mystical processes that override the apostolic tradition preserved in the New Testament. Just as described in Deuteronomy from which Paul is paraphrasing, it is not a difficult, strange nor exclusively mystical process.

Once again, what is the difference between biblical Christianity and the mystery traditions? Christianity contains mystical rituals of descent into death and resurrection, namely baptism, and teachings about mystical identification with the savior, all of which superficially resemble pagan beliefs and practices. Paul is not saying we should reject these valid Christian principles and practices. What he is saying here, however, is that mysticism can get out of hand.

Paul characterizes salvation as a practical process that occurs in the mind and heart. Or, as Jeremiah in his time described the coming Christian reformation, *"I will put my law within them, and I will write it on their hearts; and I will be their God, and they shall be my people"* (Jer 31:34). The point at which it tends to get out of hand is when people begin to think their mystical, otherworldly religious experience imparts a private revelation that overrides the open teaching of Christ and the apostles as recorded in New Testament scripture. The inspiration of the Spirit, an important phenomenon in biblical Christianity, always is subject to the Word of God, not the other way around.

Remember the argument that Deuteronomy was making against otherworldly revelation – *'Who will go up to heaven for us, and get it for us so that we may hear it and observe it?'* In like fashion Paul is arguing that everything we need to know about conversion and transformation of the heart is openly available in the preaching of Jesus and the apostles. Christians should not be misled to turn aside into new (and here is the key point) **private** revelations from the heavens or from the Deep that pretend to overturn or exaggerate scriptural revelation. As we proceed through later chapters, we increasingly will see why Paul was concerned about this.

The Orphic Mysteries [23]

The Orphic Mysteries are an especially important topic because, for the Greek world, this is where the great pagan reformation started. Here is a brief description of some of the prominent features of Orphic belief.

Legend describes Orpheus as both human and divine. As an historical figure he was believed to be the great religious reformer who founded the Orphic Mysteries. As a divine being he was a typical Greek hero figure. Unlike most other heroes, however, he always was depicted as peaceful, a patron of the arts and a great musician. This was part of his image as a reformer, turning man towards the inner life of peace and harmony, and away from violent passions and the materialistic concerns promoted by the older mysteries.

Orphism claimed to be a reformed version of the Dionysian mysteries. These earlier mysteries were a typical materialistic, pre-reformation fertility cult. Orphism insisted it had found a hidden inner truth within the Dionysian mysteries that explains the misery of the human condition, the fate of the soul and hope of salvation via liberation from material existence.

Dionysus was, among other things, a god of wine. As such he was given to fits of wild ecstasy. In the celebration of his mysteries his followers often acted that out. In some myths Orpheus, the reformer, dies when the followers of Dionysus tear him to pieces during a fit of their religious ecstasy. Thus Orpheus sacrificed his life at the hands of the followers of the religion he came to reform.

The standard account of Orphic cosmology is preserved in what is known as the *Rhapsodic Theogony*. This is a long, complex story, with long lists of names, 'so-and-so begat so-and-so,' which we abbreviate here for the sake of clarity. In the beginning Chronos (Time) creates the One, which is the cosmos in the form of an egg. From the egg bursts forth *Dionysus-Phanes*, the First Born, the creative principle.

After more begetting down through various generations we come to Zeus. With his daughter Persephone, Zeus gives birth to a second Dionysus, this time *Dionysus-Zagreus*. This second Dionysus inherits authority

---

[23]   For information on Orphism, see Martin, *Hellenistic Religions,* p 98f, and Guthrie, *Orpheus and Greek Religion.*

over both our world and the underworld. That arouses the jealously of the Titans.

The Titans are a class of primitive, unruly, and violent deities similar to the disobedient race of giants described in the Bible. Because of their evil they have been banished to the underworld. In a Dionysian frenzy the Titans dismember, roast and eat Dionysus-Zagreus. In other words, the evil Titans with their uncontrolled passions, kill the Orphic savior Dionysus during a typical ecstatic celebration of the materialistic version of the Dionysian Mysteries.

Zeus destroys the Titans in a flash of lightning. From their ashes arises the race of mortal man. Because of this, humans embody two natures. There is an evil nature inherited from the ashes of the earthly Titans. But there also is a spark of divine soul from Dionysus-Zagreus whom the Titans had just consumed when they were incinerated. Orphism used this to illustrate its new doctrine of how divine souls became imprisoned within human bodies.

Human salvation means purifying the soul from the stain of its mixture with the Titans' materialistic nature. It means restoration of the spark of divinity within man to its true unsoiled state. In life, individuals must be taught to reject their base and earthy Titanic nature in order to nurture and liberate their inner, spiritual Dionysian nature. Accordingly, they must also reject the materialistic celebration of the original Dionysian mysteries and practice the new, reformed, spiritual version promoted by Orphism. (Pre-reformation Dionysian worship is the despised and materialistic 'Old Testament' of Orphism.)

Fortunately, when the Titans devoured Dionysus-Zagreus they failed to eat the heart. The goddess Athena recovers the heart and Zeus swallows it. Zeus thereby is impregnated and gives birth to the third and final *Dionysus*. This Dionysus, the reborn savior, works to help men purify themselves from their Titanic nature. Salvation – the return of human souls to their origin in heaven – ultimately then becomes the spiritual ingathering and reunification of the savior with his own body, which had been scattered throughout the material world by the Titans' sin.

Like most of the reformed mystery cults that followed in their footsteps, the Orphics took a dim view of the material world. In the Orphic hymns we find a frequent theme dwelling on the world as a debased place, on human misery and on being subject to the capriciousness and bondage of Fate and Fortune. The Orphic hymns commonly portray the pain and suffering of human life as punishment and a means to purification.

Not much survives to inform us about Orphic ritual and cult practice. What we have mostly are literary references to their philosophic beliefs and how they reinterpreted the Dionysian mystery system. However, gold plates buried with the dead from the early centuries B.C. suggest that a system of rituals did exist.

The gold plates boast that Orphic believers trust in a salvation that gives them immortal life by transforming them into heros after death. What that meant is that by mystical identification with their hero-savior Orpheus-Dionysus, they will become like him after death. As he was re-born following his sacrifice at the hands of the evil Titans, so his follow-ers too will escape death and live forever.

At this point we are near the end of our review of Hellenistic religion. There remain only a few additional notes about what ultimately happened to the original sponsors of the great pagan reformation.

Pythagoreanism to Neopythagoreanism

What happened to the early, key players in the great pagan reforma-tion? Here I am referring to Orphism, Pythagoreanism, and the philoso-phy of Plato, all of which played key roles in the formation and spread of Hellenistic religion in ancient Greece.

Orphism disappeared as a distinct religious movement. Orphism was only a shadowy, mystical religious cult, even in the early days of the pa-gan reformation in ancient Greece. Apparently it never became a wide-spread, organized movement.

In contrast, Pythagoreanism was a more visible and materially success-ful movement. It continued to play an important role right into the Chris-tian era.

Pythagoreanism's presence is felt in many ways yet today. Those who have studied geometry in high school will remember the Pythagoran Theorem (the sum of the squares of the two sides of a right-angle triangle equals the square of the hypotenuse). This and many other mathematical discoveries came from the same Greek cult that played a major role in the religious reformation in ancient Greece.[24]

---

[24]   The principle of right-angle triangulation, the basis of the Pythagoran Theorem, actually was understood in ancient Egypt and used in the

Why would Pythagoreanism, a supposedly philosophic cult, be interested in math and science? Isn't that all the more strange if they actually were a religious cult as well, as the evidence clearly shows? However, there is nothing strange about it at all. Mathematics, science, music and philosophy were all believed to be expressions of the intelligence and order radiating down from the heavens. Intelligence and order are manifestations of a great Intelligence residing in the highest heaven, in other words God himself. Therefore math, science and music are spiritual and heavenly. To study the intelligent relationship of numbers in mathematics, or the harmony in music, or to participate in the pure reasoning of philosophy, is to learn the character and nature of God, and draws the soul closer to him. It revives one's inner spiritual nature, awakening and reconnecting the soul to the heavens from whence it came.

What happened to the movement founded by Pythagoras? It first took root in southern Italy in the late sixth century. Here it flourished for only a brief time, little more than half a century. Small, esoteric Pythagorean groups spread throughout the region. By virtue of their prowess in science and medicine, and the prestige of their learning in philosophy and religion, they attached themselves to the ruling aristocracies of various Greek colonies across southern Italy. Their knowledge could be a tremendous advantage. Some Pythagoreans applied their skill to the science of warfare where they were instrumental in the invention of catapult machines.

Their political success proved their undoing, however. Local political factions whom they had displaced began to fight back. Many Pythagoreans were run out of town by mobs and some even killed. By the mid-fifth century their political power was broken. This, however, served only to spread their surviving members and teachings to other parts of the Greek world.

After the great Pythagorean dispersion of the fifth century, some returned to southern Italy and established the town of Tarentum as the center of their cult. It was here in the fourth century B.C. at Tarentum that Plato visited Archytas, a noted Pythagorean philosopher and politician. It was Archytas who played the key role of introducing the pagan religious reformation to Plato, who in turn passed it on to classical Greek philosophy. Around the middle of the fourth century, however, the trail comes to an end. Shortly after fulfilling the fateful historical function of supplying the doctrines of the great Greek religious reformation to Plato, Pythagore-

---

construction of the pyramids. But the Pythagoreans were the first to develop it as a formal mathematical theory.

anism disappears from the historical record as a distinct philosophic school.

What happened to the Pythagorean cult? Did it just fade away as a distinct group or blend into other groups as its ideas were assimilated by Greek and Hellenistic culture at large? Did they survive as small, esoteric groups, as they originally had been, not leaving distinguishable tracks or attracting attention in a culture that already had adopted much of their teachings? We simply don't know. However, in the first century B.C., some 300 years later, they reappear in Rome as what is now called Neopythagoreanism. Once again they are a philosophic and religious cult, still embracing the same reformation of religion as they did in the sixth century B.C.

Platonism to Neoplatonism

What happened to the philosophy of Plato? As we saw above, he played such an important role in spreading the new religion by embedding it in Greek philosophy. And further, as we saw, this came about when Plato came into contact with Pythagorean teachers in southern Italy.

By a curious quirk of history, the contact and cross-fertilization between Pythagoreanism and Plato in the fourth century B.C. repeated itself in the early centuries of the Christian era. A latter day descendant of Pythagoras' original religious sect, Neopythagoreanism, once again influenced a corresponding latter day descendant of Platonic philosophy, called Middle Platonism. The merger of these two resulted in a new form of Platonism called, appropriately, Neoplatonism.

The importance of Neoplatonism is two-fold. First, it took Platonic philosophy back to its religious roots. Under the influence of Neopythagoreanism, Platonism once again more openly merged philosophic reason with religion. Second, it merged Hellenistic religion with the Chaldean Mysteries, another strain of religion inherited directly from ancient Babylonia. The final result of this mixing of philosophy and religion within Neoplatonism was called "theurgy." And the ultimate importance of theurgy and Neoplatonism is that they profoundly influenced the development of what became the theology of the Roman church.

Hellenistic Paganism to Hellenistic Christianity

What happened to Hellenistic religion in general? Scholars frequently refer to the form of Christianity practiced today as Hellenistic Christianity. And they talk about what happened to the church in the early centuries after Christ as the Hellenization of Christianity. The reason for that, very simply, is that modern, mainstream Christianity is a blend of the original (primitive) Christianity of the first century and the pagan Hellenistic religion described in this chapter. How did this happen and what is its significance?

Remember from the beginning of this chapter how the Apostle John talked about an apostasy forming inside the church during the first century. And that apostasy was identified as the religion embraced by the Hellenistic culture of that time (*what they say is from the world*), and its wide popularity (*the world listens to them*) – see above, page 3.

Christianity was born into a world totally infused with Hellenistic religious ideals. A collision between the two was inevitable. The impact of this on the early church was spread over two waves. Neoplatonism, which we noted in the previous section, was a key ingredient of the second wave of influence that completed the Hellenization of Christianity in the fourth century A.D.[25] This second wave is the subject of *Spirit of Antichrist,* volume two of our series The World of Primitive Christianity.

The scope of volume one, *Primitive Christianity in Crisis,* is limited primarily to the first wave of contact, which began in the first century almost immediately after the founding of the church. It is this initial contact between Hellenistic religion and Christianity to which the Apostle John refers in his epistles.

The rest of this volume is devoted to detailing the devastating impact of that first encounter, and how the theology it spawned flourished, nearly died out, but was resurrected and flourishes again in our time.

---

[25] Theurgy, a key ingredient of later Neoplatonism, for example is the origin of sacramental religion, which became the primary tradition of the Roman church.

– 2 –

Gnostic Christianity
in History

What does Hellenistic religion have to do with Christianity? It has everything to do with it because some Christians in the first century combined Hellenistic religion with New Testament Christianity. This produced a hybrid called Gnostic Christianity. Gnosticism was a collection of teachings that essentially proclaimed the basic principles of pagan Hellenistic religion under the name of Christianity.

According to Gnosticism, spirit originates in the heavens. Through sin the perfection of life in the heavens has been disrupted. Tainted by sin, spirit descends through the planetary spheres to earth where it becomes trapped as individual souls in human bodies. There it wanders, lost and suffering from the chaos and disorder of the material world. Human passion and materialistic pleasure have caused man to forget his true inner nature, that his soul is divine and immortal, that it originated in the heavens and is destined to return to heaven after death. Thus Gnostic Christians viewed the fall, entrapment and suffering of man essentially the same as in Hellenistic religion.

In Gnostic Christianity, salvation means several things. First it means that the knowledge of the immortal soul, its origin and destiny must be restored. (The name Gnosticism comes from the Greek word *gnosis*, meaning 'knowledge.') The soul is made of the same substance as the heavens, and because it is heavenly it is immortal. Man's destiny is for his soul to return to a life of perfection and peaceful stability in the heavens. For that to happen, however, human ties to materialistic life must be broken. The inner life of the spirit must be nurtured and developed. Man must grow into a full spiritual being so his soul can escape from the material world and ascend to heaven after death.

The need for *gnosis* (knowledge) of man's inner composition and origin, so central to Gnostic teaching, goes all the way back to the Orphic reformation of the seventh century B.C. Some of the Orphic gold plates recovered from burials instruct the dead on how to recover the lost memory of spiritual things that will give them success in the hereafter. In these texts the soul of the dead is exhorted to recognize that man is a hybrid of earth and the heavens. But man's most important component, it explains, is heavenly.[26]

Gnostic Christianity began inside the apostolic church in the first century, in a form scholars today call proto-Gnosticism. By late in the first century there was a substantial backlash against proto-Gnosticism and most Gnostic Christians left the church to found their own independent movements.

It is important to understand there is no single body of Gnostic doctrine. There were dozens of individual sects, each offering conflicting ideas on the fall of man, what spirituality means, and especially the practices and rules man should follow to free himself from the material world. We will see a wide range of ideas and interpretations in the survey of Gnostic sects that follows.

Gnostic Christianity in general is merely another manifestation of the reformation of Greek religion that began with Orphism and Pythagoreanism. There are differences, of course. Gnosticism is considered a more extreme example of Hellenistic religion in that it developed a passionately negative condemnation of material existence.

How did they justify combining pagan Hellenistic religion with Christianity? Though Gnosticism made liberal use of the teachings of the spirituality of a New Testament, it did not see Christianity as a reformation of Hebrew religion. Most Gnostic Christians passionately and totally rejected the Old Testament and Hebrew religion. If the material world is altogether evil, then its creator Yahweh and his religion must be absolutely evil as well. Salvation becomes possible, they insisted, only by completely rejecting the deception of the Hebrew God of creation.

Gnosticism continued the common Hellenistic tradition of reinterpreting older religious systems, but not the religion of the Old Testament. Gnostics saw themselves as a reformation not of Judaism, but instead as a reformation of the New Testament church itself. They viewed the so-called Primitive or 'Jewish' Christianity that prevailed for a time after the

---

[26]   See Hogart, *The Hymns of Orpheus,* for example "Soul Ladder", p 32.

founding of the church in the 30s A.D., as a partial step towards Hellenistic truth, which they felt reached its climax and full revelation of truth in Gnostic Christianity.

Gnostic Christians thus promoted their teachings as a second, more advanced revelation of Christianity. The problem with Primitive Christianity, they insisted, is that it had failed to completely break its ties with the deception of Old Testament religion.

Gnosticism took a unique interest in Primitive Christians, with devastating results for the history of the Christian faith. This came from the common Gnostic belief in a three-fold classification of the human race. One class, they claimed, are composed of 'natural' humans, purely material and lacking a soul. These are predestined to live and die like animals and perish forever. For them there is no hope.

Primitive Christians were assigned a special class of their own. Primitive Christians, they believed, possess souls and therefore have the potential to be saved, if only they receive the knowledge of the immortal soul within them, accept the grace and intervention of Christ and the heavenly Father, and be freed from the deception of the materialistic creation-centered religion of the Old Testament.

For some Gnostics this led to primarily targeting Primitive Christians for conversion to their more enlightened revelation of Christianity. Supposedly, only orthodox Primitive Christians had the potential to be saved. In effect, many Gnostics believed their commission in the world was to convert Primitive Christianity to a more advanced spirituality based on Hellenistic theology, at the same time weaning Primitive Christians away from their religious ties to Hebrew religion and the Old Testament.

Gnosticism's reinterpretation of biblical religion reads essentially as follows: The highest deity is the heavenly Father. He did not create the world. That task was accomplished by an emanation from the Father, generally equated with Yahweh, the God of the Old Testament. He is an inferior, deluded, and often evil being. His claim to be the supreme God is a wicked delusion, and man must by all means reject him and his religion. For Gnostics, the Old Covenant and the Old Covenant God are evil. The religion of the Old Covenant is a false religion based on materialistic animal sacrifice. It deceives man into seeking spirituality in the material world, keeping him in bondage to this world.

A process of emanations or fall from a higher state has trapped spirit in the material world. The true heavenly Father sent Christ to rescue the spark of spirit that exists in some men. He reveals the knowledge (*gnosis*) that will rescue these souls from the God of the Old Testament and material creation, enabling them to escape after death and re-enter heaven.[27] So Gnosticism viewed its improved Hellenistic version of Christianity as a spiritual teaching, a religion focused exclusively on the heavens, on the immortal soul, that divine spark which is from the heavens and which takes us back there after death.

Some Gnostics especially relied on the writings of Paul because of his emphasis on inner spirituality. However, Gnosticism also relied heavily on theories of progressive revelation, insisting theirs was a more advanced, second revelation of the Christian faith. To that end they often claimed special private revelations to support their reinterpretation of New Testament Christianity. Many Gnostic texts, for example, proclaim a special revelation from Christ from after the resurrection, which replaces his earthly ministry as recorded in the four gospels.

---

[27]   Compare Hultgren, Haggmark, *The Earliest Christian Heretics,* p 37–38.

First Century Gnostic Christians

Various passages in the New Testament indicate there were many Gnostic groups already in the first century, but very little evidence remains from this early period. We have substantial information on only two Gnostic sects – the Simonians and the Nicolaitans – and one additional Gnostic teacher. Of these it is the Nicolaitans who hold a special interest for us today because they are the only ones mentioned in the Bible by name (Revelation 2:6 and 2:15).

Individual Gnostic sects had considerably different practices and theologies. Therefore, if we can identify Nicolaitan theological positions, we can better understand exactly what the book of Revelation is trying to say to us when it talks about them.

Nicolaitans [28]

The Nicolaitans are believed to have been founded by the biblical Nicolas mentioned in Acts 6:5. He was one of the deacons in the Jerusalem church, ordained by the 12 apostles shortly after the founding of the church in the early 30's. It is possible he had personal contact with Jesus before the crucifixion.

The Nicolaitans are mentioned twice in Revelation. The Ephesian church is praised for hating Nicolaitan immorality and for shutting them and their leaders out of the church. The church at Pergamum is criticized for tolerating the presence of church members who embrace Nicolaitan doctrines.

The only other evidence we have for Nicolaitanism is from the early church fathers. They preached and warned against a wide range of groups they considered heretical, including many Gnostic sects. At one time they were the only source available, and they frequently depicted Gnostic

---

[28]   Hultgren and Haggmark, *The Earliest Christian Heretics,* p 28 ff.

Christians as a wildly licentious and debauched group of people. Then a sizable collection of Gnostic texts was found at Nag Hammadi in Egypt.[29] From that source we obtain a picture of a much more sophisticated movement. They often appear as seriously dedicated to spirituality and moral conduct. The moral teachings of many Gnostic groups would be quite acceptable and in some aspects even exceptional by modern cultural standards.

For Nicolaitans we have only evidence from the early church fathers. But even here, there is evidence of genuine dedication to spirituality.

Three church fathers talk about the Nicolaitans – Irenaeus (*Against Heresies* 1.26.3), Hippolytus (*Refutation of All Heresies* 7.24) and Eusebius (*Ecclesiastical History* 3:29).

Irenaeus appears to repeat only what he has read in Revelation. Hippolytus does not offer much more, but gives one important piece of evidence: *"But Nicholas departed from sound doctrine, and was in the habit of inculcating indifferency of both life and food."* Here, 'indifference' refers to the common Gnostic tendency to focus exclusively on the inner life of the spirit, and thereby become indifferent to our conduct in the material world. This is typical of much of Gnostic Christianity. It is a distinct departure from Judaism, which sees spirituality as involved with all aspects of life, including material conduct.

Eusebius provides the most information, and just enough to piece together the basic principles of Nicolaitan Christianity. He quotes from a now lost text by another church father, Clement of Alexandria:

---

[29] The Nag Hammadi library is composed of twelve leather bound books containing 52 individual texts, in Coptic but apparently translated from Greek originals, dating from the third and fourth centuries A.D. It is a highly eclectic collection of mostly Gnostic texts written by mostly unknown authors working in different locations around the eastern Mediterranean. Though the majority are Gnostic there are some Hermetic (an Egyptian Jewish/pagan form of Gnosticism), Platonic, purely Christian and some exhibiting greater and lesser degrees of Christianized Gnosticism. Peasant workmen discovered them in a buried jar while excavating fertilizer deposits in 1945 near the village of al-Qasr in upper Egypt. Unfortunately, before they were recovered by scholars, part of the find was lost when it was used as fuel in a stove for baking bread in the home of one of the workmen. The surviving material has contributed tremendously to understanding Gnostic theology and practice, and also sheds much new light on the Hellenistic Jewish roots of Gnosticism. For a full description, see The Anchor Bible Dictionary, article Nag Hammadi.

He had, they say, a beautiful wife; but after the ascension of the savior the apostles accused him of jealousy. So he brought her forward and proclaimed that anyone who wished might have her. This action, they say, came from the injunction 'the flesh must be treated with contempt'; and by following this example simply and crudely the members of his sect practice total promiscuity. But I know that Nicholas had nothing to do with any other woman than his wife, and of his children his daughters remained virgins till the end of their days and his son was never corrupted.

How do you make sense of that? Many of his followers used his teachings as an excuse for sin. Nicolas, however, practiced biblical chastity, and he taught it to his children. The incident involving Nicolas' wife is further clarified by Clement as he tries to explain the motive behind this strange event:

Such being the case, his bringing the wife whom he loved so jealously into the midst of the apostles was the renunciation of desire, and it was mastery of the pleasures...that taught him the rule "treat the flesh with contempt." For in obedience to the Savior's command, I imagine, he had no wish to serve two masters, pleasure and the Lord.

The underlying, primary teaching of Nicolaitanism, then, is that to achieve inner spirituality one must ignore outer (material) concerns (*treat the flesh with contempt*). That does not mean, however, that we should be blatantly immoral. Nicolas obviously did not intend for anyone to take the offer of his wife seriously. He was merely making a show of his contempt for the material pleasure that comes from marriage.

What Nicolas was saying is, to be successful you must pursue inner spirituality *exclusively*. If you do that, then your outer morality will take care of itself. Spirituality is not to be found in the material experience of life nor in any of the rules that the Bible or any persons use to try to legislate material conduct.

As Hippolytus said above, Nicolas cultivated an indifferent attitude toward material life and food. Taking that as the starting point, one might interpret it to mean totally breaking away from material lust. That clearly is what Nicolas intended. Nicolas himself was a shining example of purity and dedication to non-material, inner spirituality. On the other hand, one could argue it means that material issues have no spiritual relevance, so do whatever you want. The description of Nicolaitanism in the book of Revelation confirms the accusations of promiscuity against Nicolas' followers. Clearly, much of the Nicolaitan membership at some point chose to view indifference to material life as a license to indulge.

Understanding the interplay of those two applications of Gnostic spirituality – indifference in order to devote one's self to inner spirituality, and indifference as an excuse to indulge – is an important key to understanding Nicolaitan Christianity.

The problem of Nicolaitanism and Gnostic Christianity in general is the error of its radical theories about separating inner and outer spirituality. This developed from the classic Hellenistic attitude towards the material world that we saw in the previous chapter.

Simon Magus [30]

Simon Magus (Simon the Magician) was a native Samaritan from Palestine. He had made a living as a professional religious charlatan for some time before converting to Christianity in the 30's A.D. The story of his conversion and questionable motives for becoming a Christian are recorded in the Bible (Acts chapter 8).

The early church fathers said the founder of the Simonian sect of Gnosticism is this same Simon Magus, and the evidence generally supports that conclusion. The same church fathers generally give Simon credit for founding the entire Gnostic Christian movement. This is a more questionable conclusion. The weight of the evidence, however, suggests Gnosticism did originate in Palestine among heretical Jewish sects. So it would not be surprising if Simon was at least involved in the birth of Gnosticism if not the sole person responsible. Like many other seekers after fame and a following, Simon relocated to Rome, sometime in the reign of the emperor Claudius (42–54 A.D.).

Simon and his disciple Menander, another Samaritan by origin, taught a "docetic" theology. Docetism is the name used to signify the doctrine that Jesus Christ is a composite of two beings. Jesus, they believed, was a mortal man. Christ is a spirit who merged with Jesus at conception or at his baptism. Some Gnostics believed that Christ separated from Jesus before the crucifixion so that only the man Jesus died on the cross. Because of Gnosticism's extreme antagonism towards the material world,

---

[30] Hultgren and Haggmark, *The Earliest Christian Heretics,* p 15 ff.

they could not conceive of God becoming a material man and suffering death. Many but not all Gnostic sects taught Docetism in some form.[31]

Docetism is a key to understanding Gnostic theology. For example, most Gnostics considered the earthly ministry of Jesus to be defective, and this was based on their belief in Docetism. The idea was that Christ's spirituality was confined to the spiritual half of his nature. His material half, the human man Jesus, was not spiritual. Jesus was a good man but nevertheless only a material creature, and he happened to be a Jew. Therefore, they reasoned, Jesus' earthly ministry, as recorded in the four gospels, was influenced in part by the material half of his nature. This supposedly contaminated his preaching with faulty teachings carried over from his Jewish heritage.

The description of Simon in Acts chapter 8 as a self-serving showman is confirmed by the historical sources. Simon was thoroughly given to self-promotion. He claimed to be both the Holy Spirit and the Son of God destined to save man. He traveled with a woman named Helen whom he supposedly had redeemed from a life of prostitution in the city of Tyre, in present-day Lebanon. Simon claimed she originally had descended from heaven and gave birth to the angels who created the material world. But then her angelic children, led by Yahweh, turned on her out of envy and prevented her from returning to the Father. By this story Simon taught the typical Hellenistic concept of human bondage in the material world. Through the ages Helen's soul had been repeatedly reincarnated, continuing in bondage to the material world. Finally it came to rest in Helen's body, where Simon found her. Now Helen had become the first to be redeemed by Simon from bondage to the material world, and he offered the same hope of liberation to any who would follow him.

The sect's ritual focused on obtaining spiritual power. This, they believed, transformed them into spiritual beings who would endure eternally after death. Magic and sorcery were employed as part of the means to obtain the spiritual power that transforms them into immortal beings.

Both Simon and his disciple Menander insisted that only they taught the genuine and true revelation of Christianity.

---

[31] The term docetism implies giving the appearance of something other than what one is. A composite being, including a spirit that masquerades in appearance as only its human half, fits that definition. However, some Gnostics apparently claimed that Christ was a spirit that sometimes manifested itself as though it had a material human form, in the sense of phantom. Therefore when the crucifixion occurred, it only appeared that he died, but that in fact was only a false impression.

Cerinthus [32]

All the major first-century Gnostic teachers originated or taught along the eastern Mediterranean coast, near or in Palestine. This is also true of Cerinthus, who lived and taught in Asia Minor. Though little is known of his background and his following if any, he was an early Gnostic teacher of the first century of whom we have a little evidence.

Cerinthus was said to have been the first Gnostic to propose the docetic idea that Christ is a spiritual being who descended upon the man Jesus. According to his teaching, Jesus was a natural human being, the son of Joseph and Mary. Jesus the man was crucified and he did rise again, but only Jesus experienced this, not Christ.

Cerinthus also taught that the creator of the material world was an inferior angelic being. Remarkable for a Gnostic, however, he taught that Christ would bring his kingdom to rule on earth for a thousand years after the resurrection of the saints.

---

[32] Hultgren and Haggmark, *The Earliest Christian Heretics,* p 34 ff.

Second Century and Later Gnostic Sects

Neither of the two leading first-century Gnostic sects survived long. The Nicolaitans had disappeared by 200 A.D., and the Simonians by 250. In any event, many more Gnostic sects appeared in their place to carry on the tradition. As time progressed, Gnostic Christianity flourished in many new forms as it continued to mix and match ideas from the broad range of Hellenistic religion and New Testament Christianity.

Carpocrates [33]

The Gnostic teacher Carpocrates founded his movement in Alexandria, Egypt, in the mid-100's. He taught that inferior angels created the world. Jesus, because of his pure soul, could remember things he had experienced in his previous existence in the heavens.[34] So Jesus was given the task of revealing the saving *gnosis* (knowledge) to mankind.

Carpocrates was extreme in his opposition to Hebrew religion. To become free from the material world, he said, one must aggressively insult the God of the Old Testament and his angels by flagrantly violating his law. He was adamantly antinomian as well. According to Carpocrates, there is no fixed standard of morality. It is after all, he claimed, only a matter of opinion, as witnessed by the multitude of opinions on the subject found throughout the world. Instead, he insisted, salvation is by a more general and higher standard:

> We are saved, indeed, by means of faith and love; but all other things, while in their nature indifferent, are reckoned by the

---

[33] Hultgren and Haggmark, p 49 ff.

[34] Likewise Pythagoras' spirituality was demonstrated by his ability to remember his existence in prior lives.

opinion of men some good and some evil, but there is nothing evil by nature. [35]

Once again, this does not mean they totally abandoned morality. The argument was that nothing is intrinsically good or evil but depends on the situation and especially its relation to the issue of materialism.

According to Hippolytus, Carpocratians believed in conquering material lust. By aggressively hating and despising all spirit beings associated with creation, they felt they could liberate themselves from the material vices that keep man in bondage to the world. That is not quite as silly as it sounds at first. What they were saying is that when you participate in religious practices oriented towards material creation, that naturally stimulates your material lusts. By breaking free from Jewish religion you enable your mind to reorient itself towards the inner soul and its connection with the heavens and the spirituality that comes from above.

This is essentially the same argument used today by those who carry on the Gnostic Christian tradition, when they claim it is impossible to express spirituality through obedience to biblical law and Old Testament, creation-centered forms of worship. The underlying belief, then and now, is that the two are by nature incompatible. Only if you invent something new on your own can it be deemed spiritual, rising spontaneously from the divine spirituality of your inner soul.

The Carpocratians believed that all souls ultimately will be saved. If a soul fails to accept the gospel of Gnostic Christianity it will be reborn repeatedly in the material world where it continues to experience sin. Finally, when a soul has fully exhausted its suffering because of sin, it returns to God.

In this hodge-podge of libertinism and subjective morality, it is not surprising some Carpocratians figured out they could 'milk' the system. And so they earned a reputation for excessive immorality. It was reported that one faction among them built onto the teaching that the soul returns to God when it has completed its full allotment of suffering from sin. Therefore, they said, participating in sin merely speeds up the process of salvation!

---

[35]   Irenaeus, *Against Heresies,* 1.25.5

Saturninus [36]

Saturninus was a teacher from near Antioch, Syria in the second century. He began as a student of Menander, the disciple of Simon Magus mentioned above. He taught that Christians can obtain freedom from the material world by practicing asceticism. For the followers of his cult, this included rejecting marriage.

According to Saturninus, Christ came to destroy the worship of the God of the Jews and he will save all who merely believe in him.

Marcion [37]

Marcion is one of the greatest Gnostic teachers. He was born the son of an orthodox Christian bishop in the city of Sinope, on the southern shore of the Black Sea. He started his professional life in the shipping trade and became a wealthy businessman before turning to religion. He moved to Rome around 130 A.D. There he bought his way into the church with a large donation. In 144, however, he broke with the Roman church to found his own Gnostic Christian movement.

Marcion was a tireless and skilled organizer. By 155 A.D. his church was described as present in all nations. Ultimately it spread as far as Persia.

Marcion was a devoted antinomian. He taught that Jesus brought us the revelation of the true Father in heaven. The Father is absolute goodness and love, totally without anger. Therefore, Marcion insisted, the wrathful God of the Old Testament cannot be the same as the true spiritual Father. Christ came to destroy the law and the prophets, indeed, to destroy all the works of the Old Testament God. Still, Marcion did not condemn Yahweh as severely as many other Gnostic teachers did. Instead he merely characterized the God of the Old Testament as judgmental and harsh, compared to the unlimited love and grace of the true heavenly Father and Jesus.

---

[36] Hultgren and Haggmark, *The Earliest Christian Heretics,* p 56 ff.
[37] Ibid., p 101f.

The early church fathers rejected Marcion's pure-love theology. One of them, Tertulian, criticized Marcion in the following words:

> For if he [God] displays neither hostility nor wrath, if he neither condemns nor disdains, if...he never makes himself a judge, I cannot see how his moral law...can have stability. ... Why does he forbid the commission of an act he does not penalize when committed? ... In real life an act forbidden without sanctions is tacitly permitted....[38]

Marcion's theology is an excellent example of preaching against sin and licensing it at the same time by removing the penalty. Through the influence of the apostles, and later the early church fathers such as Tertullian, the Roman church never adopted the radical 'grace alone' antinomianism of Gnosticism. After the demise of classic Gnosticism this teaching did not reappear in Christianity with its original prominence until the Protestant Reformation.

Marcion accepted ten books of the New Testament attributed to Paul, plus part of the Gospel of Luke. He did not follow the usual Gnostic practice of interpreting the Bible allegorically. Marcion understood Scripture to be literal. To make this fit with his Gnostic beliefs he simply edited those scriptures that he accepted. Epiphanius quipped that after Marcion got through with his editing, what was left looked *"like a garment eaten by many moths."*

As for Old Testament scripture, Marcion simply dismissed it as having no spiritual value for Christians. Other Gnostic teachers often used Old Testament scripture, interpreting it allegorically to make it condemn creation and even the religion of the Old Testament itself. Some claimed Old Testament scripture was the product of the evil Jewish people and their evil God, but the Holy Spirit had slipped clues to spiritual truth into the Old Testament, which the Jews had missed and failed to edit out.

In rejecting the Old Testament, Marcion demonstrated a uniquely stubborn single-mindedness. What happened, according to the early church fathers, is Marcion first became obsessed with several individual biblical passages, one of which was Mark 2:21–22 (*no one patches an old garment with new cloth, nor puts new wine in old wineskins*). On this

---

[38] Tertulian *Against Marcion,* 1.26.1–4. Tertulian's last quoted statement above could easily be phrased "In real life an act forbidden without sanctions is tacitly licensed," for this indeed is the essence of licentiousness in the world of Gnostic Christianity and its modern survivals.

single foundation, he insisted we must reject anything to do with the Old Testament (the *old garment* and *old wineskins* spoken of by Mark). The Roman clergy met with him numerous times to plead with him, but he simply wouldn't budge. He stubbornly defended his position on that single scripture. For Marcion it didn't matter what other passages of the New Testament say, that is what those verses mean, end of discussion![39]

The Marcionite church practiced baptism and the sacraments. Marcion taught a docetic Christology that separates Jesus and the Christ. His followers practiced a fairly radical, ascetic lifestyle, in which marriage was forbidden.

Apelles [40]

The Gnostic teacher Apelles began his career as a student of Marcion, but they had a falling out. Apelles moved to Alexandria, Egypt, and then back to Rome after Marcion's death.

Apelles carried accommodation with orthodox theology much further than most. He rejected Docetism. Jesus and Christ are the same being, he said. Jesus came in the flesh, was crucified and resurrected. He also accepted that the creator of the material world is good rather than evil. On the other hand, he continued the Gnostic line that the God of the Old Testament and the heavenly Father are not the same, and he rejected Old Testament scripture.

Basilides [41]

Basilides was active in Alexandria, Egypt in the early 100's. He was one of the most influential writers of the second century, though none of his books survive. Under the influence of Greek philosophy and religion

---

[39] This passage from Mark is more accurately understood to refer, not to the Old Covenant or Old Testament scripture, but to those Jewish leaders in the first century who were so set in their ways and antagonistic to the Messiah, that Christ found it necessary to start over again with new religious leaders and a completely new organization, the apostolic church.

[40] Hultgren and Haggmark, *The Earliest Christian Heretics,* p 77 ff.

[41] Ibid., p 60 ff.

he elaborated a full cosmology typical of his time. Angels created the heavens, comprised of 365 levels, one for each day in the year. The lower levels of heaven, those we can see from earth, and the earth itself, were created by one special group of angels led by Yahweh.

Yahweh rules over the seven planetary spheres where matter is first encountered as one descends from the starry heavens. From this place, midway between heaven and earth, he rules over everything below including the earth.

Yahweh himself is ignorant of the cosmic levels above him and the existence of the heavenly Father in the highest heaven. Salvation comes by Christ, who is sent to man to reveal the mystery of that heavenly world that exists above the God of the Old Testament. Simply receiving that knowledge (*gnosis*), frees man from the ignorance that keeps us in bondage to Yahweh and his materialistic angels.

The process of salvation, in addition to liberation from Yahweh and his angels, is to develop the spirituality of the soul. Thereby, when the soul sheds its material body at death, it will ascend to heaven. If you become spiritual (heavenly) then at death your soul automatically rises to the heavens. The duty of a follower of Basilides is to *"order, train, correct, and perfect our souls,"* in order to become 'heavenly.'

Salvation is a matter of the soul alone. Morality, according to Basilides, is another matter entirely. Morality concerns only the body, which at death the soul sheds and leaves behind to decay. Therefore it is philosophically impossible to link salvation with moral rules and regulations that govern material conduct. But once again, this does not mean that man should wantonly sin, only that salvation technically is not linked to one's material conduct. The command to perfect one's soul, as we saw above, implies that man will come out of material lust in some general sense as a by-product of becoming 'spiritual.'

In the final restoration of all things, there will come a profound ignorance on all beings of the existence of other parts of the cosmos. This is done to relieve all beings of suffering and pain, which comes from longing for things one does not and cannot have. The point of salvation, it would appear, is to gain access to the best part of the cosmos before everything is sealed off.

Valentinus [42]

The Valentinian school of Gnosticism is important both for its wide geographic spread and influence, and the close ties it established with the early Roman church.

Valentinus began in Alexandria, Egypt, but moved to Rome where he joined the orthodox church and became one of its leading members. He was highly educated and a skilled writer. Many orthodox Christians at Rome were impressed by his work. Some claimed that Valentinus had received a special revelation of spiritual truth from Paul, supposedly passed on by a person named Theudas, a disciple of Paul.

According to Irenaeus, Valentinus came very close to being selected as head of the Roman church, and left the church only when he was passed over for that job.[43] After that he founded his own school of Gnostic Christianity in Rome, which he maintained for approximately three decades in the mid 100's.

In Valentinian theology the highest spiritual realm is composed of 30 male-female pairs of angels, called *aeons*. This is the *pleroma,* a Greek term that means 'fullness.' The sense of *pleroma* is completeness and perfection, which for Valentinus is the highest heaven, the realm of the true, spiritual Father.

The perfection of the *pleroma* is maintained by a state of submission and interdependence, symbolized by the pairing of the *aeons*. This perfection is broken by the fall of one of the youngest *aeons*, Sophia. She tries to create on her own, without working through her *aeon* partner. So she gives birth to a deformed being. This is Yahweh, who in turn creates the world. The creation story borrows heavily from Plato. Yahweh unknowingly is inspired to create all things according to eternal patterns that exist above. He is foolish and silly, however, thinking he is the only God, not knowing everything he did was controlled by powers above him.

Redemption comes from the descent of another angel, Christ, who unites with the man Jesus. Some said this occurred at his baptism, others at conception. In typical Gnostic fashion, Christ's work is to reveal the *gnosis* of man's origin, the heavenly, immortal soul within, and the destiny of the soul to return to heaven.

---

[42]   Ibid., p 82 ff.

[43]   See Tertullian, *Adv. Val.* 4.

Mankind is divided into three groups. First are the *pneumatics* (spiritual ones). At death they enter directly into heaven. These are the enlightened Valentinian Christians.

Second are the *psychics*, persons with souls who have not achieved the advanced spirituality offered by the Valentinians. These are the various groups of orthodox Christians. They are deluded into believing salvation is attained by faith *and* good works. Some Gnostics considered that a fatal mistake. Others, such as the Valentinians, followed a different argument, reasoning that orthodox Christians are merely spiritually weak. Therefore they required the assistance of faith and good works to be saved.

Valentinians taught that orthodox Christians will be saved in spite of their failure to reject all vestiges of Hebrew religion. However, it is a lesser salvation. Their reward is to spend eternity in the seventh heaven with the creator. In contrast, the spiritual Valentinian faithful at death go directly to the Ogdoad, the eighth level of heaven, and at the end of time are inducted directly into the *pleroma* (the highest heaven) where they enjoy the full fellowship of the heavenly Father.

The third class of beings are the *hylics* (materialists). They are like animals, having no soul and no hope of salvation.

Valentinian theology was classically antinomian. Epiphanius, speaking of their religious practices, says:

> ...they do not need to labor, but need only knowledge and the incantations of their rites. Each of them does anything whatsoever without fear or concern, for, they say, their class [the Pneumatics], being spiritual, will be saved from everything. However, the next class of humans in the world (referring to psychics), which they call 'natural', cannot be saved on its own, unless it saves itself by labor and just deeds. [44]

The typical Gnostic three-fold classification of man led some groups to exclusively target orthodox Christians in their evangelistic outreach. Ordinary pagans, having no soul, were without hope. Orthodox Christians, having souls, were considered potential candidates for the Gnostics' supposedly more advanced revelation of Christian spirituality.

Valentinians especially targeted and infiltrated the Hellenistic Roman church in the second and third centuries. Some early writers in the Roman

---

[44] Epiphanius, *Panarion*, 31.7.8 .

53

church bemoaned the fact they seemed to sprout in their midst faster than they could excommunicate them.

Valentinianism in the Tripartite Tractate

Several Gnostic texts recovered from Nag Hammadi in Egypt appear to have been written by Valentinus himself or members of his sect. One of these, *The Tripartite Tractate,* is a classic example of how some Valentinian Christians adopted a modified Gnostic theology surprisingly close to Hellenistic Roman Christianity.[45] In this text we find a surprising movement away from classic Valentinian theology towards the orthodox Roman position, as follows:

In *The Tripartite Tractate,* the heavenly Father himself is responsible for creation of the entire universe. Creation is in some sense deficient, but not evil in the classic Gnostic sense. Yahweh creates the world, but in so doing he is merely carrying out the will of higher beings, and he is no longer depicted as evil.

The *pleroma* of 30 angelic *aeons* is gone, replaced by a trinity of the Father, Son and Church. The three-fold classification of man into material, lawful and spiritual is muted. 'Works-oriented' orthodox Christians have been promoted to the same stature as liberated spiritual Gnostics. They now are depicted as belonging to the same church and receive the same salvation.

The Tripartite Tractate is a significant glimpse into the adaptability of Gnostic sects. As we will see again with Manichaeism in the following section, Gnostics were always willing to adapt their theology and practices to blend in with whatever religious environment in which they found themselves.

---

[45] See *The Tripartite Tractate,* **NHLE**, p 60f, especially the introduction by Attridge and Pagels, p 58f. See also Perkins, *Gnosticism and the New Testament,* p 177–178.

Manichaeism [46]

Manichaeism is significant for its amazing geographic spread, for surviving the longest of all Gnostic sects, and for its demonstration of the Gnostic trait of reinterpreting earlier religious traditions.

It began in the third century in the Near East, which was then under Persian control. The founder Mani was born of Persian parents in a Gnostic family. His father was a member of the Elkasites, a Jewish-Christian Gnostic group.

From Babylonia, Mani's new sect spread as far as Spain in the west and China to the east. In the West it died out in the sixth century. In Babylonia it survived into the tenth century. In China, it was not until the fourteenth century that the spread of the Mongol empire snuffed out the last vestiges of the sect.

Manichaeism's durability and spread is credited in part to its ability to reinvent itself to suit any environment. In the West Mani styled himself as the Christian Holy Spirit. In Persian cultures he was a Zoroastrian messianic figure descended from Zarathustra, and in China he claimed to be the Buddhist messianic figure Maitreya.

In the West, Manichaeism imitated many beliefs and practices of Roman Christianity. However, it emphatically rejected both Judaism and the earthly ministry of Jesus. At the same time it venerated the spiritual or 'heavenly' Jesus, which Manichaeism viewed as the source of a more advanced revelation of Christianity. Like many other Gnostic teachers, Mani also especially venerated the writings of the Apostle Paul.

Another factor in the success of Manichaeism is its use of a two-tiered structure for the spiritual requirements it demanded of its followers. These two groups were called the 'elect' and the 'hearers.'

The elect were a priestly caste who followed a strict practice in which they renounced marriage, meat and wine. Missionary work was an important part of their function, which promoted the historical spread and success of their religion.

The hearers were allowed to marry and lead fairly normal secular lives. They were required to be moral and just in all of their dealings, and to refrain from attachment to materialism as much as possible. Their func-

---

[46] See Perkins, *Gnosticism and the New Testament,* p 192–193, and **EB**, article "Manichaeism."

tion in the church was to finance the spiritual work of the elect. Because the hearers followed a less religious life, after death they must endure a purgatory-like process of purification before entering heaven. Employing the merit earned by their superior religious practice, the elect could intercede for the hearers, to bless them and so shorten their stay in purgatory. Thus the hearers were strongly motivated to financially support the work of their priesthood.

Manichaeism was organized quite differently from most other Gnostic movements. Many of the classic Gnostic cults of the early centuries did not thrive. Most died out within a few centuries after Christ. The reason often is easy to identify. Some Gnostic sects practiced asceticism, which held little appeal for the masses. Those that banned marriage could not count on new generations of children to carry on their work. On the other hand, the Gnostic cults that became involved in licentious antinomianism often fared little better. In place of asceticism, they emphasized individuality, private revelation and personal experience of God, all of which detracted from an effective, united church organization.

Manichaeism in effect anticipated the success of the medieval Roman church and its similarly two-track system of lay members, topped by spiritual orders of monks, nuns and priests. You could achieve salvation while still living a materialistic secular life, but doing so required strict loyalty and monetary support of a centralized, hierarchical organization. Supporting the organization was the means to obtain the intervention of the church hierarchy on your behalf, so you could be saved in spite of your less spiritual life. The success of the Manichaean church was due in large part to the fact its two-tier structure made it one of the best financed and well organized of all Gnostic movements.

Manichaean worship was simple, consisting mainly of prayers and hymns. Salvation comes from knowledge (*gnosis*) and leading a virtuous life. There was a fairly developed system of fasting, including a nearly month-long fast resembling the modern Islamic Ramadan. Confession was a weekly practice. The main weekly cycle of religious activities took place on Sunday and Monday.

– 3 –

The Hellenistic Sabbath

In the history of Christianity one topic more than any other has become a centerpiece of the controversy over Hebrew religion and the transition to a New Covenant. That topic is the Sabbath. The antagonism and controversy over this issue today is little changed from what we find in the early centuries of the Christian era.

Just stop and consider. In the context of Hellenistic religion, using the number seven is like waiving a red flag in front of a bull. To say in those days you meet to worship God on the seventh day, in modern terms would be like saying you meet every Friday the thirteenth. Seven stands for the seven planetary spheres, the material world, entrapment of souls, misery, suffering and pain. Eight, on the other hand, stands for the starry heavens, escape from bondage, happiness, spirituality and immortality.

For Gnostic Christians it all made sense. After all, the Old Testament God whom they despised, himself admitted he created the world in seven days. Worse, his primary day of worship is the seventh day of the week. All the more evidence the Old Testament is the religion of bondage. True liberation and spirituality can be achieved only by rejecting all things Jewish and looking forward exclusively to the heavens, the world of the spirit, the future home of the saved.

Gnostic Christianity pioneered the conversion from Sabbath to Sunday. As Gnostic Christians began to leave the apostolic church and found their own sects, beginning late in the first century, their absorption of Hellenistic theology accelerated. The apostolic church followed their lead beginning early in the second century. But for them conversion to Sunday proceeded much more slowly, stretching over three centuries during which many local churches continued Sabbath observance and some observed both Sabbath and Sunday.

Sunday is the first day of the week, but they didn't call it that. Creation took all seven days of the week. Though the seventh day especially was celebrated in honor of creation, the entire week itself and the very concept of the week smell of creation. Really they couldn't pick any day of the week. So they chose Sunday, but not Sunday the first day of the week. They called it the "Eighth Day." Coming one day after Sabbath, the seventh day, Sunday could be counted as the eighth day. What that meant is that it is outside of the week and therefore divorced from creation.

It was all symbolic of course, and what Sunday worship symbolized for Gnostic Christians was rejection of the material world, rejection of the creator God, and freedom from the bondage of the Old Testament. Since the number eight also symbolizes the eighth level of the cosmos, the starry heavens, Sunday also therefore symbolized salvation and escape of the soul back to heaven after death.

Clearly the transfer of worship to Sunday had tremendous theological significance for Gnostic Christians. However, did it have any of the same meaning for their more moderate, Hellenistic Christian cousins? They too referred to Sunday as the Eighth Day, and the term is used occasionally in mainstream Hellenistic Christianity yet today. Still, we must ask the question: Does use of the term *Eighth Day* really have the same religious significance in Hellenistic Christianity? Historically this is an important distinction.

Was conversion to Sunday worship in the early church a theological event directed against the Sabbath and Hebrew religion in general?

Clement

One of the first Christian scholars of the early church was Clement of Alexandria, who lived 150–215 A.D. As a scholar in the Egyptian metropolis of Alexandria, one of the most famous cities and the greatest center of learning in the Roman Empire, he was well versed in Hellenistic philosophy and the learning of his time.

In his writings Clement preaches observance of Sunday, and he does so with the typical pagan Hellenistic symbolism of the numbers seven and eight. Remember, as we discussed in an earlier chapter, eight represents heaven. This is the home of the stars whose steady, regular orbits symbolize permanence, immortality and everything good. Seven represents the seven planets whose more irregular orbits symbolize instability and change, in effect everything that is wrong with the material world.

Clement connects the material world with the irregular orbits of the seven planets. Both of these he then associates with the seven days of the week and its promise of Sabbath rest. To that he contrasts the stable motions of stars found in the heavens, to demonstrate that the 'Eighth Day' is the superior and more proper day for Christian worship.

Clement's writing can be difficult to follow, but we will analyze it step by step as we go. In the following passage Clement talks openly about the pagan Hellenistic symbolism of his day and its religious significance for Christians:

> ...and by the seven days the motions of the seven planets...which strives to attain its **true end** in rest. But after the wandering orbs [planets] the journey leads to heaven, that is, **the eighth motion and day.** [47]

Note Clement's argument that the *"seven days"* and *"motions of the seven planets"* both 'strive' to attain rest. What he means is that the seventh-day Sabbath attempts to lead Christians to rest, but fails. Why? What is wrong with the Sabbath?

In Hellenistic theology the number seven represents the evil side of the material world, especially the planets and their unstable orbits – as Clement here calls them *"the wandering orbs."* According to Clement, the *"true end"* of our quest for Christian rest does not lead there. In other words true Christian rest is not Sabbatarian rest. Instead, he says, our spiritual quest leads *beyond* the unstable planetary world and its symbolism of the number seven, as he says *"after the wandering orbs."* True rest is found only when the journey leads to heaven and its stability, which Clement here identifies as *"the eighth motion and day."*

This is important. The biblical seventh-day Sabbath and Hellenistic Eighth Day both symbolize rest, each within its own unique religious tradition. The Sabbath promotes both physical and spiritual rest, while Hellenistic rest is exclusively spiritual and non-material. What Clement is saying is that Christians must make a choice. And the basis of that choice, for him, is pagan Hellenistic theology. In Clement, Hellenistic symbolism triumphs over Hebrew symbolism. Sabbath may symbolize rest in biblical religion, but Clement rejects that. He does so because Hellenistic religion

---

[47]   Strom. 5.106.3–4.

associates the number seven with materialism (*the wandering orbs*) and he therefore considers it inferior. Because Hellenistic paganism associates the number eight with heaven and promotes a purely non-material rest, Clement concludes that Sunday the Eighth Day is the only spiritual choice for Christians.

For Clement, however, the issue of Sabbath versus the Eighth Day is not merely a matter of symbolism, as we see in this additional passage from his writings:

> Whether it be a question of time which, after passing through the seven ages, leads to **the final rest**, or of the seven heavens, which some count in ascending order; and of the fixed sphere ...which is called the **Ogdoad**, it means that the gnostic ought to rise out of the sphere of becoming and of sin. [48]

Clement often used Gnostic terms to signify Christian ideas, and his use of the term *gnostic* here only signifies enlightened Christians. However, his theology of Sunday rest is thoroughly Hellenistic and almost any Gnostic believer would feel entirely at home with it.

Notice in this passage that achieving "*final rest*" means rising above the realm of material creation (above *the seven heavens* and the *sphere of becoming*). The "*sphere of becoming*" is the material world, which is subject to instability and change (*becoming*) in comparison to the un-changing, eternal nature of the heavens (*the fixed sphere*). The *seven heavens* is a reference to the orbits of the seven planets. The "*fixed sphere*" (heaven), Clement explains, is called the *Ogdoad* (Ogdoad means "eight," in this case a reference to both heaven and the Eighth Day).

But the important point of this passage is how Clement attaches it to the issue of sin. He says that Christians "***ought** to rise out of*" (avoid) the "*sphere of becoming **and of sin**.*" In Hellenistic religion, materialism is the source of all evil and sin. It is material lusts that lead to sin. Therefore, in Hellenistic thinking, the solution is to turn to religious practices that are purely non-material, in other words oriented exclusively to the heavens. [49]

In this passage Clement is arguing that Christians ***must*** rise above the materialism of Sabbath symbolism in order to come out of sin. For Clem-

---

[48]   Ibid. 4.159.2.

[49]   In Primitive Christian theology, God gives the spiritual power to Christians to rise above material temptation, so they can lead spiritual lives within a material environment. The goal is to master material existence, not to hide from it.

ent this is more than just Hellenistic symbolism. Indeed this is Hellenistic theology with its typical insistence that true spirituality is exclusively heavenly and non-material.

Clement's Hellenistic rationale for Sunday observance requires rejection of the Sabbath. He admits the seventh-day Sabbath seeks to give man rest, but it fails, he believes, because it is materialistic. According to Clement, true spiritual rest is found only in the symbolism of the Eighth Day because the Eighth Day encourages us to come out of sin by pointing to a purely non-material spirituality and rest. This is classic Hellenistic and Gnostic theology. The conversion from Sabbath to Sunday, in Clement's view, indeed was a theological event.

Epistle of Barnabas

An even more significant appearance of the Eighth Day is found in the Epistle of Barnabas. This supposedly was written by Barnabas, the companion of Paul. Its importance lies partly in the early time frame of its composition. Scholars fix the date as somewhere between 70 and 135 A.D., well before Clement.

One purpose of the letter is to warn Christians against a Jewish interpretation of the Old Testament. Using allegorical interpretation, the author argues that the Old Testament really teaches New Testament spiritual principles. It specifically warns against a literal interpretation of Jewish law, so that *"we should not be shipwrecked by conversion to their law."* [50] However, it is not arguing for tolerance of immorality. It merely emphasizes the need to replace Hebrew law with what the author considers a more spiritual, allegorical interpretation of God's commandments:

> Let us be spiritual, let us be a temple consecrated to God...and let us strive to keep his commandments in order that we may rejoice in his ordinances. [51]

When the topic turns to Sabbath, the author argues for an allegorical interpretation that replaces Sabbath with Sunday the Eighth Day. His argument runs as follows:

---

[50] *Epistle of Barnabas*, III, 6.

[51] Ibid. IV, 11.

The seven days of creation are symbolic of the time frame of human history. Each day of the week indicates a thousand years, so the first six days indicate six thousand years allotted to man. Christ returns to earth at the end of six thousand years, judges the wicked and initiates millennial rest with the resurrected saints. The seventh day points to that seventh period of one thousand years – the millennial rest. In spite of the connection between the seventh day and millennial rest, however, the author argues that Sabbath still is not appropriate for honoring Christian rest.

Why? As the epistle explains, when Christ comes he will:

> ...change the sun and the moon and the stars, and then he will truly rest on the seventh day. Furthermore he [God] says, 'Thou shalt sanctify it [the Sabbath] with clean hands and a pure heart.' If, then, anyone has at present the power to keep holy the day which God made holy, by being pure in heart, we are altogether deceived. See that we shall indeed keep it holy at that time, when we enjoy **true rest**....[52]

Notice the phrase *true rest*, the same terminology used by Clement above. 'True rest' is a code word for exclusively spiritual rest, the basis for rejecting Sabbath. Sabbatarian rest is not 'true' rest because of its involvement with the material world.

The author of Barnabas engages in some clever sleight of hand. First he implies that the seventh-day Sabbath symbolizes the seventh 1,000-year period of human history, the time of millennial rest after Christ returns to earth. Nevertheless, he says, that future time is a completely different world than the material creation in which we live today. This is emphasized by his claim that Christ will *"change the sun and the moon and the stars, and then he will truly rest."* In effect he is saying that Christ will create a new world when he comes, and only in that new world will we find the rest symbolized by the seventh day. *"True rest,"* he insists, is possible only in the coming spiritual world.

Even though that future world supposedly is the seventh 1,000-year time period of human history, the epistle explains, Christians can't honor it today by observing the seventh-day Sabbath. Why? Because it is a different world, a different creation, which is yet future. Only when that future time period arrives can we, as it says, *"truly rest on the seventh day."*

---

[52]   Ibid. XV, 5–7.

Until that time arrives, therefore, we must celebrate *"true rest"* with a different day. As the author explains:

> The present sabbaths are not acceptable to me, but [instead] that which I have made, in which I will give rest to all things and make the beginning of an eighth day, <u>that is the beginning of an-other world.</u> Wherefore we also celebrate with gladness the eighth day....[53]

For the author of Barnabas, the Eighth Day is ideally suited for Christians specifically because it *"is the beginning of another world,"* symbolizing the exclusively spiritual world to come. The Eighth Day, being outside the seven-day week, is divorced from creation and therefore symbolically points to something outside our present material world. Indeed, in Hellenistic theology it symbolizes *'another world'* – the heavens.

The author's reasoning is somewhat tortured – he claims the Eighth Day begins with the seventh time period of world history, when Christ returns. This serves an important purpose, however. Connecting the two rest days (Jewish and Hellenistic) emphasizes that the Eighth Day is the spiritual continuation and true fulfillment of the old materialistic seventh-day Sabbath. The author seems to be arguing that, Yes, it is the seventh time period, but the fact it starts with a new creation (*change sun, moon and stars*) makes it *"another world."* That in turn means it can be symbolized only by the Eighth Day, because only the eighth day represents that 'other world' that is not materialistic.

Through the rest of this chapter, we will see repeatedly how Hellenistic Christians equated Sabbath and Eighth Day in order to say one fulfills the other, but at the same time separates them so as to require that one be rejected in favor of the other.

The Epistle of Barnabas was widely circulated and respected in the early centuries of the Christian era. Some church leaders, including Origen and Jerome, considered it a canonical book of the New Testament. The early church fathers generally attributed the epistle to Barnabas, the companion of Paul, which lent it substantial authority and credibility. Today, however, scholars agree that Paul's companion Barnabas was not the author, but instead an unknown person writing from Alexandria, Egypt.

---

[53] *Epistle of Barnabas*, XV, 8–9, emphasis mine.

Inaccurately ascribing documents and letters to names other than the real author was common in ancient times. We see this reflected in Paul's warning against Christian apostasy in 2 Thessalonians chapter two, when he urged Christians in the first century *"not to be quickly shaken in mind or alarmed, either by spirit or by word or by letter, as though from us"* (2 Thess 2:2). By saying "us" Paul undoubtedly includes Barnabas, his frequent companion. It appears that already in Paul's time there were apostate Christians who forged letters and attributed them to Paul, Barnabas and others, in order to promote their own religious ideas. The Epistle of Barnabas is one example of this, and suggests this ancient practice may indeed have played an important role in the apostatizing of the early church.

I think the only possible conclusion is that Sunday and Eighth Day worship did have significant theological meaning when it was first introduced in the early church. Though less radical in condemning material existence, Hellenistic Christian Eighth Day theology takes the same general form as in the Gnostic and pagan Hellenistic mainstream. It rejects the material world and looks forward exclusively to a non-material spirituality of the heavens. We see this in the Epistle of Barnabas when the author argues that true rest cannot be associated with this world. Clement expressed the same idea by associating coming out of sin with rising above the seven spheres of the material world and passing beyond the enumeration of time into seven periods, finding true rest in the Eighth Day rather than in creation rest. This is classic Gnostic theology.

In the early centuries after Christ, just as today, the distinction between material and spiritual was presented as a primary justification for discarding the Sabbath. Hellenistic Roman Christianity was less extreme in its separation of spirituality and materialism than classic Gnosticism. Yet they used the same distinction to achieve the same goal. The Sabbath, because of its attachment to creation, was considered materialistic and therefore inferior and spiritually dangerous.

Here is an example from the purely Gnostic side. The Nag Hammadi Valentinian text, *The Gospel of Truth*, presents the same argument for Sunday worship in these words:

> Even on the Sabbath, he labored for the sheep which he found fallen into the pit. ...that you might know interiorly – you, the sons of interior knowledge – what is the Sabbath, on which it is not fitting for salvation to be idle, in order that you may speak from the day above, which has no night, and from the light which does not sink because it is perfect.

> Say, then, from the heart that you are the perfect day and in you
> dwells the light that does not fail. [54]

Here we find emphasis on *'interior knowledge,'* which reveals the true Christian Sabbath. For Gnosticism, the interior world is the non-material world of the immortal soul. It also says that Christ himself labored on the Sabbath (*on the Sabbath, he labored for the sheep*). This signifies that the true Sabbath has nothing to do with work, for the real Sabbath is spiritual.

Further, the day associated with spirituality is described as *"the day above"* which *"is perfect."* That means the day associated with the heavens, the world of spiritual perfection to come, i.e. the Eighth Day, the same idea expressed in the Epistle of Barnabas. The author goes out of his way to make clear that Christian rest cannot be associated with creation when he describes it as composed purely of *"light that does not fail,"* and *"that has no night."* Genesis defines the days of material creation as a composite partly of day and partly night (*God called the light Day, and the darkness he called Night. And there was evening and there was morning, the first day* – Gen 1:5.) The Eighth Day, being purely spiritual, is composed only of light.

Is 8th Day Theology Significant?

Still, does any of this really matter? Was Eighth Day theology only a sideshow? After all, the most important significance attached to Sunday in modern Hellenistic Christianity is the resurrection, not the Eighth Day.

What role did the Eighth Day play in the conversion from Sabbath to Sunday observance? Was Eighth Day theology merely a Gnostic phenomenon, with little involvement in the history of mainstream Hellenistic Christianity?

First, it should be noted that Eighth Day theology did not appear until Christianity. The symbolism of the numbers seven and eight appeared in Hellenistic paganism long before the birth of Christianity, but it was not applied to the idea of the week until that symbolism infiltrated Christianity. Before then it was limited to the number seven symbolizing planets and the material world, and the number eight symbolizing the heavens, stability and immortality.

---

[54]   **NHLE**, 46–47.

There is no direct reference to the Eighth Day in New Testament scripture. However, at least by the second century A.D. it appears in the writings of both Roman and Gnostic Christianity, with Gnostic Christianity leading the way. Jean Danielou, the famous Jesuit scholar and expert on Primitive Christianity, has this to say: [55]

> While the typology of the eighth day was developing in orthodox gnosis [Roman Christianity], it was having a considerable success in...heretical gnosis [Gnostic Christianity].
>
> The Gnostics, who were decided enemies of Judaism, were carried away by this theme.

What Danielou is saying is that it caught on first, like wild fire, among Gnostic Christians, while it developed more slowly in the orthodox Roman church. As we noted earlier, it took nearly four centuries for it to gain the upper hand in the Roman church.

The theology of the Eighth Day was tailor made for Gnostic Christianity because it insisted on trashing Hebrew religion and the Old Testament as the religion of materialistic bondage. In Roman Christianity, the earliest texts dealing with the Eighth Day likewise were those that had a more anti-Judaic character. This includes *Dialogue with Trypho* as well as the *Epistle of Barnabas*, from which we quoted above.

There is one notable difference between Eighth Day theology in Gnostic Christianity and its counterpart in the Roman church. The Gnostics, always more radical and Hellenistic, tended to apply Eighth Day theology to the cosmological structure of the universe, in other words the seven planetary spheres, and the eighth sphere, Heaven. For Gnostic Christians, salvation was intimately connected with separating themselves from the material world so that after death they could successfully ascend past the seven planets to reach heaven.

In Hellenistic Christianity the number seven more frequently was associated with the seven ages of human history within the material world. Eight therefore refers to eternal life in the heavens, the promised reward of the saved after the completion of human history in our material world.

So we see two distinct approaches. For Gnostics it symbolized the structure of the universe. In the Hellenistic Roman church it depicted primarily the time periods of human history. The two ideas roughly come together, however, in their common interpretation of the number eight as

---

[55]   Danielou, *The Bible and the Liturgy*, 258–259. Bracketed text added.

heaven and the goal of the saved, and interpretation of the number seven as materialistic and inferior.

Though Roman Christianity favored the interpretation of Eighth Day theology in terms of historical ages, the Gnostic interpretation in terms of the levels of the cosmos is found in the writings of the Roman church fathers. Some of them speak of the Eighth Day in the same astral, cosmological sense as the Gnostics did. Both Origen and Proclus touch on these Gnostic themes in their writings.[56] Origen, for example, accepted the Gnostic idea of the ascension of the soul through the seven planetary spheres after death.[57]

Sometimes the Christian and Gnostic approaches are paired together by the same author, and we find this among both Gnostic and Roman Christian writers. Notice how the two traditions were combined by Clement (see above, pages 58 and following): "**_Whether_** it be a question of **_time_** which, after passing through the **_seven ages_** [ages of human history], leads to the final rest, **_or_** of the **_seven heavens_**, which some count in ascending order [cosmic levels]...it means the gnostic ought to rise out of the sphere of becoming and of sin." Here Clement validates both traditions. He is arguing that whether you interpret it by one or the other scheme it means the same thing – that Christians should rise above the material world (the sphere of becoming). For Clement, both traditions mean essentially the same thing – get rid of the materialistic seventh-day Sabbath and look instead to Sunday the Eighth Day.

Both Gnosticism and Hellenistic Christianity understood the Eighth Day to signify breaking away from Hebrew religion and the Old Testament. Gnosticism took it to a more extreme degree only because of their total rejection of the God of the Old Testament. For a more moderate Hellenistic Christian view, note the following assessment by the famous Jesuit theologian and historian, Jean Danielou:

> The substitution of the eighth day for the seventh appears, therefore, to be the expression, at once symbolic and concrete, of the substitution of Christianity for Judaism. This leads us to touch on the primary aspect of the symbolism of the eighth day. ...it was used by the Christians to exalt the superiority of the Sunday over the Sabbath, and thus it became an instrument of Christian polemics. The passage from the religion of the seventh

---

[56] Origen *Contr. Cels.* 6, 22. Proclus *Co. Tim. 3*; 355, 13.
[57] See below, pages 119 and following.

day to that of the eighth was to become the symbol of passing from the Law to the Gospel.

What Danielou is saying in effect is that Eighth Day theology was a key weapon in the larger battle over the Hellenization of Christianity and destruction of the Hebrew heritage of the apostolic church. Thus he affirms this was an issue of great theological significance.

Eighth Day and the Weekly Cycle

The primary symbolism of Sunday observance is the resurrection. And the resurrection generally is believed to have occurred on Sunday, the first day of the week. But the importance of Sunday lay in its interpretation not as the first, but rather the Eighth Day. Symbolically that means it is *outside* the weekly cycle. It symbolically represents the eternity of our existence in heaven, which comes after the end of the material world. How then, if it is outside the week, could the Eighth Day be integrated into the weekly cycle? It was necessary to do so, since first of all a weekly celebration was needed to replace weekly Sabbath observance. In reviewing the historical evidence, Danielou assures us again of the central importance of Eighth Day theology, saying that in joining the resurrection to the weekly cycle, *"...this symbolism of the eighth day took a preeminent place."*[58]

So, how do you get the Eighth Day, from outside creation, to correlate with something inside the seven-day cycle? How do you get the Eighth Day to equate to the first day, as well as the seventh day, which it must do in order to replace it, but without validating the seventh day? And, if the seventh and eighth days are linked, how does the Eighth Day relate to creation when it actually symbolizes freedom from creation? The way this was done is sometimes strangely complex but superbly clever.

The end result is a series of arguments, often fragmentary and contradictory, but each rich with Hellenistic, Christian and Gnostic symbolism. In the end, it ties together the eighth, seventh and first days, all in one.

As the early Roman church father St. Hilary observes, all three days are linked:

---

[58]   Danielou, *The Bible and the Liturgy*, 262.

> Although the name and the observance of the Sabbath had been established for the <u>seventh</u> day, it is the <u>eighth</u>, which is also the <u>first</u>, that we ourselves celebrate, and that is the feast of the perfect Sabbath.[59]

For St. Hillary, the eighth and first days *are* the Sabbath, which previously had been celebrated on the seventh day. So, how do we connect the seventh day Sabbath, but leave out its previous mode of observance?

The answer is creation. Sabbath always symbolized creation by honoring God's rest at the **completion** of creation. In that context, the Hellenistic church fathers observed that the first day also is involved in creation, but in this case obviously, as the first day it is the **start** of creation.

Therefore both first and seventh days are involved in creation. But not necessarily the same creation, however! It was necessary to equate first and seventh days, but also to differentiate between them so that one can replace the other. Here we come to the idea of the 'second' creation and its special role in the argument over Sabbath observance.

The material world was the first creation. New Covenant salvation is the second creation. This is based in part on New Testament scripture, in which Paul describes Christians as a 'new' creation:

> So if anyone is in Christ, he is a new creation: everything old has passed away; see, everything has become new! (2 Cor 5:17)

Of course, one might argue that if Christianity is a second, spiritual creation, then Sabbath as a traditional symbol of the first creation should be retained as the symbol of the second creation as well. New Testament scripture in fact supports the use of Sabbath as a symbol of Christian salvation.[60] That, however, the church fathers insisted, would not do. (Remember, it was important to incorporate the seventh day so the first day becomes a fulfillment of the seventh day, but at the same time not validate the seventh day for continued use within Christianity.)

The problem, they insisted, is that the second creation has not ended. Christian salvation is on-going, while the seventh day celebrates the *end* of material creation.[61] Since the second creation so far has only a begin-

---

[59]   St. Hilary, *Inst. Ps.,* 12.

[60]   See below, Appendix B, "Hebrews 4 and the Sabbath."

[61]   Carrying this reasoning one step further, the idea was floated in the early church that the symbolism of the end of material creation itself

ning, they insisted, it can only be honored by celebrating its beginning. That of course means using the first day, the historic beginning of creation, to symbolize Christian salvation. As St. Ambrose explains:

> But the new creation was not commanded to observe the Sabbath, so that [by recognizing] its beginning on the Lord's Day, it would know also that the grace (of the second creation) has no ending. [62]

Therefore, they reasoned, Christians must be loyal to a different standard and different symbolism that depicts only the start of creation.

Nevertheless, Sabbath and Sunday are connected because both represent creation. The closer they could tie the two together, the easier it was to justify the change by arguing Sunday is the natural fulfillment of Sabbath. They were not really abolishing Sabbath, they insisted, only fulfilling its true spiritual intent. They were not even abandoning the symbolism of creation, just re-pointing Christian rest to the spiritual creation of the New Testament.

Until the fourth century when Sunday observance was mandated by law, much of the church continued to observe the seventh-day Sabbath. By showing that Sunday in effect symbolizes essentially the same thing, only in an improved and more spiritual fashion, the easier it was to entice the church to make the transition.

St. Basil saw another connection between the description of creation in Genesis and the Eighth Day. The Hebrew text of Genesis refers to the second through seventh days of creation as just that – second, third, fourth, etc. But in Genesis 1:5, a literal rendering of the Hebrew text refers to the first day as *"day one."* [63] From this fact, Basil constructs the idea of a hidden truth encased in this passage. It is a classic example of the mystical numerology preached by the Pythagoreans. Pythagorean theology survived in the Roman Empire alongside Christianity as Neopythagoreanism and Neoplatonism,[64] and it is not surprising to see it show up in the thinking of the early church fathers.

---

was a prophecy that seventh day Sabbath observance would someday come to an end.

[62] P.G. 26, 133 B-C.

[63] Many modern biblical versions, including the King James, render this as "the first day", but Basil is correct in that the original Hebrew says "day one".

[64] As described above, pages 32 and following.

According to the Pythagoreans, the entire cosmos came from a first principle called the One. When the universe was in its state of Oneness, symbolized by One, there was no differentiation of form and matter, in other worlds there is just Oneness. If that sounds confusing, don't struggle with it. It is a subtle, mystical concept. The point is, when Genesis refers to the first day as "day one" instead of "first day," Basil believed it was a hidden reference to the 'Oneness' of Pythagorean theology. So, he argued, the first day of creation was not really composed of day and night, even though Genesis 1:5 mentions day and night. On the first day of creation, he insisted, the dual traits of day and night mystically were still contained within a state of Oneness – *"day one"* as the Hebrew text says.[65] Since day and night were hidden within a state of 'Oneness,' Basil reasoned, the first day of creation actually was composed only of light.

Why is it important that the first day of creation be composed only of light, and not separate day and night portions? Because that also happens to be the nature of the Eighth Day. So this shared trait connects the first day of creation with the Eighth Day. Thereby Basil makes the account of creation in Genesis 1:5 into a reference to the superior nature of the Eighth Day, and a prophecy of the future observance of the Eighth Day by Christians.

This is classic Gnostic theology. Remember the Gnostic description of their rest day quoted above, *"that you might know...what is the Sabbath...that you may speak from the day above, which has no night..."* (see above, page 64). So Genesis itself supposedly sanctions Hellenistic Christianity's conversion to Sunday observance.

St. Basil explicitly makes this point when he speaks of the Eighth Day as:

> ...the day without end...which will have <u>neither evening</u> [night portion], nor succession, nor cessation, nor old age.[66]

This is further explained by another clever argument, this time involving Easter. (Sunday in essence is a 'weekly' Easter in that both celebrate the resurrection.)

Easter generally was seen as a replacement for Passover. Once again, exactly as with Sabbath and Sunday, the church fathers believed they had found mystical signs within Passover that pointed to the Eighth Day and

---

[65] See Danielou, *The Bible and the Liturgy*, p 63 ff.

[66] Basil, *De Spir. Sancto*, 27.

therefore, they believed, sanctioned its eventual replacement by Easter Sunday.

Here's the argument, which is quite simple. The Hebrew calendar is lunar, so the beginning of each month coincides with the appearance of a new moon. Therefore the middle of the month coincides with the full moon. Passover is celebrated in the middle of the first Jewish month, called Nisan. Therefore Passover always occurs at full moon. So, they observed, at Passover the entire 24 hour day is lighted, the evening portion by the brightness of a full moon. Thus in theory it too is a day without night. As John Chrysostum preached regarding Passover on the 14th of Nisan:

> ...he who is saved enjoys a perpetual light, the moon shining all night long and the sun following her: this happens indeed on the fifteenth day, which is that of the full moon. The fourteenth day is, therefore, to be understood symbolically.[67]

The fact Passover is supposedly a 'day without night' was taken as a prophetic sign it would someday be replaced by Easter, which like Sunday is supposed to be purely spiritual and therefore points forward to the time after the end of the material creation when there is only light and no darkness.

What's Wrong with the Sabbath?

We now turn to a number of additional issues promoting the depiction of the Sabbath as inferior. First, the church fathers insisted, there is a problem with the very idea of Sabbath rest. Physical rest is one thing. But when described as 'idleness' it becomes something else entirely.

So, the church fathers asked, Should Christians be 'idle'? Over time, it became popular to condemn cessation of work on the seventh-day Sabbath because it promotes idleness.[68] On Sundays it was proper to cease from work sufficiently to give time for spiritual worship, they said. But that is entirely different from what they viewed as the 'excessive' idleness associated with Sabbath observance.

---

[67] See Danielou, *The Bible and the Liturgy,* p 299.
[68] See Danielou, *The Bible and the Liturgy,* p 227.

But there were other problems as well. Both Hellenistic Christians and even some Hellenistic Jews observed in their writings that the stars continue to revolve through the skies during Sabbath. Therefore, they said, even creation itself is not subject to the Sabbath. Worse still, when Jesus was criticized by the Jews of his day for healing on the Sabbath, he responded, *"My Father is still working, and I also am working"* (John 5:17). Therefore, they reasoned, if Jesus and the Father perform spiritual works on the Sabbath and even the creation itself is not idle, how then can we tell mankind to be idle on Sabbath? [69]

How then is Christian rest to be understood? What is the essence of spiritual rest compared to the material idleness of the Sabbath, which they condemned?

Non-material, Internal Rest

A key idea in both Gnostic and Hellenistic Christian thinking about the Sabbath is its supposed materialistic orientation. Sabbath focuses on material creation, while the New Testament is about a second, spiritual creation. Sabbath demands physical rest, while the New Testament, they said, teaches spiritual rest.

This shows up in anti-Sabbatarian theology in various ways. The obvious argument was to say that only the Eighth Day points to heaven and therefore it is the only choice if you want to observe a day that is spiritual. But there was also the idea that spirituality exists internally, which for Gnostic Christianity was especially associated with the immortal soul. Thereby, Christians become 'living Sabbaths,' possessing rest within themselves. Origen, for example, expressed this idea as follows:

> The perfect man, who is always occupied with the words, the actions, the thoughts of the Word of God, is always living in His Days, and all His Days are the Lord's Days. [70]

So, spiritual rest sometimes was presented as an on-going spiritual state not associated with any day. As we will see throughout this volume, Gnostic Christianity always favored the idea that spirituality is solely internal. But orthodox Christianity also championed internal spirituality.

---

[69]   Ibid. 232.

[70]   Origen, *C.Cels.* 8, 22.

Jesus himself emphasizes the magnification of the law to encompass one's internal state, for example in his famous Sermon on the Mount in Matthew chapter 5. The difference is that Gnostic Christianity, always the radical, took an either/or approach – you must reject the outward, material aspects of religion in order to focus exclusively on the internal, spiritual side.

In the end, it always comes back to the original Gnostic/Hellenistic concept of rejecting the material world. For example, the great Hellenistic Christian churchman and historian Eusebius, in the fourth century, expressed the essence of the argument in the following words:

> ...indeed, the perfect Sabbath and perfect and blessed rest is found in the kingdom of God...outside everything sensible (material)...where, freed from the realities of the body and the slavery of the flesh...we shall celebrate the Sabbath and we shall rest. [71]

The key importance of Eighth Day theology is pointing Christians away from material concerns and towards the future life in heaven. Everything we do in this life must be a preparation to guarantee that we successfully achieve the goal of return to the heavens to be with Jesus forever. As Danielou observes, for Gregory, St. Basil and others, the underlying purpose is *"keeping our eyes fixed on the future life."* [72]

Augustine explicitly describes Sunday observance in exactly those terms. For him, Christian rest must point to eternity, which is outside our world:

> ...it is one thing to rest in the Lord while yet being in the midst of time [the weekly cycle] – and this is signified by the seventh day, that is to say, the Sabbath; and another thing to go beyond all time (eternity) and to rest endlessly...which is signified by the eighth day. [73]

The Eighth Day Today

Eighth Day theology is not just an historical phenomenon. Hellenistic Christian churches today, both Catholic and Protestant, still openly preach

[71] Co. Ps. 91; P.G. 23, 1168D.
[72] Danielou, *The Bible and the Liturgy,* 271.
[73] Ibid.

veneration of Sunday as the Eighth Day. One example is *Dies Domini, On Keeping the Lord's Day Holy,* an apostolic letter released by Pope John Paul II in 1998. In it we find many of the same arguments from Gnostic and early Roman Christian theologians cited above.

Pope John Paul II echoes many of these same ancient arguments, including especially the idea that Sunday marks a new, spiritual creation for Christians. He argues, for example, that Sunday is the true Christian fulfillment of creation rest, because it honors the spiritual creation. When it comes to Eighth Day symbolism, the Pope confirms its importance in the theology of the early Roman church. He describes it as *"much loved by the Fathers* [the church fathers from the first centuries after Christ]."

"Sunday is not only the first day," says John Paul II, *"it is also 'the eighth day' ... in a unique and transcendent position which evokes not only the beginning of time but also its end in 'the age to come.' "* Referring back to St. Basil, whom we quoted above, John Paul explains, *"...Sunday symbolizes that truly singular day which will follow the present time, the day without end which will know neither evening nor morning...; Sunday is the ceaseless foretelling of life without end which renews the hope of Christians...."*[74]

Just as in Gnostic theology, John Paul sees the Eighth Day as a symbol of the age that exists outside of the present material world (*that truly singular day which will follow the present time*), when there is no longer alternation of day and night (*which will know neither evening nor morning*).

Conclusions

Eighth Day theology formed inside the world of Christianity under the influence of pagan Hellenistic religion. It received its first and most enthusiastic response from Gnostic Christianity. Here it focused more on cosmological ideas about the planetary spheres that surround the earth. According to Gnostic Christianity, the goal of man is to ascend through the planetary spheres, to return to the soul's original home in heaven. This by its very nature was diametrically opposed to Hebrew religion. Return of the soul to heaven was seen as escape from the material world. And escape, they reasoned, is possible only by rejecting the God of creation,

---

[74]   John Paul II, *Dies Domini,* 32

rejecting his angels who govern the material world, and rejecting his inferior, deceptive, seventh-day symbolism of rest.

If you could talk to a Valentinian Gnostic today, he would ridicule the Sabbath: "Don't you know the Sabbath died with the Old Covenant? It has to do with creation. It's hopelessly materialistic. It relates only to external, physical existence. The Sabbath can't save you! I believe in the spiritual way of heaven. The spiritual Sabbath, the Sabbath of the inner man, the Sabbath that looks forward to the future spiritual world and salvation, is Sunday the Eighth Day!"

In the early centuries of Christianity, just as today, the Sabbath and its replacement by Sunday the Eighth Day was a major theological marker for the rejection of Old Testament religion and its replacement by a supposedly more spiritual Hellenistic Christian theology. Remember the argument of the Epistle of Barnabas. It openly argued that the purpose of reinterpreting Sabbath as the Eighth Day is to separate Christians from Hebrew law – *that we should not be shipwrecked by conversion to their law.*[75] Indeed, have things changed that much in the past 1900 years?

Hellenistic Christianity adapted Eighth Day theology to its own scheme of historical ages. But here as well the Eighth Day continued to symbolize spirituality, eternity and the heavens, and rejection of the materialism of Sabbath observance in Hebrew religion, exactly as it did for Gnostic Christians.

Many of the same ideas surrounding the symbolism of the Eighth Day flowed freely between mainstream Hellenistic and Gnostic Christianity. For example, notice how Eighth Day theological themes from the mainstream Roman church show up also in the Gnostic text from Nag Hammadi that we quoted on page 64, above:

Jesus worked on Sabbath
Hellenistic Roman church:
> Jesus performs spiritual work on the Sabbath, so even Jesus does not observe Sabbath.

Gnostic text:
> *"Even on the Sabbath, he labored for the sheep"*

---

[75] *Epistle of Barnabas,* III, 6.

Idleness

Hellenistic Roman church:

The seventh-day Sabbath should be rejected because it promotes idleness.

Gnostic text:

"the Sabbath, on which it is not fitting for salvation to be idle"

Sabbath rest is an interior state rather than literal rest

Hellenistic Roman church:

Sabbath rest is an interior, spiritual state.

Gnostic text:

"that you might know interiorly – you, the sons of interior knowledge – what is the Sabbath"

Day of rest must equate to heaven

Hellenistic Roman church:

The Eighth Day is spiritual and heavenly in contrast to the Sabbath of material creation. The purpose of the Eighth Day is to keep our minds focused on our future life in heaven.

Gnostic text:

"in order that you may speak from the day above"

Day without night

Hellenistic Roman church:

The Eighth Day is pure light, not composed of separate day and night portions as are the material days of creation, including the seventh-day Sabbath.

Gnostic text:

"the day above, which has no night"

Christians live the Sabbath within themselves

Hellenistic Roman church:

Christians live the principle of Sabbath rest at all times within themselves. Sabbath is not a defined time. Christians <u>are</u> the Sabbath, by virtue of their state of spiritual rest.

Gnostic text:

"Say, then, from the heart that <u>you are</u> the perfect day and <u>in you dwells</u> the light that does not fail."

77

It seems abundantly clear that Eighth Day theology was a complex of anti-Sabbatarian ideas, broadly shared by both the mainstream Hellenistic Roman church and Gnostic Christianity. Both used these same arguments to paint seventh-day Sabbath observance as irredeemably materialistic and inferior. On the other hand, the Eighth Day was manipulated to achieve two important goals. First it was positioned to symbolize the same biblical ideas about rest, but in a supposedly superior, more spiritual fashion. Thereby the church could argue it was not abandoning anything by transitioning to Sunday worship. Rather, it was only fulfilling the true, spiritual meaning of rest. Secondly, it very effectively replaced Hebrew religious symbolism with the symbolism of Hellenistic religion. I.e. it materially advanced the Hellenization of the church.

Did the early church fathers know what they were doing when they freely stitched together Christian and Hellenistic religion to concoct Eighth Day theology and the rationale for converting to Sunday worship? In fact, they knew exactly what they were doing, and they felt perfectly correct in doing so. Many of the early church fathers openly believed that Hellenistic religion and philosophy were a partial revelation of truth from God (See below, pages 119, 322 and following). In fact some of them were quite proud of the Hellenistic origins of what today has come to be known among scholars as Hellenistic Christianity.

Consider for example Jean Danielou, the famous Jesuit scholar, prolific author, and for many years professor of Primitive Christian History at the *Institut Catholique* in Paris. Given his specialty, he had ample opportunity to ponder this question. And like the early church Fathers, he saw no problem with Hellenistic paganism. In his famous text, *The Bible and the Liturgy,* he lays out the following justification for incorporating Hellenistic religious concepts and symbols in the worship of the early church:[76]

Danielou is aware of the many New Testament injunctions for Christians to keep separate from the world. However, he interprets this solely in the sense of preserving the church's identity. In other words, the purpose of keeping separate from the world was to prevent the church from being destroyed by merging into other movements. This, he says, was a special concern when the church was still small and its existence precarious. Before the Hellenistic church received the official endorsement of the

---

[76] Danielou, *The Bible and the Liturgy,* 243–245.

Roman emperors in the fourth century, holding beliefs in common with pagan religion might have led the church to be absorbed by pagan cults that held similar Hellenistic beliefs. In fact, he explains, that is the very reason the church found it necessary to reject the seventh-day Sabbath!

As he explains it, the principle of physical rest was not confined to Hebrew religion. In Hellenistic Roman society of that time, there were similar ideas of a weekly day of physical rest. In this Danielou is correct. The Roman week originally had ten days. But in the first centuries of the Christian era, Roman society gradually replaced that with the seven-day planetary week. This was based on astrology and Hellenistic religious ideas about the spheres of the planets, which we covered in previous chapters. Some of our modern day-names survive from that same Roman planetary week, such as Sun-day, Moon-day (Monday) and Saturn-day (Saturday).

It so happens Saturn was a god of war, and as such he was a rather negative figure. Because of astrological superstition, Romans generally believed the god presiding over a given day exerted his influence on all activities carried out on that day. And therefore, given Saturn's war-like personality, Saturday came to be regarded as an unlucky day. It was considered unlucky to begin commercial projects on that day. In fact business in general was thought inappropriate on Saturday, and so it became an unofficial non-work, leisure day for many Romans.

To this Danielou adds the fact that even pagan Greek philosophers sometimes promoted the idea of stopping work in order to devote time to philosophic and spiritual contemplation. The Greek historian Strabo specifically mentioned this in the first century B.C. Danielou even implies that the Jewish practice of ceasing from work on the Sabbath was derived in part from pagan beliefs. Therefore, he concludes, because the Sabbath and its practice of physical rest was to some degree shared by pagan society, the church could not use the Sabbath as a symbol of New Testament salvation. To do so would have violated the command to keep separate from the world, he claims, and so the church was forced to start over with something new.

The problem with that reasoning is that what it started over with was not new at all, but a blatantly pagan and key doctrine of Hellenistic and Gnostic theology. It was as much a part of 'the world' as anything could be. Danielou has that covered, however. After the church was officially recognized by Rome in the fourth century A.D, he says, it no longer was at risk of losing its identity by being absorbed by other groups. Remember, according to Danielou the injunction to keep separate from the world was only intended to protect the church from being absorbed into other groups. When it had gained official recognition, therefore, that was no longer a problem. At that point the church supposedly became free to adopt pagan practices. Danielou views the eventual incorporation of Eighth Day pagan theology, its symbolism and spiritual teachings, as a very positive development and praises it for enriching the symbolism of Christian rest.

As clever as it is, there are glaring holes in Danielou's theory. If it was wrong to continue Sabbath observance because of its similarity to some pagan practices, why was it not wrong at the same time to adopt Eighth Day theology with its glaring connections to pagan Hellenistic religion? Keep in mind that Eighth Day theology was adopted as early as the second century, some 200 years before the church achieved official recognition by Rome. In addition, if after achieving official recognition the church no longer risked losing its identity and could allow free reign to the import of Hellenistic religious ideas, why didn't it also grant free reign to Sabbatarian theology at the same time?

What is the real issue behind the Sabbath–Sunday controversy? There are so many intriguing details, of which we have reviewed only a portion here. But the essence always comes back to the question of whether the seventh-day Sabbath is spiritual, or hopelessly materialistic and incapable of expressing Christian values. Further, is it the will of God that the Sabbath be used in Christian worship as it was in the apostolic church in the first century, or was it divine will that it be replaced with pagan Hellenistic symbolism and practices?

The church fathers claimed to find prophetic clues pointing to the Eighth Day in such obscure facts as the brightness of the moon on the night before Passover, and the wording of Genesis 1:5 where the original text says 'day one' instead of 'first day.' They interpret every reference to the number eight in scripture, such as the apostle Peter's reference to the eight persons saved in Noah's ark (1 Peter 3:20), as mystical expressions of the Eighth Day. They even enlist the following passage from Ecclesiastes as a reference to the Sabbath and its replacement by the Eighth Day:

> Send out your bread upon the waters, for after many days you will get it back. Divide your means seven ways, or even eight, for you do not know what disaster may happen on earth. (Eccl 11:1–2)

I suggest the whole idea is a house of cards, a grossly artificial construction that cannot stand the light of reasoned examination. However, in the end, the issue is not what any man thinks. For those who believe there is a God in heaven, the question is divine will. What does God think? Is it his will that New Covenant Christians continue to use Sabbath both for its practical benefits of rest and worship, and as a symbol of New Testament salvation? The first-century apostolic church clearly thought so. Were they mistaken, as modern Hellenistic Christians today maintain? Were they only marking time until a more complete revelation of God's will unfolded through the Hellenistic church fathers?

The final answer for those who regard the New Testament as definitive of New Covenant Christianity is found in the book of Hebrews, which directly addresses the question of continuity of Christian rest between Old and New Covenants. Appendix B, "Hebrews 4 and the Sabbath," beginning on page 379, explains in detail the New Testament link between Sabbath and Christian salvation.

– 4 –

The Origins of Gnostic Christianity

Where did Gnosticism come from? Scholars have filled books with arguments over this, and it is still hotly debated today.

Hellenistic religions habitually claimed to be the revelation of a universal truth hidden within earlier religious traditions. Gnostics, however, rarely claimed a connection with religious traditions earlier than Christianity, in spite of their obvious use of Hellenistic teachings that go back earlier than Christianity. Nearly all Gnostics regarded themselves as Christian, and claimed they had received the true revelation of a hidden and more advanced tradition from within Christianity.

The Roman church fathers tended to trace all Gnostic sects back to the Gnostic teacher Simon, in the first century A.D., whom they identify as Simon Magus from the book of Acts. Though possibly exaggerated, this is an important clue that agrees with the latest evidence and research into Gnostic origins, which places the origin of Gnosticism in Palestine.

The earliest Gnostics came mostly from Palestine or near Palestine. Simon was from Samaria, a region within Palestine, Nicolas from Antioch and possibly Palestine, and Cerinthus from Asia Minor (modern western Turkey). This geographic focus is significant because linguistic evidence and various Gnostic mythic themes indicate Gnosticism sprang from heretical Jewish sects in Palestine.

At its core, Gnosticism is essentially a Hellenistic reinterpretation of biblical religion. As we look back in history we also see that Hellenistic religion first came into contact with the religion of the Bible before Christianity. This occurred when Alexander the Great first conquered the Near East, including the land of Israel. This was more than three centuries before the advent of Christianity, so when we say biblical we mean the Old Testament.

The Greek attitude toward religion was highly intolerant. In conquered lands the Greeks pursued a policy of reinterpreting local religions in terms of Hellenistic beliefs and aggressively imposing that on the local population. In Israel this produced a tradition of Hellenistic Judaism that already had several centuries of development behind it by the time Christianity appeared on the scene.

When we compare Gnostic texts and myths with Jewish texts and stories, we find many similarities and obvious borrowings. The merging of Hellenistic belief with the Bible led some Jewish sects to the same ideas that appear later in Gnosticism. As a result, much of the foundation for Gnostic belief was already in place well before Christ was born. The pattern and time line paint the following picture:

The introduction of Hellenistic culture into Palestine spawns heretical, Hellenistic Jewish sects well before Christ. These mingle Hellenistic belief with Old Testament biblical themes to create an apostate Hellenistic Jewish theology. Gnosticism proper is born when Jewish Christians rework and reinterpret teachings from these sects as a new revelation and more advanced form of Christianity. That is why we find so much evidence of borrowing by Gnostic writers from Jewish texts.

In the remaining part of this section we review two examples of the connection between Gnosticism and Hellenistic Judaism.

Giants

The book of Genesis and its stories held a special fascination for Gnostic Christians. This is especially true of the story in Genesis chapter six about giants fathered by a mysterious race of beings called "the sons of God." These commonly were assumed to be angels who entice and subvert mankind through materialistic greed and sexual lust.

Gnostics often identified the sons of God as Yahweh and his angels, who, they claimed, use the material world to enslave mankind.

Some of the features in these Gnostic stories about the giants appeared first in Jewish apocryphal writings. The first book of Enoch (6–10) and Jubilee (4–7), Jewish texts dating from the second and first centuries B.C., talk about the same fallen angels that pollute human society by sexually defiling themselves with women.

Jewish tradition claims these fallen angels revealed secrets to women that became the source of great evil in human history. That included the making of jewelry, cosmetics and various arts that assist in seduction; gemstones and metallurgy that favor the accumulation of wealth and production of weapons; and the arts of magic, astrology and medicinal herbs. In other words, the fallen angels fostered human materialism as well as religious practices such as astrology, all associated with human bondage in Hellenistic belief.

Some objected that it is impossible for angels to mate with humans. One Jewish text from the second century B.C., resolves that by saying the women lustfully defiled themselves by envisioning the angels as they were having intercourse with their husbands.[77]

Those same ideas appear later in Gnostic mythology. In the following passage from the Nag Hammadi text *Apochryphon of John*, notice how Gnostics used the same Jewish themes of angels tricking women by assuming the appearance of their mates, and imparting civilized arts that bring human bondage:

> He sent his angels to the daughters of men.... And the angels changed themselves in their likeness into the likeness of their...mates, filling them with the spirit of darkness.... They brought gold and silver and...copper and iron and metal and all kinds of things.[78]

The Gnostic *Apochryphon of John* from Nag Hammadi appears to copy Jewish material directly from 1 Enoch about angelic seduction and the giants. In addition there are many books used by the Gnostics, some of which have been lost, which are believed to have been Jewish pseudepigraphic works. Both Gnostic and orthodox Christian writers refer to Gnostics using the books *Gospel of Eve*, various works attributed to Adam and Moses such as *Testament of Moses* and *Assumption of Moses*, as well as *The Ascension of Isaiah*, and many others.[79]

---

[77] See Testament of Reuben 5.7.

[78] *NHLE*, 121.

[79] See Perkins, *Gnosticism and the New Testament*, p 22 ff.

Planets

In classic Hellenistic philosophy the planets usually help the soul return to heaven, or at worst play a neutral role. By contrast, Jewish writings generally take a more negative view of the heavenly bodies. Because of their preoccupation with evil, the Hellenistic Jewish sects tended to aggressively interpret the role of the planets as evil. This is significant because Gnosticism later promoted the same negative view.

The heterodox Jewish books of Enoch[80] link angels with the stars and planets. 2 Enoch 4 refers to *"rulers of the stellar orders"* and to *"angels, who rule the stars and their services to the heavens."*

Sin among the stars is described in 1 Enoch 80:6 where the stars are said to *"alter their orbits and tasks"* and *"not appear at the seasons prescribed."* This leads to the punishment of the 'seven stars,' i.e. the planets. 1 Enoch 18:15–16 describes this further and reads, in part:

> And the stars...are they which have transgressed the commandment of the Lord in the beginning of their rising, because they did not come forth at their appointed times.

In this ancient time, both planets and stars are called stars. Planets are identified as the stars that follow irregular paths. Not coming forth *'at their appointed times'* is a reference to the irregular movement of the seven planets. Hellenistic Judaism interpreted that irregularity as rebellion against God.

Again, in 1 Enoch 21:2–6 there is a description of the seven stars (planets) who have been confined for their sins:

> And I saw...a place chaotic and horrible. And there I saw seven stars of the heaven bound together in it.... These are of the number of the stars of heaven, which have transgressed the

---

[80] There are three books of Enoch. 1 Enoch was composed sometime in the fourth through first centuries B.C. Fragments of many sections were found at Qumran. 2 Enoch's dating is contested. It may have been written from the first century B.C. in Egypt to the early centuries A.D. in various locales. In any case it contains an eclectic collection of earlier Jewish traditions. 3 Enoch is a late composition, probably from the sixth to seventh centuries A.D. in Babylon. See Anchor Bible Dictionary article: ENOCH, First/Second/Third Book of.

commandment of the Lord, and are bound here till ten thousand years....

1 Enoch 80:7–8 warns against failing to recognize that some heavenly bodies are sinful and so mistakenly worship them as gods. That, it says, leads to great evil and destruction.

As we see in all the above, early Hellenistic Judaism interpreted planetary irregularity as much more than inferiority. It was viewed as sin and evil, and linked to the fallen angels. This is the same teaching found later in Gnosticism.

The themes of fallen angels, introduction of evil to the world by sexual misconduct of angels, interest in Hellenistic cosmology, evil among the planets and other religious themes, all are fundamental to Gnostic Christian mythology but appeared first in Hellenistic Jewish apostasy before the Christian era.

Why do we think the transition from heretical Judaism to Gnostic Christianity occurred mainly in Palestine? There is substantial linguistic evidence linking Gnostic mythology to a Palestinian background. That consists mainly in the use of Semitic names and word-plays that point solely to the Hebrew culture of Palestine. There are many linguistic features that could not reasonably have originated from Christianity. Nor would it have come from the Egyptian-Jewish culture of Alexandria, which used Greek instead of Hebrew.

The summation of the evidence suggests that Gnosticism originated within Jewish heretical sects, probably in Palestine and possibly Samaria. The Samaritan magician Simon Magus certainly would have been familiar with these traditions, especially given his profession before adopting Christianity. However, it is likely he was only one of the first among many who saw the potential for fame and monetary reward by packaging Christianity with the most popular and accepted religious tradition of that time, namely Hellenistic philosophy and religion.

The blending of Hellenistic religion with biblical tradition had already begun within heretical Jewish sects several centuries before Christ. Among the flood of Jewish converts that poured into the first century church were many individuals like Simon Magus who injected these ideas into Primitive Christianity almost immediately after the founding of the church. Gnosticism was the product of the combination of this heretical, Hellenistic Jewish tradition with New Testament Christianity.

It is surprising how quickly apostasy developed within the early church. Some even argue that proves it was not apostasy, but rather a genuine feature of Primitive Christianity and should be accepted as God's will. The Apostle Paul, however, argues exactly the opposite. He said the Gnostic antinomian tradition, which he condemned, was already present in the first century. And, he said, it was going to blossom immediately after he (Paul) was removed from the scene (2 Thess 2:7). Paul was martyred at Rome in the 60s AD. Therefore here, in his letter to the Thessalonian church, we have a prophecy that apostasy would flourish within the church in the latter part of the first century A.D. And when we look at history, the only meaningful fulfillment of this prophecy is the flourishing of Gnostic Christianity in the church in the second half of the first century, exactly as Paul predicted.[81]

Advances in historical research in recent years confirm this New Testament prophecy. It also explains why it happened so quickly. Gnostic Christianity enjoyed such early and rapid success because it was founded on an existing Jewish tradition with several centuries of development behind it. When the New Testament church was founded in the 30's A.D., the Hellenistic Jewish faction was already in place and hit the ground running. It was the arrival of Christianity that triggered the explosion of an already existing heretical tradition into a large-scale movement. The result was truly impressive. Classic Gnosticism spread as far as Spain in the West and China to the East, and endured for the equally impressive time span of more than a millennium.[82]

It has been suggested that one of the sources of Gnostic hatred of Hebrew religion was antagonism between Samaritan Judaism and the orthodox temple religion in Jerusalem. There certainly was antagonism between those two. However, there was antagonism as well between Jewish temple religion and the multitude of other Hellenized Jewish sects in Palestine at the time of Christ.

---

[81] In the larger sense, the prophesy of 2 Thessalonians is fulfilled by both of two waves of apostasy that attacked the Primitive Church, the first, Gnostic Christianity, beginning in the first century, and the second, the development of Catholicism at Rome beginning in the second century. This is outlined later in this volume, but explained in detail in *Spirit of Antichrist,* the second volume in our series The World of Primitive Christianity.

[82] In a future volume of our series, The World of Primitive Christianity, we will cover the unusual tale of how Gnosticism survived in the eastern Mediterranean and Balkan areas, spread across southern Europe not long before the Protestant Reformation, and how a few isolated sects survive yet today in the Middle East.

Start with unprincipled leaders of Hellenistic Jewish sects, grasping after power and glory, competing against the official temple worship in Jerusalem. To that add Christian ideas about the end of the Old Covenant, together with Hellenistic aversion to material creation and its natural bias against creator deities, which by nature led to condemnation of orthodox Hebrew religion. Then, on top of all that, the fact that mixing Hellenistic ideas with the biblical tradition provided an avenue for political and social acceptance by the new Greek ruling class, and it is not difficult to see how it all came together.

This brief look at the origins of Gnostic Christianity is provided here to lend historical perspective to Gnosticism and its role in Christian apostasy. A more detailed study of the Jewish heretical sects and how they evolved into Gnostic Christianity must await a future volume in our series, The World of Primitive Christianity.

– 5 –

Gnosticism in the Bible

It is surprising how frequently the New Testament directly refers to Gnostic Christianity. Scholars did not fully pick up on this in the past because Gnosticism itself has not been well understood until recently.

It was not called Gnosticism in its day. The term *gnosis* sometimes was used by Gnostics to refer to their spiritual path of salvation, but rarely as a name for themselves. As we know, they almost universally called themselves Christians. Further, there was no single body of Gnostic doctrine, nor even a harmonious community of Gnostic Christianity. They regularly condemned and fought among themselves, at the same time denouncing their external enemies – the Hellenistic mystery cults, Hellenistic philosophy, and Hellenistic Roman Christianity.

The New Testament sometimes refers to them by one of their most common doctrines. That is the docetic teaching that Jesus and the Christ are not the same person. Many but not all Gnostics believed that Christ was a spiritual being who combined with the man Jesus, but then withdrew just before the crucifixion and it was only Jesus who died on the cross. That is the natural product of Gnosticism's extreme interpretation of Hellenistic cosmology. If God is perfect and eternal, and matter is changeable and evil, then it is philosophically impossible that God could literally mix with matter and suffer death.

When you find a reference to not believing Jesus is the Christ or Jesus is not come in the flesh, that is an almost automatic indication of Gnosticism. This is not the final, absolute test, however. Some Gnostics did not teach Docetism, and there are biblical passages referring to Gnostic beliefs that do not mention Docetism. Ultimately one must carefully analyze the text in terms of Gnostic theology to make a final determination.

Before proceeding, it may be helpful to remind ourselves of the context. This is the New Testament. This is the body of literature most Christians believe was inspired by God through the Holy Spirit to teach us about Jesus Christ and our relationship to him. It would seem, therefore, the choices the New Testament makes in recording Jesus' criticism of Gnostic Christianity are both revealing of his will and very relevant to us today. To that end, after this review we will try to summarize what the New Testament indicates are the major features of Gnostic Christianity that arouse Jesus' anger.

Jude

The entire book of Jude is a warning against Gnostic Christianity as it infiltrated the primitive church with its message of liberation from the Old Testament and the law of Yahweh. How do we know it is talking about Gnosticism? Once analyzed in light of recent discoveries, we find it is loaded with references to Gnostic theology and symbolism. For example:

Verse 13 Jude slams apostate Christians as *"wandering stars."* Who are the wandering stars? In Hellenistic cosmology wandering stars are the seven planets. Because planets follow more irregular orbits compared to the perfect regularity of stars, they sometimes were described as 'wandering.' The English word "planet" in fact comes from the Greek *planetes*, which means wanderer or nomad.

Why would anyone be insulted by being called a planet? For Gnostic Christians the term planet carried special meaning that made it a grave insult. The irregularity of the planets was understood as a symbol of increasing instability and evil as you proceed from the perfection of the heavens through the planetary orbits down to the chaos and evil of material existence on earth. The seven planets were part of an evil system that keeps man in bondage to the material world. Gnostics associated all of this with Yahweh, the seven days of material creation, Hebrew religion and the seventh-day Sabbath, all of which they hated.

What Jude is doing is using the Gnostics' own symbolism and theology to insult them. By calling them planets he is implying that Gnostics, not Yahweh, are the real source of evil and bondage.

Verse 10 Jude blasts them with the label of *"irrational animals."* Recall that some Gnostics divided humanity into three categories, the lowest of which are material beings without a soul whom they compared to mindless animals. This is the worst insult you could throw at a Gnostic. In the same verse Jude carries the point even further by comparing their knowledge, their precious *gnosis*, to animalistic instinct.

<u>Verse 8</u> Jude condemns them for slandering God's faithful angels:

> Yet in the same way these dreamers also defile the flesh, reject authority, and slander the glorious ones.

"The glorious ones" is a traditional designation of faithful angels. This is a reference to typical Gnostic theology in which Yahweh's angels were condemned for their involvement in creation and the administration of the Old Covenant. Recall the example of the Carpocration Gnostic Christians who believed they must aggressively insult Yahweh and his angels in order to free themselves from the bondage of Old Testament religion (see above, page 46).

<u>Verse 14</u> Jude warns that these false teachers were prophesied to come, and he supports his warning with a quote from the writings of Enoch. Remember from the previous chapter that the apocryphal Enoch literature was an important source of inspiration for the Gnostics. Now Jude is coming after them with their own favorite literature.

<u>Verse 15</u> Jude warns that the Lord's judgment will fall on false teachers because of *"all the harsh things that ungodly sinners have spoken against him* [the Lord]*."* The *'harsh things'* is a reference to the slander and bitter condemnation the Gnostics constantly heaped on Yahweh for being the creator and for his working with the Hebrew nation under the Old Covenant. This was a common theme among nearly all Gnostic Christian groups. It was especially prominent, for example, among the Carpocratians who taught that Christians must boldly proclaim their rejection and hatred of Hebrew religion (see above, page 46).

<u>Verse 19</u> Jude says they are *'devoid of the spirit.'* To the Gnostics, spirit is everything!

<u>Verses 12–13</u> Jude calls them *"waterless clouds"* and *"wild waves of the sea."* Once again Jude is insulting them with their own religious terminology. In Gnosticism, water typically symbolized Spirit. Calling them waterless implies that their claim to be filled with and guided by the private inspiration of the Spirit is false.

"Wild waves of the sea" depicts Gnostics as unstable. Remember that Gnosticism equated spirituality with the stability and regularity of the

heavens. This is another classic example of how Jude, throughout his letter, carefully borrows from Gnosticism itself to slam them with their own symbolism and terminology.

Jude on Antinomianism

The most important issue for Jude, however, is Gnostic lawlessness. This appears immediately and runs through the entire book, beginning in verse four:

> For certain intruders have stolen in among you, ...who pervert the grace of our God into licentiousness and deny our only Master and Lord, Jesus Christ.

The last part of the verse, *"deny our only Master and Lord,"* is a reference to classic Gnostic theology. Gnosticism indeed denies and rejects Jesus Christ, on various levels. The doctrine of Docetism rejects the true incarnation of Jesus Christ by its theory that he was a composite being, composed of a spirit named Christ and a human named Jesus. Thus Jesus Christ supposedly had two natures, one spiritual and one human, which never mixed. That means, for example, that his human side was not spiritual. Based on this theory, they also rejected much of his earthly ministry, claiming his spiritual teaching (coming from the spirit Christ) was contaminated by the influence of his material side (from the human man Jesus).

The reference to "licentiousness" reflects Gnostic rejection of Yahweh and his Law. One of the problems with Christ's earthly ministry, they reasoned, was its validation of Hebrew religion, as seen for example in his teaching the correct spiritual observance of the Sabbath. This they attributed to the influence of Jesus. Though a good and moral man, Jesus was a Jew, and his materialistic nature supposedly polluted our savior's earthy ministry with his Hebrew heritage. After the resurrection, and some said only after he ascended back to heaven, his earthly nature was discarded and now the restored, fully spiritual Christ revealed a more spiritual version of Christianity that replaces his earthly ministry. The Gnostics, of course, claimed their unique mixture of Christianity and pagan Hellenism was that second, more spiritual revelation of Christianity.

In verse 8 we are told they *'reject authority.'* This refers to the classic Gnostic teaching that all law died with the end of the Old Testament. According to most Gnostics there is no law nor punishment nor authority under the New Testament, only love and kindness and a spirituality that proceeds naturally from one's inner being – the now-awakened, heavenly immortal soul.

Jude directly replies to this Gnostic doctrine by recounting a series of Old Testament examples of disobedience and punishment – Sodom and Gomorrah, and rebellions during the exodus from Egypt (vs 5–7). Jude explicitly links these Old Testament examples to what is happening in the New Testament church and the eternal destruction that will be handed out to these latter-day rebels:

> Yet in the same way these dreamers also...reject authority...for whom the deepest darkness has been reserved forever. (verses 7–8, 13)

What Jude is doing is demonstrating that law and punishment did not end with the Old Testament. Under the New Testament willful disobedience still leads to destruction, just as it always has.

Jude includes something not found elsewhere. Towards the end he gives a clear and distinct command to the church to protect its members:

> But you, beloved, must remember the predictions of the apostles of our lord Jesus Christ.... It is these worldly people, devoid of the Spirit, who are causing divisions.   ... And have mercy on some who are wavering; save others by snatching them out of the fire; (vs 17–19, 22–23)

What can *'save others by snatching them out of the fire'* possibly mean, except to instruct and warn, to combat the spread of Gnostic theology within the primitive church and rescue those who are being led astray by antinomian teachings.

Colossians

Paul's letter to the Colossians has come to be regarded by some scholars as an essentially anti-Gnostic document. This is based on many scholarly textual issues, for example the frequent use of favorite Gnostic terms such as light and dark (1:12–13), hidden treasures of knowledge (2:3), powers and authorities (1:16; 2:10), and Christ in whom dwells the "fullness"[83] of God (1:19). Paul emphasizes throughout the book that Christ has authority over everything and everyone. What he is doing is countering common Gnostic teachings that tended to make Christ less important, sometimes only one of many angelic beings from the heavenly realm.

Colossians is also famous for the passage in chapter 2, verse 16, which many interpret as rejection of Sabbath observance and other Old Testament practices:

> Therefore let no one pass judgment on you in questions of food and drink or with regard to a festival or a new moon or a sabbath.

When you read the entire passage in light of Gnostic beliefs, however, the result is an astounding reversal of the common assumption. Indeed, Colossians 2:16 is one of the most misunderstood passages in the Bible today.

Paul says *"let no one pass judgment on you."* So, what were those judgments? It is commonly assumed someone was telling the Colossian Christians to observe Old Testament customs, and that Paul is taking the opposite side and saying they shouldn't. Actually, the text doesn't specifically say who was on which side of the argument. However, in light of Gnostic teachings and the context of the entire chapter, it is not difficult to figure out.

As we have seen above, Gnostic theology led to many ascetic practices. Gnostic Christians believed the material world is evil and you have to reject it either literally or psychologically in order to escape from it. Those who believed in literal rejection of the world engaged in various ascetic practices. It is not hard to imagine the type of judgments raised against the Colossians *"in questions of food and drink."* The critics were telling the Colossians they should **not** indulge in feasts of food and drink. Indeed, just a few verses further down, Paul directly refers to it: *"Why do you submit to regulations Do not handle, Do not taste, Do not touch...?"* (2:20–22)

But what about the judgments concerning *"a festival or a new moon or a sabbath"?* Were the critics telling the Colossians they should or should not take part in those things?

---

[83] 'Fullness' is the translation for *pleroma*. For the use and importance of the same term in Gnosticism, see description of the Valentinian Gnostic sect, above p 52 ff.

Once again, we easily know what Gnostic Christians were saying about this as well. They universally rejected and despised the Old Testament and all things Jewish. In many Gnostic sects, rejection of the Old Testament and Hebrew religion and law was an absolute requirement for salvation.

To fully understand what was going on, we need first look at other topics in the background of early Christianity. Among New Testament Christians there was a traditional belief that the Old Testament was governed and administered by angels, because angels executed punishment on people who sinned against it. This is based on Old Testament accounts of angels used by God to punish Israel, for example the angel of death that Israel escaped by observing the first Passover in Egypt. Paul himself refers to it in Galatians 3:19, speaking of the Old Covenant as *"ordained by angels through an intermediary."* The author of Hebrews also mentions it: *"For if the message declared by angels was valid and every transgression or disobedience received a just retribution, how shall we escape...?"* (Heb 2:2–3). Again, in Acts 7:53, *"You [Jews] are the ones that received the law as ordained by angels, and yet you have not kept it."*

The Gnostics essentially were saying: "Look at Old Testament scripture and see for yourself what happens to people who are in bondage to the law. If you try to keep the Sabbath, and then some Friday evening you happen to forget and work a few minutes past sundown, what's going to happen? The angels will come after you! You may be stricken with a dread disease; they may even kill you! Is that the kind of religion you want? Or do you want to be under grace? However, you can be under grace only if you free yourself from Yahweh and his punishing angels by rejecting everything Jewish, especially the Sabbath."

It's the age-old argument – law OR grace. According to Gnostic Christianity you can't have both. If you want to practice spiritual Christianity, they said, you have to throw out the Old Testament and the law.

Understanding the Gnostic obsession with freedom from materialistic angels,[84] we now can understand the verses preceding Colossians 2:16. In

---

[84] Archons, aeons, etc. Gnostic cosmology invented a plethora of intermediate beings under various names, generally corresponding to the Christian concept of angels. In the world of late antiquity (the early centuries A.D.), these intermediate beings frequently were called 'elemental spirits', and Paul uses that term several times in Col chapter 2 (see NRSV translation). This term is used broadly to refer to any intermediate beings, including good and evil angels in the biblical tradition as well as the angelic beings that control the flow of energies into the world in pa-

verses 13–15 Paul explains that the only power angels had over man was through sin and the penalty of sin. This was removed by Christ's death on the cross, which wipes out our sins. This, then, explains the strange reference in verse 15: "*He disarmed the principalities and powers and made a public example of them, triumphing over them in him.*" Who are the principalities and powers? From the biblical point of view they are Yahweh's angels who punish lawbreaking. They are part of the ministry of condemnation and death to which Paul refers in 2 Corinthians 3:7–9. From the Gnostic point of view they are the same angelic powers, but viewed as evil beings who keep man in bondage through Old Testament creation-based, materialistic religion.

In Colossians 2, Paul responds to this by saying the whole thing is nonsense. The only hold the Mosaic Covenant and law had on us is because of sin, and if our sin is forgiven by Christ's sacrifice then we are not under the condemnation of the law. It is a moot point, because the angels who administered the Old Testament no longer have any legal claim on us. They have no power to punish us. The whole Gnostic argument about having to free ourselves from Old Testament religion and its angels collapses on that one point.

The full context of Colossians chapter two indicates the church was being told they must reject the full list of Jewish practices listed in verse 16 in order to achieve a state of Christian liberation from the material world. Paul is countering that by insisting that in Christ we are *already* free.

So, Paul turns the argument right back against the Gnostics. By saying we have to free ourselves from the angels of the Old Testament, the Gnostics in effect were placing man in continued subjection to angels. That is why, in verses 20–21 Paul argues Hellenistic/Gnostic asceticism puts us in bondage to "elemental spirits":

> If you with Christ died to the elemental spirits of the universe, why do you live as if you still belonged to the world? Why do you submit to regulations, Do not handle, Do not taste, Do not touch?

'Elemental spirits' is a typical Greek term referring to angels as they were viewed in Hellenistic/Gnostic theology – spirits who rule over the mate-

---

gan Hellenistic religion. For Gnosticism, the evil angels are those associated with Yahweh who both participated in creation and administer the Old Covenant.

rial creation and subject man to materialistic bondage. By using the Greek term 'elemental spirits' rather than angels, Paul is signaling that he is talking about some kind of Hellenistic Christian theology in which Yahweh's angels are merged with the Greek concept of materialistic spirits who subject man to bondage.[85]

The Gnostic doctrine of salvation says we are still in bondage and have to free ourselves by practicing asceticism and rejecting Sabbath, whereas the true Christian doctrine of grace says Christ already has freed us.[86] Judaeophobic antinomianism and ascetic rejection of material creation are nonsense. The Sabbath and other Jewish customs, the law and material existence in general, are no threat to spiritual Christians.

Here is the striking conclusion concerning Colossians: Many Christians today continue to use Colossians 2:16 to argue we must reject Jewish practices such as Sabbath in order to free ourselves from Old Testament religion. Paul, however, actually was saying *exactly the opposite!* Paul was defending the Colossians against the criticism of Hellenistic/Gnostic teachers. He was saying they had no right to condemn Christians for participating in Jewish celebrations and engaging in material feasting on those days.

Now we also better understand what Paul meant when he says these things are only *"shadows of things to come"* (vs 17). Some believe Paul was saying Jewish customs are frivolous and insignificant so we should not observe them. However, remember that escape from the material world was the core argument in Gnosticism. For them, rejection of Hebrew religion and its creation-centered rituals was an absolute requirement for accomplishing that escape.

Paul is merely continuing his argument against the Gnostics' foolish belief that Jewish practices are inherently evil and we have to be worried about bondage to evil angels. Instead, Paul insists, the real substance of salvation is Jesus Christ (vs 17).[87] Jewish religious institutions support New Testament salvation by symbolically pointing toward the real core issue, which is Jesus.

---

[85] Once again Paul is expressing himself with Hellenistic/Gnostic terminology, indicating the nature of the apostasy involved at Colossae.

[86] The Gnostic view of Old Testament religion described in Colossians is essentially the same as that found in modern Hellenistic Christianity, which still today argues that participating in Jewish customs automatically subjects one to bondage.

[87] A complete explanation of 'shadow' and 'substance' (or body) appears below, in appendix A, "The Full Story behind Colossians 2".

In Colossians Paul is neither arguing for nor against the observance of any Jewish custom. What he is doing is refuting and ridiculing the typical Gnostic argument that rejecting Jewish customs and practices is a core issue of salvation. The whole idea is nonsense, he says, because Jesus is the core issue of salvation and those customs and practices merely point to Jesus.

Throughout the book of Colossians Paul constantly emphasizes the superiority of Christ over all things, greater than the principalities and powers, greater than the angels, greater than the power of sin, greater than man himself. *"He* [Christ] *is before all things, and in him all things hold together"* (1:17).

Gnostic Christianity, according to Paul, constantly derails itself over secondary issues about freeing Christians from bondage, which simply don't make sense and detract from the real issue, Christ himself. And what is it that leads Gnostic Christianity into that error? What is the source of Gnostic Christianity itself? Paul lays it out very clearly: *"See to it that no one makes a prey of you by philosophy and empty deceit, according to human tradition"* (Col 2:8). What could Paul have meant by *'philosophy'* and *'human tradition'*? What was the single dominant philosophy and human tradition in Paul's time and place? Can this possibly be a reference to anything other than Hellenistic philosophy and religion, the dominant human cultural tradition at the time Paul was writing this?

Paul's letter to the Colossians did not have to wait until our day to be misinterpreted and turned on its head. This first appears among the Gnostics themselves. In the *Gospel of the Egyptians*, an ancient Gnostic text from the Nag Hammadi library, the cross is portrayed in a way probably patterned on this misinterpretation of Colossians 2:14–15.[88] In this Gnostic book, Jesus is described as nailing 13 great angels to the cross. These are the evil angels of creation that keep man in bondage to the material world through the religion of Yahweh. Nailing them to the cross symbolizes liberation from the Old Testament God and his law, which for these Gnostics was the very substance of their salvation.[89]

What really was nailed to the cross? Modern Hellenistic Christianity perpetuates ancient Gnostic theology by saying this New Testament passage means Hebrew religion and its law was nailed to the cross. The text,

---

[88] See ***NHLE***, 208 ff.

[89] See Perkins, *Gnosticism and the New Testament,* p 154.

however, indicates it is not the law but our sins that are nailed to the cross. According to Paul,

> ...God made you alive together with him, when he forgave us all our trespasses, erasing the record [*our criminal record, the written list of charges against us*] that stood against us with its legal demands [*the demand for punishment*]. He set this aside, nailing it to the cross. (Col 2:13–14, see NRSV translation; bracketed explanations added))

Because of the poor translation of some versions, which read *"handwriting of ordinances that was against us,"* this passage often has been misunderstood to refer to the law itself. In the Greek text, however, the *"handwriting of ordinances"* implies a written legal 'indictment,' in other words a legal document listing the charges brought against us, in other words a list of our sins.

Submission to Angels, Colossians 2:18

There remains another important historical issue involving Colossians 2. This concerns verse 18: *"Do not let anyone disqualify you, insisting on self-abasement and worship of angels...."* This is an apparent reference to the Hellenistic tradition of subjecting Christian believers to angels, a prominent doctrine among Valentinian Gnostics.

In Valentinus' theology all emanations from the heavenly Father are pairs of beings with male and female attributes.[90] This has important psychological implications. Sexual pairing represents a state of submission, interdependence and wholeness that makes possible the peace and bliss of heaven. When spirit fell into the material world, they explained, the evil Yahweh separated the sexes and that condition was broken.[91] This refers

---

[90] This theme appears in some other Gnostic writings in the guise of androgynous beings. Androgyny, as the merging of male and female qualities, in general represents perfection and freedom from the bondage of material passion, exactly as the pairing of male and female angels represented perfection and harmonious interdependence in the Valentinian *pleroma*.

[91] The idea is that the defectiveness of the material world resulted from a violation of the principles of submission and interdependence that supports the bliss of the heavenly *pleroma*. This was expressed mythically in the story of one of the aeons (Sophia), who wanted to produce further emanations on her own, without consulting and participating with her

to the biblical passage in which Yahweh separated the genders by creating Eve from Adam's rib. This supposedly is the underlying cause of evil passions within human beings. If mankind were not distinctly separated into male and female beings, Valentinians reasoned, there would be no lust, no jealousy, no greed, in short none of the dysfunctional urges of the human mind that lead to sin. This is especially true of sexual desire, which the Valentinians viewed as the deceptive echo of an inner spiritual longing for unification with one's spiritual mate. The solution, therefore, is to return man to his original state that combines both male and female traits in one spiritual being.

To that end, upon conversion Valentinian Christians took part in sacraments that culminated in a divine marriage ceremony in which they were spiritually married to angels.[92] A male convert would be married to a female angel, and a female convert to a male angel. In this way the original sin of the breaking of submission and interdependence is reversed in the life of individual Christian converts, and the original perfection of the heavens is restored. The evil passions and lust of their materialistic nature are miraculously healed. Henceforth they live in a spiritual state of love and peace, no longer in bondage to the evil passions that afflict the rest of mankind. There is no need for law nor striving against sin, which they equate to bondage. Their salvation is based on a miraculous transformation of the inner spirit, secured by their submission to and spiritual union with angels. This automatically produces sweetness and gentleness and an outpouring of goodness that occurs naturally, without human effort.[93] So

---

partner. Thus the offspring of her (original) sin was defective, resulting ultimately in the creator Yahweh who in turn is responsible for the mess in which we find ourselves today.

[92] The Valentinian theology of marriage to angels and the spiritual transformation that produces, is most clearly expressed in the Nag Hammadi text *The Gospel of Philip*. See also the introduction to *The Gospel of Philip* in **NHLE** by the translator, especially p 140.

[93] One can only assume that these Gnostic rituals did not really produce the lasting and total resolution of the human urge to sin that they claimed. For those Valentinians who experienced shortcomings in this area, there always was the traditional Gnostic antinomian 'out' – if I do fall short, no matter, it is only a problem in my material life and body which I will leave behind at death. It has no relevance for salvation, which is spiritual and affected only by my inner spiritual state. As Epiphanius depicted the Valentinians, they boasted that they are totally free and have no need to conform to any standard of righteousness or good works (see above, p 52 ff).

they gained a reputation in the early church for preaching antinomian liberation.

The Valentinian doctrine of inner transformation is strikingly similar to the genuine New Testament doctrine of Christian transformation. The difference between the two is the Gnostic addition of antinomian rejection of the law as a guide to God's will, and the imbalance in their radical separation of inner and outer spirituality. Valentinians believed that their outward conduct in the material world is not significant, because within their souls they had achieved heavenly perfection.

Upon death a Valentinian looked forward to ascending to heaven and being formally joined with his or her angelic partner, to spend eternity in the perfect unity and bliss of the heavenly *pleroma.*

The Valentinian belief in union with angels is alluded to in several Gnostic texts. One example is from the *Gospel of Philip.* Here in one passage it explains that evil spirits come in genders, and tempt humans of the opposite sex. However, if a Gnostic Christian is united with an angelic partner, they cannot be tempted sexually: *"So if the image and the angel are united with one another, neither can any* [demon] *venture to go in to the man or the woman."*[94] The 'image' refers to a Valentinian Christian, whose union with an angel has healed his sexual and materialistic desires and so prevents demons from tempting him.

Colossians chapter two is a very complex passage of scripture. The Colossians to whom Paul addressed his letter were immersed in the Hellenistic culture of their time. They would have recognized immediately what Paul was talking about. Elemental spirits, submission to angels, asceticism and Gnostic antinomianism were all common ideas and controversies in the Hellenistic Christian culture of the first century A.D. For us today it is difficult because of our lack of understanding of that same Hellenistic cultural background. For a more detailed review of Colossians, see Appendix A, "The Full Story Behind Colossians 2."

---

[94] **NHLE**, 149.

2 Thessalonians 2

2 Thessalonians chapter 2 records a prophecy about a great lawless personality who rises to the head of the church and is destroyed by Christ at his second coming. He may proclaim himself to be divine and the embodiment of Christ. This is the culmination of a great rebellion (vs 3) that had already appeared in the church in Paul's time. This individual's lawlessness, his belief or religious tradition, is described as already at work in the world of the primitive church:

> For the mystery of lawlessness is already at work, but only until the one who now restrains it is removed. And then the lawless one will be revealed, whom the Lord Jesus will destroy with the breath of his mouth, annihilating him by the manifestation of his coming. (2 Thess 2:7–8)

Notice it says the *mystery* of lawlessness, by which we know it is talking about religious doctrine rather than perhaps just a rising incidence of crime and social lawlessness at the time 2 Thessalonians was written. By this time nearly all religions of the Hellenistic world had downgraded the God of creation to a defective angelic being or subordinate deity from whom we must free ourselves. Rejection of the authority of the God of creation was not limited to Gnostic Christianity. In fact it had achieved wide acceptance in the Hellenistic world in late antiquity.

Within first-century Christendom, however, there is only one Hellenistic tradition teaching a mystery of lawlessness that rejects the authority of the God of creation. That is Gnostic Christianity and its central doctrine that one's conduct in material life is completely separate from salvation, teaching in addition that turning away from the Old Testament creator God and rejecting biblical law are a requirement for Christian salvation.

2 Thessalonians 2 is an extremely important text. It specifically prophesies that Hellenistic rejection of the creator God, along with the attendant religious baggage of liberation and lawlessness introduced by the Gnostics in the first century, will not die out. It will continue and grow through time, even up to the very second coming (vs 8) when it is finally destroyed by Christ himself. This passage thereby also indicates the final religious apostasy of the beast power described in Revelation will be an outgrowth of the Hellenistic religious tradition.

Note carefully, it does not say Gnosticism itself will continue till Christ returns. It says only that one of the primary doctrinal packages pioneered by Gnosticism – the mystery of lawlessness – will continue and must still be present in some prominent form of religious teaching in our world today.

2 Peter chapter 2

This entire chapter is aimed directly at Gnosticism:

> But false prophets also arose among the people, just as there will be false teachers among you, who will secretly bring in destructive opinions. They will even deny the Master who bought them.... Even so, many will follow their licentious ways....
>
> Bold and willful, they are not afraid to slander the glorious ones, whereas angels, though greater in might and power, do not bring against them a slanderous judgment from the Lord.
>
> They are blots and blemishes, reveling in their dissipation while they feast with you. (vs 1–2, 10–11, 13)

"Deny the master who bought them" is a reference to Docetism and its companion theology that rejects Jesus' earthly ministry (see below, section "2 John," pages 107 and following). *"Licentious ways"* is Gnostic antinomianism, the mystery of lawlessness. *"Slander the glorious ones"* refers to Gnostic condemnation of Yahweh's creating angels. *"They feast with you"* reflects the conditions in the first-century primitive church in which proto-Gnostic Christians mixed freely with orthodox New Testament Christians.

> They promise freedom, but they themselves are slaves of corruption; for people are slaves to whatever masters them. (vs 18–19)

Freedom is one of the great themes of Gnosticism – freedom from the bondage of the Old Testament, from Yahweh and the external control of his law. Spirituality is a matter solely of the inner man, the soul. Well, yes, most Gnostics said you shouldn't engage in many kinds of immoral conduct. They steadfastly maintained, however, that morality, at least those aspects dealing with material life, technically plays no role in salvation. It cannot block salvation. It is not a criterion of salvation. In contrast, notice how Peter uses a string of examples from the Old Testament – the fallen angels, Noah, and Sodom and Gomorrah (vs 4–8) – and insists that in the same fashion God continues to punish and destroy willful evildoers under the New Testament yet today (vs 9–10).

> ...the Lord knows how...to keep the unrighteous under punish-
> ment until the day of judgment – especially those who indulge
> their flesh in depraved lust, and who despise authority.

For Peter, authority, punishment and rulership are aspects of God's dealing with man that distinctly carry over from the Old into the New Testament.

2 Peter 2 is closely patterned after the book of Jude, so that one appears almost to be a copy of the other. Notice that neither Peter nor Jude
are talking about unbelievers. They specifically refer to apostasy among
believers inside the New Testament church (2 Peter 2:2, compare Jude 3).
The nature of that apostasy is specifically a licentious interpretation of
grace (note especially Jude 4).

What Peter and Jude are directly saying is that the principle of law and
punishment in general survives from the Old into the New Testament.
Faithful, repentant Christians are under grace and don't have to worry
about that. In contrast, Jesus regards antinomian Christians as under the
law. They have fallen from grace and will bear the full force of the punishment of the law because of their willful disobedience.

2 Peter 3:15–17

In chapter three Peter carries forward the same themes from chapter
two about antinomianism and licentious grace. Here he adds the detail
that these false teachers regularly misuse the writings of Paul to support
their radical ideas:

> So also our beloved brother Paul wrote to you...as he does in all
> his letters. There are some things in them hard to understand,
> which the ignorant and unstable twist to their own destruc-
> tion.... You therefore...beware that you are not carried away with
> the error of the lawless and lose your own stability. (2 Peter
> 3:15–17)

Notice how Peter describes Gnostic teaching as unbalanced (losing stability). That is an important point. Gnostic Christians were, after all, Christians. They understood and taught a great deal of genuine biblical truth.
This is especially true of proto-Gnosticism as it developed inside the
church in the first century. Gnostic theology focused on many true teachings from Paul's writings about the spirituality of the inner man. But in
Gnosticism they are exaggerated and isolated from other equally impor-

tant teachings about overcoming, self-control and obedience to written biblical standards. The result is a highly spiritualized but unbalanced teaching that licenses and facilitates lawlessness.

Does chapter three refer to Gnosticism?

The context of 2 Peter chapter 3 is widely misunderstood by Bible commentators. The opening to the chapter, in verse 4, refers to scoffers who doubt the return of Jesus to earth and claim the material world continues on without end. They say: *"Where is the promise of his coming? For ever since our ancestors died, all things continue as they were from the beginning of creation!"* On this basis many interpret chapter three as a reply to atheists. Some relate it to the Epicureans, a Hellenistic religious group that taught an atheistic-like doctrine of a God who is not concerned with or involved in the material world.

This interpretation necessitates a sharp departure from the obviously Gnostic issues addressed in chapter 2, to which Peter returns at the end of chapter 3. Atheists may be included, but the Apostle's criticism is aimed primarily at something else. The text indicates he is thinking about those who deny that God brought Noah's Flood and who deny that God will judge the world in the end time to punish evil. As he says, *"They deliberately ignore...*[that] *the world of that time was deluged by water and perished"* and *"the present heavens and earth have been reserved for fire, being kept until the day of judgment and destruction of the godless"* (vs 6–7).

In chapter 3 Peter is continuing his theme about those who reject the idea of divine authority and judgment. Recall for example the Gnostic teacher Marcion, who insisted that the heavenly Father is not judgmental and never condemns man as Yahweh did under the Old Testament (see above, pages 48 and following). We also see this kind of reasoning in the Gnostic teacher Basilides (see above, page 50). He claimed the material world goes on without end, with people surviving on various levels of the cosmos for eternity.

Many Gnostics rejected the idea that God has ever condemned and visited divine punishment on the world. Some claimed the heavenly Father had nothing to do with Noah's Flood. He would never do that, they insisted! The heavenly Father is pure love, mercy and grace. Actually, they claimed, the Flood was an attempt by the evil Yahweh to stamp out the true spiritual followers of the heavenly Father. Gnostic teachers were fond of pointing out that Noah, his wife, his three sons and their wives total eight. This they said was one of those hidden clues from the Old Testament that validates their system of belief. Remember, for Gnostics eight points to the Eighth Day, a symbol of the heavens, a sign of those who have rejected the materialistic and judgmental Yahweh. For them this was proof that Noah and his family were enlightened and instead worshipped the true heavenly Father of love and mercy, who never condemns.

Still, for orthodox Christians the question remains: If God does judge, then why does he allow the world to go on in spite of the evil we see about us. Peter interprets this as an expression of Jesus' grace and mercy, giving man time to repent:

> The Lord is not slow about his promise, as some think of slowness, but is patient with you, not wanting any to perish, but all to come to repentance. (vs 9)

It is in this context that we find Peter continuing in chapter three to build the same argument against lawlessness as in chapter two. His point is that the continuation of the world through God's forbearance should not be interpreted in an antinomian sense that condones disobedience, as though God is too nice to condemn anyone even for willfully evil conduct.

The Gnostic teacher Carpocrates is an example of those who specifically link antinomianism with the idea of God's forbearance, virtually identical to what Peter warns against. Carpocrates argued that Christians should try to conquer material lust. If you fail in that, however, hope is not lost. In fact, man's ultimate hope specifically rests on the fact that the world does not end. According to Carpocrates, those who are evil will continue to be reborn endlessly in this world, until finally every soul completes its full allotment of suffering from sin. At that point the soul returns to God. (For Carpocratian theology see above, pages 46 and following.)

In the Carpocratian religious system the continuity of the world – the absence of a specific end to the world – is a key factor in an antinomian teaching of universal salvation. If you have a problem with temptation, don't worry. You will have unlimited chances in the future to complete the process of salvation. The heavenly Father is so loving he never condemns anyone – in the end everyone will be saved. This is exactly the type of thing Peter is warning against. Do not regard the continuation of human history as an excuse for lawlessness, he says. The unlimited opportunity taught by some Gnostic Christians is untrue. There will be a final end, at which point everyone will be judged.

The overall theme in both chapters two and three of 2 Peter is that the true God still judges and punishes. That aspect of God's personality did not end with the Old Testament as Gnostic Christianity claimed.

2 John

Notice John's urgent command to reject and separate from Gnostic Christians as they infiltrated and infected the apostolic church with their Hellenistic theology:

> Many deceivers have gone out into the world, those who do not confess that Jesus Christ has come in the flesh; any such person is the deceiver and the Antichrist! ... Everyone who does not abide in the teaching of Christ, but goes beyond [transgresses] it, does not have God.... <u>Do not receive into the house or welcome</u> anyone who comes to you and does not bring this teaching; for <u>to welcome is to participate in the evil deeds</u> of such a person." (2 Jn 7, 9–11)

In this passage we also have a critical phrase referring directly to the doctrine of progressive revelation as it was misused in Gnostic theology. Notice how John says, *"Everyone who does not abide in the teaching of Christ, but goes beyond it, does not have God..."* (vs 9). (See NRSV translation; the Greek text uses the term "transgress" which implies to go outside or beyond.) What is it that we are to not "go beyond"? It says don't go beyond *"the teaching of Christ,"* but what exactly is the teaching of Christ? Theologians argue over the question of whether this means the "teaching <u>about</u> Christ," i.e. the doctrine of Christ's nature, whether he has a docetic nature as the Gnostics claimed, or does it mean "the teaching <u>of</u> Christ," i.e. Christ's ministry. Most translations read "of Christ," but, for example, the Revised English Bible opts for the translation "about Christ."

It is significant that this passage closely follows after a reference to Gnostic Docetism, in verse 7. (This is the Gnostic doctrine that Jesus is composed of two separate beings, one divine and one human.) But verse 7 is also part of a larger passage beginning in verse 5, which refers to the problem of Gnostic rejection of Jesus' earthly ministry. In verses 5 and 6 John refers to love and the commandments, and repeatedly makes the point that this is the teaching of Christ that was *"from the beginning."* John uses this phrase repeatedly in his first letter. And in 1 John 1:1–3 he defines it as Jesus' earthly ministry. That is when Jesus taught the future apostles in person, when they personally experienced him, directly seeing, listening to and even touching him (*We declare to you what was from the beginning , what we have heard, what we have seen with our eyes…and touched with our hands* – 1 John 1:1).

In fact, in interpreting 2 John we do not need to choose between these two ideas – Jesus' nature versus what Jesus taught. They are part of one theological package, and in 2 John the apostle is referring specifically to both. Many Gnostics used Docetism as their justification for rejecting much of what Jesus taught during his earthly ministry. Their argument was that Jesus is a combination of a Spirit named Christ and a mortal man named Jesus. The problem is that Jesus happened to be a Jew. That, they reasoned, is why Christ's earthly ministry is defective. It was contaminated, they insisted, by the Hebrew heritage of his materialistic, human side. That is how they explained away the many lawful teachings recorded in the gospel accounts of Jesus' life and ministry, such as his teaching the correct spiritual observance of the Sabbath.

The important point here is understanding that when John warns to not "go beyond" the "teaching of Jesus," he is criticizing the full complex of docetic doctrine preached by Gnostic Christianity. This specifically includes their rejection of Jesus' earthly ministry. We know that is true because this was a doctrinal package in Gnosticism. It is significant, therefore, that John specifically mentions the entire package in verses 5–7 as a prelude to his statement to not "go beyond" the "teaching of Jesus." The fact that he mentions both ideas together, indicates he understood Gnostic Christianity much better than the many theologians today who argue over what the 'teaching of Jesus' means. But that is not surprising, since he witnessed Gnostic theology first-hand.

Why is this important? It is extremely important because the same Gnostic concept of rejecting large parts of Jesus' earthly ministry is found in modern Hellenistic Christianity today as part of a doctrinal complex called dispensational theology. With this, Evangelical Protestantism teaches that much or all of Jesus' earthly ministry is Jewish and does not apply to Christians today. We will return to this issue, and its application to modern Protestant theology, in later chapters.

1 John

In **1 John 2:18–23** John characterizes Gnostics as the Antichrist, and mentions two important things. First, he affirms the existence of many such groups. Indeed the historical record shows a splintered world of many Gnostic Christian groups.

John also says these groups formed within the New Testament church and then went out from it. This also agrees with the historical record. Separate, organized Gnostic groups appeared mostly in the second century. In the first century most Gnostics were practicing Christians within the New Testament church. This is reflected in various other biblical passages such as Jude 12 (*These are blemishes on your love-feasts*) and 2 Peter 2:13 (*reveling in their dissipation while they feast with you*). Scholars often refer to the development of Gnosticism inside the first-century church as "proto-Gnosticism."

In **chapter 4** of his first letter John takes up the theme of Docetism again:

> ...every spirit that confesses that Jesus Christ has come in the flesh is from God, and every spirit that does not confess Jesus is not from God. And this is the spirit of the Antichrist, of which you have heard that it is coming; and now it is already in the world. (1 John 4:2–3)

And what is the source of the spirit of Antichrist? John says it is the product of the non-Christian world surrounding the church:

> ...the one who is in you is greater than the one who is in the world. They [Gnostic Christians] are from the world; therefore what they say is from the world, and the world listens to them." (1 John 4:4–5)

The last part of this passage is especially interesting. Where does Gnostic religion ultimately come from? (*"What they say is from the world"* – the world of Hellenistic culture and religion.) The world surrounding the New Testament church was Hellenistic, in all its many forms – from Greek philosophy to the newly Hellenized mystery cults to the popular superstitions of astrology. The term *Hellenistic* comes from *Hellene*, a designation of the Greeks. Remember that Hellenistic religion, which by the time of Christ had spread throughout the Mediterranean and Near East, began with the great pagan religious reformation in ancient Greece. That is why the New Testament sometimes refers to anyone who is non-Christian and non-Jewish as "Greek." (See Romans 1:16 and Acts 14:1.) By the time of Christ, virtually all of paganism had become Hellenistic.

Everyone in those days, from government leaders and university professors to chariot drivers and construction workers were totally immersed in the ideas and language of Hellenistic religion. The purpose of religion was to awaken your immortal soul and get to heaven. Everyone knew that's what it was all about. If you went to the masses to invite them to meet with you on the seventh day to learn about the (ugh!) creator, or spoke about the coming eternal kingdom of God on earth, people would laugh: "What a bunch of hayseeds! Did you guys drop out of second grade?"

(*"And the world listens to them"*) On the other hand, if you can Hellenize the Christian message just enough to include such basics as, say, the immortality of the soul, the promise of ascent to heaven at death, antinomian liberation, and symbolism of the number eight, then, together with other features shared in common between the Bible and Hellenistic religion such as a focus on the life of the spirit, you have a real winner.

Notice that 1 John repeats the message of 2 Thessalonians chapter 2:

> 2 Thess 2:7–8 – <u>For the mystery of lawlessness is already at work</u>.... And then the lawless one will be revealed, whom the Lord will destroy...annihilating him by the manifestation of his coming)

> 1 John 4:3 – And this is the spirit of the Antichrist, of which you have heard that it is coming; <u>and now it is already in the world</u>.

These passages in John's letters together with 2 Thessalonians chapter 2 mark the Hellenization of Christianity as a critically important historical event. It signals the first appearance of the primary vehicle for religious deception by Satan during the Christian era.

Given the Gnostic context, we now better understand some of the other passages in John's letters. Earlier in his first letter John warns against arguments that Christians cannot sin: *"If we say that we have no sin, we deceive ourselves.... If we say we have not sinned we make him a liar...."* (1 John 1:8,10). Remember that many Gnostic sects believed spiritual liberation means becoming free from all the evil lusts of material life, resulting in a genuine state of spiritual perfection **now**, in this life.

Valentinians, for example, attributed this to a spiritual union with right-eous angels.[95] Other Gnostics such as the Nicolaitans emphasized indif-ference to sins they regarded as physical matters, which they claimed have no effect on inner spirituality. If their inner soul was unaffected by external sin, then they had achieved sinless perfection regardless of what was happening in their material life. John, however, says that Christians continue to sin and cannot shrug it off as many Gnostics did.

In **chapter two** John preaches doctrines of knowledge (*gnosis*) of God and mystical union with God, which are shared by both Gnostic and or-thodox Christianity. Gnostic Christians, however, added an antinomian dimension by claiming you have to reject Old Testament religion and the law in order to obtain *gnosis* and mystical union with God. John explains the orthodox version in a way specifically designed to counter the Gnos-tics' antinomian misinterpretation of these Christian truths. He does this by directly tying them to obedience:

> Now by this we may be sure that we **know** him, if we **obey** his commandments. Whoever says 'I have come to **know** him,' but does not **obey his commandments**, is a liar...but whoever **obeys his word**, truly in this person the love of God has reached perfection. By this we may be sure that we are **in him**: whoever says, **'I abide in him,'** ought to **walk just as he walked**. (1 John 2:3–6)

John says those who possess spiritual *gnosis* also must imitate Jesus' righteous conduct during his earthly ministry (*walk as he walked*).

In 1 John **chapter 3**, John continues the theme of obedience that recurs over and over in his letters:

> Everyone who commits sin is guilty of lawlessness; sin is law-lessness. You know that he was revealed to take away sins, and in him there is no sin. No one who abides in him sins; no one who sins has either seen him or known him.
>
> Little children, let no one deceive you. Everyone who does what is right is righteous, just as he is righteous. Everyone who com-mits sin is a child of the devil; for the devil has been sinning from the beginning. The Son of God was revealed for this pur-pose, to destroy the works of the devil.
>
> Those who have been born of God do not sin, because God's seed abides in them; they cannot sin, because they have been born of

---

[95] See above, section Submission to Angels, Colossians 2:18, p 99.

God. The children of God and the children of the devil are revealed in this way: all who do not do what is right are not from
God, nor are those who do not love their brothers and sisters. (vs
4–10)

How many ways can you say it? Forwards, backwards, sideways. God
and sin do not mix! No one can approach God nor have a relationship
with him if he believes and practices the great antinomian lie.

I never fully grasped this passage until I understood its Gnostic context. At one point it seems almost to say that after conversion a Christian
is incapable of sin (*they cannot sin, because they have been born of God*).
However John himself in chapter one, as quoted above, clearly says that
Christians continue to experience sin. The resolution is that chapter three
actually is talking about Gnostic liberation theology. It is referring to the
Gnostic belief that openly and willfully rejecting the Old Testament God
and his law is the way to approach the heavenly Father. John rejects that
as nonsense. You cannot know God and abide in him while willfully rejecting his revealed standards of material conduct.

In verse 7 John warns against persons who would "deceive you." Exactly what is their deceptive argument? In the remainder of the verse John
refutes the deception he has in mind, saying, *"Everyone who does what is
right is righteous, **just as** he* [God] *is righteous."* The deception, then,
must be the opposite of John's rebuttal. That deception is the classic antinomian argument that Christ liberated us from the need to obey God, so
we can be righteous without God's righteousness being reflected in our
conduct. In modern terms, it is the argument that Christ obeyed the law in
our place, therefore we don't have to. According to John, however, the
purpose of religion is for us to become like God, to be righteous exactly
as he is righteous.

Can a man really become righteous like God? If so, how? In verse 9
John addresses that question, saying "Those who have been born of God
do not sin, because God's seed abides in them...." So it is the indwelling
of God's Spirit that enables man to become righteous.

In this passage the New Testament directly brands as children of Satan
those who believe willful sin does not ultimately break our relationship
with God (*a child of the devil*). That is not a pleasant idea, yet it is a basic
New Testament teaching revealed through the apostle John.

If I were to summarize John's message for Christians, it would be
"Just say NO to antinomianism." The basic idea is a fraud. Theological
justification of willful lawlessness is a deception of Satan.

Revelation chapters 2 and 3

Here we come to the end of the New Testament and its final book. Revelation chapters two and three have a special significance for us because of their prophetic nature. They are talking not only about what happened in the first century church. It is a presentation of seven churches with both positive and negative traits, given as a warning and instruction to all Christians through all time:

> Let **anyone** who has an ear listen to what the Spirit is saying to the churches. (Rev 2:7)

It is also here that we find, for the first and only time, references to a Gnostic sect by name – the Nicolaitans. In an earlier chapter we learned that this was one of the typically spiritual but licentious Gnostic sects from the first century. (See Nicolaitanism, above, pages 40 and following.)

The **Ephesus** church is praised for joining Christ in hating the works of the Nicolaitans (vs 6) and not tolerating evildoers (vs 2). Despite exalted teachings of inner spirituality, Gnostic theological licensing of sin always became an excuse for sin among many of its followers. The Ephesians were not fooled by the show of spirituality in which Gnostic Christians encased their licentious teachings, and they didn't tolerate the disobedience that came from it. The Ephesians are praised for having the spiritual discrimination to recognize and reject ministers who teach antinomian spirituality: *"...you have tested those who claim to be apostles but are not, and have found them to be false"* (vs 2).

The message to the second church, **Smyrna**, makes no mention of Nicolaitans, but it does refer to *"slander on the part of those who say that they are Jews and are not, but are a synagogue of Satan"* (vs 9). The early New Testament Christians for some decades referred to themselves as Jews. Pagans and orthodox Jews also referred to the earliest Christians as Jews. Scholars today sometimes refer to the primitive New Testament church as Jewish Christianity because of its continuity of the biblical religious tradition from the Old Testament. In the context of the first century, the claim to be Jews can be the same as claiming to be Christians.

Why does Revelation say these critics really are worshippers of Satan? One biblical definition is 1 John 3. Here Christians who believe in the antinomian doctrines of Gnostic Christianity are described as unwittingly worshipping Satan.

The slander experienced by the primitive church at Smyrna comes from some group that sincerely believes and claims to follow the true God of the Bible, but in reality practices a deviant form of biblical religion. That potentially points to many groups in the first century. Most prominent among many candidates, however, are Gnostic Christians who traditionally claimed they have the true and more advanced revelation of Christianity. So they slander Primitive Christians as backward, inferior, or false Christians. The slander Primitive Christians experience today is only a continuation of what was happening in the first century, and it will continue until Christ returns and puts a stop to it as described in the message to the Philadelphia church.

The third church, **Pergamum**, also is expressly involved with Nicolaitan Gnosticism. Here the church has been less successful than before. Pergamum has been infiltrated by Nicolaitan Christians (vs 15). The problem is compared to the story of Balaam, where Israel was seduced by a foreign religious system that led to a loosening of moral standards. (The significance of Balaam as a symbol for Hellenistic apostasy in the church is described at length in Appendix D.)

The problem at Pergamum is identified as fornication and eating food sacrificed to idols (vs 14). Eating food sacrificed to idols may be a reference to ecumenical acceptance of non-Christian religious practices. Fornication may refer to immorality or, once again, it may symbolically represent mixing with foreign religious practices and beliefs. In any case, this description cannot mean the church openly promoted sexual immorality, else how could it still be a church ruled by Christ? The historical evidence from Nicolaitan and Gnostic theology in general supports the logical conclusion it could be talking only about *tolerance* of sin.

Those are the symptoms. The underlying cause is *"the teaching of the Nicolaitans"* (vs 15). We know what that is – a sophisticated antinomian spirituality that produces goodness magically, by breaking the natural human psychological obsession with the material world. Although antinomian spirituality does not overtly teach immorality, and in fact is intended to bring man out of sin, we know from the writings of the early church fathers as well as from Revelation that it resulted in immorality for the Nicolaitans, as it always ultimately does. (See Nicolaitanism, above, pages 40 and following.)

Note that the Pergamon church itself did not adopt Gnostic theology. Their error is ecumenical tolerance of Gnostic Christians within their church (vs 14). Christ calls for them to repent. If not, he will arrange a persecution and personally orchestrate it to physically destroy those who have become involved with Nicolaitan Gnostic doctrines and practices (vs 16).

The fourth church, **Thyatira,** also is troubled by false teachers, led by a great prophetess called Jezebel. That may have been her actual name, or it may be a symbolic reference to the Canaanite queen in ancient Israel who seduced God's people to mix worship of Yahweh with the pagan worship of Baal. What was the foreign religion with which Thyatira had become involved? It doesn't specifically say, but notice the wording is identical to the description of the Nicolaitan problem at Pergamum: *"teaching and beguiling my servants to practice fornication and to eat food sacrificed to idols"* (vs 20). This suggests it was the same type of problem, though not necessarily the same antinomian sect. There were plenty of Gnostic and other Hellenistic sects to go around, as there are yet today. God warns them, and warns us today:

> Beware, I am throwing her on a bed, and those who commit adultery with her I am throwing into great distress, unless they repent of her doings; and I will strike her children dead. And all the churches will know that I am the one who searches minds and hearts, and I will give to each of you as your works deserve. But to the rest of you in Thyatira, who do not hold this teaching, who have not learned what some call 'the deep things of Satan', to you I say, I do not lay on you any other burden.... (vs 22–24)

The situation at Thyatira is extremely serious. The church has become divided on the basis of whether they accept or reject the antinomian teaching of their own apostate leader. This becomes the means of separating those who will be preserved and those who are killed in an unspecified *'great distress,'* perhaps a severe persecution. Part of the Thyatira message is that in serious situations of apostasy, Christians cannot hide behind a church or minister. Jesus holds us individually responsible for staying clear of grossly antinomian apostasy.

What specifically is this apostasy, so serious that each individual member of the church can mark himself for death if he does not recognize and keep separate from it? Notice the reference to the *"deep things of Satan"* (vs 24). This often is taken as a reference to one or the other religious mystery, including the mystery of lawlessness. What does it really mean, however, in its historical context?

Today for the first time, the history and meaning of the doctrines that spiritually destroyed the church at Thyatira, *the deep things of Satan,* can be known. It is an antinomian teaching about mystical union between man and God that taps into a divine reservoir of spiritual power known as the

Deep, bypassing material life and physical obedience. It started as a religious mystery tradition in ancient Babylonia and was picked up by Gnostic sects who introduced it into the New Testament church. The full account of this fascinating story, and the modern Christian theologies that perpetuate the same teachings, occupies the entirety of a later chapter of this book.

The fifth and seventh churches, **Sardis** and **Laodicea**, are the only two churches that appear not to have been noticeably bothered by heretical Christians.

The sixth church, **Philadelphia**, is a model for Christians who are troubled by Hellenistic Christianity. What they are praised for, more than anything else, is what they don't do. They just don't give in. They refuse to bend. Hear their description and praise:

> I know that you have little power, and yet you have kept my word and not denied my name.

Though they have few tangible signs to substantiate their beliefs, they stand their ground. Many of us experience religious fervor only when our church group has just launched a new building project, or there is a miraculous healing, something tangible we can rally around. These people rise above that.

Notice that Philadelphians are praised for not denying his name. Why would they be tempted to deny his name? Are they being harassed by Gnostics as seems to have happened at Smyrna? The same synagogue of Satan is mentioned:

> I will make those of the synagogue of Satan who say that they are Jews and are not, but are lying – I will make them come and bow down before your feet, and they will learn that I have loved you. (Rev 3:9)

We know that in the first century it was Hellenistic Christians, specifically the Gnostics who were prominent in harassing the primitive church with their claims to be the true and more spiritually advanced Christian church. Jesus is described as intervening to make them *"learn that I have loved you."* Why would he do that? Is it not because they constantly claim God is displeased with and does not love those who practice Primitive Christianity, that he only loves Christians who have converted to Hellenistic beliefs, as they continue to say to this day? In the end, when Christ returns he will make Hellenistic Christians come and bow down and admit who is the genuine, true church of God.

The description of the spiritual challenge of the seven churches, as it relates to apostasy and contamination from outside influences, uses a complex of interrelated terms – the teachings of Balaam, Nicolaitan Gnosticism, the synagogue of Satan, and the deep things of Satan. All of these trace back through other historical and biblical evidence to the single largest heretical movement of the New Testament world and its primary doctrine of antinomian liberation. As such, Revelation presents a uniquely unified overview of the challenge to the church mounted by Satan.

Christ's View of Gnosticism

What is Gnosticism from the Bible's point of view? Based on the New Testament evidence, what does Jesus think of Gnostic Christianity? Here are some of the Gnostic doctrines, traits and issues that stand out:

Among the heretical doctrines Christ inspired his ministers to condemn in his Word, Christian antinomianism takes first place – both willful disobedience and immorality, and the theology behind it, the 'mystery' of lawlessness. The apostle John in 1 John 3 couldn't say enough about it – God and willful disobedience is nonsense, a logical impossibility.

After lawlessness comes Docetism, mentioned frequently. As we have seen, Docetism includes the key rationale by which Gnostics justified their rejection of Jesus' earthly ministry (see above, section "2 John," pages 107 and following). If Jesus had two distinct natures, one of which was human and unspiritual, then his earthly ministry was contaminated and must be replaced by a second, more spiritual revelation of the faith. Docetism also denies Christ's sacrifice, frequently claiming that the spirit Christ withdrew before the crucifixion, and only the physical man Jesus died on the cross. Further, Docetism denies that spirituality involves material life and our material conduct, claiming that spirit and matter do not mix.

Gnosticism is also characterized as 'going beyond' the teachings of Jesus (2 John 9), in other words, teaching a progressive revelation of Christianity that contradicts Jesus' earthly ministry. That was a striking feature of Gnosticism, as it still is for Hellenistic Christianity today.

Next comes asceticism, mentioned in several scriptures, and rejection and misinterpretation of Jewish religious practices, given special treatment in Colossians 2.

There is praise for those who recognize Hellenistic theology for the lawless evil it really is. That is significant. Why does Jesus make a special point of praising the Ephesian church for hating Nicolaitan immorality and not tolerating its licentious teachers, as though that were such a special thing? The presence of those statements implies some Christians have a problem recognizing antinomian theology and thereby are misled into tolerating it. The church at Pergamum is a prime example.

The relationship between Primitive and Hellenistic Christians is a recurring theme. There is a huge amount of shared belief between the two. How should Primitive Christianity relate to its Hellenistic cousins? There are a number of New Testament passages that directly respond to this vital issue, indicating that Primitive Christians should not participate religiously with Hellenistic Christians. Primitive Christian churches are openly criticized both for allowing themselves to be seduced by Hellenistic theology and for tolerating factions within the church that have accepted it.

We see that Hellenistic Christianity commonly infiltrates the true church. This includes antinomian preachers operating inside the primitive church. The Ephesians are praised for recognizing and shutting their doors to false apostles associated with the Nicolaitan sect (Rev 2:2). In the Thyatira church, rejecting openly antinomian teachers inside the church is a sign separating those who are spared from those who will be destroyed (Rev 2:22).

Antinomian Christians are depicted as hounding and slandering God's people with their false claims to be more spiritually advanced and the only true Christians accepted by God. Revelation 2 and 3 in general demonstrate that Jesus regards dealing with the problem of the synagogue of Satan – both resisting its teachings and withstanding its slander and persecution – to be one of the primary challenges of the primitive church.

Gnosticism is depicted as a religion of Hellenistic culture (1 John 4), which indeed historically it was. Many Hellenistic doctrines not specifically mentioned in the New Testament, such as the immortality of the soul, survive today in mainstream Christianity. This too is significant in light of John's characterization of religious apostasy as Hellenistic.

Scripture depicts the appearance of Gnostic theology in the first-century church as the beginning of a great Hellenistic Christian religious tradition, which is prophesied to become the primary vehicle of apostasy and opposition to God until Christ returns. Subsequent history amply confirms that view.

The religious heritage of Gnosticism and Hellenistic Christianity, as it survives in its present-day forms, incorporates all the primary traits described in the New Testament. To say that "all" primary Gnostic traits survive today is a controversial statement. Most assume that the Gnostic teaching of Docetism has not survived. Certain important aspects of ancient Docetism indeed did not survive, such as the idea that Jesus' nature was so radically dualistic he really was a composite of two beings, the spirit Christ and the human Jesus. The radical idea held by some Gnostics that Christ separated from Jesus before the crucifixion and only Jesus died, also has not survived. The question, however, is the exact nature and complete teaching woven around Docetism. This is a topic covered in *Spirit of Antichrist,* volume two of our series The World of Primitive Christianity, in which it is demonstrated that Docetism indeed continues as one of the primary and most important teachings of Hellenistic Christianity today.

Nearly all serious scholars – Protestant, Catholic and Jewish – freely admit the historical veracity of the Hellenization of Primitive Christianity. This only confirms God's word spoken through John. It historically, factually, and provably links modern Hellenistic Christianity with the New Testament's description of the infiltration of Hellenistic beliefs into the New Testament church, beginning with Gnostic Christianity in the first century. It links the historical Hellenization of Christianity with the great subversion of the church foretold by Christ. It is a rational, historically and biblically proven fact.

The earliest intellectuals of Roman Christianity did not dispute this. In fact, they were quite proud of their Hellenistic roots! Clement, Origen, Augustine and others believed that Hellenistic philosophy, and specifically its religious component, was given to the pagan world by the will of God as an intermediate revelation of truth, to prepare pagans for the full revelation of God's (Hellenistic) truth in Roman Christianity.[96]

Origen, one of the most prominent early church leaders and theologians, is a striking example of the influence of Hellenistic religion in the early Roman church. Some of his doctrines are strikingly Hellenistic. For example, Origen believed that souls originate in the realm of *ether* among the stars, and return to their original home after death. As they ascend through the seven spheres they stop at each level to receive instruction, preparing them for entry into heaven. According to Origen, stars possess

---

[96] See Scott, Origen and the Life of the Stars, pages 106 and 132.

souls. Both stars and angels are intermediate forms of beings between God and man. The state to which souls have fallen, whether they became stars, angels or humans, depends on the degree of sin committed in their pre-existent state in the heavens.[97]

Taking this to its logical conclusion, modern Hellenistic Christianity is only the final stage in an evolutionary chain extending back to Orphism, Pythagoras and the great pagan religious reformation in ancient Greece. Historically, the claim that Hellenistic religion is a precursor to modern Hellenistic Christianity is entirely accurate. The only question is whether the Hellenistic conversion of Christianity was God's will.

Should we embrace the Hellenization of Christianity as a second, more spiritual revelation of the Christian faith, or is it the subversion of the church that the New Testament repeatedly warns us to reject?

---

[97] Origen was so radical that much of his teaching about the stars was formally declared anathema by the Roman church in the sixth century, when Hellenistic Roman Christianity increasingly turned away from Platonism in favor of Aristotelian philosophy. See Scott, Origen and the Life of the Stars, p 104 ff.

– 6 –

Gnostic Spirituality

Natural Human Spirituality

It is impossible to consider this topic without including the question of natural human spirituality. This is the phenomenon to which Paul refers in Romans chapter 2:

> When Gentiles who do not possess the law do instinctively what the law requires...(they) are a law to themselves. (Romans 2:14)

According to Paul, people who do not know the true God are by nature able on their own to understand many godly principles:

> They show that what the law requires is written on their hearts, to which their own conscience also bears witness; and their conflicting thoughts accuse or perhaps excuse them. (vs 15)

Paul affirms that even persons who do not know God can have God's law *'written on their hearts.'* Virtually all societies throughout the world, from the most primitive tribes in the jungle to the most advanced, teach that murder is wrong, the sixth of God's Ten Commandments. Equally the principle of faithfulness between marriage partners, the seventh commandment, is taught almost universally, as well as various standards of truthfulness, the ninth of God's Ten Commandments.

What does it mean to have God's law written on your heart in a carnal, natural sense? Why would God do such a thing? Wouldn't it be better to let the natural man be as evil as he can be, so there is no mistaking who is who?

The answer comes partly from the very nature of human existence. The basic nature of man has been constructed to fulfill the will of God in various ways. Some of this is vital for the survival of the human species. Other aspects are vital in providing a foundation for fulfilling God's spiritual plan for man.

Some kinds of conduct that fulfill God's will are encoded in the human gene pool. Consider for a moment the implications for survival of the species if God had to come down and talk to each young man at the age of 18 and explain the importance of being fruitful and multiplying. Given our record of obeying God, do you think we would last more than a single generation? However, God doesn't have to do that. As any young man at age 18 knows only too well, God has designed it so there is little risk of the human species dying out from lack of fruitfulness. So we see that man has been genetically programmed to carry out the will of God.

This first example admittedly involves conduct not normally classified as spiritual. Yet, there are other types of conduct, shared among all peoples of the earth, which manifest decidedly spiritual aspects of the natural human personality. Consider the following:

Man was created as an intellectual, perceptive, and emotionally complex being. A human child requires extensive mental and emotional development to become a successfully functioning adult. Providing the care to make this work often involves conduct with distinctly spiritual implications. Just one example among many is the emotional nurture of children by mothers. What if God had to come down and personally talk to every first-time mother and present her with a long list of guidelines? What if mothers had to be instructed they must emotionally support their children, else their offspring will become sociopaths and murderers and fill mental institutions till no sane persons are left to care for them, and God's plan is totally ruined and the human species itself becomes extinct?

Given the human record of obedience, half of us would be in mental institutions and the other half murdering each other and the world would have ended long ago. Yet, throughout the world, women for millennia have fulfilled this vital role with a substantial degree of success. Can anyone question the genuine spiritual qualities involved in a mother's love and nurture of her children? Yet it goes forward on its own without overt intervention by God. We see it throughout the world, a truly universal phenomenon, in countries that in name worship the God of the Bible and equally in non-Christian nations. Notice how these qualities are given distinctly more to women than to men. That and the universality of the phenomenon clearly are the product of God encoding spiritual tendencies in human genetic material. The conclusion to which one comes is that man was created with a basic capacity for spirituality, sufficient to allow him to more or less successfully survive as an intellectual, perceptive being, without direct reliance on God.

Here is another striking pattern: as one goes further up the ladder to more sophisticated spiritual issues, human conduct becomes increasingly more deficient.

Consider the record of mankind in obeying the godly standards mentioned above – refraining from murder, adultery, and lying. Once again, the record between Christian and non-Christian cultures is remarkably similar. Nearly all people around the world refrain from murder. Statistically very few persons give in to their anger and actually murder someone, however often we are tempted and consider doing it. It doesn't take that much spiritual sophistication to sense the shocking vulgarity of killing a human being. On the matter of marital fidelity the record is much more spotty. In fact some non-Christian cultures, especially in Asia, have a better track record than supposedly Christianized western society. Many studies in America place the incidence of infidelity among the married at greater than 50 percent. And lying! Truly we have here a universal sin, practiced by some of us on a weekly if not daily to hourly basis. For the natural human mind, the outward effect of lying is so insignificant compared to murder. It takes substantial spiritual sophistication to perceive the vulgarity of deceiving another human being.

So we see that natural human spirituality is woefully deficient. Our natural spiritual perception is limited and somewhat basic. Man's motive for promoting spirituality also can be quite selfish. We perceive the benefits that come from certain kinds of spiritual conduct, and we understand it is in our best interest to construct a society that promotes it. We all want spirituality, especially for other people so they won't abuse us!

Man has the capacity not only to perceive but also to grow spiritually. It would appear that the natural spirituality of human nature is in effect a spiritual launching pad. Indeed the very nature of the human experience confirms that. Human existence functions as a vast spiritual classroom. It is virtually impossible for humans to reach old age without becoming to some degree more spiritual than when they embarked on life as young adults. The very nature of marriage, child rearing, the constant necessity for social interaction of all kinds, our natural craving for love and approval, turns life into a long spiritual lesson from which we all learn, with varying degrees of success, whether we believe in God or not.

How far an individual advances in natural spiritual growth depends on many factors. Personality type, childhood experiences and training, general environmental factors, the culture, and individual choices along the road of life, all play a role. Throughout the world one finds a similarly wide range of spiritual progress and failure. You find criminals and social misfits, and you find sweet caring grandparents who want to spend their last years loving and helping their children and grandchildren. We find the same varying degrees of success and failure among those who worship the God of the Bible and equally among those who worship Buddha or Krishna. The striking thing about it is the universality of the phenomena.

The bottom line is that God created all human beings with the ability to reason and function spiritually. He put us here on earth in hope that as we experience life we will develop those natural spiritual tendencies. To the degree any person learns and practices godly principles of conduct, that individual life will be more happy and successful, as also disregard of those truths leads to pain and suffering.

Man is created as a spiritual embryo. He can grow and develop on his own, and the world is full of the evidence of this. What God wants of us as Christians, however, extends far beyond that. Whether an individual makes an umbilical connection to God and is born into a complete spiritual existence with him is another story, not to be confused with natural human spirituality.

Is it any wonder then, when humans express spirituality they overlap to such a large degree with biblical teachings, since many of God's basic principles already are built into the very structure of human existence?

What would a Gnostic Christian naturally do when he is told he has been liberated from the bondage of the material world, from the evil God of the Old Testament, indeed from all rules and laws imposed externally on man? He is told, however, he must henceforth live a spiritual life, to do the will of the spiritual Father above, to follow pure love and kindness.

Gnostic Christians believed they were lawful, not lawless, because they obey the spiritual Father from above. For example, we read in the Gnostic text, *The Gospel of Truth* :

> For the Father is sweet and in his will is what is good.[98]

> Therefore, if one has knowledge, he is from above. ... Having knowledge, he does the will of the one who called him, he wishes to be pleasing to him....[99]

---

[98]   Gospel of Truth, **NHLE**, 47.
[99]   Gospel of Truth, **NHLE**, 42.

What are the Gnostic good works that come from obedience to the Father above? Typically, among Gnostics it tended to be a general collection of obvious good deeds a person of any culture naturally would understand. Once again, from *The Gospel of Truth*:

> Feed those who are hungry and give repose to those who are weary....[100]

So what would a newly converted Gnostic Christian resolve to do? Well, probably he is going to resolve to be a much better Christian in the many ways that any natural person knows he should. He may resolve henceforth to be scrupulously honest. Why? His mother and father told him from childhood he shouldn't lie. No parent likes to be lied to, whether they believe in God or not. They have complained often enough to their child that it bothers his conscience. He may resolve to never again steal. Everyone knows that's wrong. Society can't function if everyone is allowed to steal, so there is plenty of natural societal pressure against that. He certainly doesn't want to ever murder anyone. And so in short order he will reinvent a large portion of God's law. Gnostic Christians would accept that as long as they do it because of the internal spiritual feelings of their heavenly, immortal soul, and not because the dreaded Yahweh commanded it.

Does that mean natural human spirituality is phony and we should make light of it? Absolutely not.

In various countries of Asia there are Buddhists and Hindus, and followers of Shintoism, Shamanism, and numerous other 'isms,' who know nothing of Christ. Yet every day they struggle with profound and basic spiritual issues just as we do. Every day multitudes of people of non-Christian faiths decide to sacrifice their lives to help a wayward child, to continue in faithfulness to a troubled, unresponsive spouse, to turn the other cheek in the face of abuse and pain; alcoholics climb on the wagon and sinners of all kinds repent and embark on new and better lives. And they do it all in the name of the Buddha or Krishna, or the sacred ancestors, the Great Spirit, and many other names.

Does that mean all religions are a valid approach to God? I think not. The religions of the world essentially are embodiments of natural human spirituality, all shaped by historical and cultural processes into unique individual forms, incorporating much truth along with a large assortment

---

[100]   Gospel of Truth, **NHLE**, 47.

of error. As sponsors of natural human spirituality they frequently guide their followers into genuinely godly conduct. They often do much good.

We should applaud spirituality and the manifestation of godly conduct in all its many forms. At the same time we need to understand the difference between natural human spirituality and living in a true relationship with God. As Paul witnesses in Romans chapter 2, as we saw above, every manifestation of godly conduct is not necessarily evidence of God's direct involvement. Likewise every religion or church that teaches some biblical truth is not necessarily from God. Failure to make that distinction, failure to base our distinctions on the guidance of the New Testament and its explicit warnings, can lead to serious error.

Gnostic Theories of Non-material Spirituality

Here we attempt to discuss the most common traits of Gnostic spirituality, and of those the two primary features are asceticism and libertinism. At first glance that seems such a contradiction. How can you believe in both asceticism and libertinism? Most Gnostics emphasized one more than the other, but some seem to have combined both in their religious experience. How can that be?

The answer brings us back to the primary driving force behind Gnosticism – its belief in Hellenistic cosmology – and the effect this had on Gnosticism's reinterpretation of Christianity. Hellenistic cosmology demands a dramatic separation between material or worldly existence on the one hand, and spiritual or heavenly existence on the other. For Gnosticism the material world is diametrically opposed to the spirituality of heaven.

This led to an emphasis on spiritual revelation from within.[101] Hellenistic religion says that man possesses an immortal soul made of the same spirit substance as heaven. The soul thereby is a gateway or window to spiritual knowledge from above. One of the themes of Gnostic salvation was that developing and enhancing inner spirituality creates a mystical connection between the soul and the heavens. Therefore looking deep within yourself brings spiritual revelation about heavenly things.

If spirituality is found within the soul, then what springs *naturally* from the soul is spiritual. Spiritual growth is not so much a matter of learning how to live outwardly in this world, but turning inward to dis-

---

[101]   Martin, *Hellenistic Religions,* p 140f, especially 143.

cover one's natural, inner self. At the same time that you turn inward you also turn away from the outside world and all of its regulations and temporal controls. Anything imposed from outside, that one does because one has to, especially if it relates to material existence, is inferior to outright evil.

In classic Gnostic theology, material pleasure is not necessarily evil in the moral sense as we often think of it. As we saw in a previous chapter, some Gnostic teachers claimed that morality is only a matter of opinion. In classic Gnostic thought, the problem with material pleasure was more the fact that it distracts from the spirituality of the inner soul. That is the essence of human bondage. If a man chases women or indulges in feasting, in other words, if he focuses on the outer world, he will never develop his inner, spiritual self.

Rejecting rules of normal human conduct as binding is just another method of rejecting the world. That is especially true if the rules in question are rules that govern man's conduct in the material world. For example, if you are talking about Old Testament laws that deal with the sexual conduct of marriage partners, you have a law that in effect encourages involvement in the material world by virtue of the fact it regulates it. Generally, Gnostic libertinism was not a question of rejecting morality as much as it was simply a question of rejecting the distraction of the material world. If you believe your material conduct has no effect on salvation, then you will not experience the anxiety of trying to control your external conduct. In effect it was a means to *psychological* freedom from the material world.

That kind of thinking led to a curious and very important phenomenon within some Gnostic sects, which uniquely illuminates their antinomian beliefs. If you sincerely try to flee from materialistic sin such as adultery, then your emotional reaction, your 'fear' of sin, creates an obsessive emotional involvement with material life. It is only by completely divorcing yourself from concern about material sin, completely wiping it from your mind, that you truly become free from lust and are able to pursue inner spirituality. According to Gnosticism, biblical law only tends to excite fear and worry over materialism. Therefore, law by its very nature is a materialistic psychological trap that keeps man in bondage to sin.

Gnostic spirituality is strikingly similar to the mystical traditions of India (both Hinduism and Buddhism), in which true release from the material world is achieved by breaking all emotional ties to the world, removing both positive **and** negative attachments, sinking into a quiet detached state totally focused on the spirituality from above.[102]

This is mentioned in several Gnostic texts. *The Second Treatise of the Great Seth* is one example. Here it ridicules the orthodox concern about sin, which it describes as *"...their doctrine to fear and slavery, worldly cares...."*[103] Elsewhere it makes the same point with a direct reference to biblical law: *"...always being slaves of law and earthly fear."*[104] The Valentinian Gnostic *Gospel of Philip* spells it out even more clearly:

> Fear not the flesh nor love it. If you...fear it, it will gain mastery over you. If you love it, it will swallow and paralyze you.[105]

For many Gnostics, bondage to material things could occur either through lust for material pleasure, or through the emotional worry stimulated by struggling against temptation. Freedom from sin, they believed, comes from psychological detachment. In other words, as long as your heart and mind, your inner man, are totally devoted and fixed on the things above, and what happens on a material level does not distract you from devotion to God, then it can't hurt you. If you foolishly turn back to worrying about obedience to law, however, you will forever be locked in a battle with material existence you can never win.

That is the very idea contained in the common Gnostic teaching that morality is a matter of **indifference**. Remember how the early church fathers universally criticized Nicolas and many other Gnostics over this issue. Now perhaps we can begin to understand what Gnostic indifference really means. Gnosticism did not intentionally promote sin. Quite the opposite! What they actually were saying is that it is only by turning off all emotional response to material sin – both positive and negative – that

---

[102] It is very interesting to observe the similarities between a number of Gnostic systems and the religious thought of India as regards emotional liberation from the material world. Both Hinduism and Buddhism teach a mildly ascetic cessation of emotional involvement with material existence, a quiet passionless state considered necessary for spiritual development. Interestingly, within Buddhism this led to their own antinomian tradition.

The similarities are not accidental. See Appendix C for a further comparison of Hellenistic and Indian religion.

[103] **NHLE**, 367.

[104] **NHLE**, 369.

[105] **NHLE**, 149. See also introduction to the Gospel of Philip by the translator Wesley W. Isenberg, p 140.

one can hope to truly escape from it. Recall Clement's description of Nicolas offering his wife to anyone who wanted her:

> ...his bringing the wife whom he loved so jealously into the midst of the apostles was the renunciation of desire, and it was mastery of the pleasures so eagerly sought that taught him the rule 'treat the flesh with contempt.'[106]

Even Clement recognized that Nicolas' demonstration of indifference to sin actually was a demonstration of how Gnostics believed we can escape from material lust. Gnosticism's antinomianism actually is a system for rescuing man from sin. The source of this thinking was Hellenistic religion and philosophy. Remember, for example, the Stoics of ancient Greece who believed something similar. For them, becoming indifferent to the material passions, in other words becoming '*stoic*,' was the means to purify the soul from lust and so return to the heavens (see above, pages 16 and following).

Despite the fact it didn't work very well and was widely misused, the antinomian grace of Gnostic Christianity actually is very idealistic. For some it was essentially well intentioned. One could imagine a conversation between a Valentinian Gnostic and Primitive Christian as follows:

Gnostic: I understand you believe in trying to please God by obeying the law. How is it going? Have you achieved spirituality, or are you still in bondage to lust and sin?

Christian: Well, I can't say I have fully arrived. I am much happier now and much more at peace with myself. Still, sometimes it's a struggle. Even now sometimes I am tempted to sin and I have to exercise self-control in order to obey God.

Gnostic: And how long has it been?

Christian: Well, I was converted when I was very young. I guess it's been nearly forty years now.

Gnostic: Forty years, and you still haven't achieved liberation from sin? When are you going to wake up? How long does it take till you figure out legalism doesn't work? The more you worry about obeying and feel guilty and approach God in fear, the more your mind becomes fixated on material things and the more you get bound up with temptation. You have all these silly rules. Your stupid law about di-

---

[106] See above, p 40f, Nicolaitans (Gnosticism in History).

vorce forces people to stay in unhappy marriages, and all it does is tie them in emotional knots and make them focus on their physical situation. Look at me. I've been liberated from all that. I don't have to struggle and fight battles. That isn't what spirituality is about. I worship every Sunday with God's people and I feel the Spirit moving mightily within me. I have learned the most profound feelings of love for Christ and the Father. I volunteer and serve my fellow man. I have achieved a level of spirituality I never could if I were still trying to do it with all that legalistic nonsense. My righteousness comes from God; it flows naturally from within me as Christ heals and restores the natural spirituality of my immortal soul.

Now perhaps we can better understand the Gnostic doctrine that *gnosis* (knowledge) imparts salvation. In Gnostic Christianity, as in Hellenistic religion and Orphism and Pythagoreanism before it, saving knowledge is the knowledge of the organization and nature of the universe. At first glance that seems rather silly, but you have to look at the deeper meaning to get the point. Salvation comes from the knowledge there is a God in heaven and how spirit fell and became trapped in our bodies as immortal souls. The key piece of knowledge is that, therefore, our souls are immortal and divine. Our soul is made from the same substance as God and the heavens. Restoring the knowledge of the link between our inner being and God awakens and stimulates the soul, restoring a mystical union with God that causes us to fully express the qualities of God in our lives.

This type of reasoning is found, for example, in the Gnostic Valentinian text *The Gospel of Philip*.[107] This is a very complex passage, but we will tackle it in three parts, and as we step through it piece by piece the meaning soon becomes clear.

The main idea is that achieving knowledge (*gnosis*) of God automatically transforms you into a godlike person.

> It is not possible for anyone to see anything of the things that actually exist unless he becomes like them.

In this first sentence, the phrase *'things that actually exist'* means spiritual things.[108] So what it says is that you can't see or know spiritual things

---

[107] *The Gospel of Philip*, **NHLE**, 146–147.

[108] To 'actually exist' means real, eternal. Only spiritual things are real and eternal, as only the things in the heavens are unchanging in contrast to the constant change and impermanence of the material world.

unless you become spiritual too, as it says *"unless he becomes like them."* In other words, you have to be spiritual in order to see or perceive spiritual things.

Next the author reverses the logic. If being spiritual lets you know spiritual things, then it is equally true that simply knowing spiritual things automatically makes you spiritual (if A equals B, then B must equal A):

> But you...saw something of that place, and you became those things. You saw the spirit, you became spirit. You saw Christ, you became Christ.

In other words, once you obtain knowledge of something spiritual, you automatically absorb the spirituality of that thing. Notice how the Gnostic text phrases it, *'You saw* [have gnosis of] *the spirit, you became spirit. You saw* [have gnosis of] *Christ, you became Christ.'*

That is why *gnosis* (knowledge) is the key to salvation in Gnostic Christianity. The foundation of Gnostic Christianity is mystical connection to God through *gnosis.* The mere act of learning the mysteries of the construction of the heavenly world and the connection between the immortal soul and the heavens, the mere act of knowing God, imparts spirituality automatically, magically transforming humans into spiritual beings.

The text next specifically applies this to obtaining spiritual perception of the inner soul:

> So [in this place] you see everything and [do] not [see] yourself, but [in that place] you do see yourself – and what you see you shall [become].

This is phrased rather obscurely. However, notice how it says *"in this place"* you see things but *"do not see yourself."* With this the author is arguing that in our material lives (*this place*) we see many things but are ignorant and blind to the real self within (*do not see yourself*), meaning the soul. This is the ignorance into which man has fallen, having lost *gnosis* of the inner spiritual nature of our immortal soul and its destiny to be liberated and return to the heavens.

"But in that place you do see yourself" refers to receiving knowledge (*gnosis*). In other words, in a spiritual state of knowledge (*that place*) we

spiritually perceive our immortal soul (*you do see yourself*).[109] "*And what you see you shall become,*" means that just achieving perception (*gnosis*) of your soul and believing this doctrine that your soul is immortal and divine, made of the same substance as the heavens, causes the soul to be awakened, and you naturally and automatically take on the goodness of the divinity residing within yourself.

This is why the Hellenistic doctrine of the indwelling immortal soul was so central to Gnostic theology. It is a key to their claims of an advanced spirituality that proceeds from the inside out, without the need of guidance from biblical law.

Those who do not base their relationship with God solely on magical regeneration of the soul through mystical union with God, it says, are still living in the Old Testament. As the following text warns: "*He who has received something other than the lord is still a Hebrew.*"[110]

This implies that Primitive Christians, whose belief has not fully liberated them from their Jewish roots, have not received the lord in their hearts. As it says, they receive '*something other than the lord.*' Remember the Gnostic passage cited above, in which it is the mystical connection established by *gnosis* that mystically brings us into contact with Christ. (*You saw Christ, you became Christ.*) Using any other means in the process of becoming spiritual, such as the law as a guide to God's will, is '*something other than the lord.*' So they are condemned as being '*still a Hebrew.*'

And so the destruction of Old Testament religion and removing it as the underlying heritage of Christianity became one of Gnosticism's primary objectives. True spirituality, receiving the Lord in your inner man, they believed, cannot occur as long as Primitive Christians continue to believe in Christianity as a substantive continuation of the Hebrew faith, perpetuating the fear and worldly cares of Hebrew law.

Mystical union with the heavenly Father and Christ was an important theme for Gnosticism. But it is also a valid New Testament doctrine, prominent in Paul's writings. The problem with Gnosticism is that it combined this valid New Testament teaching with their theology of law-

---

[109] The term "that place" is commonly used by Valentinian Gnostics as a code word for mystical connection to the *pleroma* or Depth of the Father. It is that mystical experience of God's pure love that connects them to the spirit that flows out from God's Depth, which awakens the soul. See Thyatira and 'the Deep Things of Satan', pages 140 and following.

[110] **NHLE**, 147.

lessness. The key idea in Gnosticism is that the inner working of the Spirit is **exclusive**. One must not seek spirituality or righteousness through external striving to obey the law. The following passage from the Valentinian text *The Gospel of Truth*, pointedly explains that seeking spirituality from external sources is to be avoided:

> Rest in him who is at rest, not striving nor being involved in the search for truth. But they themselves are the truth and the Father is within them. [111]

Consider the implications of this Gnostic text. Through mystical connection to God (*the Father is within them*), Gnostic Christians recognize that truth is revealed solely from within (*they themselves are the truth*). They must **not** strive nor get involved in searching externally for the truth (*not striving nor being involved in the search for truth*). Instead, just lean back in grace and let it happen (*rest in him who is at rest*).

Renouncing Old Testament religion generally was an absolute requirement of Gnostic salvation. Involvement in any Jewish practices, they believed, automatically subjects a person to the bondage of Yahweh and his angels. Some Gnostic sects taught an aggressive, confrontational approach in which their followers purposely flouted Jewish practices. One must by all means work on the Sabbath and disrespect all Jewish customs. Some believed that by insulting and denouncing the creating angels and their leader Yahweh they would become free from the passions of material life.[112] It was Yahweh who created the material world and set up laws about how to live material lives. All that was destroyed with the end of the Old Covenant, they believed, and liberated Christians must by all means establish their freedom from that religious system.

On the other hand, Gnostics saw no problem with participating in the pagan religious customs of the day. In so doing they escaped much of the persecution that fell on the primitive church. Hellenistic Roman Christianity followed the same path, only much more slowly. Gnostics from the start generally had no problem with pagan religious customs. For them it was one of those issues of outward conduct that has no effect on inner spirituality. Besides, by the early centuries A.D. nearly all of paganism

---

[111] Gospel of Truth, Robinson, *Nag Hammadi Library*, 1977 edition, 48.

[112] For example, the Carpocratians. See above, page 46, Carpocrates (Gnosticism in History). Recall also the several New Testament passages that criticize the Gnostics for slandering the holy angels.

had become typically Hellenistic and shared much of the same religious belief as Gnostic Christianity.

Gnostic Immorality

Distinguishing between material and spiritual can be slippery. Lying, cheating, greed, etc. might be viewed as matters involving the intellect and therefore were valid concerns of spiritual life. Sexual lust, on the other hand, often was viewed as purely materialistic. It was something to be avoided but more in the sense of ignoring it rather than overcoming or controlling it. Of course, in the flexible antinomian environment of Gnostic Christianity you could craft distinctions according to your taste. As we saw above, some Gnostics emphasized that specific rules of morality are only a matter of personal opinion,[113] so one cannot lay down a rigid standard of right and wrong. Instead, just be dedicated to the heavenly principles of faith and love, which some believed is all that really matters.

History records the presence of fringe groups within some Gnostic movements that carried antinomian beliefs to excess. When we refer to Gnostic immorality, however, we are not necessarily talking about vulgar displays of animalistic, drunken carousing. Remember that Gnostic Christians were religious people. They went to church on Sunday, sang hymns and participated in sacraments that promised them freedom from sin. Their ideal was a peaceful existence in which they are not touched by the frustrations and cares of life, in which their inner being is flooded with spiritual power and love that naturally enables them to rise above temptation.

They believed that codified biblical regulations regarding marriage and divorce, premarital chastity, and many other material issues have no binding authority over Christians. Under Christianity, they insisted, there is no law, but still you should be a good person and avoid sin. There is no need for external guidance such as the law, they insisted, because God and the Spirit working through your soul heals your evil lusts and leads you into right conduct, all achieved naturally and without effort. The problem with law is it only leads to frustration. In the end it actually stimulates lust and thwarts the inner process of spiritual healing.

---

[113] For example, the Carpocratians. See above, pages 46 and following.

As a Gnostic Christian you should lead a 'good' life. In theory you cannot lose salvation, but nevertheless sin is wrong and the intent of Gnostic Christians clearly was to escape from sin. What does that mean, however, on a practical level? In real life it means your religious world is substantially vague and flexible, however well intentioned it might be. What if you meet someone who really excites you? Well, if you look deeply enough inside your soul you probably will find some new inspiration and guidance to accommodate your desire. It is clear from the historical record that many individual Gnostics, when needed, found the 'inner guidance' to justify breaking whatever rule was in the way of getting what they wanted.

Of course, different people obviously will come up with different interpretations of the inspiration from within, even though they supposedly all come from the same Spirit. If your new-found spiritual excuses do not wash with your fellow Gnostic churchgoers, you might have to find a new congregation. No problem. Within the Gnostic Christian world you could pick and choose, from the radical antinomian liberation of the far left where seemingly anything goes, to the far right Gnostic sects that took their asceticism seriously. Early Christianity was highly diverse, not unlike today. Some Gnostic churches allowed marriage and accumulation of wealth, while the conservative groups that didn't, damned to hell their more liberal brethren.

Those focusing on antinomian liberation naturally would give more latitude than other groups. In either case, however, the underlying theology is similar. Both demand detachment from material life, whether literal or merely psychological. For liberal Gnostics, you could participate in sin, though it was frowned on, as long as you didn't make the mistake of becoming either positively or negatively obsessed by it. This is the full fruition of Gnostic indifference to sin, the idea that only inner spirituality matters. This they regarded as complete liberation, a necessary step leading to true inner spirituality.

Gnostic Ascetic Spirituality

Now for the other side of the coin. Ascetic rules are compatible with Gnosticism if you consider ascetic rules not as the rules of the world, but the rules of heaven. Ascetic rules promote inner spirituality. Old Testament law only promotes materialism, they insisted, because it regulates material life.

Asceticism and libertinism share the common goal of breaking man's ties to the material world. Asceticism demands literal separation from the world. Libertinism only demands psychological detachment.

Gnostic asceticism allowed the open use of rules we might consider highly legalistic. In fact, some modern theologians mistakenly label Gnosticism as legalistic, or describe its error primarily as the promotion of salvation by works. Therefore, they claim, biblical condemnation of Gnosticism is only condemnation of salvation by works. That is a critical mistake.

Ascetic Gnosticism, one important branch of Gnostic Christianity, indeed was a religion based on works. Yet, it too was entirely antinomian from a biblical perspective. Both ascetic and libertine Gnosticism were united in their condemnation of Yahweh and Hebrew religion. All of Gnosticism, both libertine and ascetic branches, condemned biblical law as evil and a materialistic trap.

Remember that Hebrew religion focused on teaching man how to live righteously within the material world. Gnostic asceticism, in contrast, focused exclusively on the heavens and its rules were designed to block man's involvement in and enjoyment of the material world. Thus, Gnostic asceticism could substitute its own rules that sometimes were even more strict, and at the same time rail against the Old Testament, the evil creator God Yahweh, and proclaim antinomian liberation from biblical law. So even ascetic Gnosticism is antinomian from the biblical perspective.

As we saw in the previous chapter on "Gnosticism in the Bible," the New Testament focuses most of its condemnation of Gnosticism on the issue of antinomianism (for example 2 Peter 2, Jude, Revelation and many other passages). However, it also addresses the question of ascetic Gnostic theology. Remember the problems with ascetic teachings at the church of Colossae, described in Colossians chapter 2. More about ascetic Gnosticism and its theology of salvation by works, can be found in Appendix A, "The Full Story behind Colossians 2."

Gnostic ascetic practices varied widely. Marriage often was forbidden, also wine and eating of meat. Water usually was substituted for wine in celebrating the Lord's supper. A few practiced severe asceticism, withdrawing from society to live as hermits. One interesting ascetic exercise was to remain completely still for some length of time in a rigid standing posture. The idea was to imitate the peaceful repose and regularity of the stars.[114] Anything that imitates the heavens, they believed, increases the natural attraction of the soul to its true home and will help it ascend after death.

There were many additional means to acquire spirituality and spiritual power within Gnosticism. Some relied on the passion story of Jesus and the cross for their liberation to spiritual life. As we saw above, some Gnostics developed a theology based on the classic misinterpretation of Colossians chapter 2, which claimed the act of salvation was nailing the evil creating angels and their power to the cross.[115] In their case apparently, ritual reenactment of the passion story provided liberation from Old Testament law and materialism.

The Spirit was extremely important for Gnostic Christians. Some emphasized the acquisition of spiritual power to overcome and escape from bondage to the materialistic angels of creation. Some sought this power in magical charms and various magical rituals. Through these means, they believed, they could thwart Yahweh's evil angels who want to prevent their souls from ascending to heaven after death.

Valentinian Gnostics believed that their sacraments provided them with a spiritual body of light that makes them invisible to the evil angels. They claimed that the sacrament of communion clothes them with the spiritual body of Christ, and this is the guarantee they are spiritual and will be saved.[116]

Gnostic Imbalance

Many Gnostic ideas about spirituality are strikingly similar to genuine teachings from New Testament scripture. This is especially true of the writings of Paul. He frequently refers to the building of spirituality in the

---

[114] A practice found also within Hellenistic Christian monasticism.
[115] See above, page 98, Colossians (Gnosticism in the Bible).
[116] See *NHLE*, 144 ff.

inner man through mystical union with Christ and the power of the Holy Spirit. Here is just one example, from his letter to the Ephesians:

> ...that you may be strengthened in your inner being with power through his Spirit, and that Christ may dwell in your hearts through faith, as you are being rooted and grounded in love. ...

> ...who by the power at work within us is able to accomplish abundantly far more than all we can ask or imagine.... (Eph 3:16–17, 20–21)

Remember, Gnostics were Christians, and they used New Testament scripture liberally to justify their Hellenistic beliefs. They especially loved the writings of Paul. However, one must balance this against many other New Testament passages warning against the antinomian grace that Gnostics incorporated in their radical misinterpretation of Paul. Gnostic Christianity made the classic mistake of isolating a portion of the New Testament and ignoring the rest of Jesus' inspired word, including even Paul's many other writings such as his admonition to *"Work out your own salvation with fear and trembling..."* (Phil 2:12). Fear and trembling! How very un-Gnostic. How very unspiritual in the eyes of some.

From the Primitive Christian point of view, as expressed in the New Testament and by Paul himself, **both** internal and external forces play vital roles in God's plan for mankind – **both** the power of the Spirit working from within **and** personal character, self-control and obedience to external standards.

Gnostic Christianity took a portion of the genuinely biblical message dealing with inner spirituality, isolated and exaggerated it, combined it with Hellenistic teachings about the immortal soul, and packaged it as an advanced form of Christian spirituality that circumvents biblical law. It is a perversion of the New Testament message of salvation. It is the very thing Peter was talking about when he warned against those who pervert Paul's writings into an unbalanced message that leads to lawlessness (2 Peter 3:16–17).

Gnostic spirituality is *tremendously* appealing. On the one hand it incorporates a large body of biblical truth. But in the Gnostic reinterpretation of Christianity, you attain spiritual perfection immediately, without having to struggle against sin. There is no law, no punishment, no anxiety nor fear, just a flood of spiritual peace and love from God channeled through your immortal soul by the Holy Spirit. It magically frees you from sinful lusts with zero effort on your part, naturally and gently turning you to righteous conduct. And if God's power does not succeed in turning you from evil, even that doesn't matter. As a truly spiritual being, loved and chosen by God, connected directly to God through your immortal soul, you are above all that. The true heavenly Father is pure love and mercy. He will never condemn you regardless of how evil your conduct.

Aside from the fact it doesn't really work and is roundly condemned by the New Testament, what can you say against it? On the surface it is absolutely beautiful.

– 7 –

Thyatira and
'The Deep Things of Satan'

We come now to the culmination of our historical quest for the principles of Gnostic Christianity. Here we seek to unravel a mystery that
uniquely illuminates the significance of that elusive term, the 'mystery of
lawlessness.' This is the question of the identity of the mysterious apostasy that afflicted the church at Thyatira, as described in the book of
Revelation.

Thyatira, in the first century A.D., was a city in Asia Minor in what is
now western Turkey. Nearly two thousand years ago it was the location of
one of the seven Christian churches held up by the apostle John as examples of the problems New Testament churches in general experience over
time. What was special about Thyatira was its problem with antinomian
apostasy, which John described as *the deep things of Satan.*' This was a
theology described as promoting tolerance of sin (Rev 2:20–23). Notice
the description of the faithful remnant in this church. Notice how John
defines the faithful as those who refuse to accept the theology embraced
by the majority of their own church:

> But to the rest of you in Thyatira, who do not hold this teaching,
> who have not learned what some call 'the deep things of Satan'
> (Rev 2:24)

First, keep in mind that John is not saying the Thyatira church literally
worshipped Satan. He is criticizing people in a troubled but genuinely
Christian church. I think we can assume they did not believe they actually
were worshipping Satan. As Christians they undoubtedly considered
themselves to be worshipping the true Christian Father. The problem is

they had begun to mix their worship with foreign religious ideas, which John describes as really coming from Satan.

John is not that precise. He says simply "some," in other words some persons or groups in the religious landscape of that day, had teachings involving the terminology "deep" or "depth" of God, and the Thyatira church had incorporated this into their Christian teaching. Can we identify what John was talking about? We start with only two clues. The church had gotten involved in antinomian tolerance of sin (vs 20), and the underlying theology was something from the religious culture of that time described as the Deep or Depth of God (vs 24). So, who in that time was using those religious phrases? Indeed, if we scan the Hellenistic religious landscape of the early centuries A.D., we find examples of that very terminology.

The Chaldean Connection

The Chaldean Oracles are short fragments of text preserved in the writings of various pagan Hellenistic authors. The fragments themselves are believed to go back to the Chaldean priesthood of ancient Babylonia, hence the name.[117] It is in the Chaldean Oracles that we find numerous

---

[117] The Chaldean Oracles are based on ancient teachings of the astrologer priests of Babylonia. (The name Chaldean refers to the southern Mesopotamian tribes that dominated the Neo-Babylonian Empire.) They survive as quotations in texts written by Neoplatonic philosophers. Neoplatonism did not take formal shape until the third century A.D. However, it was the outcome of a substantial evolutionary process over several centuries that intertwined Platonism and Neopythagoreanism from as early as the first century B.C.

The Chaldean Oracles themselves were composed in the early second century, and were discovered and used by Neoplatonists nearly a century later. The religious mixture that produced the Chaldean Oracles may have been fomenting much earlier than the actual writing of the Oracles. Hermetism, which shares many of the same traditions and beliefs, dates from at least the first century A.D. and possibly earlier.

The same Paternal Depth symbolism and associated cosmological beliefs appear in Valentinian Gnosticism, which dates to the mid second century. The heresiologist Epiphanius attributed Valentinian Paternal Depth theology to Hellenistic philosophy and specifically to Hesiod. If Epiphanius is to be believed, and indeed the context of his attribution is quite plausible, then these ideas have roots that go back in time long before that. Thus the comparison of Paternal Depth expressions in the Chaldean Oracles and Gnosticism, with their occurrence in Revelation, believed to have been composed in the mid-70s to 90s A.D., is temporally plausible.

references to spiritual depth in relation to the highest God, the supreme Father.

One of the terms we find is 'Paternal Depth.' This is equivalent to the Depth of God the Father (or Deep Things of Satan, as John insisted it really was). It refers to a reservoir of pure spirituality that exists in God and flows out into the world to nourish man spiritually. Neoplatonism considered this to be the source of intelligence and reason in man, and so they sometimes referred to it as *Mind*. Therefore we find one Chaldean oracle that says:

> Such is the Mind...while yet it had not gone forth, but abode in the **Paternal Depth**, and...**nourished silence**.[118]

The intelligence present in the human mind was believed to have emanated from heaven as part of the immortal soul. Rational thought was viewed as a reflection of the intelligence found in the regularity of the movement of the stars, and so was considered heavenly or spiritual. So here it is talking about Mind or Intelligence before it had descended from heaven, when it still existed in a totally pure state, unmixed with the materialism of our world.

The place of this highest spirituality is called "Paternal Depth." So now we know that the Depth of the Father is the location and source of spirituality in its purest form. It is the highest essence of spirituality, in the heavens, *before* it flows out from the Father to sustain spiritual qualities found in our world.

This is further clarified by another oracle, which says:

> Ye who understand, **know** the **Super-mundane** [non-material] **Paternal Depth**.[119]

This passage comes surprisingly close to John's statement in Revelation 2:24. Those who have attained spiritual enlightenment have come to *"know"* the Paternal Depth – in other words, have "learned" the 'Deep Things of Satan,' as stated in Revelation. Notice again that it describes a spirituality that is totally non-material (*Super-mundane*). This lofty spirituality is the goal, something one can learn or come to know.

---

[118] **CO**, number 12.
[119] **CO**, number 168.

Super-mundane means above the world, in other words non-material. That is why the previous oracle, quoted above, mentions that it *'nourished silence.'* Hellenistic religion in late antiquity commonly taught that as one progresses towards full knowledge of God, one's worship becomes less and less materialistic.[120] This begins, at the lowest level, with rejection of animal sacrifice. From there it progresses up a ladder of increasing spirituality towards prayer and adoration of God. In the end even oral prayer is discarded, for oral prayer involves the material functions of sound and hearing. The highest worship is believed to be totally silent, thereby completely non-material and internal. It is experienced only as an ecstatic mystical sensation of knowing or merging with God. That is the primordial 'silence' of the Paternal Depth – pure, non-material spirituality.

The idea of tapping into a primordial reservoir of spirituality goes back to the ancient Babylonian concept of the abyss, also called the 'Deep.' [121] The Babylonian abyss was an underground storehouse of spirit power. In those ancient times, before the great pagan religious reformation, spirit power meant fertility. This primarily meant the life-giving waters that annually renewed and supported human life. The abyss was a vast underground storehouse of fresh water controlled by the savior god Dumuzi (Tammuz), from which his life-giving fertility returned each year at the start of the wet season.

The Babylonian concept of the abyss in turn goes back to the Genesis creation. Recall that Genesis describes a time just after creation when the land of Eden was nourished by water flowing up in streams from inside the earth (Genesis 2:6, compare NRSV). Elsewhere in Genesis this underground water that flooded the land is directly referred to as 'the deep' (Genesis 1:2, also 7:11).

In the aftermath of the great pagan religious reformation in the seventh to sixth centuries B.C., the Chaldean religion of Babylonia underwent a process of spiritual reinterpretation just as occurred in Greece and elsewhere. The Babylonian 'deep' or abyss originally was a storehouse of fresh water buried deep within the earth, flowing out from a mystery-cult savior to sustain physical life. Now it was reinterpreted as the source of spiritual energy, flowing out from the spiritual Father, to awaken and renew the immortal soul within man.[122]

---

[120] This is especially true, for example, of Neoplatonism and Hermetism.

[121] See above, pages 21 and following, The Mystery Cults.

[122] The Chaldean Oracles actually retained the term 'Deep,' using it to designate a deep subterranean location where they believed matter exists in

The goal of this latter-day Chaldean religious tradition is to regenerate the soul by means of a mystical union with the spiritual Father, tapping into his spiritual storehouse (the 'abyss' or Depth of the Father). "Knowing the Father" signifies becoming fully alive spiritually by mystical union with him, connecting Christians to the spiritual power flowing out from his Paternal Depth.

The implication derived from Chaldean theology is that the religious apostasy of Thyatira was a teaching about attaining an advanced state of non-material spirituality by tapping into God's storehouse of spirituality. This is obtained specifically by a mystical experience of union with God. It is similar to biblical teachings about the Holy Spirit and Christ living his life within his followers.[123] What most dramatically differentiates the two, however, as we will see, is the presence or absence of antinomianism.

At Thyatira it was attached to antinomianism, which led to disobedience and tolerance of evil (Rev 2:20). Though similar in some aspects, it is not the inner spirituality taught in the New Testament. Instead, it emphasizes spirituality solely as a non-material phenomenon. It is encased in ideas about divorcing spiritually from the material world and its temporal concerns and from control exercised from outside. Instead, it operates by connecting the soul to a heavenly reservoir of spirituality that works mystically and exclusively from within, not seriously concerned with one's external, material conduct.

That sounds very similar to some of the antinomian Gnostic theology we reviewed in previous chapters. In typical Gnostic thinking, non-material spirituality requires rejection of Hebrew religion and law, because of their involvement with material creation. Indeed, as we next discover, Gnostic Christianity was very much involved in the mystery tradition of the Deep.

---

its pure, unformed state. Now, after the great pagan reformation, this was considered a source of evil and a place of punishment for sinners, i.e. Hell. The source of life-giving substance, which had been reinterpreted as in the highest heavens, they differentiated by renaming it the Depth. See Lewy, *Chaldaean Oracles and Theurgy: Mysticism, Magic and Platonism in the Later Roman Empire*, pages 169 ff and 295 ff.

[123] For example, 1 Cor 2:10 refers to *"the depths of God"*, speaking about profoundly spiritual knowledge perceived only through the Spirit.

The Chaldean Gnostic Connection

How did Chaldean theology get into a first-century Primitive Christian church? The evidence that remains is fragmentary. We do know, however, that the same terminology of *Paternal Depth* and *primordial silence* was used by Gnostic Christians in the second century among the Valentinian sect.[124] The evidence from Gnosticism also provides important new details about Paternal Depth theology.

It appears that Gnosticism borrowed its teachings about the Depth directly from Hellenistic religion. The heresiologists made a major point of the fact that Valentinian Gnostics borrowed much of their teachings from earlier Greek sources, especially the idea of Depth.[125] So we are not surprised to find that the concept of the Deep among Valentinian Gnostics is very similar to what we encountered in the Chaldean Oracles.

In Valentinian cosmology the highest and most spiritual heaven is called the *pleroma*. This is the resting place and source of pure spirituality, in effect the Valentinian counterpart of Paternal Depth in Chaldean theology. Within the Valentinian *pleroma* the first pair of archangels are called Depth and Silence. As we saw in the previous section, these were also two primary characteristics of spirituality in Chaldean theology.[126]

The first angel, the one called Depth, is also named Progenitor, Profather, or simply Father.[127] Combine those names and you get an angel called Paternal Depth. His partner Silence also carries the name Grace. So the Valentinian heavenly *pleroma* is headed by a lead pair of angels called Paternal Depth and Silent Grace.

---

[124] The 'deep' appears among other Gnostic sects, most importantly the Naassenes. This sect, and its similarly significant relationship to the apostasy at Thyatira, appears in *Spirit of Antichrist,* the second volume of our series The World of Primitive Christianity.

[125] For example, Epiphanius, *Panarion* 31.2.4, and Hippolytus, *Refut.* 6.24. Further, Epiphanius credits Greek Chaos as the direct source of the Valentinian concept of Paternal Depth (*Panarion* 31.2.5). The ancient Mesopotamian abyss and various concepts of the primal state are equivalent to Chaos in Greek religion. A watery primal state in which basic matter was undifferentiated, i.e. there was no 'form' is common in the Near East. The Greek idea of 'chaos' conveys the same sense of primal lack of differentiation or formlessness. As the primal state, this is the ultimate source of all being, thereby equating to God, and the source of the power that sustains all things.

[126] Epiphanius, *Panarion*, 31.2.5 and 2.9.

[127] See Desjardins, *Sin in Valentinianism*, p 14.

There is already a whiff of antinomianism in the second angel's name. Remember, as we saw in the previous section on Chaldean theology, the silence of heaven is an expression of its non-material nature. Therefore 'Silent Grace' signifies Non-material Grace, in other words a grace that is divorced from and unconcerned with material existence.[128]

Our starting point, then, is the fact that Valentinian Gnostics identified Chaldean Paternal Depth with their own concept of the heavenly *pleroma,* whose lead angel also bore the name Paternal Depth. Fortunately, we know a lot more about Valentinian Gnosticism than Chaldean theology. And, most significantly, now we have crossed over into the world of Christianity.

What does this mean in practical terms for Christian worship and belief? What are the specific religious teachings attached to Paternal Depth theology in Valentinian Christianity? And how did that produce tolerance of immorality at Thyatira? The answer to that is both surprising and highly significant for us today. It is found in one of the Valentinian texts from Nag Hammadi, *The Gospel of Truth.* We will now be looking at a series of passages from this Gnostic Christian text that reveal the full range of religious beliefs involved in ancient Paternal Depth theology.

First we are told that Christ, "the Son," came forth from the Depth itself:

> ...his Son ...who came forth from the depth, he spoke about his secret things, knowing that the Father is a being without evil. For that very reason he brought him forth in order to speak about the place and his resting-place from which he had come forth, and to glorify the pleroma...and the sweetness of the Father.[129]

Nag Hammadi texts can be difficult reading. This passage at first may seem hopelessly confused. Let's take it one piece at a time.

We learn several important things from this passage. First, notice that the Depth is designated as the *"resting-place"* of Christ – Christ came

---

[128] The entire Valentinian *pleroma* of thirty pairs of archangels also is described as *"enveloped in silence,"* (Irenaeus, Against Heresies, 1.1.3).

Elsewhere, Hippolytus recounts the Valentinian story of a certain mythological figure, Sophia, and tells how she at one point *"hurried back into the depth of the Father."* (*Refut.* 6.25) Here it appears that Paternal Depth refers either to the safety of the heavenly *pleroma* in general or to a special state or spiritual power within the *pleroma.*

[129] The Gospel of Truth, **NHLE**, 50.

forth from this place (*his resting-place from which he had come forth*). So now the Depth is also identified with divine rest in Christ. Recall that the Depth traditionally was depicted as at rest – unchanging, peaceful, silent – pure spirituality at rest, unburdened by the chaos of the material world.[130]

In this passage also, Christ is depicted as having come to reveal the existence of the Depth and to glorify the *pleroma* (*to speak about the place...and to glorify the pleroma*). This is talking about spiritual regeneration, the central doctrine of Gnostic salvation. In Gnostic theology, man has fallen into a helpless state (total depravity) by having forgotten his origin in the heavens. Thereby the connection between the heavens and the immortal soul has been severed. In Gnosticism, Christ brings salvation by restoring the knowledge of the heavenly *pleroma*, which automatically reconnects the soul to Heaven's spiritual power. Thus the *pleroma* is 'glorified' for its central role in salvation.

Next, notice how this passage talks about the Father as *"a being without evil."* What does it mean that the Father is without evil? That is explained in another passage from the same text. Speaking of the Father, it says:

> ...nor did they think of him as small nor that he is harsh nor that he is wrathful, but (that) he is a being without evil, imperturbable, sweet....[131]

This is the typical Gnostic teaching that the true heavenly Father is pure love, nonjudgmental and without anger, in contrast to the harsh, punishing and demanding God of the Old Testament. Gnostic rejection of divine anger and punishment is in part the result of the influence of Greek philosophy. Remember that in typically Hellenistic Greek thinking, spirituality and God are associated with the eighth level of heaven. This is the abode of the stars, where the peaceful, unchanging movement of the stars represents immortality and the presence of God. Anger was associated with the instability and chaos of the material world. The idea that God could be angry implies that God has mixed with the material world, which was foreign to Greek sensibility.

For Valentinian Gnostics, resting in the Depth of God was viewed as a beautiful state of peaceful communion with the all-loving Father. He of-

---

[130] This is the heavenly Rest depicted by Eighth Day theology, and the reason Gnostics and Hellenistic Christians insisted the day of rest must point to the heavens rather than creation of the material earth.

[131] The Gospel of Truth, **NHLE**, 50.

fers access to his spiritual Depth freely, by his grace (*the sweetness of the Father*), not placing demands or requirements on his worshippers as Yahweh does.

In the earlier passage quoted above we were told that Christ came to reveal both the existence of spiritual rest (the Deep) and the Father's grace (his *sweetness*). But exactly how do Christians access the Paternal Depth? It is through Christ. In the following passage the phrase *"The one who made them all grow up in himself"* is a direct reference to Christ. It is a takeoff on Ephesians 4:15 where it expressly refers to Christ.[132]

> Therefore, all the emanations of the Father are pleromas, and **the root** of all his emanations **is in the one who made them all grow up in himself.** [133]

Here Christians are described as rooted in Christ *(the root...is in the one who made them all grow up in himself)* . And it says that by being rooted in Christ we also become actual *pleromas* ourselves (*all the emanations of the Father are pleromas*). What is that about?

Again this is talking about the Gnostic concept of spiritual regeneration through mystical union with God and the heavens. If we are 'rooted' in Christ then we are connected through Christ to the heavenly *pleroma* and draw on the power of the Paternal Depth. By connecting to the heavens, our immortal soul magically takes on the spirituality and perfection of the *pleroma* itself. Thereby those who are rooted in Christ themselves become copies of the heavenly *pleroma,* as it says, *"all the emanations of the Father are pleromas."*

Recall from our discussion of Colossians that Valentinian Gnostics believed their Christian sacraments magically heal the human urge to sin (see above, pages 99 and following, section *Submission to Angels, Colossians 2:18*). Valentinians claimed this regenerates the soul of individual Christians to the state of perfection found in the *pleroma.* Hence the *pleroma* is duplicated and established in your own soul.[134] Since *pleroma*

---

[132] The biblical version is Ephesians 4:15, *"...we must grow up in every way into him who is the head, into Christ...."* The more Christianized Nag Hammadi texts often copy verses and phrases from New Testament canonical books.

[133] The Gospel of Truth, **NHLE**, 50.

[134] Valentinian theology made extensive use of the idea of shadows, i.e. spiritual forces, process, conditions etc. in this world that are imperfect instantiations in the material world of angelic archetypical realities in the *pleroma*. This is explained in more detail in Appendix A, see below,

and Depth are synonymous, that means the Depth itself is planted in your soul. In other words, by having Christ come into one's heart (to be rooted in Christ) a Christian comes to "know the Depth (*pleroma*) of God." This is an almost exact copy of the description of the apostasy at Thyatira, where it talks about "learning what some call the Depth of God," or as John phrased it, the "deep things of Satan." What John expressed as "learning" can also mean "knowing," the central doctrine of Gnostic Christianity.

Valentinians also expressed it as a mystical ascent to Heaven in order to obtain direct experience and knowledge of God:

> For the place to which they send their thought, that place, their root, is what takes them up in all the heights to the Father. They possess his head, which is rest for them....[135]

In this passage, the *'root'* is Christ, through whom we have access to the *pleroma* (Depth) of the Father (*what takes them up...to the Father*). By meditating on the heavenly Depth and on Christ (*the place to which they send their thought*), we mystically ascend to him and are united to the Father (*possess his head*). Union with the Father leads to spiritual rest (*which is rest for them*). Once again we encounter the term 'rest.'

What does it mean for Christians to be 'at rest,' to mystically exist in union with God in the Depth of the Father? The following passage describes the Gnostic concept of spiritual rest, and in the process reveals the underlying antinomianism embedded in this theology:

> ...but they rest in him who is at rest, not striving.... But they themselves are the truth; and the Father is within them and they are in the Father, being perfect, ...being in no way deficient in anything, but they are set at rest, refreshed in the Spirit. And they will heed their root. They will be concerned with those [things] in which he will find his root and not suffer loss to his soul.[136]

This final passage is very revealing. Again we encounter mystical union with the Father (*the Father is within them and they are in the Father*). The start of this passage also says Christians who are at rest in him no

---

page 331 and following. In effect, the restored soul of a Valentinian Gnostic is a shadow of the perfection that exists in the *pleroma*.
[135] The Gospel of Truth, **NHLE**, 50.
[136] Ibid., 51.

longer "strive" (*not striving*). So entering God's rest means no more *'striving.'* But what exactly does that mean?

As the passage continues, it says Christians who have come to know the Depth of God are *'perfect'*, *'being in no way deficient.'* Remember how enlightened Christians earlier were described as copies of the heavenly *pleroma,* which means spiritual perfection. The word *pleroma* itself means fullness in the sense of *complete* and *perfect.* Therefore, to know the Depth of God means you have been spiritually regenerated. Your immortal soul is reconnected to the heavenly *pleroma.* You have become spiritually complete and perfect. There is no need to strive for perfection by obedience to the law, nor anything external, because you are already perfected, already sinless and spiritually complete in your soul, possessing the very Depth of God within yourself.

This means that spiritual truth is revealed exclusively from within, as it says, *"they themselves are the truth."* Truth therefore is an exclusively internal revelation and process. It is not something outside of yourself that you 'strive' after. Indeed, as it says, you _are_ the truth!

The passage above ends with the statement that if a Christian is mindful of the heavens in which he is rooted he will *"not suffer loss to his soul."* This is a reference to the Gnostic teaching of eternal security. If you are connected to the Father and the spirituality of the *pleroma,* nothing can hurt your soul. You are literally immune to the material world. Once you have been spiritually regenerated and the perfection of the heavenly *pleroma* had been duplicated in your soul, you become eternally secure.

The early church fathers criticized Valentinians for believing they are spiritually complete and have no need to perform good works as more traditional Christians believed.[137] As we have seen, that does not mean they believed it is just fine to engage in evil, only that good works have nothing to do with salvation. It is this grace alone, antinomian theology of regeneration and eternal security through mystical union with God that is being paraded in *The Gospel of Truth.* It is also essentially the same concept of antinomian mystical union with God that is preached today in much of modern Hellenistic Christianity, as we will see in following chapters.

The concepts of rest in Christ and not striving are biblical. But as usual, the Gnostics appropriated Christian truth and Christian terminology

---

[137] See above, p 53f, Valentinus.

from Paul's writings, and then bent it to their own antinomian purposes. In Romans 9:30–33 Paul talks about the folly of striving after salvation in a carnal fashion, trying to earn salvation by works. He says:

> ...but Israel, who did strive for the righteousness that is based on the law, did not succeed in fulfilling that law.

Why did they fail?

> Because they did not strive for it on the basis of faith, but as if it were based on works.

Paul clearly argues against striving **in the wrong fashion**. Gnostic Christians eagerly jumped on that as they habitually did many other individual statements in Paul's letters, but typically exaggerated and misinterpreted it. Gnosticism claimed the real point is to not strive at all. Spirituality and goodness, they said, come exclusively through a magical regeneration of the soul. Today, Hellenistic Christian theology carries forward a tradition of similar and sometimes virtually identical exaggeration and misinterpretation of Paul's writings, as Peter warned was happening already in the first century (2 Peter 3:16). Today millions of Christians in Reformation churches are taught to just lean back in grace and let the regenerating power of the Father solve all their problems. Striving or trying to participate in the process, they say, will only make you fail, because salvation is performed solely by God. Man plays no role in salvation.

Notice the balanced message from the original passage by Paul in Romans 9. He argues against striving in the wrong way, by piling up works as proof of our good standing before God. But at the same time he does endorse striving, except that it should be based on faith rather than counting the merits of our actions (vs 32). Elsewhere in the New Testament, the author of Hebrews likewise endorses striving to enter the spiritual rest:

> Let us therefore make *every effort* to enter that rest, so that no one may fall through such disobedience as theirs. (Hebrews 4:11)

The New Testament specifically endorses effort and 'striving,' and clearly states that the result of that striving is obedience. The issue for Paul is the proper manner and attitude behind striving.

Scholars have commented on the profound religious sentiment in Valentinian texts – the sweet love of the Father, mystical unity with God and Christ, the power of the Spirit to magically heal the human urge to sin, the guaranteed security of our spiritual rest in him. Paternal Depth theology indeed is tremendously appealing.

What if you believed the Valentinian claim that you can validly choose between their more advanced Christian revelation and traditional Primitive Christianity? On the one hand you have to sincerely seek to obey God's written standards as well as the Holy Spirit. You are empowered by the Spirit, but it is neither automatic nor irresistible. You must struggle against the world and your own human nature. God promises he will never abandon you nor let anyone forcibly take you away from him, but in the end there is a possibility you could turn away from God and fail. There is no absolute, blanket guarantee.

On the other hand, if you choose the supposedly more spiritual Paternal Depth theology it is all done for you. Just sink back in the Father's sweet love, be a generally good person but don't worry too much about those assorted 'external' failings you experience. The only thing that really matters is what is inside, your immortal soul that now exists in a state of perfection through mystical connection to God and his power. Spirituality is non-material. If you are terribly tempted, or if the pressure from the world gets too difficult and you feel you must compromise, not to worry. You should be a good person in your material existence but it cannot affect or block your salvation, because salvation is non-material. You possess a salvation that can never be lost.

If you believed you had the option to go either way, which would you choose?

Eighth Day Theology
and
The Deep Things of Satan

The 'deep things of Satan' helps explain why Eighth Day theology was so popular among Gnostic Christians. To understand this, we look again to the Gnostic text, *The Gospel of Truth*. This is a portion of one of the passages quoted earlier, where it is talking about being rooted in the heavenly *pleroma* through Christ.

> And they will heed their root. They will be concerned with those [things] in which he will find his root and not suffer loss to his soul.[138]

As we saw above, the phrase *"not suffer loss to his soul"* is a reference to Gnostic belief in eternal security. Notice however, that Gnostic Christians have this guarantee only because they *"heed their root"* and because they are *"concerned with those (things) in which he will find his root."*

For Valentinian Gnostics, maintaining focus on the heavenly *pleroma* in which they are rooted is what produces eternal security. Therefore the primary purpose of their religious practice was this very thing – constantly maintaining their mystical connection to the heavens. This allowed them to draw spiritual power from the *pleroma*, which they believed maintains the state of perfection of their souls. If your soul is secure through its connection to the heavens, then nothing else such as material conduct can interfere with salvation – in other words you are eternally secure.

This is the underlying motivation for the transfer of worship from Sabbath to Sunday in Gnostic as well as much of Hellenistic Christianity. Recall from our previous discussions that the whole point of Eighth Day theology was to orient and connect Christians to the heavens.

Valentinian Gnostics taught that there was a special class of inferior Christians, called *psychics*. These were orthodox Christians who had not fully freed themselves from the worship of Yahweh. In part because of their bondage to Hebrew religious practices, they did not have the perfection of the heavenly *pleroma* implanted in their hearts. Therefore they were required to perform good works to earn salvation, and so their salva-

---

[138] *The Gospel of Truth*, **NHLE**, 51.

tion could be lost. If you want the salvation that cannot be lost, however, you have to reject everything with a materialistic connection to this world and focus exclusively on the heavenly *pleroma*.

Once you understand the Hellenistic reasoning that underpins Gnostic theology, it all makes sense. Eighth Day theology, eternal security, and the mystical, heavenly theology of Hellenistic religion, all go hand in hand. Once the early church was infected with Hellenistic thinking, beginning in the first century through the influence of Gnostic Christianity, it was only a matter of time before the transfer to Sunday observance would occur. Why would you want to continue observing a day that points to material creation? Once the new theology was in place, correspondingly new religious practices supporting that theology inevitably followed.

Definition of Paternal Depth Theology

Here is the summation of Depth of God theology as it was developed in Valentinian Christianity:

The Depth represents a state of spiritual perfection and rest in Christ. Christ himself came forth from the Depth. The purpose of his coming was to reveal the existence of the Depth and the potential for man, through him and the Father's sweet grace, to enter it and thus be regenerated spiritually. The Depth offers a spiritual rest based on God's nonjudgmental love, and salvation by grace and faith alone. The Father is pure love and sweetness. He is not an angry God, neither judgmental nor demanding like the God of the Old Testament. He does not place conditions on entering his rest.

Connection to the Depth is maintained by turning away from the material world, instead connecting to the heavenly Depth through Christ. Connection to the Depth creates a state of spiritual perfection in the soul. Possessing the Depth in this manner provides a guaranteed salvation that cannot be lost.

In brief, Paternal Depth theology means accepting God's unlimited love, entering a mystical, heavenly relationship with him through Christ by grace alone. It means spiritual regeneration imposed exclusively by God, without effort on man's part. It means turning away from the materialism of Hebrew religion, rejecting the external guidance of law, instead yielding yourself completely and exclusively to the private revelation of the Spirit. Thus Christians become self-sufficient, possessing the perfection of the heavenly Depth within themselves.

That is what it means to learn or know the deep things of Satan. This is the essence of Paternal Depth theology that the Primitive Christian church at Thyatira had absorbed from their Gnostic Christian neighbors. It is also the essence of the latter day Gnosticism that continues to plague Christianity yet today.

Why was this a problem at Thyatira? Unfortunately, Gnosticism's unbalanced theories of heavenly spirituality simply don't work very well. Rejecting the role of divine law in defining moral conduct, and depending exclusively on private revelation from within, inevitably leads to immorality, as it did at Thyatira, and as it still does today.

Conclusions

The Valentinian sect came into existence as an organized body early in the second century. This is at least several decades after Revelation was written. Therefore the Valentinians themselves could not have been involved directly with the apostasy at Thyatira. However, we know it was proto-Gnostics leaving the New Testament church who formed the Gnostic sects of the second century.[139] So the presence of this theology in a major Gnostic sect, just a few decades after Revelation was written, strongly suggests it would have been present in proto-Gnostic circles inside the primitive church late in the first century. This is only confirmed by Revelation 2:24, from which we know it was present in at least one Primitive Christian church in the 70s to 90s A.D. and formed the basis in that church for typically Gnostic tolerance of immorality.[140]

---

[139] I John 2:19

[140] Paul's choice of words – Deep (KJV) or abyss (NRSV) – in Romans 10:7 likely signifies more than the underworld or the grave, and if so may hint at the presence of Paternal Depth apostasy in the Roman church as well.

It is significant also that we find Paul in the very middle of the first century warning the New Testament church at Colossae (a near neighbor to Thyatira) against Gnostic false doctrines strikingly reminiscent of Valentinian theology, including a direct reference to the *pleroma* (Col 2:8–10) which the Valentinians identified with the Deep.

It appears that the spiritualized reinterpretation of the mystery tradition of the Deep may have been fairly widespread in the first century

There are striking similarities between the spirituality of Paternal Depth theology and genuinely biblical New Testament spirituality. At the same time, however, Paternal Depth theology obviously went beyond biblical spirituality – shall we say, it goes off the 'deep' end.

This is the great mystery, the *mystery* of lawlessness whose lawless nature is hidden beneath claims of obedience to a higher spirituality. According to Paternal Depth theology, lawlessness is not evil. Instead, by connecting to the heavens one receives power to achieve an even higher spirituality. Its modern proponents generally insist it is not lawless at all because it teaches obedience to the inspiration of the Spirit coming from the spiritual Depth within. In fact, this theology claims that obedience to 'external' codified law is a source of evil. All things external tend to block inner spirituality. Therefore, they say, written law actually is a deception and spiritual trap.[141]

In the next four chapters we now turn to examining the survival of this very same supposedly more advanced antinomian theology as taught in the Christianity of our world today.

---

and perhaps played an important role in the development of proto-Gnosticism within the primitive church.

[141] Compare this to radical Evangelical theology; see discussion below, pages 171 and following, in section *Pauline Mysticism*.

Part 2

Gnosticism for Our Time

New Testament warnings against apostasy are all the more significant because they often appear as prophetic messages. Most significant of all, perhaps, is 2 Thessalonians chapter two, in which the mystery of lawlessness is presented as a single religious tradition stretching from the first century to the end time when it is finally put down by Jesus Christ at his second advent.

We now know what the mystery of lawlessness was – a very sophisticated, spiritual Christian theology. We also know the group behind it – Gnostic Christianity – and when and where it started – in the first century A.D. inside the newly founded apostolic church. We know what happened to the Gnostic Christians who started it – they departed en masse from the apostolic church beginning late in the first century to establish their own independent churches and sects. We also know these classic Gnostic Christian groups had mostly died out by the sixth century.

The New Testament does not say that Gnosticism itself would survive. What is prophesied to survive is the complex of antinomian doctrines known as the mystery of lawlessness. If New Testament scripture is true, then we must find the fulfillment of those prophecies somewhere within the world of Christianity today.

The prophecies to the seven churches, in Revelation chapter two, contain multiple references to Gnosticism and antinomian apostasies. These are depicted as warnings for all Christians throughout the entire church era. Once again, if the New Testament is true, then this is a very serious issue for Christians today.

Given the historical background presented in part one of this volume, it should not be that difficult to identify the same super-spiritual antinomian doctrines in our day. Thus, over the next four chapters, we now embark on the incredible story of the survival of Gnostic Christian theology in our time, a story so unusual it seems almost surreal.

– 8 –

The Mystery
of Lawlessness Today

In his second letter to the Thessalonians Paul specifically prophesies that the mystery of lawlessness would continue until Christ returns:

> For the mystery of lawlessness is already at work.... And then the lawless one will be revealed, whom the Lord Jesus will destroy...annihilating him by the manifestation of his coming. (2 Thess 2:7–8)

Who, then, is promoting the same mystery of lawlessness today? Speaking loosely, who are the 'Gnostics' for us today? I have never met anyone who said he is a Gnostic. It appears the only thing we have to go on is doctrine. After all, it was only certain Gnostic doctrines that were prophesied to survive into our time. Let's consider then, what would they be preaching today, based on what history shows they were teaching in the early centuries after Christ?

First, we should know they wouldn't be calling themselves Gnostics. That is a label invented by modern scholars. Most Gnostics considered themselves Christians.

Not only would they be calling themselves Christians, they would be claiming to be an advanced and more enlightened form of Christianity. The Gnostics emphasized progressive revelation. They regularly claimed to have received special revelations from after the resurrection that override and modify Jesus' earthly ministry and the New Testament itself. They openly embraced the Hellenization of Christianity as that second, more spiritual revelation of Christianity.

They would view Primitive Christians as partially enlightened, but confused and in bondage because they have failed to completely free themselves from the Old Testament and its law.

Some Gnostic churches would claim to find their more advanced teaching of salvation in the letters of Paul. The Marcionite Gnostic church, for example, used a New Testament composed only of letters ascribed to Paul and part of the Gospel of Luke (written by Paul's companion).

Gnostics today would condemn Sabbath observance as spiritually backward, as a carryover from a primitive stage of Christianity practiced by those who have failed to be enlightened by the new revelations they claim to see in Paul's letters. Remember, for Gnostics anything Jewish automatically signifies bondage.

They would be teaching the substitution of Sunday for Sabbath worship. Sunday symbolizes heaven, spiritual rebirth, liberation, and the Hellenistic Eighth Day that exists outside the Old Testament seven-day cycle.

Gnostic Christians would be teaching many Hellenistic doctrines, especially the immortality of the soul. They would teach a radical interpretation of grace versus law, claiming the two are incompatible.

We know, however, that Gnostics would not openly advocate immorality. For them rejection of the law was only a gateway to a higher spirituality and Christ-centeredness that brings man out of sin naturally, without effort or participation by man himself. And rejection of the law does not mean they had no standards. What Gnosticism did, as Paul describes in Colossians, is substitute their own human sensibility about godliness, *"after the commandments and doctrines of men"* (Col 2:22). As we saw in an earlier chapter, much of natural human spirituality overlaps with God's teachings and there is a great deal of good in it.[142]

So far we have people who:
- call themselves Christians and follow a second, supposedly more spiritual revelation of Christianity
- teach a doctrine of progressive revelation based on Pauline theology
- condemn Sabbath observance and Primitive Christianity in general as backward

---

[142] See above, chapter 6, Natural Human Spirituality, pages 121 and following.

- substitute Sunday for Sabbath
- believe in a grace that requires rejection of law
- substitute moral standards based on philosophic reasoning and natural human judgment
- believe in an immortal soul that ascends to heaven at death
- embrace the Hellenization of Christianity as God's will

Has anything really changed in the past nearly 2,000 years?

And what is the most central doctrine of this tradition? The key teaching, then and today, is the mystery of lawlessness, the teaching that man not only can but **must** exclude obedience to Old Testament practices and law, most of all the Sabbath, in a new inner spirituality of love and liberation that separates salvation from obedience.

Is This an Exaggeration?

But, is this really 'Gnosticism'? Are we playing loose with the evidence in making such a bold claim? There are differences, of course, especially if you compare modern Christianity to the more radical Gnostic sects of the second and third centuries A.D. For some of these, grace was primarily the Father's love and mercy revealed to mankind by Christ, but not mediated through Christ's sacrifice.

Remember, however, that when the New Testament talks about Gnosticism it is referring to proto-Gnosticism, i.e. Gnosticism as it first appeared inside the apostolic church. When Gnostic Christians left to form their own churches and sects in the second and third centuries, freed from the restraint of their peers in the apostolic church, they became much more radical and dominated by pagan theology.

Further, the New Testament does not say Gnosticism itself would survive. New Testament prophecy specifically identifies what will survive as Gnosticism's most prominent set of doctrines, the mystery of lawlessness. The key to understanding the importance of Gnosticism is recognizing its historical role of injecting the mystery of lawlessness into Christianity and initiating the subversion that culminated in the Hellenization of the church.

If we look to New Testament prophecies about the survival of some of those teachings into our time, then we understand precisely why Hellenistic Christianity exists in the form it does today. It is no real surprise. New Testament prophecies of the continuation and spread of the doctrine and spirit of lawlessness are completely fulfilled in our time. Look in any direction. The evidence is everywhere about us.

In this chapter we review a collection of religious teachings from mainstream Christianity, which factually demonstrate the survival of the mystery of lawlessness in our time. After establishing that foundation, in the following chapters we methodically analyze the theology and historical processes that brought modern Christianity to such radical and surprising beliefs.

Eternal Security

In the year 1521 Martin Luther wrote a letter in which he advised the recipient *"Be a sinner, and let your sins be strong, but let your faith in Christ be stronger.... No sin can separate us from Him, **even if we were to kill or commit adultery a thousand times each day.**"* [143]

Could Luther really mean what he appears to be saying? Does Protestantism openly and intentionally advocate evil? To understand Luther, we need merely turn back to the first century and Nicolas, the founder of the Nicolaitan sect of Gnostic Christianity.[144] Remember how Nicolas made similarly shocking statements when he publicly offered his beautiful young wife to anyone who wanted to possess her sexually. From the historical evidence we know Nicolas was not advocating sin. Instead he was merely making a dramatic show of his contempt for material life. By doing so he believed he could rid himself of lust and thereby more completely devote himself to inner spirituality.

We also know that despite Nicolas' good intentions his theology didn't work very well. His followers soon caught on to the fact it could be used as an excuse for willful sin. Given this common starting point, it is entirely appropriate to ask if Reformation (Protestant) theology has in fact espoused essentially the same antinomian theology taught by Nicolaitan Gnosticism in the first century.

---

[143] Martin Luther, Saemmtliche Schriften, Letter number 99, 1 August 1521, translated by Erika Flores in "The Wittenberg Project, The Wartburg Segment", as published in Grace and Knowledge, Issue 8, Sept. 2000, Article "Ecclesiasticus: The Wisdom of Ben-Sirach", page 27.
[144] For description of Nicolaitans and their founder Nicolas, see above pages 40 and following.

How did these ideas unfold for Reformation (Protestant) Christianity? As we will see, it has followed a track very similar to Gnostic Christianity in the first centuries after Christ.

Reformation theology actively promotes various standards of good conduct that overlap extensively with biblical morality. Reformation theology does not officially endorse sin. Yet, Luther's statement does mean that one has the *option* to indulge, literally, in the most bizarre evil, to unimaginable excess, without repentance, and still be saved.

The sentiments expressed by Luther still echo today through many modern advocates of the doctrine of eternal security. This is the doctrine that claims salvation is "eternally secure" for Christians, regardless of conduct.

Here is a brief selection from contemporary Hellenistic Christian preachers and theologians:

John Ankerberg and John Weldon:

> To say that any sin, no matter how bad, can cause the loss of salvation, is to deny the infinite value of the atoning death of Christil.[145]

Charles Stanley:

> ...God's love for His people is of such magnitude that even those who walk away from the faith have not the slightest chance of slipping from His hand.[146]

John MacArthur (leading advocate of Lordship salvation):

> ...someone says, but can't Christians put themselves outside God's grace? What about those who commit abominable sins? Don't they nullify the work of redemption in themselves? Don't they forfeit the love of God?

> Certainly not.... It's preposterous to think that we can forfeit it [salvation] by anything we do.[147]

---

[145] Ankerberg and Weldon, *Knowing the Truth about Eternal Security*, p 30.

[146] Stanley, *Eternal Security*, p 109.

[147] MacArthur, *The Love of God*, Word Publishing, 1966, p 159, quoted by Corner, *The Believer's Conditional Security*, p 182–3.

A More Spiritual Christianity?

Nicolas never intended his theology to be used as an excuse for sin. Quite the opposite, he saw it as a means of liberation from lust, a theme shared by nearly all Gnostic Christians. Nicolas argued that putting aside concerns about material things was only one part of a process enabling Christians to totally devote themselves to a higher form of inner spirituality. Do we find the same idea in Hellenistic Christianity today?

Advocates of eternal security today argue essentially the same thing, claiming that eternal security, though it can be misused, actually is a gateway to a superior relationship with Jesus. For example:

John Ankerberg and John Weldon:
> ...we believe that the doctrine of eternal security glorifies God – that is, inspires love and obedience to God – far more than...the doctrine that a Christian can lose his salvation.[148]

Charles Stanley:
> Where there is no assurance of God's acceptance, there is no peace. Where there is no peace, there is no joy. Where there is no joy, there is a limitation on one's ability to love unconditionally. Why? Because a person with no assurance is by definition partially motivated by fear. Fear and love do not mingle well. One will always dilute the other. Furthermore, fear spills over into worry. Let's be realistic for a moment. If my salvation is not a settled issue, how can I be anxious for nothing (see Phil 4:6)?[149]

Like Stanley, Gnostic Christians also saw avoiding fear as an important benefit of their antinomian theology. Recall the discussion of Gnostic theology and avoiding fear (see above, pages 126 and following).

For Stanley, unconditional love requires that God will never reject his followers, regardless of any degree of sin, perversion or unfaithfulness.[150] Is that really unconditional love? Are there two standards, one for the saved who are allowed to get away with anything, and another for the unsaved who are sent to hell for doing the same things the saved get away with? Why are the saved loved 'unconditionally,' but not the unsaved?

---

[148] Ankerberg and Weldon, *Knowing the Truth about Eternal Security*, p 6.
[149] Stanley, *Eternal Security*, p 13,15.
[150] Ibid. p 16–17.

Isn't this simply licentious grace, licensing the same sins to the saved for which the unsaved are condemned? Hellenistic Christianity insists it is not. They consistently and vociferously insist it is a more spiritual form of Christianity.

But, back to the original question – Is Reformation theology today duplicating the same ancient Gnostic teaching which claims that ignoring material sin is a gateway to a higher form of spirituality? Indeed, some today hold that very same antinomian view. According to Stanley, for example, removing worry about sin – by abolishing conduct as a requirement in salvation – is a key to becoming Christ-centered:

> As long as I have an ongoing role in the salvation process, my natural tendency will be to focus on my behavior rather than on Christ. ... We are never completely free to fasten our gaze on Him until we are sure our relationship with Him is secure.[151]

This is precisely the same idea espoused by Nicolas in the first century. Offering his wife to anyone who wanted her was only a means to dramatically illustrate his belief that one can focus on spirituality only by putting material concerns about sin completely out of mind.

Stanley makes some valid observations regarding focus on self and the problems of legalism. He accepts that a certain amount of self-examination is appropriate, and I would agree with him that excessive self-focus is a common companion to legalism.

On the other hand, however, does such an extreme interpretation of inner spirituality really work? Remember, the underlying theory both then and now, is that ignoring or licensing sin actually makes sin go away. Therefore it seems eminently reasonable to ask, Does it work any better today than the same theology worked for Nicolas' followers in the first century when they fell into immoral conduct? Does it really make sin go away as they claim? Consider the following:

The Carnal Christian

In recent Reformation theology, the antinomian doctrine of salvation for willfully sinful Christians has come under the title, the "Carnal Chris-

---

[151] Ibid. p 18.

tian." The name is derived from the following passage in Paul's letter to the Corinthian church:

> For you are still carnal. For where there are envy, strife, and divisions among you, are you not carnal, and behaving like mere men? (1 Corinthians 3:3, NKJV)

From the starting point of this single verse, the argument has evolved that Christians can be not only 'human,' but totally depraved as well, indistinguishable from the unsaved. And based on this single verse it is argued that Paul validates the inclusion of such people in the church as Christians who are 'in Christ.'

The doctrine of the Carnal Christian is associated with what is called extreme eternal security. This extreme form of eternal security says that absolutely no positive change in a person's character is required for salvation. It is the type of doctrine now very popular in Evangelical circles in America, and is typified for example by the preaching of the nationally known American Baptist minister Charles Stanley.

Once again, this does not mean they officially encourage evil. They teach it only as a viable option. Keep in mind as well that persons who believe in this doctrine commonly apply it selectively to their own specific failings. In other words, they may pursue good conduct in some areas, but willfully omit it in those aspects of their lives in which they have a particular weakness.

But, do advocates of the Carnal Christian doctrine really believe one can show absolutely no positive change and still be saved? Here is a brief selection of opinions from leading theologians and ministers:

Charles Stanley:
> ...you can't tell a carnal believer from a lost man.[152]

Chuck Swindoll:
> That explains how a Christian can steal and lie. That explains how a Christian can lack integrity and commit adultery and turn against the very things he or she once taught.[153]

---

[152] Robert Stanley (Atlanta, GA: In Touch Ministries, 1982), *Spiritual Vs. Carnal: Study in 1 Corinthians,* audiotape #8, PQ092, as quoted in Corner, *The Believer's Conditional Security,* p 153.

[153] Chuck Swindoll, *Clearing the Hurdle of Carnality: Selection from 1 Corinthians,* audiotape CHH 5-A, as quoted in Corner, *The Believer's Conditional Security,* p 155.

Robert Gromacki:

> To an unsaved person or to an untaught, critical Christian, he [the Carnal Christian] will look like an unsaved person and may even be called such.[154]

When applied correctly these ideas have some validity. A converted Christian indeed can fall into evil, even gross evil. Where there is an attitude of repentance God will forgive any sin, however evil. The Apostle Paul murdered Christians before he was converted. King David committed cold, premeditated murder to cover up his adultery, but in the end he repented and turned back to God. The problem is that these ideas are applied in the typically extreme antinomian sense that such "Carnal Christians" are still saved regardless of whether they ever repent or produce a single positive change in their lives.

Look again at the biblical passage on which this teaching is constructed. The problem Paul is addressing at Corinth is social disunity and petty quarreling, involving pride and grasping for status in the church. Such conduct is wrong, but it is a far cry from the stealing, adultery, murder, and openly willful evil to which many Reformation theologians apply it. What is Paul's attitude towards gross sin? Is it as tolerant as supposedly implied in this one passage?

Later in the same letter Paul names a list of gross sins, including stealing and adultery, and warns *"Do not be deceived! ...none of these will inherit the kingdom of God"* (1 Cor 6:9–10). Paul commands the same Corinthians, *"Drive out the wicked person from among you"* (1 Cor 5:13).

What is the result of Carnal Christian theology? I am sure none of the churches that espouse this theology actually advocate that their members practice wanton evil. Yet, is there an antinomian effect to these doctrines? If you tell people they *should* be good, but in the end they can do literally anything they want and still be saved without ever repenting, does it have an antinomian effect? Do people today react the same way Nicolas' followers did in the first century? If similar antinomian theories are preached today, do they produce the same results?

I relate the following events from personal experience exactly as they occurred. The first story unfolds many years ago when I was staying at

---

[154] Robert Glenn Gromacki, *Salvation Is Forever* (Chicago: Moody Press, Third Printing, 1976), p 173–174, as quoted in Corner, *The Believer's Conditional Security,* p 155.

my parents' home during a summer break from college. My parents were lifelong conservative members of various Reformation congregations. At this time they attended a church I consider representative of moderate Reformation theology. One day two ministers from their church came to the house. As they knocked I was ordered to leave. I knew something was up, so I walked through the kitchen towards the back door, but didn't leave. Through an open door I listened to a profoundly tragic story.

In the midst of a respectable middle-class Protestant church, the choir director had been caught in an affair with the church organist. Both were married. Apparently it had been known for some time by a few, but nothing had been done about it. Finally the choir director's wife became so distraught she put a gun to her head and committed suicide. Now everyone knew about it. Yet, weeks later the choir director still was standing up in front of the church every Sunday and the organist was still playing.

My parents were demanding to know what was going on. According to them, neither the choir director nor the organist had expressed repentance and the affair was still in progress. Neither of the ministers disputed this. However, these men followed the belief system typical of the doctrine of the Carnal Christian found in a large part of Reformation Christianity, rejecting the idea that repentance is required for a saving relationship with Jesus. They defended their decision not to remove these two people from their posts on the basis it was better to keep them in the church and pray for them. By the principles of love and grace they were still Christians and were still saved, and we should approach them with an accepting attitude as does Jesus, in spite of their sin.

To my parents' credit they left that church. Unfortunately, at that time and afterward, they themselves embraced the doctrine of eternal security. But like so many who espouse that theology, they applied licentious grace to only their own particular weaknesses and not the sins of others. So we often witness the strange and irrational spectacle of conservative Christians who believe in eternal security, condemning their fellow Christians to hell for violation of a rule that particularly upsets them, which technically cannot happen if eternal security is true.

The second story occurred not many years ago, taking the form of a conversation with an acquaintance who is a liberal but far from radical Protestant Christian. He and I have disputed the issue of Christian premarital sexual morality on various occasions, and on this day he described for me the experience of his daughter with a college roommate. The roommate was described as a sexually active girl who regularly brought men back to her room to stay overnight. At the same time she also was a devoted church-going Christian. This girl was described as defending her conduct by saying she knows it isn't right, but she finds sex so tempting she feels she simply can't stop. Still, she is a good person. She loves her parents. She is kind to others. She goes to church every Sunday. She has a nice personality. So, she believes that God understands and by grace she is saved. She is a Carnal Christian in that one aspect of her life. What is a little indiscretion compared to the higher principles of love and goodness? This is a classic example of the ancient Gnostic Christian compartmentalizing of inner and outer religiosity. Outward sin cannot derail your salvation as long as your inner spirituality and relationship with Jesus are intact.

My friend, who related the story, noted that young people sometimes find it difficult to abstain from premarital sex because of peer pressure. He expressed sympathy for young girls who feel they have to be sexually active to achieve social popularity, and suggested that in those circumstances it might be a valid choice. He also stated the typical antinomian Reformation idea that when a person is converted, in many cases it doesn't produce any change in conduct, but that cannot mean they are not saved.

Are these isolated incidents? Does Reformation theology today produce the same results as the theology of the Gnostic teacher Nicolas? Is Reformation theology implicitly included in the New Testament's condemnation of the immorality of Nicolaitan Christians in the first century? Consider what some Hellenistic Christians themselves say about it:

Hellenistic Christians Bemoan Antinomianism

Many Hellenistic Christian leaders themselves openly recognize and condemn the problem of antinomianism in Reformation Christianity. Many are troubled by the teachings of their own churches. For example Charles Stanley quotes arguments he frequently encounters from people who criticize his own teaching of eternal security:

> "A holy God demands holy living from His children," they argue. "A man or woman whose lifestyle in no way demonstrates a desire for Christ-likeness could not possibly have the Holy Spirit within, regardless of what was prayed or confessed in the past."

Those who hold this view perceive the doctrine of eternal security to be a **license for sin.** For this reason they consider eternal security a dangerous doctrine.[155]

Stanley frankly admits many Christians do make use of the Reformation license to willfully sin, as he continues:

And to be honest, the behavior of many "Christians" provides them [Stanley's critics] **with ample evidence to make such a claim.**[156]

Speaking of the doctrine of the Carnal Christian, Vic Reasoner is horrified by what he sees as the results of this theology:

Sexual immorality among Christian leaders and congregations full of divorce are a fruit of this **antinomian teaching.**[157]

Charles Spurgeon, the famous Calvinist theologian, also condemned extremist views within Reformation theology with these words:

...they overlaid it [Reformation theology] with an incrustation of something that approached **Antinomianism....**[158]

My heart bleeds for many a family where **Antinomian doctrine** has gained sway. I could tell many a sad story of families dead in sin, whose consciences are seared as with a hot iron, by the fatal preaching to which they listen.[159]

Zane Hodges is a Protestant theologian typical of those who support what is called extreme eternal security. He argues, for example, that repentance is not required for salvation. Repentance is a good thing, he says, and it makes possible fellowship with God, but it absolutely is not required for salvation. Reacting to that, the prominent theologian R. C. Sproul says:

---

[155] Ibid. p 154, emphasis added.
[156] Ibid, emphasis added.
[157] Dr.Vic Reasoner, in foreword to Corner, *The Believer's Conditional Security,* vii.
[158] Quoted by Iain Murray, *Spurgeon v. Hyper-Calvinism: The Battle for Gospel Preaching,* 126–127, in Geisler, Chosen But Free, p 132.
[159] Ibid. Murray p 155, Geisler p 132.

I can hardly believe Hodges means what he says. This is **anti-nomianism** with a vengeance.[160]

Reformation theologians espouse many different shades and degrees of belief in the theology bequeathed by Luther and Calvin. They eagerly debate the issues and often condemn those who do not embrace their own interpretation. What I find ironic is the way they frequently condemn interpretations more extreme than their own as antinomian, while justifying their own ideas that logically suffer from only a slightly lesser degree of the same problem.

Again note the striking similarity between the first century and today. Morality on the material level is downplayed; in fact unlimited sin becomes a viable option. Still, sin is not officially recommended. Quite the opposite, the entire theology, both then and now, is designed to bring man out of sin. Their point is that it is only by removing worry about salvation, only by removing worry about sin, that man can be psychologically freed from material lust in order to achieve a greater spirituality of the inner man.

It didn't work that well in the first century. And today? In view of the Carnal Christian doctrine, invented to explain why so many Christians take the willful sin option, and widespread open criticism from Hellenistic Christians themselves, I think we can fairly say it doesn't work any better today than it did then.

The Excuse

Telling a Reformation theologian he preaches antinomianism is almost certain to provoke a hostile reaction. I speak from experience. The near universal argument is they do nothing of the sort. However, that begs the question: Is Reformation theology excused by the fact it officially recommends people not take the willful sin option? Is it excused by the fact its theology really is intended to bring man out of sin? If you answer yes, then you must answer one additional question. If that is a valid excuse, then why does the New Testament so severely condemn Gnosticism for arguing essentially the same thing in the first century?

---

[160] Sproul, *Faith Alone,* p 171.

The New Testament condemns antinomianism from various points of view. Scripture condemns the Nicolaitans for <u>practicing</u> immorality. On the other hand, the apostle Jude condemns Gnostic Christians from the <u>doctrinal</u> point of view, for teaching the doctrines of antinomian grace that license and facilitate that kind of conduct (Jude 4–8). So just teaching the doctrine of unlimited sin as an option, itself is biblically condemned.

As we have seen in previous chapters, there is a spirit of lawlessness, the natural proclivity of man to do whatever he wants. And there is also the **mystery** of lawlessness, which is a theological system that facilitates willful sin.

The term "mystery" of lawlessness implies something that is hidden, as in a mystery. Both ancient Gnosticism and mainstream Christianity today exemplify that very trait, promoting licentious grace under the guise of a more spiritual relationship with Jesus.

Pauline Mysticism

One branch of Protestant theology bears such a striking resemblance to Gnostic spirituality it deserves special mention. That is Pauline mysticism, one of the pillars of antinomianism within Evangelical Protestant theology. Many Protestants today are unaware of the unusual, mystical nature of the 'grace alone' and 'faith alone' theology taught in some of their own churches.

Paul frequently talks in mystical terms of the power of the Spirit working from within to produce Christian morality in individual lives. Sometimes he expresses it as Christ living his life within us. As in Galatians 2:20,

> ...it is no longer I who live, but it is Christ who lives in me.

The early Protestant reformers, and many Evangelical theologians today, interpret this to mean man plays no role in the formation and expression of Christian character. That is not a relative statement. When they say no role, they really mean nothing – absolute zero.

The Christian life, therefore, is essentially a matter of leaning back, resting in grace and letting the natural, mystical process do its work. According to this reasoning, to try to make any effort on your own, or to believe you play a cooperative role, is a violation of the principle of grace and faith alone.

Primitive Christianity traditionally has held that biblical law, as amended and magnified by Jesus, continues as a moral standard and guide for Christian conduct and good works. According to some modern Evangelical theories, however, it is wrong to even look at the law to learn what good works will please God. To do so, they say, implies you are trying to do works on your own, to play a cooperative role in salvation. Therefore it is a tacit violation of faith in the mystical power of Christ working within you.

We see this graphically illustrated by the contemporary Evangelical writer Steve McVey in his book *Grace Walk*.[161] This is especially pertinent, as this book has been promoted as a true exposition of Christian doctrine in some Primitive Christian churches that are in the process of converting to Evangelical theology.

In his book McVey argues that trying to conform to rules will always fail, because law only stimulates the desire to disobey. Here he quotes from Romans 7:5,

> While we were <u>living in the flesh</u>, **our sinful passions, aroused by the law,** were at work....

The point he makes is quite valid. What he fails to distinguish, however, is that Paul clearly specifies he is describing how persons *"living in the flesh"* react to the law. Paul is not suggesting that spiritual Christians react in that manner.

This reasoning is strikingly similar to Valentinian Gnosticism, which used the very same argument that law must be rejected because it only stimulates lust and sin (see above, pages 127 and following). Valentinians insisted that if you use the law as a guide to God's will, it will only entrap you.

The solution according to McVey is to get rid of the law, the same solution proposed by Gnosticism. There is no law under the New Testament, McVey argues, because Jesus kept the law for us, and when he lives his life within us he will mystically reproduce his obedience in us. Therefore it is necessary for Christians to ignore the law in order to focus ex-

---

[161] Mr. McVey and other modern Christian writers teach many very godly principles and express them eloquently, and frequently with excellent psychological insight. The problem we are discussing here is the tragedy of the antinomian component in this theology. The mystery of lawlessness is a 'mystery,' often enshrined in a genuinely spiritual context that obscures its real nature.

clusively on Jesus living his life within you.[162] Remember the Valentinian Gnostic teaching that mere *gnosis* of the divinity residing in the soul mystically transforms us and manifests the goodness of God in our lives. (See above, pages 130 and following, and pages 99 and following in section "Submission to Angels".)

Primitive Christians generally regard this as a gross exaggeration of the genuine Pauline mysticism of the New Testament. Indeed, it is not difficult to find fault with the Evangelical position. First, if the individual truly plays absolutely no role, how then can Paul and other New Testament authors criticize Christians as they frequently do? Are they really preaching to Christ inside those Christians and admonishing Christ to get with it?

Evangelical Obedience

Does modern Evangelicalism replicate the antinomianism of Gnostic Christianity from the early centuries after Christ? Consider the following:

Steve McVey describes legalistic Christians as those who look to God and his law, saying,

Lord, help me to do the things You want me to do.[163]

That is wrong, he insists! It is wrong, he says, because it means focusing on rules, even if they are God's rules. In contrast, he argues, spiritual Christians say,

Express Your life through me in any way You desire.[164]

The last part of that sentence is the key to understanding Evangelical obedience. When they say Christ obeyed the law and he reproduces his obedience in you, one might reasonably assume that means Jesus leads us to obey the law the same way he did. That is what the Apostle John preached when he wrote, *"...whoever says, 'I abide in him,' ought to walk just as he* [Jesus] *walked"* (1 John 2:6). Notice that John uses "walk" in past tense, referring to Jesus' conduct (walk) during his earthly ministry.

---

162 McVey, *Grace Walk*, p 81, 87–89.
163 McVey, *Grace Walk*, p 35.
164 Ibid, emphasis added.

In the end, however, what Evangelical theologians such as McVey really are saying is that the obedience Christ will inspire within you is in no way tied to the obedience he practiced during his life here on earth. Evangelical obedience is a mystery, based on a private revelation of the Spirit. Whatever you do in response to your conscience and inner spiritual feelings, as long as it is in some sense 'good,' and is **not** done in response to an externally recorded command from God, that is obedience.

That leaves the door fairly wide open. Yet, technically it can be argued it is not antinomian. It teaches obedience to a private inspiration attributed to Christ. The problem is there is no standard to judge whether the private inspiration working within you really is from Jesus or is the product of your natural mind. As a practical matter, if your 'inspiration' is too strange, if it differs too much from the inspiration of the leadership of your church, it probably will be condemned as erroneous. Still, this provides for overturning the teachings of Jesus and the apostles as recorded in the New Testament, whenever and wherever needed.

What does Evangelical transformation of the heart really mean? In practical terms what it comes down to is natural human spirituality. If you personally feel Jesus wants you to emotionally renew your life by dumping your troublesome spouse, if your inner self says you can observe any day you wish, regardless of what God says in his recorded Word, if you feel your volunteer work at the homeless shelter fulfills the magnification of the law by demonstrating Jesus' love and after that you can do anything you want, who is to say you're wrong and that really isn't from Jesus? There is no real standard other than your personal spiritual feelings and a general sense of goodness.

Is there a concrete standard by which Christians can judge their private inspiration? Can Christians determine when the inspiration they and others feel is from Jesus and when it is merely human reason and the Hellenistic philosophy that swirls around us? The apostle John directly addresses this issue in his letters to the primitive church, where he indicates there is indeed a very tangible standard:

> Whoever says, "I have come to know him," but does not obey his commandments, is a liar, and in such a person the truth does not exist.... (1 John 2:4)

In the first century, just as today, there were antinomian Christians who claimed to have an inner experience and walk with Jesus (*to know him*) without obeying his commandments.

174

In contrast to this I see Paul preaching to the Philippians, exhorting them to *"work out your own salvation with fear and trembling"* (Phil 2:12). **Work** out you own salvation! With **fear** and **trembling**! How could Paul say that, and at the same time have intended the extreme mysticism of faith alone in the way Evangelical theologians interpret him? Why didn't Paul just warn the Philippians to stop trying so hard, lean back in grace and let it happen? Paul follows this admonition, in the very next verse, with another reference to the mystical power of God working from within:

> ...for it is God who is at work in you, **enabling** you both to will and to work for his good pleasure. (Phil 2:13)

For Paul the mystical work of the Spirit *enables* us to will and work for what God wants in us. It does not do it for us, as he also quite clearly demonstrates in verse 12, where he exhorts Christians to get serious and do their part. There is no indication here of the antinomian Evangelical teaching that obedience to God is a purely mystical, internal phenomenon that excludes biblical law, or that man plays no role in the process.

Either Paul suffers from a split personality or theologians who interpret him have been carried away with exaggeration and don't really understand what he taught. Today they are still misusing selected passages from Paul's writings to create strangely mystical, unbalanced theologies that lead to lawlessness, exactly as Peter said they were doing already in the first century (2 Peter 3:15–17).

Protestant Gnosticism

Primitive Christians are not the only ones to make a connection between modern antinomian theology and ancient Gnosticism. Some modern religious leaders and scholars, including Hellenistic Christian theologians themselves, raise a cry of warning against the survival of Gnosticism in their own churches.

One example of this is a widely distributed book, *Against the Protestant Gnostics,* first published in 1987 by Oxford University Press. The author Philip Lee is a Presbyterian minister and accomplished scholar. In his book Lee issues a plea for the Protestant movement to reject the errors of Gnosticism and return to a more traditional Christian theology and practice. Primitive Christians would not agree with all he says – for example he believes the church should accommodate practicing homosexual believers – but they would tend to find much common ground in his assessment of the survival of Gnostic error in modern Christianity.

Lee attacks problems in many branches of the Protestant movement, but some of his most severe criticism is directed at Evangelical Protestantism. As we saw earlier in this chapter, Evangelicalism today has evolved into a super-spiritualized teaching of mystical union with Christ and a private revelation from the Spirit for each individual Christian.

This affords interesting comparisons with ancient Gnosticism. The idea of hidden truth and private revelation always was a major theme in Gnostic Christianity. In reply to Evangelical perpetuation of these Gnostic themes, Lee observes:

> **Evangelicalism also requires secret gnosis** because, despite all its repetition of the Lord's name, the content of the Evangelical Christ remains undisclosed.[165]

Lee is referring to the same ideas we saw expressed above by McVey. Evangelicalism's secret *gnosis* is this same private revelation of the Spirit. It is the same secret *gnosis* which they claim replaces rather than complements New Testament scripture and the written commandments of God.

Remember also Paul's warning to the Roman church against a spiritual tradition in his day of seeking a private spiritual revelation by mystically encountering Christ in the heavens or the Deep, rather than looking to the open teaching of Jesus and the apostles in New Testament scripture as the source of divine truth. (See above, pages 25 and following, "Paul and the Mystery Cults.") In this same fashion, the ancient Gnostics also believed that by the Spirit they received the secret revelation of an advanced form of Christianity. That allowed them to disregard those portions of the Bible with which they disagreed, or interpret them allegorically to draw out whatever was needed to support their supposedly more spiritual revelation of Christianity.

Of all that Lee writes, I most treasure his definition of heresy, which so keenly goes to the heart of the matter, both for ancient Gnosticism and its latter day incarnation in Evangelicalism:

> ...heresy involves a truth being carried to an illogical or dangerous degree.[166]

---

[165] Lee, *Against the Protestant Gnostics*, p 192. Bracketed words are my explanatory comment.

Mystical identification with Christ is a true Christian teaching recorded in New Testament scripture. Paul preaches it throughout his letters. He repeatedly asks Christians to look to Christ as their inspiration and source of power to lead righteous lives. But, does that mean internal connection with Christ is the only source of spiritual guidance for Christians?

Does the mystical connection to Christ contradict and override the open teachings of Jesus and the apostles from the apostolic era, recorded for us as the New Testament? Must Christians reject biblical standards of conduct merely because they have been written on paper, just to avoid blocking the mystical work of Christ from within? Evangelicalism indeed has taken an important New Testament teaching and illogically and dangerously exaggerated it to the point of heresy.

The Fruit of Private Revelation

What happens when people decide private inspiration of the Spirit overrides the open revelation of New Testament scripture?

Extreme doctrines about private revelation more than anything else facilitated the deviations of Gnostic Christianity and the Hellenization of the church in the first centuries after Christ. And who can refute its claim? It is, after all, a *private* revelation.

Roman Catholicism believes it comes through one man, God's representative on earth, the Pope, who has God-given authority to change biblical revelation. *"I will give you the keys of the kingdom of heaven, and whatever you bind on earth will be bound in heaven"* (Matthew 16:19). Protestantism believes it comes through the entire church, as the Spirit brings converted Christians to a consensus understanding of how the scriptural revelation has been changed. *"When the spirit of truth comes, he will guide you into all the truth"* (John 16:13).

Sola scriptura was one of the great rallying cries of the Protestant Reformation. It means "scripture alone." Many mistakenly think it means Truth comes from accepting all scripture, especially the entire New Testament. That is quite mistaken. How could Truth be based on harmonizing all New Testament scripture when Reformation ministers preach the New Testament is superceded by the private revelation of a more spiritual Christianity?

---

[166] Lee, *Against the Protestant Gnostics*, p 45.

Martin Luther, the great leader of the Protestant Reformation, did *not* believe in the spiritual value of *all* New Testament scripture. Luther praised the writings of Paul and the Gospel of John. Here he found the teachings of grace on which he built the radical grace and faith alone theology that became the rallying cry of the Reformation.

The problem is that he and other reformers took it to such an extreme it contradicted other New Testament passages, especially the book of James. It is here the Apostle James warned that faith without works is not really faith. But Luther along with other Reformation theologians denied that faith without works could block salvation.

For Luther, James was a real problem. This he solved by rejecting the book of James, dismissing it as a 'letter of straw.' Luther went so far as to accuse James of proclaiming false teachings in his letter[167] and suggested it should not be used in Protestant schools.[168] Luther's ambiguity towards accepting all of New Testament scripture is widely shared among Hellenistic Christian teachers yet today.

Whether in theory or practice, *sola scriptura* means only that spiritual ideas espoused by the church should be found 'somewhere' in scripture. Truth can still change, only the church must find some allusion to, or support for those changes somewhere in the Bible.

This is a pattern typical of Gnosticism, a pattern that extends all the way back to the great pagan religious reformation in ancient Greece. Recall how so many of the early religious movements, from Orphism to Stoicism to Plato, all insisted their new Hellenistic religion was a hidden truth established by allegorical, sometimes obscure interpretation of earlier religions.

Gnosticism employed this same scheme to paint itself as a later, more advanced Hellenistic revelation of Christianity. In like fashion it sought justification for its Hellenization of Christianity through obscure and allegorical interpretation of single pieces of scripture rather than embracing the whole of God's word.

Mainstream Christianity today follows essentially the same pattern. In doing so it preserves the very error described by Paul in the first-century (Romans 10:6-8), upholding a secret, otherworldly, private revelation of Christianity instead of holding to the original, apostolic revelation of the faith in the first-century church.

---

[167] *Luther's Works*, Fortress Press, Philadelphia,1967, 4, 26.
[168] Ibid., 54,424–425.

Time after time, we find the ideas and principles of ancient Gnostic theology repeated in modern Hellenistic Christianity. Prophecies of the survival of the mystery of lawlessness indeed are amply fulfilled in our time.

We now turn to a more systematic review of the Protestant theology of salvation. Did the Reformation resurrect the balanced New Testament theology of the apostolic church? Or did they resurrect a different but equally ancient theology that also dates from the first century?

– 9 –

Reformation Theology
Part 1

(Eternal Security)

Basic Outline of Reformation Theology

How did Reformation theology come to embrace such controversial doctrines? Before proceeding further, we need to grasp the fundamentals of Reformation theology and see how it all fits together. There are only a few key ideas on which the entire structure rests. Before even that, however, we need to understand the problem Reformation leaders were trying to solve with their new theology.

The Protestant Reformation was a reaction against the abuses of medieval Roman Christianity. Beginning with St. Augustine in the late fourth century, Roman Christianity elaborated a theory of church authority that sanctioned church tradition as the revelation of God's will. Through this the Roman church introduced many new teachings that some came to regard as salvation by works.

The Roman church actually teaches that man is saved by grace. Still, salvation is viewed as a cooperative undertaking in which both God and man participate. To begin, this means that man has free will. God offers salvation to all mankind. Man has the freedom and the ability to accept or reject the offer. Primitive Christians generally would agree and find nothing wrong with that position. However, the Roman church did not stop there.

Roman theology says that salvation begins with the sacrament of baptism. Through baptism one's sins up to that point in life are forgiven. But what about sins committed after baptism? For ongoing sin, Christians are forgiven through the sacraments of confession and penance. Penance means a priest prescribes various works tailored to the specific sin involved. The purpose is to educate and correct the sinner and prevent the recurrence of sin in the future. Here one begins to encounter serious questions about salvation by works. Eventually this evolved into theories about 'merit.' The church taught that monks, nuns and priests could achieve a high degree of perfection in their lives, and the merit they earned was a sort of spiritual commodity that could be accumulated and stored by the church. This store of merit, accumulated through the works of righteous men, could then be drawn upon by the faithful in their struggle for justification and ultimate entry into heaven.

In medieval times it was also believed that the common man can accumulate merit through good works, including the contribution of money to church projects, and the merit earned from that can be used to cancel the negative effects of sin. Eventually this evolved into the practice of selling indulgences. The 'contribution,' in other words the price of the indulgence, would be set at an amount designed to earn sufficient merit to cancel the negative effect of a specific sin. Eventually the practice evolved of making such contributions in anticipation of committing that sin in the future.

How was the Reformation to deal with this? Today, many assume Luther's rallying cry, salvation by 'faith alone,' is the essence of Reformation theology. In actual fact it is much more complex – and strange. The two most fundamental doctrines of the Protestant Reformation, according to both Luther and Calvin, are the doctrines of eternal security and predestination. These two doctrines are the primary means by which the Reformation sought to combat the problem of legalism.

Eternal security, sometimes called 'once-saved always-saved,' means that once you are chosen or experience salvation, it is locked in. Once granted, salvation cannot be lost. You are "eternally secure."

Predestination means that before the world began God knew the names of all human individuals who would be born on earth, and from those he individually pre-selected everyone he wants to save. It has nothing to do with their conduct, whether good or evil. They have no choice in the matter. Those he has selected he will save, like it or not. Those not chosen eventually will be born, live and die, and spend eternity in the torments of hell. God's decision to not select them equally has nothing to do with their conduct, whether good or evil. Their fate is determined before the world began and there is nothing they can do about it.

Calvin became famous for his devotion to predestination, and so the term *Calvinism* has become almost synonymous with predestination. Many do not realize that Luther also espoused the doctrine of predestination. He wrote a treatise on predestination entitled *On the Bondage of the Human Will,* which he later claimed was his most important work. Throughout his life, however, Luther seemed much more concerned with the ideas surrounding eternal security, which has led to his name being associated more with ideas of *grace alone* and *faith alone.*

What we are talking about here are not side issues. This is the very heart and foundation of the Protestant Reformation.[169] How could that be? Wasn't the essential issue of the Reformation the relation of grace to works and fixing the legalism of medieval Roman theology? What do eternal security and predestination have to do with that?

No Free Will

Martin Luther and John Calvin did not invent the Reformation's solution to Roman legalism. Indeed, they based their solution on an ancient religious tradition borrowed from St. Augustine, from more than a thousand years before the Reformation. This religious tradition had a highly developed theology, including eternal security and predestination, that offered ready-made solutions for some of the problems confronting the Reformation.

What did that ancient religious tradition offer that made it so attractive to Luther and Calvin? As it turns out, the critical issue was whether man has, or does not have, free will. As we saw above, the Roman church's explanation of salvation is based on the idea that man has free will, and therefore man is able to cooperate with God. The legalism that came out of that, all depended on the underlying concept that salvation is a cooperative process. If man cooperates with God by choosing to be good, then in some sense being good can be viewed as a contributing factor in salvation.

---

[169] Predestination and eternal security literally were the theological foundation of the Protestant Reformation. E.g. see White, *The Potter's Freedom,* p 34 ff.

But man can participate cooperatively in salvation only if he has free will. Augustine taught that the human race lost free will when Adam sinned in the Garden of Eden. From this teaching, borrowed from Augustine, Reformation theology elaborated its radical solution to the problems of medieval Roman legalism.

If man lacks free will, then whatever he does must be the result of some other power working in him. In one bold stroke the problem is solved. Legalism is impossible. If man does anything, it is not really him doing it, so the credit goes entirely to God. There is no participation by man, and salvation cannot in any sense be regarded as tainted by human works.

Total depravity is the name the Reformation gave to the doctrine that man lacks free will. Total depravity means that man is by nature hopelessly corrupt. This is much more than saying man is incapable of pleasing God. It means man is literally incapable of any good thought or act. Therefore if salvation were offered, he would have no way to appreciate what it means and accept it. Thus the argument that man lacks free will. Being totally depraved, he is literally incapable of choosing to follow God.

But, how does the concept of no free will lead to predestination and eternal security? In fact, these two primary doctrines of the Protestant Reformation are required in order to solve complications introduced by the concept that man lacks free will.

If man is incapable of choosing God, then how can anyone be converted and start on the path of Christian salvation? Given those assumptions, the only answer that holds together philosophically is that God does the whole thing. God must choose who will be saved because man, lacking free will, is literally unable to choose to follow God. And that is how predestination came to be.

How does God choose those he will save? God cannot pick individuals on the basis of their good qualities. He can't even choose people based on foreknowledge of their future conduct. To do so might imply that a person, to whatever small degree, plays a role in his or her own selection. So, philosophically you have to assume people are chosen *arbitrarily*, all to protect the extreme Reformation position that man plays no role in salvation.

If a person has been predestined to be saved, at some point during their life God intervenes to regenerate their soul. **Regeneration** is a healing of the state of total depravity. It imparts spiritual perception, a natural desire and love for God, and the ability to choose God. This automatically leads to that person accepting God's offer of salvation and starting down the path of a Christian life.

Advocates of predestination often complain their theology is unfairly criticized and maligned. Some argue that regeneration actually imparts free will. Therefore God really does not forcibly impose himself on anyone. However, the fact remains that when people are regenerated they *always* turn to God and become Christians. There is no other possible outcome. True, it is not imposed violently. Yet God acts without consent. (Since man is totally depraved and without free will, it is impossible for man to give consent.) Once predestined and regenerated, you are facing an offer you literally can't refuse.

This leads to another vital principle of Reformation theology. God's will is **sovereign** and **irresistible.** Very simply, that means nothing can thwart God's will. After regeneration there is nothing man can do to change his fate. If God chooses you to be saved, you will be saved, like it or not. Equally, there is nothing you can do if you are one of the unfortunate not selected for salvation. No matter how good or bad, you will be tortured in hell for all eternity.

In today's world where individualism and free choice are so highly prized, predestination has gained a rather negative reputation. Use of the word *irresistible* often is replaced by terms such as 'effectual,' as in effectual grace and effectual salvation. This is done to soften and hide the true implications of predestination theology. But the meaning remains the same.

How does eternal security fit into this picture? Predestination always includes eternal security. If God arbitrarily selects and forcibly regenerates you, his irresistible power also forcibly preserves you as a Christian until you die. Therefore those predestined to be saved automatically are eternally secure as well.

This is **traditional predestination theology**, the prevalent teaching at the time of the Reformation in the 16th century and continuing for several centuries after that.

Extreme Eternal Security

By the beginning of the 1900s, it was assumed the radical ideas on which the Protestant Reformation was founded were on their way out. In fact, predestination theology has declined markedly in popularity, though it still enjoys a huge following.

Today, predestination is the official doctrine of a number of major Protestant denominations with members numbering in the millions. The Presbyterian Church, counting some three million members, mostly in the United States, is one. Another is the Reformed Church, a mostly European Protestant denomination. A substantial portion of Baptists also officially espouse some form of predestination.

Despite the decline in traditional predestination belief, however, Reformation theology has made a remarkable comeback since the early 1900s. The movement that rejuvenated Reformation theology and adapted it to modern culture is American Evangelicalism. Their specific brand of theology encompasses what is called **extreme eternal security.**[170] What much of Evangelicalism did was to eliminate or mute the doctrine of predestination, the most objectionable aspect of Reformation theology in today's world.

That however led to serious problems. The mechanism by which man is prevented from playing any role in salvation is God's sovereign will and the irresistibility by which God arbitrarily selects people and imposes himself on them. In predestination theory, faith, belief in Jesus, and good works all are the irresistible effects of regeneration. They always happen because God forcibly imposes those qualities through regeneration. Though good works are a necessary part of salvation, this is not salvation by works. Everything is credited to the irresistible effect of God's will, nothing to man, and the philosophic purity of the idea that man plays no role in salvation is preserved. Take away predestination and you have to find some other way to explain why Christians must be good but get no credit for it.

On the other hand, you could argue that technically it doesn't matter if you are good. And that is how they solved the problem of maintaining that man plays no role in salvation, even after predestination was removed. In effect they took Luther's famous statement that you can murder and commit fornication a thousand times a day and still be saved, at face value. You should be good, they reasoned, but you have the option to indulge literally in any sin however evil, to whatever outrageous degree, and still be saved. Therefore it is all right to encourage and even demand

---

[170] Extreme eternal security is a subset of Dispensational Theology, which is covered in detail *in Spirit of Antichrist*, volume two of our series, The World of Primitive Christianity.

that people be good. But since Christians under this theology are licensed to participate in unlimited sin, technically there is no way that could be considered a *requirement* of salvation.

Under extreme eternal security, man now has free will to accept or reject God's offer of salvation. However, once one accepts the offer, salvation still becomes locked in, just as with predestination. The only difference is the point at which this occurs – at conversion rather than, for predestination, from before the world began. Faith and belief usually are required, but only for the initial moment of conversion. After that, when salvation is locked in, Christians can immerse themselves in the worst evil, deny God, curse his name and never return to the faith. They can murder, rape and pillage, and never repent, but they will be saved, irresistibly, like it or not.

Once again, it should be made clear this does not mean Protestantism officially promotes sin. Reformation churches universally urge their members to follow some standard of righteousness. Reformation theologians sometimes talk about the church's mission to bring about repentance among those of their members who are already saved but have never repented. Nevertheless, their theology requires that Christians technically possess an unlimited license to sin, all because of their philosophically strict interpretation of man playing no role in salvation.

Belief and faith is required for the initial experience of salvation. Repentance, however, may or may not accompany that faith. If repentance does occur it can lapse at any time and may never be renewed. But that has no effect on salvation. Repentance implies obedience and good works. Therefore it too must be entirely optional in order to preserve the philosophic integrity of man playing no role in salvation.

There is a third modern tradition worth mentioning. That is **lordship salvation.** This is a latter day reaction against the excesses of extreme eternal security. Lordship salvation insists that repentance and good works are required for salvation. But it is not what most people think. In fact, as we will see, lordship salvation actually is nothing more than a recycled form of predestination in which God forcibly imposes repentance and good works on those he arbitrarily chooses to save.

So we have the following key ideas and movements involved in Reformation theology:

- Total depravity (no free will)
- God's will – sovereign and irresistible
- Regeneration (the healing of total depravity)

- Predestination
- Traditional eternal security – with predestination
- Extreme eternal security – without predestination
- Lordship salvation

The underlying principle of all Reformation theology, however, is the one most critical point by which they neutralize Roman legalism. Salvation at some point becomes locked in, eternally secure. This occurs either before you were born or at the point you accept the offer of salvation. Either you have no free will and therefore get no credit for being good, or it doesn't matter if you are good and so no credit is granted for being good, as far as salvation is concerned. Either way, if there is absolute and total separation between human conduct and salvation, then it is both true that it can't be lost, and there is no danger you could be considered to have earned it.

Literally NO Role in Salvation

The following is a statement by R. C. Sproul, a nationally famous American predestination theologian. Here he talks about regeneration and how man plays absolutely no role in the process:

> Since the grace of regeneration...requires no cooperation from us, its efficacy lies in itself and not in us. We can do nothing to make it effective; we can do nothing to make it ineffective. We are passive with respect to our own regeneration.[171]

Whether espousing predestination or extreme eternal security, Reformation theology always comes back to the concept of man playing literally NO role in salvation. That is not a relative term. 'No' means nothing in the most complete sense. This is such a sacred element of Reformation theology it will be protected by going to any extreme, even to the point of reasoning that the saved are licensed to get away with all the sins for which the unsaved are sent to hell. As extreme as that sounds, it is literally true.

---

[171] R.C. Sproul, *Grace Unknown*, (Grand Rapids, Baker Books, 1997) p 184, quoted by Vance, *The Other Side of Calvinism*, p 523.

We see this idea perpetuated plainly by modern Reformation theologians. The following authors express the extreme view espoused by most Reformation theologians:

John Ankerberg and John Weldon, criticizing those who believe in a co-operative role for man:

> God may even do 95 percent, but unless that 5 percent is there, [they say,] even the 95 percent is useless. But again, doesn't that take us back to the false beliefs of...other religions that, although they claim salvation is by grace, also stress the necessity of individual performance for achieving salvation?[172]

In Reformation theology it is all or nothing. In that vein, the following nationally famous American Evangelical preacher reiterates how eternal security is necessary, without which their concept of salvation by faith is lost:

Charles Stanley:

> If salvation is not forever [eternally guaranteed], salvation cannot be through faith alone.[173]

In these quotations we see clearly the philosophic element at work. Introducing the smallest amount of human participation is assumed to be a violation of the philosophic principle of grace and faith alone. Only when salvation is transformed into an irreversible guarantee do these theologians feel they have protected the purity of the concept.

Primitive Christians generally insist such issues be settled by scriptural revelation and the harmonizing of all scripture, rather than philosophic reasoning based on a limited selection of scripture. Primitive Christians immediately point to the book of James where the apostle says *"faith apart from works is barren"* and therefore *"a person is justified by works and **not** by faith alone"* (James 2:20,24). These are the passages that led Luther to condemn James for teaching heresy and to try to ban this New Testament book from Protestant schools.

Luther's treatment of James reflects the style of biblical interpretation characteristic of Gnostic Christianity. Gnostic theologians traditionally viewed scripture, especially Jesus' earthly ministry, as defective and

---

[172] Ankerberg and Weldon, *Knowing the Truth about Eternal Security,* p 8.
[173] Stanley, *Eternal Security,* p 16.

therefore suspect. Truth could be found in scripture, but only by selectively assembling limited portions of scripture and manipulating them by human reason to bend them to coincide with Hellenistic beliefs. Remember from an earlier discussion the limitations of the Reformation concept of *sola scriptura*. Religious truth generally must be found somewhere in the Bible, but not necessarily be a distillation of all scripture.

In that light, consider the following admission of the existence of "problem passages" in the effort to biblically justify eternal security:

> Many others do not believe the doctrine [of eternal security] because of the existence of problem passages. But biblically, this is easily resolved, because only one teaching can be true. Either Christians can lose their salvation or they cannot. ... If one teaching can be proven, then any Scripture that would seem to deny that position must be interpreted in light of the truth that is already established.[174]

What that means, in effect, is as follows: If a number of scriptures can be interpreted to support eternal security, then eternal security can be declared a proven doctrine. Therefore the entire list of scriptures that appear to contradict eternal security can be dismissed. In effect, advocates of eternal security begin with the assumption their doctrine is present in scripture and therefore is true. Scriptures to the contrary must then be bent forcibly to make them agree. And there is nothing wrong with that, they insist, because it already has been established that eternal security is true. The result of that approach can be quite unusual, as we shall see.

While that may seem a harsh assessment of those who teach eternal security, I invite you, the reader, to judge for yourself in what follows.

The Scriptural Battle over Eternal Security

A full account of the scriptural wars surrounding the doctrine of eternal security would fill multiple volumes by itself. Here we must confine ourselves to a limited selection that samples the style and approach used by both sides.

---

[174] Ankerberg and Weldon, *Knowing the Truth about Eternal Security,* p 10.

One of the classic arguments involves the significance of the word "gift." In Ephesians 2:8, Paul writes, *"For by grace you have been saved through faith, and this is not your own doing; it is the gift of God...."*

Charles Stanley, among others, makes a special point of this verse, insisting that *"To place conditions on the permanency of our salvation is to say it is not a gift."*[175] If you analyze the technical meaning of the word "gift," according to Stanley, you will realize it means a recipient of a gift becomes its new owner, and therefore it cannot be taken back. Since it is yours you can misuse it, abuse it, trash it, anything you want, but by the philosophical definition of the word *gift* it is still yours. Stanley explains:

> What we do with the gift is another matter entirely. The fact that I don't take advantage of a gift says nothing about who it belongs to. It still belongs to me. You can take a gift and bury it in the backyard, but it still is yours. Once you accept a gift, you are stuck with it, like it or not![176]

On the other hand, we have many opposing scriptures, including for example, the two cases in the book of Matthew where the unprofitable servant and the unprepared guest at the wedding of Christ are cast into *"outer darkness, where there will be weeping and gnashing of teeth."*[177] The phrase "weeping and gnashing of teeth" is used frequently by Matthew. It is the same phrase found in Matthew 13:42 where it clearly is talking about the final judgment, *"...and they will throw them into the furnace of fire, where there will be weeping and gnashing of teeth."*

Both parables seem to refer to unproductive Christians being cast into hell. Not so, say the advocates of eternal security. "Outer darkness" is not a place, i.e. it is not hell. Instead, they say, it is a state of lesser reward in heaven, outside the inner circle where the saints enjoy direct contact with Jesus. In fact, Stanley exhorts, we must read the text surrounding Matthew 22:13 much more literally. Technically, he says, the unprepared guest is only cast out of the building where the wedding takes place, so this has nothing to do with losing salvation. The term 'outer darkness,' he says, is explained by the fact this happened at night and it was dark outside where he was thrown.[178] The weeping and gnashing of teeth is not literally pain as one might experience in hell, Stanley adds, but merely an

---

[175]   Stanley, *Eternal Salvation,* p 121.
[176]   Ibid.
[177]   Matthew 22:13, see also 25:30 .
[178]   Stanley, *Eternal Security,* p 191,194.

outburst of frustration caused by the servant's realization his conduct has cost him a substantial part of his reward. This will soon pass and turn to joy as even the unprofitable servant enters the glorious kingdom of God.[179]

However, we find numerous New Testament passages that refer to Christians being rejected for various serious problems. Paul witnesses that even an apostle can fail if he does not exercise control of his material lusts:

> But I discipline my body, and bring it into subjection, lest, when
> I have preached to others, I myself should become disqualified.
> (1 Cor 9:27, NKJV)

The real question here is whether a semantic, philosophic argument over the meaning of the word gift overrides the plain teaching and harmonizing of all scripture. Do we assume the word gift means salvation cannot be taken back because of the technical implications of that single word, and then bend other starkly plain scriptures from the Apostle Paul to accommodate that?

Does use of the term gift in relation to salvation really imply what they claim it does? Have you ever heard of a gift being taken back by the giver, or returned by the recipient? Politicians regularly return contributions when caught taking them from questionable sources. I know of parents who have retrieved gifts from children because they were caught misusing them. Is it reasonable to create dogmatic truth on the basis of such a shaky argument?

Gnosticism and the Gift Argument

Gnosticism was the first major Christian movement to teach that salvation, once granted, cannot be lost regardless of one's conduct. In the early centuries A.D., Valentinian Gnostics promoted the same argument that if we receive salvation and the Spirit as a gift then it cannot be taken back. In the Gnostic text *Gospel of Philip* we read:

---

[179] Ibid. p 190–195.

> But if he receive the holy spirit, he has the name as a gift. He who has received a gift does not have to give it back....[180]

"He who has received a gift does not have to give it back," sounds almost like a quote from some modern Reformation theologians.

Scriptures Cited to Support Eternal Security

Here are additional scriptures cited in favor of eternal security:

Ephesians 1:13

> ... marked with the **seal** of the promised Holy Spirit; this is the pledge of our inheritance

Use of the term 'seal' implies protection and guarantee. Based on this one verse, some assume salvation is irreversibly guaranteed. But does this necessarily mean the guarantee is irreversible and cannot be voided? Like the term gift, above, this is a philosophic argument based on the technical definition and implications of a single word. If there are other scriptures that pointedly say salvation can be lost, should they all be harmonized together in order to arrive at truth?

John 10:28

> I give them eternal life, and they will never perish. No one will snatch them out of my hand.

Is this an irreversible promise that Christians can never lose salvation – *"No one will snatch them out of my hand"* ?

Opponents of eternal security point to the preceding verse (vs 27) where it explains to whom Jesus directed these words: *"My sheep hear my voice. I know them, and they follow me."* If we turn a deaf ear to Jesus' voice and do not follow him, does the promise of verse 28 still apply to us?

This is part of the true promise of Christian security, that no one can forcibly snatch his followers out of his hand. But does that mean Jesus' followers cannot themselves make the choice to turn away, or stumble and drift away?

---

[180] **NHLE**, 148, *Gospel of Philip.*

Romans 8:1

> There is therefore now no condemnation for those who are in Christ Jesus.

This passage is addressed to those who are *"in Christ,"* and explains Jesus' attitude of forgiveness to his followers. As always, the question is whether a person who turns away from God is still "in Christ Jesus." Can a person, voluntarily or by willful or egregious sinfulness, exit the state of being in Christ Jesus?

Hebrews 10:14

> For by a single offering he has perfected **for all time** those who are sanctified.

Here the atoning grace of Christ's sacrifice is described as applying to Christians *"for all time."* For some advocates of eternal security, to believe salvation can be lost is a violation of this truth that Christ perfected his followers "for all time."

Opponents of eternal security point out that the context of this statement is the contrast between Old Testament animal sacrifices, which had to be repeated constantly, and Jesus' sacrifice, which occurred once "for all time." Therefore this is merely a statement about the scope of Christ's sacrifice and the fact it does not have to be continually repeated.

1 Corinthians 3:13–15

> ...and the fire will test what sort of work each has done. If what has been built on the foundation survives, the builder [Christian] will receive a reward. If the work is burned up, the builder will suffer loss; **the builder will be saved, but only as through fire.**

This is part of the genuine New Testament teaching about rewards. It describes Christians who have produced so poorly they will lose much or all of their reward, but still be saved.

Advocates of eternal security say this applies to any degree of sinfulness. In other words it indicates that all Christians will be saved, and the only thing that can be lost is one's reward. But, does this passage by itself exclude the idea that a Christian can do even worse, in fact so badly it leads to not being saved at all?

Scriptures Cited to Refute Eternal Security

The book of Hebrews is a special problem for advocates of eternal security. Here we find several major passages that appear to contradict this teaching:

Hebrews 6:4–5

> For it is impossible to restore again to repentance those who have once been enlightened...and then have fallen away....

This seems to say that those who have 'fallen away' are truly lost. Advocates of eternal security sometimes get around this by saying it refers only to persons who were not truly converted. However, it clearly is talking about those who had "once been enlightened."

Stanley agrees this passage refers to converted Christians. However, he points out, it only says they cannot be restored to repentance. And that, he says, has nothing to do with salvation.[181] Remember that many advocates of eternal security believe repentance is desirable but entirely optional.

Therefore, they say, the fact that some Christians cannot be restored to repentance has nothing to do with salvation.

Hebrews 10:26–31

> For if we willfully persist in sin after having received the knowledge of the truth, there no longer remains a sacrifice for sins, but a fearful prospect of judgment, and a fury of fire that will consume the adversaries.

This appears to say that willfully sinful, unrepentant Christians are truly condemned to hell fire.

Stanley, however, says this too has nothing to do with salvation. The phrase *"no longer remains a sacrifice for sins,"* he says, refers only to Old Testament sacrifices, not Christ's sacrifice. And the reference to judgment by fire (*a fury of fire*) does not refer to the fire of hell, he explains, but to the judgment in which Christians lose only their rewards. What the whole passage really means, he explains, is that Christians can

---

[181]   Stanley, *Eternal Security,* p 247 ff.

no longer avoid losing their reward by performing Old Testament sacrifices.[182]

However, the fire in this passage is said to consume people (*the adversaries*) not just their works. Stanley's interpretation is not consistent with the subject and context of the passage.

Romans 8:12–13   (See also **Revelation 21:8,**
Galatians 5:19–21,
James 1:14–15, Ephesians 5:5–7)

So then, brothers and sisters, we are debtors, not to the flesh, to live according to the flesh – for **if you live according to the flesh, you will die;** but if by the Spirit you put to death the deeds of the body, you will live.

There are numerous New Testament passages such as these that warn of the fatal consequences of willful sin. Some are phrased more generally and are open to the interpretation they refer only to the unconverted. But some, such as this passage from Romans, clearly refer directly to Christians whom Paul addresses here as *"brothers and sisters."*

Some advocates of eternal security claim the reference to dying in this passage only means physical, not spiritual death.[183] In other words, God may punish you by physically killing you, but still save you.

Some Hellenistic Christians themselves criticize this interpretation. They note that for them, death means immediate ascent to heaven to be with Jesus. Punishing willfully evil Christians by killing them doesn't seem like a very serious punishment if they ascend immediately to be joyfully united with the savior.

Matthew 10:22

...and you will be hated by all because of my name. But the one who endures to the end will be saved.

This and numerous other passages in the New Testament refer to 'enduring to the end' in the sense of a requirement or mark of those who will be saved. By contrast, advocates of extreme eternal security emphatically teach that salvation is a momentary event and there is no requirement to continue in faithfulness after that point.

---

[182] Ibid. p 260ff.

[183] Corner, *The Believer's Conditional Security*, p 134 ff.

As Charles Stanley explains, *"God the Father and God the Son have you in...their hand. And my friend, whether you let go or not hasn't got anything to do with it* [salvation]. **The Bible nowhere says, 'Hold on'.** *"* [184]

Look up the word endure, endures, etc. and see how many times this idea is "nowhere" espoused in New Testament scripture. Or, if one insists on a more exact terminology, look up the term 'hold fast,' such as in 1 Corinthians 15:2,

> By which also you are **saved, if** you **hold fast** that word which I preached to you; unless you believed in vain." (NKJV)

Galatians 5:21, after a long list of specific, seriously sinful acts, Paul says:

> ...and things like these. I am warning you, as I warned you before: those who do such things will **not inherit the kingdom** of God.

"Inherit the kingdom" is a term frequently used in the New Testament in reference to salvation. Advocates of eternal security, however, deny this passage is talking about losing salvation.

The way around this and similar verses is to argue that there are two classes of people entering the kingdom. Those who remain faithful enter the kingdom as inheriting sons, possessing it as owners. Unfaithful Christians still will be saved, they say, but when they enter the kingdom they do not possess it as 'an inheritance.' [185] Exactly what that means is somewhat vague, but it seems perhaps like the difference between inheriting your own mansion in heaven versus entering heaven but being stuck in a rented condo. In effect, they turn this verse into a reference to punishing Christians by downgrading their reward in heaven.

---

[184] Charles Stanley (Atlanta, GA: In Touch Ministries, 1990), *Eternal Security: You Can Be Sure!,* audiotape #3, MH190, quoted in Corner, *The Believer's Conditional Security,* p 172.

[185] See discussion in Corner, *The Believer's Conditional Security,* p 519ff, involving this interpretation of Galatians 5:21 by Hodges, Evans and Kendall.

Conclusions and Overview

The pattern I see developing from the lists of scriptures quoted by advocates and opponents of eternal security is as follows:

On the one hand we have numerous scriptures that contradict eternal security. These scriptures contain substantive terminology and specific references indicating that man can walk away from or lose salvation. These generally indicate that loss of salvation may be caused by a pattern of willful sin or neglect over time, or because of knowing and willful rejection of Jesus and his offer of salvation.

On the other hand are the numerous scriptures used to support eternal security. These contain substantive arguments that God is faithful and guarantees his promises for those who are faithful to him.

Do these two sets of scriptures contradict or complement each other? Indeed, are there any 'problem' scriptures on this subject at all? I submit that these scriptures are entirely compatible exactly as is.

The scriptures cited in favor of eternal security outline the true doctrine of Christian security. God is faithful and we can trust his promises and should have no fear that anyone can forcibly snatch us out of his hand. There is nothing substantive in these texts, however, on which to base the radical interpretation that salvation is irreversible and we are saved regardless of anything we do.

Those who advocate eternal security appear to be doing exactly what Ankerberg and Weldon advocate, as we saw earlier in this chapter (see above, page 189.) They assume scripture contradicts itself, so we must make a choice to accept eternal security, and then forcibly reinterpret the supposedly 'contradictory' passages to make them agree with that truth. The scriptural evidence, however, argues forcefully for the opposite approach.

The contradictory scriptures are contradictory only if you begin with the *assumption* that eternal security is true. Once we quit trying to force eternal security on the New Testament there no longer are any contradictions. There are passages that clearly and pointedly reject eternal security, and there are other passages – the ones used to support eternal security – which really only support Christian security. They contain nothing requiring the extreme interpretation involved in eternal security.

Two-Track Salvation

In one of the greatest contradictions of eternal security theology, many Reformation theologians argue that you can be saved without experiencing fellowship with Christ. According to this line of reasoning, the only result of even the most horrific, unrepentant sin is loss of fellowship with Christ and the Father.[186] Thereby, many biblical passages that talk about losing salvation are reinterpreted to refer only to losing fellowship with Christ.

Some believe this means disobedient Christians will be punished by being excluded from the inner circle of the saints in heaven. In other words, there are two paths of salvation and reward. Those who persevere in the faith will be with Jesus and enjoy personal fellowship with him in heaven. Those who turn away from the faith or who never repent and develop Christ-like qualities in the first place, will be saved but will never enjoy the direct presence of Christ. For example, biblical passages such as Revelation 3:21, which promises the saints will reign with Christ, sometimes are interpreted as a promise of personal contact with Christ reserved exclusively for only those who remain faithful.[187]

Some Gnostic Christians similarly split salvation into two tracks, reserving a better reward for more spiritual Christians. For example, Valentinian Gnostics believed that the saved are split between two such groups (see above, pages 52 and following). Valentinians fancied themselves as the *pneumatics*, the more spiritual group that are able to rise above material sin more effectively. At death, they believed, they ascend to the eighth level of the heavens, and ultimately at the end of time they participate in the marriage supper of the lamb and finally ascend with Christ into the *pleroma*, the highest heaven where they directly experience the presence of the heavenly Father.

The inferior group of Christians are the *psychics*. These are Primitive Christians whom they regarded as spiritually weak and more prone to sin. Because of that weakness they need the help of rules and regulations to be saved. When they die, they ascend only to the seventh heaven, where they spend eternity with the creator God, Yahweh. Given the Gnostic attitude towards Yahweh, this was a decidedly inferior state, yet on the other hand

---

[186] See Corner, *The Believer's Conditional Security,* p 126–127.

[187] Ibid. p 140.

better than what awaits the unsaved. Because of their inferior spirituality and failure to fully free themselves from the material world, they will never directly experience the presence of Christ and the heavenly Father.

Once again we see Gnostic spirituality and doctrine mirrored in Reformation Christianity.

The New Legalism

The Protestant Reformation started as a movement to resolve problems of legalism in medieval Christianity. Its ministers continually harp on this subject. To be sure, it is a valid issue, addressed prominently in scripture.

There is, however, a truly strange phenomenon in Reformation theology today in regards to legalism. On the one hand you find an overwhelmingly biased and exaggerated concept of Old Testament legalism, to the point that some claim it is evil to even look at the law as a guide to God's will. On the other hand, however, legalism is held up as the very foundation of the doctrine of eternal security.

Reformation theology is legalistic? Surely that cannot be! Yet it is. Consider the teaching of its own theologians.

One of the most common arguments of those who espouse extreme eternal security is that Jesus' sacrifice for sin provides *forensic* justification. The term *forensic* means 'judicial' or 'legal.' What that means is that when God forgives you, he legally wipes the slate clean. That is a true doctrine taken directly from New Testament scripture. But how it is applied in Reformation theology is truly fascinating.

Consider the teaching of the nationally famous American theologian Charles Stanley. Here Stanley illustrates the idea of eternal security by comparing it to the legal concept of a marriage contract:

> A man and woman are married by entering into a legal contract. Obtaining a divorce is a legal matter as well. Whether they ever act married or not is irrelevant. ...
>
> In the same way, we don't become saved by acting saved. Neither do we become unsaved by acting unsaved. Salvation, as we have seen, occurs at a moment in time.... At that point in time God declares us "not guilty."
>
> Just as there are married people who act as if they are not [married], so there are Christians who show no evidence of their

Christianity as well. But that does not change their eternal status....[188]

Stanley's argument is that salvation is a 'legal' issue. If we are justified 'legally,' then our salvation can only be viewed from a legal point of view. And, specifically, he is arguing that is why our conduct has no effect on salvation.

It is like two prisoners standing before a judge. Both have been found guilty of murder. The judge lectures on the horrifying evil of murder and sentences the first man to eternal torture in hell. The judge begins to lecture the second man. But this one has a lawyer who raises an objection on technical grounds. This man, the lawyer points out, came forward in church at the age of six and gave his heart to the Lord. He never actually repented, and since then has wallowed wantonly in sin. He is now a serial rapist and murderer. He stands here smirking and still has not repented. But the law is the law – this man is under 'forensic' justification.

"Oh," says the judge, "in that case I can't touch you. Enter into the eternal bliss of heaven."

Here is what I find so strange. The argument constantly raised against the concept of law is that it leads to legalistic attitudes in which there is no real change of the inner man. That is an entirely valid issue. People of all kinds comply technically with the external requirements of both religious and secular law, while inside they are full of lust, hatred, and every imaginable evil. The New Covenant addresses this issue. In his prophecy of the coming New Covenant, Jeremiah foretold that God would *"put my law within them, and I will write it on their hearts"* (Jeremiah 31:33).

But then a large part of the Reformation movement reinvents their own theology of salvation as a legal technicality. If you have professed belief in Jesus at one brief moment in time, then you are irreversibly saved and it doesn't matter if you ever repent. It doesn't matter if there is any change in the inner man. If you teach that salvation is a technical legal issue and has nothing to do with the inner man, is that not legalism of the same order?

How can anyone trash Hebrew religion as legalistic and superficial, and in the same breath say that Christians are licensed to get away with literally unlimited sin and never repent? Is it just me? Am I missing something? Or is the issue of legalism truly one of the most irrational contradictions of Reformation theology?

---

[188] Stanley, *Eternal Security,* p 104–105. Bracketed words added for clarity.

In the space of just a few hundred years, what started as an attempt to resolve the problem of legalism in the medieval Roman church has come full circle. The medieval Roman church said it possessed the legal authority to do anything it pleased, and to a large extent it did just that, despite its sometimes very spiritual teachings. Today, Reformation theologians likewise say individual Christians possess the same option, to do literally anything they please, despite genuinely spiritual teachings and urging that it is better to be good.

The original intent of Roman Christianity was that Christians be transformed in the inner man. Penance, for example, was intended to educate and reform so that Christians would cease from sin. Likewise the Reformation originally was devised as a means to return Christianity to a genuine inner religious experience.

The medieval church eventually came to believe that technical performance of its rituals and contributions to the church would bring salvation, regardless of your inner spiritual state. Likewise today, Reformation theologians say you will be saved automatically by a momentary past expression of faith in Jesus, regardless of your inner spiritual state.

How tragic that within just a few centuries the Reformation has evolved into the same legalistic error it was intended to correct.

– 10 –

Reformation Theology Part 2

(Predestination)

Predestination is another Reformation doctrine first taught by Gnostic Christianity. Predestination emphasizes God's "sovereign will." That is the term used to represent the idea that God's rule is absolute. It is a cardinal principle of Reformation theology that God's will cannot be compromised by human will. If God wants something to happen, then it *will* happen.

God never allows man's will to override his own. And therein lies the problem. If man has the option to accept or reject God's offer of salvation, philosophically that gives man the power to thwart God's will. In Reformation theology that is unthinkable. If God predestines a person for salvation, then he will be saved, like it or not. Likewise if God chooses not to save someone, his destiny was sealed before the world began and there is no hope. The point is that God is in charge and his will is irresistible and absolute.

That is one mechanism by which Reformation theology justifies its radical solution to the legalism of the medieval Roman church. If God's will cannot be thwarted, then man has no choice. If man has no choice then nothing he does could possibly affect his salvation. Therefore man does not cooperatively participate in salvation as taught by the Roman church. Therefore man truly cannot be saved by works; it is logically impossible.

Irresistible (Forcible) Grace, Pro and Con

On the surface, predestination theology is more compatible with Primitive Christianity. It accepts repentance, faith and works as 'requirements' or 'necessary' elements of salvation. But it is important to understand how faith and works come to be.

If you have been predestined to be saved, at some point in your life God applies his grace to you. You don't ask for it. You are not even able to understand that you need it. But when that grace is applied, it irresistibly "regenerates" your soul. It is a sort of spiritual awakening of the soul that leads to conversion.

God's intervention continues on past conversion. Regeneration irresistibly produces faith, repentance and good works, and these appear immediately upon conversion. For example, R.C. Sproul, a nationally famous American radio minister and predestination theologian, writes, *"Those who possess saving faith necessarily, inevitably, and immediately begin to manifest the fruits of faith, which are works of obedience."*[189] Indeed, Sproul condemns as "antinomian" those who believe that God saves people who show no change in their conduct.[190] That is very attractive to Primitive Christians, who often do not realize it comes from predestination theology, which claims Christians are forcibly imbued with those qualities without any participation on their part.

Predestination believers are not troubled by requiring some degree of good works. If God imposes everything forcibly, then it's not really you doing it, so it still is not salvation by (your) works.

Forcible grace, however, brings up a pertinent comparison with the gift argument mentioned in the previous chapter. It is as though a stranger walks up to you on the street and thrusts a package in your arms. "This is a gift," he announces, "but don't try to give it back, or I'll shove it down your throat." Is that really a gift?

Here is what one modern critic of predestination says:

> Salvation is God's gift, God's free gift. ...But by its very nature a gift has to be received or rejected. There is no such thing as an irresistible gift.[191]

---

[189] Sproul, *Faith Alone,* p 103.
[190] Ibid. p 111.
[191] Vance, *The Other Side of Calvinism,* 516–517.

Total Depravity

At the beginning and very foundation of predestination theology is the idea that man is totally depraved. This is understood in the truly radical sense that man is helplessly evil, literally unable to do anything good, unable to love God, and therefore (here is the key point) totally unable to respond to God. God cannot offer salvation to man and let him choose. Not only would that imply salvation depends on a man's good conduct by virtue of his accepting God's gift, but in fact man is so totally depraved he is literally incapable of choosing to follow God. This is developed from a number of biblical passages, such as the following:

> You were **dead** through the trespasses and sins in which you once lived.... But God, who is rich in mercy, out of the great love with which he loved us even when we were **dead** through our trespasses, **made us alive** together with Christ. (Eph 2:1–2,4–5)

> For this reason the mind that is set on the flesh **is hostile** to God; **it does not submit** to God's law – **indeed it cannot** (Romans 8:7)

The question, of course, is what "dead" and "hostile to God" really mean. Once again we fall into the pit of philosophical speculation. For traditional predestination theologians it means total depravity. For others, it means nothing of the sort. Consider the sharp contrast of the following two views:

The traditional predestination view, by William Ames:

> ...God determines to save whomever He wishes regardless of whether they choose to believe or not. In fact, God gives the faith to believe to whomever He wills. Without this God-given faith they could not and would not believe. In fact, fallen human beings are so dead in sin that God must first regenerate them before they can even believe. Dead men do not believe anything; they are dead![192]

Once again we get into philosophical arguments about the meaning of a single word, in this case the word *dead*, arbitrarily fixing the meaning so as to dictate an entire theology.

---

[192] Geisler, *Chosen But Free,* p 47, a summation of the view proposed by William Ames, a traditional predestination theologian.

A more moderate view, by Normal Geisler:

> This extreme Calvinistic interpretation of what is meant by spiritual "death" is questionable. First of all, spiritual "death" in the Bible is a strong expression meaning that fallen beings are totally separated from God, not completely obliterated by Him. As Isaiah put it, "your iniquities have *separated* you from your God" (Isaiah 59:2). In brief, it does not mean a total destruction of all ability to hear and respond to God, but a complete separation of the whole person from God.[193]

The radical doctrine of total depravity is a key part of the foundation of predestination theology. It is because man cannot choose for himself that we must believe that God arbitrarily chooses who is saved and who is lost. Yet, by contrast the Apostle Paul witnesses that the natural mind *is* capable of perceiving spiritual issues. Recall our discussion of natural human spirituality from an earlier chapter (see above, pages 121 and following). According to Paul:

> When Gentiles who do not possess the law do <u>instinctively</u> what the law requires...[they] are a law to themselves. ...what the law requires is written on their hearts, to which their own conscience also bears witness; (Romans 2:14–15)

The doctrine of total depravity is analogous to the ancient Gnostic Christian teaching of the hopeless and helpless state of the soul in its fallen state. Gnostics generally believed that when spirit fell into matter and became captivated by material lust, they entered a state of total ignorance, totally separated from the heavens from which they had fallen. The soul is in a state of death, unable to do anything to extricate itself from its predicament. Salvation comes from the Savior who descends to impart *gnosis* (knowledge) of the heavens. That knowledge regenerates and heals the soul, magically reestablishing the mystical connection between man and the heavens.

This, in part, is the reason Gnostic and Hellenistic Christianity deemed it so important to introduce the pagan Hellenistic symbolism of the Eighth Day so as to point exclusively to the heavens. Reestablishing the connection between the soul and the heavens was, for Gnosticism, the equivalent of regeneration in Reformation theology.

---

[193] Geisler, *Chosen But Free,* p 57.

For Gnosticism, the real issue was not sin and forgiveness, but regeneration through connection to the heavenly Father and the spiritual power of the heavens. We will meet this important distinction again later in this and following chapters.

Is Salvation by Predestination Really Forcible?

Those who oppose predestination often describe it in very harsh terms. From one point of view it appears genuinely frightening and immoral. Predestination theologians, however, vigorously complain that their teaching is misrepresented and slandered. This is particularly the case in regard to the idea of forcible salvation. Indeed, many claim that predestination is compatible with free will.

Here we get into a philosophical argument about how God chooses who is to be regenerated. Is God cold and heartless, arbitrarily picking some to be regenerated and some to be condemned to eternal hellfire, even before they are born? To get around this, some predestination teachers bring in the concept of "foreknowledge." If God is all-knowing, some theologians reason, then he must know everything that will happen in the future. Therefore, he knows who eventually will accept him as savior and who will not. To say that God does not know everything that will happen in the future, they say, is to reject God's unlimited power and sovereignty.[194]

So, if God knows everything, what predestination really means is that God selects those whom he already foreknows will accept him as savior at some point in their lives, and he rejects those whom he foreknows will reject him. Therefore God really is not forcibly converting anyone, nor unjustly condemning the innocent. He is just aligning his will with what he already knows is going to happen.

There are additional philosophical problems embedded in that argument, however. For example, if God must align his will with some reality outside himself, is he still actually sovereign? On the other hand, is it philosophically accurate that God could literally know every detail of every event in the future without that compromising free will? In other

---

[194] For example, see White, *The Potter's Freedom,* p 53ff, and Geisler, *Chosen But Free,* p 52 ff.

words, if what is going to happen is already known, hasn't it become in some sense fixed before it happens?[195]

Could God voluntarily grant free will to man by intentionally putting some future events outside his knowledge? If God gives you and me free will to accept or reject him, then in doing so doesn't that make our future decision unknowable before it happens?

Some protest that putting anything outside God's knowledge is both irrational and a blasphemous denial of God's sovereign power. Yet, how would they answer the question, Can God the Father kill himself? If you answer 'No,' then you might open yourself to a charge of blasphemy for limiting God's sovereign power to do what he chooses. But if God did exercise his sovereign will to commit suicide, wouldn't that limit his sovereign power since he would no longer exist?

I could go on, but I think the point is amply illustrated. This is the kind of nonsense that comes from compromising biblical revelation with human philosophy. Some questions are beyond human comprehension and are essentially unanswerable. Creating theology on the basis of obscure reasoning about the nature of God's foreknowledge and sovereign will is an exercise in ignorance. If the New Testament says man can choose or reject God's offer of salvation, then we can take it on faith that is so, and the philosophical details of exactly how God manages that are not important.

On the other hand, many believe that God chooses without foreknowledge of anyone's future conduct, whether good or bad. It is totally arbitrary. (This is the original Reformation theology elaborated by Calvin.) Yet they equally reject the idea of a cold, harsh God ramming Christianity down peoples' throats. How can that be?

They claim that God does not really force anything on man. He simply regenerates a person, which means he heals and removes man's depraved state. Thus man is enabled to recognize the true state of his existence, he is able to love God, to believe and have saving faith in Jesus Christ. There is nothing forced, they insist.

Problems remain, however. The outcome of the operation is always the same. You are not regenerated and then, able to understand the issues involved, make your own choice. Once regenerated it always happens – *always* the same outcome. How can anyone claim regenerated persons are

---

[195]   I.e., if it is already known what will happen, then is God prevented from changing it and does that in effect limit his free will?

acting out of free will when there is only one choice, and no one in history has ever made any other choice after regeneration? The very concept of free will implies there can be more than one outcome.

Geisler, a moderate Calvinist theologian, explains it in the following incisive and somewhat humorous fashion:

> The problem with the idea of "irresistible grace" in extreme Calvinism, according to this analogy, is that there is *no informed consent* for the treatment. ...patients are dragged kicking and screaming into the operating room, but once they are given a head transplant, they (not surprisingly) feel like an entirely different person![196]

Is God's plan of salvation a manufacturing process spewing out people who love him because they were made to automatically feel that way? If that's all there is to it, why didn't God make everyone that way in the first place?

Does God hate you?
Love and Hate in Predestination Theology

God's love for man is one of the great messages of the New Testament. The classic example, one of the most widely known and quoted verses of the Bible, talks of that love:

> For God so loved the world that he gave his only Son, so that everyone who believes in him may not perish but may have eternal life. (John 3:16)

The idea that God loves all mankind is a huge problem in predestination theology. Here's why:

If God loves you, that implies he wants you to be saved. But since God's will cannot be thwarted, that means you have to be saved. Therefore God can't love the whole world, else everyone would have to be saved. Therefore, philosophically, God's love must be limited to only those predestined to be saved, not the whole world.

Those predestined to fail are born for the sole purpose to demonstrate God's anger and justice. Therefore God cannot love those he arbitrarily chooses to fail. (What a tangled web we weave!)

---

[196] Geisler, *Chosen But Free,* p 97.

How then does predestination theology explain John 3:16 and other, similar biblical passages? Some of these even say that God loves "all men." Advocates of predestination solve the problem of John 3:16 (*for God so loved the world*) by insisting the term 'world' actually refers only to those already predestined to be saved. Therefore the term 'world' in John 3:16 does not necessarily mean every individual in the world. As proof they point to other verses such as the following, which they claim indicate God's love really is directed only to the church:

> Husbands, love your wives, just as **Christ loved the church** and gave himself up for her (Eph 5:25)

From this verse they infer that Christ loves *only* the church, though the word *only* clearly is not present in the text.

But what about those other passages that refer to God loving "all men." For example:

> ...God our Savior, **who desires *all men* to be saved** and to come unto the knowledge of the truth. (1 Tim 2:3–4, NKJV)

Predestination advocates get around these passages with the explanation that "all" and "all men" refers not to individuals, but to all races and tribes of men. In other words, by the exercise of his sovereign will, God has predestined individuals to be saved, chosen from all nations and tribes of people around the world.[197]

That, however, only leads to additional complications. Even today there are nations and tribes in remote corners of the globe that have hardly heard the Christian gospel and have few or no converted Christians among them. Go back in history only a short time and the majority of nations and tribes of the world had no converted Christians. How do you square that with this interpretation of "all" and "all men"? The answer to that is indeed fascinating. As we will see later in this chapter, some predestination advocates, following out this logic, conclude that you don't even need to hear about Jesus in order to be saved.

But back to the topic at hand. Does God really have no feeling for some people, so that he coldly condemns them to eternal torture without any opportunity to be saved? The answer is clearly laid out in the 1689 London Baptist Confession of Faith, as follows:

---

[197] See Vance, *The Other Side of Calvinism,* p 484 and following for an excellent discussion of this predestination concept.

> By his decree, and for the manifestation of His glory, God has predestinated certain men and angels to eternal life through Jesus Christ, thus revealing His grace. Others, whom He has left to perish in their sins, show the terror of His justice.
>
> ...
>
> Out of His mere free grace and love He predestinated these chosen ones to life, although there was nothing in them to cause Him to choose them.[198]

Here we see clearly stated the predestination vision. God arbitrarily chooses some individuals to be saved in order to make a show of his love and grace. Those not chosen are specifically there equally to make a show, in this case a show of his anger and justice against sinners.

It is as though God is putting on a cosmic play in which he enjoys acting out various roles. Sometimes he plays the loving Father, full of pity, stooping to save the unfortunate and helpless sinner, basking in their gratitude. At other times he plays the avenging judge of righteousness who glories in retribution, an eye for an eye, bringing the bad guys to justice. The most shocking aspect is that everyone involved is chosen arbitrarily, as the Baptist Confession says, *"although there was nothing in them to cause Him to choose them."*

Some people are born for the sole purpose to be cannon fodder in this cosmic drama, to be terrorized and tortured in hell for eternity as a show of God's justice. And there is nothing they can do about it. They are "totally depraved," literally unable to respond to God.

Is that love? Is there even justice in that? The following comments by Geisler seem so appropriate: *"...sound reason demands that there is no responsibility where there is no ability to respond. It is not rational to hold someone responsible when they could not have responded."* [199]

It amazes me how the Reformation at every turn feels compelled to debase man utterly, solely to preserve an unbalanced, extreme concept of man not participating in the minutest way in his relationship with God. Some critics, appalled by such radical reasoning, go so far as to describe forcible regeneration in predestination theology as divine rape.

I would characterize their predestinating God as an advanced case of "self-love." This God degrades man to the status of a divine toy, the ob-

---

[198] 1689 London Baptists Confession of Faith, modern language rendition, quoted by White, *The Potter's Freedom,* p 124.

[199] Geisler, *Chosen But Free,* p 29.

ject of a gratuitous childish game in which God shows off by arbitrarily imposing himself on everyone else. I think any parent who has watched their child grow, and reflected with awe and wonder as they see the beginnings of an independent personality, the first signs of the child's own sense of humor, their own opinions, and has treasured the beauty of those moments and grown in love for their child as they see a full, complete and independent human being emerging, knows instinctively how vulgar and contrived the basic tenets of Reformation theology are.

Can love be the foundation of a system that turns people into automatons, stripping them of their humanity, in a strange cosmic drama based on divine vanity? Does this God really love anyone other than himself? Geisler again criticizes the predestination concept in the following words:

> A loving God will not force anyone against their will to love Him or to worship Him. Forced love is not love; forced worship is not worship. Heaven will not be composed of robots. ... God will not dehumanize in order to save. To dehumanize is to de-create, since that is what God created – a human.... God is love, and love works persuasively but not coercively. Those whom God can lovingly persuade have been foreordained to eternal life. Those whom He cannot, are destined in accordance with their own choice to eternal destruction....[200]

The Scriptural Battle over Predestination

In the previous chapter we saw how eternal security theology was constructed as an extension of genuine biblical truth regarding Christian security, namely God's promise of salvation and repeated New Testament reassurance that we can trust that promise. In predestination theology we encounter a similar situation. Here, the biblical precedent is the New Testament teaching that the Messiah, his sacrifice for sin, and the founding of the Christian church, were part of a plan formulated before the world began. The fact that God had a plan in place before the world began is a natural hook on which to hang the idea that that plan included the arbitrary choice of who is to be saved.

---

[200] Dr. Norman Geisler, *God, Evil and Dispensations,* essay in Donald Campbell, ed., *Walvoord: A Tribute* (Moody Press, 1982), quoted in White, *The Potter's Freedom,* p 54–55.

Some of this is covered in Appendix B, "Hebrews 4 and the Sabbath." We summarize the most important points here as it pertains to predestination.

God called Abraham and created a nation from his descendants, which became the nation of Israel. He charged them with the task of creating a new and just society based on his law and theocratic rule. In order for them to do this he also promised them their own land, the Promised Land, where they could carry out their mission free from outside interference (Genesis 17:7–8).

After the passage of more than a thousand years, the results were much less than expected. As a nation, Israel had failed. By that time, Jewish religion had splintered into many forms, most bogged down in legalistic elaboration of the law. On the other hand, some turned to mysticism and antinomian ideas that played a role in the birth of Gnostic Christianity.

At this point the Messiah appears. The entire Jewish world is ablaze with Messianic expectations, but they are focused primarily on the restoration of the physical kingdom of Israel, the original kingdom promise under the Old Covenant. Jesus the Messiah, however, comes with a different message, pointing to a new covenant, the one promised in Jeremiah 31:31–34, *"It will not be like the covenant that I made with their ancestors.... I will put my law within them, and I will write it on their hearts...."*

Unfortunately, Israel as a nation did not recognize its Messiah. Because Israel rejected Jesus, the promise of the kingdom made to Israel was transferred to the Christian saints. This is the basis for the term "gospel of the kingdom," the message preached by Jesus and repeatedly mentioned throughout the New Testament (for example, Matthew 9:35; 24:14). It comes from the fact the kingdom promises were transferred to the church. Christ himself proclaimed that transfer, as recorded by the Apostle Matthew:

> Therefore I tell you [Jews], the kingdom of God will be taken away from you and given to a people that produces the fruits of the kingdom. (Matt 21:43)

There is another change in the kingdom promise. Under the New Covenant, the kingdom promise has been expanded. As described in Revelation 21, the saints are promised they ultimately will become rulers over the entire earth.

The kingdom promise, and the idea it has been transferred to the church, was a huge and contentious issue in the first century. It had a major impact on the relationship between the church and Judaism.

Remember that the early church was rooted in Jewish culture. Most of the members of the first-century church were Jews. There were Jewish communities throughout the Hellenistic world, and most Christian churches in major Gentile cities were first established in those Jewish communities. The entire early church faced constant pressure and criticism from the Jewish community at large. And Judaism especially resented the Christian claims about the kingdom promise.

How could the church claim it is the rightful owner of the promises first given to Israel? Here was this as yet tiny, struggling group of people making huge claims for themselves. If this was from God, why hadn't the majority of Israel accepted it? For most Jews the idea was simply ludicrous. It was the establishment versus the upstart. What right did they have? How could God abandon Israel after all they had been through as God's chosen people?

In response, the New Testament in various passages explained that the changes in the kingdom promise and the establishment of the New Covenant were planned before the creation of the world. For example, Paul in his letter to the Ephesians, testifies:

> ...he [God the Father] chose us in Christ before the foundation of the world.... (Eph 1:4)

As such, the calling of individuals to become Christians was purposed by God before the creation of the world. That sounds suspiciously like the claim that God selected individuals by name before the world began. Advocates of predestination claim that is exactly what this means. Is that true?

Romans chapter 9

In his letter to the church at Rome, Paul says many things that advocates of predestination hold up as proof of their doctrine. In Romans chapter 9, he talks about the transfer of the kingdom promises to the Christian church, and he justifies it on the basis that God has the right to do whatever he wills. Does that sound suspiciously like the predestination concept of God's sovereign will? Let's see how Paul develops his argument, and whether it does or does not support the predestination case.

In verses 4–5 Paul lays out the background of Israel's right to the promises. *"...to them belong the adoption, the glory, the covenants, ...and the promises"* (vs 4).

In verses 6–13, Paul refers to the transfer of the promises from physical Israel to spiritual Israel, the church. He then justifies the transfer of the kingdom promise by comparing it to Jacob and Esau. In that famous Bible story God chose Jacob to inherit the promises instead of Esau, and he did so before either was even born. Doesn't that sound suspiciously like the claim that God predestines people to succeed or fail before they are born?

Paul's purpose indeed is to demonstrate that God has the right to make choices even before the people involved are born. In this case he is specifically justifying the fact that Israel's replacement by the church was planned before the world began, before the people involved were even born.

Jewish society at that time, dominated primarily by legalism, would have insisted that their devotion to technical performance of the law earned them the right to the kingdom promises. Paul counters with emphasis on God's mercy. If all have sinned and fallen short in obedience, then anytime God grants gifts and blessings to any people, it is an act of mercy. No one has ever earned the right to the kingdom promises:

> So it depends not on human will or exertion, but on God who shows mercy. (vs 16)

Here we encounter an important question regarding God's decision to cease working exclusively through the nation of Israel. God sometimes says it was because they failed to fulfill the purpose of their covenant. But he also says he planned it from the very beginning. Is that a contradiction? If he planned it before the world began, how could he know Israel would fail?

Consider the broader picture. Man has made a thorough mess of every covenant God has ever offered. This is not limited to just the Old Covenant. Look what a mockery Gentiles have made of the New Covenant. Today millions of people claim they have the option to get away with every crime under the sun merely because they love Jesus. Other millions claim they will be saved automatically, just because they won a random lottery drawing before the world began, and to hell (literally) with the billions of suckers who didn't get picked. Is the New Covenant any less a failure than the Old?

God knew Israel would fail, not because they are worse than anyone else. No people in history have ever succeeded as a group. Relatively small numbers of Israelites successfully lived up to the spirituality of the Old Covenant. The purpose of the Old Covenant just as with the New, was to bring people to spirituality and a personal relationship with God. When Jesus was asked by a devout Jew what he must do to inherit eternal life, Jesus challenged him to look into the Old Covenant itself for the answer: *"What is written in the law? What do you read there?"* The man answered, *"You shall love the Lord your God with all your heart...and your neighbor as yourself."* Jesus concludes, *"You have given the right answer; do this, and you will live"* (Luke 10:26–28). Where did this come from? This, the very foundation of New Covenant morality, was quoted directly from the Old Testament, namely Deuteronomy 6:5 and Leviticus 19:18.

The author of Hebrews witnesses that there were thousands of individuals, not just the great names of Old Testament history, who were faithful to the spirituality of the Old Covenant in those days (Heb 11:35–38). The same pattern continues unchanged today. Comparatively small numbers of individuals scattered through many groups remain faithful to the New Covenant as originally revealed by Christ and the apostles in the first century.

Against this background of repeated human failure, we more easily understand and appreciate the point Paul is making in Romans 9:16. Knowing that organized groups of human beings sooner or later always fail, God exercises his right to choose and change the people through whom he works. Because of the human tendency to sin, all such choices by God are acts of mercy. No group has ever 'earned' an exclusive right to the kingdom promises, neither Jew nor Gentile.

But, back to Romans chapter nine. In verses 17–18 Paul continues the theme of God's right to choose, citing the case of Pharaoh who opposed the children of Israel before the Exodus. Here was a proud and evil ruler of a pagan land who openly fought against Yahweh and scorned the warnings of his prophets. The Old Testament account says that God purposely hardened Pharaoh's heart even more, so as to make a great example of his evil and God's mercy to Israel. So we see that God also sometimes chooses to react to excessively evil persons and groups, in effect rejecting them by giving them over to their evil.

Now we encounter one of the supposedly key predestination verses:

> You will say to me then, "Why then does he still find fault? For who can **resist his will**?" But who indeed are you, a human being, to argue with God? (vs 19)

Who can "resist" the will of God? Here is another key principle of predestination theory – God's "irresistible" will.

In verses 20–22 Paul also talks about some people as "objects of wrath," whom God uses to demonstrate his power and justice, as he did with Pharaoh and the Egyptians. This sounds suspiciously like those condemned to eternal torture in predestination theology. Is this talking about people being predestined to fail before they were born, who have no hope of salvation?

In verses 25–29 Paul again talks about the transfer of the kingdom promises to the Christians saints, explaining that this was ordained beforehand, being prophesied in the Old Testament in the books of Hosea and Isaiah. A Jew in Paul's day might say, "You claim that God already planned to replace the nation of Israel with the church before the world began. That's unreasonable! Look, I'm not a bad person. How does God have the right to decide to give the kingdom promises to someone else before I was born, before he even knew what kind of person I would be!"

That is why Paul raises the issue of God's right to choose the people through whom he will work even before they are born. Paul is explaining why God has that right, and gives the example of how God exercised that right when he chose Jacob over Esau before they were born. That does not mean Jews are excluded from God's plan. Remember that the majority of first century Christians were Jews. It means only that Israel as a nation lost its special position as the vehicle through which Jesus the Messiah was to be offered to the world.

The issue throughout chapter nine is who has the right to God's kingdom promises. The Jews by heritage had the right. But they sought it legalistically, and in so doing failed to fulfill the purpose of the law and their covenant, which was to produce a righteous nation that loves God and their neighbors as themselves. In contrast, Gentiles who by heritage never even tried to pursue biblical righteousness, have now been called to righteousness, which can be attained by faith, writing the law on their heart.

But here is the big question: Where in all of this is the idea that God, before the world began, singled out you and me by name and decided irreversibly whether we will be saved or damned for all eternity? Is it just me? Am I missing the point? Or is there something genuinely missing from this supposed proof of predestination?

In Romans nine I see where Paul defends God's right to make historical decisions about nations and groups of people through whom he works, even before the individuals are born who populate those groups. Because of human failure, his choice of people is always an act of grace. No one has ever earned it, and so God reserves to himself the right to pick the people through whom he works. Paul also defends God's right to be angry with seriously evil persons, to even "give them over" to their evil and harden their heart if he chooses, to make an example of them. But there is a huge leap from that to the concept of predestination as taught in Reformation theology.

In fact, the whole topic of the covenant promises and their transfer to the church contains powerful proof that predestination is not a biblical teaching. Consider this: Israel often is referred to as the "elect." This is a favorite term among predestination advocates, for it means "the people God has chosen." Israel is the elect, the chosen people. It was God's will and commission to Israel that they inherit the Promised Land and become a righteous nation, showing forth God's righteousness and goodness as a beacon to the entire world. If God's will is sovereign (irresistible) in the radical sense that God will never allow his will to be thwarted, and it was God's will that Israel become a righteous nation, then how could Israel have failed?

If the Christian elect cannot fail, how could the Jewish elect fail? If God changed his mind about working exclusively through national Israel because of the poor results he was getting, can he change his mind about working through you and me as individuals if he gets equally poor results from us?

Consider the words of the martyr Stephen. In the book of Acts he talks about the Jews of the first century and why God disenfranchised them:

> You stiff-necked and uncircumcised in heart and ears! You always **resist** the Holy Spirit; as your fathers did, so do you. (Acts 7:51, NKJV)

How could Jews resist the Holy Spirit? According to predestination theory, nothing can resist God's sovereign will.

Did God before creation compile a list of names of those he will save and those he will condemn, and there is nothing they can do about it? Is that an inherent, indispensable part of New Testament theology? Or, as we have seen before, is this a philosophical exaggeration of a true Christian doctrine? That we further answer by comparing those claims with the rest of Jesus' New Testament revelation, to which we now turn.

Scriptures Cited to Support Predestination

As before, there simply is not enough space in this volume to cover all the biblical passages and arguments pertaining to predestination. Here we cover a small number of representative passages to give the essence and flavor of the argument.

John 6:37, 44

> **Everything that the Father gives me** will come to me, and anyone who comes to me **I will never drive away;**
>
> **No one can come to me unless drawn by the Father** who sent me; and I will raise that person up on the last day.

Predestination advocates say these verses mean the Father specifically predestines and hands over to Christ those who are to be saved. In turn, Christ promises none of those will ever be lost (*I will never drive away*). Does this mean God has predestined people by name before the world began and they cannot fail?

Opponents of predestination point out that the context of these verses is a conversation between Jesus and certain Jews who are questioning his authority. Jewish leaders viewed Jesus as a usurper, building his own heretical following without justification in Jewish tradition. In verses 29–36 Jesus responds by emphasizing his connection to the Father. In verses 37 and 44, therefore, Christ is saying that his activity in gathering followers around him is strictly the product of the Father's work, not just his own doing. The point he is making is that his work is sanctioned by the Father. He, Jesus, is only following the will of the Father and will never work contrary to the Father's will. In that context, he will never refuse (*drive away*) anyone the Father gives him.

Do these verses imply that our individual fate was decided before the world began? When Jesus says, *"No one can come to me unless drawn by the Father,"* does that mean the Father gives Christ only persons preselected by name long ago, or is that reading into this passage something not really there? If the Father calls a thousand persons and only 500 respond and come to Christ, is it not still true that those 500 came to Christ only because they were drawn by the Father?

Equally, when Christ says, *"everything the Father gives me will come to me,"* does that mean God gives him all the people he calls, who are irresistibly forced to come to Christ, or only the ones who respond? Further, does Jesus with these words commit himself to keep his disciples even if they murder and practice fornication a thousand times a day, as Luther claimed? Isn't that an exaggeration of what this passage is really about?

Matthew 11:27, John 5:21

> All things have been handed over to me by my Father; and no one knows the Son except the Father, and no one knows the Father except the Son and **anyone to whom the Son chooses to reveal him.**

> Indeed, just as the Father raises the dead and gives them life, so also the Son gives life **to whomever he wishes.**

These verses also refer to *choosing* and divine *will*. Is this a reference to predestination as some claim, in which Jesus arbitrarily chooses and rejects whomever he pleases by name, before they are born? Or, is this merely preaching the key importance of Jesus, and the fact that life is obtained only by going through him? There is nothing said here about Jesus irrevocably deciding the fate of individuals before they are born.

Advocates of predestination connect the phrase *"to whomever he wishes"* with the arbitrary quality of the selection process in predestination theology. Does that phrase imply Jesus picks people arbitrarily, without reason? Or does it mean that Jesus has the authority to judge and to select those with whom he will walk in a personal relationship, and those ultimately he will save? If Jesus indeed has authority to select who is to be saved, can't he choose to withhold salvation from those who convert but then commit murder and fornication a thousand times a day (a-la Martin Luther)?

Romans 8:29–30, Ephesians 1:5

> For those whom he **foreknew** he also **predestined** to be conformed to the image of his Son, in order that he might be the firstborn within a large family. And those whom he **predestined** he also called;

> ...having **predestined** us to adoption as sons by Jesus Christ to Himself, **according to the good pleasure of His will.** (NKJV)

Here we find key Reformation terminology – predestination, foreknowledge, and God's will. The question is whether predestination refers to selection of individuals by name before they were born. Or does it only refer to God's plan to call some people to be Christians under the New Covenant?

Remember from our review of Romans chapter nine that the plan to transfer the kingdom promises to the followers of the Messiah, and to expand the calling to Gentiles, was in place before the world began. Therefore use of the term *predestined* is entirely appropriate. What is happening today – the calling of both Jews and Gentiles to participate in the New Covenant – indeed was foreseen and predestined long ago. That is what these verses are talking about.

"According to the good pleasure of his will" need not indicate that God is arbitrary in picking who is to be saved, as in predestination theology. That phrase can be understood just as easily as a description of God's love and the pleasure he derives from working with a people devoted to him.

Revelation 17:8

> And the **inhabitants** of the earth, **whose names** have not been **written in the book of life from the foundation of the world,** will be amazed when they see the beast....

This one verse comes the closest I have seen to supporting the classic doctrine of predestination. The phrasing, at least as it is translated in English, might be taken to imply that the actual names of all the saved, contained in the book of life, were written *before* the foundation of the world. However, an alternate interpretation is that these are the names that have been written *since* ('from') the foundation of the world. In other words the writing is a process that occurs throughout history, from the beginning to the end of the world, as people live and die and make decisions to follow Christ.

There are a number of references to the Book of Life in the New Testament, and predestination advocates use some of these in their arguments. Unfortunately for them however, among these is the following: *"He who overcomes shall be clothed in white garments, and I will not blot out his name from the Book of Life."* (Rev 3:5, NKJV) If a person's name were indeed written in the Book of Life before he or she is born, we know from this passage it is not be irreversible, else God would not say that entries can be removed.

In the end, the way we understand Revelation 17:8 depends on harmonizing it with many other New Testament scriptures, to which we now turn.

Scriptures Cited to Refute Predestination

Acts 14:1

> ...Paul and Barnabas went into the Jewish synagogue and spoke in such a way that a great number of both Jews and Greeks became believers.

Opponents of predestination cite this verse because it implies that Paul and Barnabas' manner of speaking had a positive effect that increased the response and conversion of their audience.

Some Protestant churches today discourage the use of altar calls.[201] This is the practice of inviting and urging the audience to make a decision for Christ. Predestination says that if a person has been chosen, God will draw him forcibly to accept Jesus, like it or not. An altar call implies that some outside force plays a role in helping a person make that decision, and so violates the philosophic concept of the irresistibility of God's will.

If those who are predestined to be saved are compelled irresistibly to convert to Christianity, then it shouldn't matter how well a minister speaks to his audience or whether he issues an altar call. Therefore the claim in Acts 14:1 that Paul and Barnabas' style of preaching increased their response, would have to be false.

John 7:16–17

> My teaching is not mine but his who sent me. Anyone who resolves to do the will of God will know whether the teaching is from God or whether I am speaking on my own.

Here Jesus clearly states that a person's own resolve plays a role in spiritual perception, in this case to recognize that Jesus' teaching is from the Father. Thus man does appear to play some cooperative role in his relationship with Jesus.

Matthew 23:37

> Jerusalem, Jerusalem, the city that kills the prophets and stones those who are sent to it! How often have I desired to gather your children together as a hen gathers her brood under her wings, **and you were not willing!**

---

[201] See Vance, *The Other Side of Calvinism,* p 543.

Here we see Jesus expressing his heartfelt desire (his will) to save the Jewish nation, but his will is overridden by the will of the people. This again demonstrates that God allows man to resist his will.

2 Peter 3:9

> The Lord...is patient with you, not wanting any to perish, but all to come to repentance.

God desires all to come to repentance. And the wording implies those who do not repent will "perish." But if God wills all to repent, and all people do not repent, then once again we see that God allows his will to be thwarted.

Advocates of predestination explain this by saying references here and elsewhere to 'all men' cannot really mean all mankind. James White explains this by noting that in the opening passage to 2 Peter (in the first three verses) the Apostle addresses his letter as a whole to the church. Therefore, White says, this individual verse also refers only to the church, not really 'all' men. So if Peter is referring only to Christians, then God's will is not thwarted.[202]

1 John 2:2

> ...and he is the atoning sacrifice for our sins, and not for ours only but also for the sins of the whole world.

Here the apostle John seems to differentiate clearly between the sins of Christians and non-Christians. And he specifically says that Christ's sacrifice was intended for both.

This directly contradicts predestination theology, which says that Christ's sacrifice is reserved only for the sins of those whom God has chosen. If Christ's sacrifice were intended for those who are predestined to be lost, that implies God wants them to be saved. And if they are not saved then God's will can be thwarted.

Advocates of predestination solve the problem of 1 John 2:2 by arguing the whole verse really is talking only about Christians after all. James White explains the traditional predestination position on this passage.[203] The phrase *"our sins,"* he says, refers only to the one specific group of Christians to whom John was writing his letter. Therefore the phrase *"sins*

---

202 White, *The Potter's Freedom*, p 145 ff.
203 Ibid., p 261 ff.

of the whole world" does not refer literally to all men, but merely all other Christians scattered throughout the world.

I find this explanation superbly clever and at the same time totally implausible.

Luke 13:24

> Strive to enter through the narrow door; for many, I tell you, will try to enter and will not be able.

This passage is a huge problem. Why? Because if a man is totally depraved, according to predestination theology, then supposedly he can't even try to enter the kingdom of God without first being chosen and regenerated. But, once he is regenerated and tries, then he can't fail, because it is God's irresistible will that regenerated persons succeed.

Some Reformation theologians resolve this by saying that man can experience a 'false faith.' [204] That means it is possible for a person to act like a regenerated, saved person, attend church, develop Christ-like qualities, but not be saved at all simply because he or she was never chosen. In fact, some say that because anyone can experience false faith, you can never be sure you are one of the chosen until you meet Christ in heaven.

I find that unsettling. One of the primary arguments advanced in favor of predestination and eternal security is that it gives peace of mind. At least in some of its flavors, however, it apparently does exactly the opposite. The idea you can never be sure you are one of the chosen until you reach heaven was common in Calvinism in past centuries.

What a tangled web we weave! In the previous chapter on eternal security we encountered Carnal Christians. These supposedly are saved Christians who act like the unsaved. Now we discover their alter ego, the falsely converted. These are unsaved people who act like saved Christians. The former are licensed to commit unlimited sin but are still saved regardless of how evil they become. The latter practice righteous conduct, but are unsaved and condemned to writhe in hell for eternity no matter how good they become.

But wait, there's more! In the following sections we encounter something that for me is the strangest of all. Not only do you not have to repent, nor have faith nor believe, you don't even have to accept Jesus to be

---

[204] For example, see Geisler, *Chosen But Free,* p 99–100.

saved. And if you follow the philosophic reasoning of Reformation theology, step by step, it makes perfect sense.

The Essence of Salvation in Predestination Theology

The doctrine of regeneration has biblical substance. The New Testament talks about the transforming power of grace and the Holy Spirit. In Christ we become a "new man." As always, however, taking a biblical truth to extremes can lead to problems.

In predestination theology the central act of salvation is regeneration. Regeneration is the application of grace, earned by Jesus exclusively for the saved. At that point you are transformed into the "new man," possessing a new mind that by nature will accept and love God. And it happens irresistibly.

Before regeneration you are so totally depraved you are literally unable to believe the gospel or make a decision for Jesus. Therefore, and here is the important point, regeneration comes *first*.[205] Until you are regenerated you can't believe, you can't have faith, you can't accept Jesus, because after all, you are totally depraved. This is the beginning of a huge problem, however, because the New Testament almost always talks about the process of salvation in the opposite order. Here are two examples:

> But these are written [the gospels] so that you may come to believe that Jesus is the Messiah, the Son of God, and that **through believing you may have life** in his name. (John 20:31)

> For I am not ashamed of the **gospel; it is the power of God for salvation** to everyone who has **faith**.... (Romans 1:16)

Both Apostles John and Paul seem to think salvation begins with hearing the gospel, believing it and having faith. Predestination, however, insists that the central and initial act of salvation is regeneration. We are not saved because we have faith. Rather, we have faith because we have been saved through regeneration.

Here we come to the heart of the confusion in predestination theology. Consider it logically. The Bible says we are saved by faith and not by

---

[205] See discussion in Vance, *The Other Side of Calvinism*, p 520–521.

works. But if faith is the automatic by-product of regeneration, and good works also are the automatic by-product of regeneration, then how can they say you are saved by faith alone and not by good works? In effect, predestination places both faith and good works on the same plane, as mere automatic, irresistible by-products of regeneration. According to that rationale it is impossible to say that either faith or good works is more important than the other.

Indeed, predestination's exaggeration of the role of regeneration wreaks theological havoc with the very concept of Christian salvation. Is this really the belief of that portion of modern Reformation Christianity that still embraces predestination? Yes, it is. For example, the nationally known Presbyterian minister and prolific author, R. C. Sproul:

> We can never trust Christ for our salvation unless we first desire him. This is why we said earlier that regeneration precedes faith.[206]

Laurence Vance sums up the *de facto* state of predestination theology by saying, *"In the Calvinistic system Irresistible Grace* [regenerating grace] *is what actually saves a man, believing on Christ is only the result of this 'grace.'"* [207]

Salvation without Christ?

Carrying out this line of reasoning further, we get into even more difficulty. If the key event in salvation is regeneration, then are any of the other things that follow regeneration actually necessary – including faith and good works. Is it even necessary to believe in Jesus? Many advocates of predestination say those things occur automatically and immediately. Others disagree.

Indeed, some argue that since regeneration is the key to salvation, anything that follows is not actually required, not even conversion and belief in Jesus. Some Baptist denominations hold to this belief, such as those designated Primitive Baptists. Their name comes from the claim they follow the original (primitive) teaching of the apostles. Eddie Garrett, a member of that denomination, explains:

---

[206] R. C. Sproul, *Chosen by God,* (Wheaton, Ill., Tyndale House Publishers, 1986) p 118, as quoted by Geilser, *Chosen But Free,* p 226.

[207] Vance, *The Other Side of Calvinism,* p 523–524.

"Primitive Baptists believe that...sinners are regenerated, or born again, independently of, or without, the gospel as a means." [208] What that means is that hearing the gospel, even believing in Jesus, plays no part in salvation itself. Regeneration is the key, and therefore only regeneration itself is actually required.

Remember how some predestination theologians explained away biblical statements that God loves all men and wills that all men be saved (see above, page 209). Supposedly, they explain, the Bible doesn't really mean *all* men, instead only some individuals within all tribes and nations of man. But, recall how that only led to more problems, because there are so many tribes and nations where, throughout history and still today, there are few or no converted Christians.

But now we have the solution! If you don't have to hear the gospel and believe in Jesus to be saved, the absence of Christianity in many tribes and nations is no longer a problem. Here is the incredible position taken by Primitive Baptists:

> The population of heaven after the end of the world **will not be determined by those who have accepted the Lord Jesus Christ,** but by those whom the Lord Jesus Christ accepted before the beginning. [209]

> God has an elect people and Christ died for them and they all will be born again and will live in heaven.... **Many of them will have never heard the gospel.** [210]

> **Salvation is NOT dependent upon gospel faith.** Indeed, it could not be so, for millions of children of God have never heard the gospel preached. [211]

After all the arguing about faith alone, trusting in the precious blood of Jesus, and how faith and belief are miraculously instilled in man by re-

---

[208] Eddie Garrett, "The Purpose of the Gospel" *The Hardshell Baptist,* December 1990, p 1, as quoted by Vance, *The Other Side of Calvinism,* p 529.

[209] Kevin Fralick, "The Idea of Acceptance," *The Christian Baptist,* June/July 1998, p 9, as quoted by Vance, *The Other Side of Calvinism,* p 529. Emphasis added.

[210] Eddie Garrett, "Two Salvations" *The Hardshell Baptist,* p 3, as quoted by Vance, *The Other Side of Calvinism,* p 529. Emphasis added.

[211] S.T. Tolley, "Is Gospel Faith Necessary in Order to Be Saved in Heaven?" *The Christian Baptist,* August 1996, p 4, as quoted by Vance, *The Other Side of Calvinism,* p 529. Emphasis added.

generation, the strictly logical reasoning of Reformation theology leads some to conclude none of those things really matter after all. They rationalize this by saying that though multitudes of 'saved heathen' have never heard the name of Jesus, regeneration has created within them a new disposition. A regenerated heathen feels sorrow for his sins, and an unfilled longing for the savior of whom he has never heard.

The doctrine of the saved heathen is a minority position within the world of predestination theology. Yet it was espoused by several historically great Reformation teachers, including Zwingli and Zanchius, as well as prominent theologians of our day such as Boettner.[212]

Even the famous Baptist evangelist Billy Graham, late in his career, adopted this radical theology. In various interviews he outlined these ideas, including the following statements during an interview with Robert Schuler on the popular Christian television program Hour of Power.[213] In that interview, referring to the body of Christ, Graham said:

> ...that is what God is doing today, he is calling people out of the world for his name, whether they come from the Muslim world, or the Buddhist world, or the Christian world, or the non-believing world. They are members of the body of Christ because they have been called by God. They may not even know the name of Jesus, but they know in their heart that they need something that they don't have, and they turn to the only light that they have and think that they are saved, and they're going to be with us in heaven.

Referring specifically to people in primitive lands who have never heard of Jesus, Graham adds:

> ...they never heard of Jesus, but they believed in their heart that there is a God, and they try to live a life that is quite apart from the community in which they [reside].

The idea is that once you have been regenerated you can turn to any religion in which you were born, including non-Christian religions, and be saved as long as you are merely in some general sense a 'good' person and believe in God.

---

212 See Vance, *The Other Side of Calvinism,* p 532–533.

213 Interview of Billy Graham by Robert Schuler, on the *Hour of Power* television program broadcast 5/31/1997, entitled *"Say 'Yes' To Possibility Thinking,"* program #1426.

Predestination Summary and Overview

Once again, the word "extreme" seems so appropriate. But it is an extreme interpretation involving real biblical truths. There is a genuinely biblical foundation out of which predestination theology is grown. As we saw in the discussion on Romans chapter nine, there are significant aspects of Christianity that were "predestined" before the world began. The New Covenant itself was foreordained and revealed through prophesy in the Old Testament. The call to participate in the New Covenant was predestined to be expanded to include Gentiles. In Romans 9 Paul defends God's sovereign will, his right to make changes and choose whom he works through, even before the individuals involved in those groups are born.

We have seen various New Testament passages that witness to the fact that God calls individuals at various times to participate in his covenants. This naturally raises questions. God chose Israel in ancient times. But he apparently didn't establish a religious work at the same time in China. Why? What would a Chinese individual from that time say about that? Would he accuse God of being unfair?

Think as well of the manner in which God called Paul by miraculously striking him blind. It's pretty hard to ignore that kind of calling. What about the other Jews of that time, some of whom merely heard Jesus speak once or twice. Can you imagine someone from that time complaining, "Well, if God had struck me blind then I would have realized how serious it is and followed Jesus too!" From that human perspective, is God fair?

God sometimes is described as becoming fed up with evil individuals, including the famous case of the Egyptian Pharaoh at the time of the Exodus, and giving them over to their evil state so as to demonstrate his justice. These are the issues Paul is addressing in Romans 9 when he defends God's right to do what he chooses with his creation.

The conclusion of the matter is that God reserves the right to react to individual historical conditions and situations as he sees fit. Those reactions are to some degree personal, and may differ significantly from case to case. All have sinned. Therefore no one has an irrevocable right to anything. Everything God does for man is an act of mercy. On that basis God has the right to choose whom to work through and what gifts and special opportunities to give to any person or nation.

As Paul was saying, it is God's creation and he reserves the right to do with it what he wills. However, to stretch that into the idea that God arbitrarily predestined individuals by name before the world began, that he forcibly turns some people into Christians and condemns the rest to eternal torture without any chance of salvation, simply does not square with the overwhelming evidence of biblical scripture. This is a strange, some would say absolutely weird overreaction against the mistakes of medieval Roman Christianity, and leads merely to a spiritual wreck in the ditch on the opposite side of the road.

Predestination and Antinomianism

Finally, is predestination theology antinomian? For eternal security alone, the case is fairly obvious. Some Hellenistic Christians label their own brothers as antinomian for espousing extreme eternal security. But what about predestination? Traditional predestination theology does not sanction wanton evil as openly as extreme eternal security. But is it antinomian as well?

Predestination theology overtly teaches righteousness. Mainstream predestination theory says that after being saved by regeneration, Christians are irresistibly compelled to have faith, to believe, and produce good works.

Is there, however, an 'antinomian effect' in predestination theology? Remember Nicolas and his teaching of a more advanced spirituality, and the unintended antinomian effect it had on his followers. Can the same thing happen with predestination theology? Consider the following:

If you believe your fate was determined before you were born, that your ability or inability to love God was fixed from the beginning, then whatever happens is in God's hands. You can't change anything, so why would you be foolish enough to try? If you don't naturally feel like going to church and being a good person, then apparently God has not chosen you, and it's a waste of time trying. You might as well indulge in worldly pleasure and enjoy yourself as long as you have time remaining in this earthly life.

On the other hand, if you think you are one of the lucky ones, then still there is nothing you can do about it. Your natural inclination to love God and do good is solely the product of regeneration and the Holy Spirit. You may reasonably conclude you can't increase or decrease what God is doing in you. If God has supernaturally intervened to make you naturally want to be kind to your children, that's wonderful. But if he hasn't yet intervened supernaturally to make you love your grumpy spouse, well there's really nothing you can do about that either. But you're going to be saved, and whatever it takes to be saved God will forcibly (read 'naturally') cause to happen. So don't worry. In the end it will all work out. You are eternally secure! Remember, predestination also automatically includes eternal security. If God has selected you, his will is sovereign and you *will* be saved.

Some advocates of predestination say that God initially causes you to produce good works, but after that you can backslide. You may sink into a life-time of terrible sin. Nevertheless you remain eternally secure. The key to making that work, they say, is God's foreknowledge. Knowing everything about the future, God knows exactly how and when you will die. And before you die, he will again intervene forcibly to bring you back to the faith. What that means is you can have your fling and still not worry about it. God is on the job and he will bring you back, if necessary in the nick of time – guaranteed!

Do some Reformed Christians really think that way? Sadly, the antinomian effect of predestination theology is only too real.

For many years during my childhood, my family attended a Presbyterian church in which mainstream predestination theology was taught. I remember listening to discussions between my parents about individuals they knew who had turned to openly sinful lives because they had become convinced they were not predestined to be saved. These included backsliding members who had left the church, as well as children of members who had gone their own way.

The common theme was discouragement from recurring problems with temptation and sin. In mainstream predestination theology, if God has predestined you to be saved then he will forcibly cause you to be good. Not perfect, but at least generally 'good' in the sense that is expected in the social context of your local church congregation. If you fail to fit in, it is very easy to conclude you are a 'bad seed' in the predestination sense. For those who come to doubt themselves, it is only natural for some to conclude God has not chosen them. Since there is nothing they can do about it, they might as well enjoy themselves with sinful pursuits during the short time that remains before descending into hell fire. Sadly, that is a common pitfall for those who posses a sensitive spirit and feel burdened with guilt by their experience of sin.

For those with a more hardened mind, it is equally easy to conclude that various sins in which they have fallen don't really matter, and instead look to what good they have achieved, and who cares about those silly gossiping church members who criticize them. Once you talk yourself into the certainty you are one of the chosen, then you must conclude that whatever good God forcibly has injected into your life, however limited, must be sufficient. After all, if you have been chosen you *are* eternally secure.

Lordship Salvation

On the other hand is lordship salvation. This is a reaction within Reformation Christianity against the excesses of extreme eternal security. Lordship salvation in part is a dispute over the relationship between law and faith. And it comes down squarely on the side of the Apostle James who preached to the first century church that faith must produce works in order to be genuine faith (James chapter 2). In essence, it says that to be saved one must accept Jesus not only as savior, but also as lord and master. There must be at least some positive change and good works when a person becomes a Christian.

There are definite limitations to the concept, however, as we will see in what follows. Remember that John MacArthur, the leading proponent of lordship salvation, also believes in eternal security (see above, page 162). So, what does lordship salvation really mean? How can someone believe in lordship salvation and eternal security at the same time?

The controversy over lordship salvation appeared in the late 20th century, as a dispute carried on publicly, largely by John MacArthur its leading proponent, and Zane Hodges and Charles Ryrie who oppose it. Both Hodges and Ryrie maintain that it is possible for a sinner to accept Jesus as savior, and live and die as a Carnal Christian without ever accepting him as Lord and master. MacArthur condemns that as antinomian. Hodges and Ryrie accuse MacArthur of legalism and teaching salvation by works.

Lordship salvation is not a problem for those who embrace predestination. Remember that Predestination says regeneration automatically produces faith and works of obedience.

R. C. Sproul, for example, is a modern predestination theologian widely known through his prolific writing. He argues that lordship salvation has been part of the Reformation tradition from the beginning.[214] Viewed in the light of history, lordship salvation really is nothing new.

By looking more closely at MacArthur, we see what really is going on. MacArthur in fact is an advocate of traditional, old school predestination theology. In his writings he even rejects modern attempts to soften predestination by claiming God knows in advance what everyone will do and so God merely chooses those he already knows will accept him. MacArthur writes, *"...if you claim that salvation is based merely on God's foresight into the decisions of individual men and women, you are actually claiming that people secure their own salvation."* [215] *"The Bible clearly teaches that God **sovereignly** chooses people to believe in him."* [216] Choosing *"sovereignly"* is a way of saying God chooses *arbitrarily,* without his choice being affected by any outside factor, such as a person's future conduct.

This is Lordship salvation according to its primary advocate John MacArthur. Those predestined to be saved also produce good works, because that is God's irresistible will, and it happens automatically. It is nothing more nor less than the same old predestination theology in which man is stripped of choice and relegated to the role of a divine toy.

Some dispute the idea that lordship salvation is nothing more than recycled predestination theology. Yet MacArthur is quite clear about this in his own writings. He declares, for example, *"What we're really saying is that grace is **efficacious**. In other words, grace is **certain** to produce the intended results."* [217] 'Efficacious' is the modern, less offensive term for irresistible. Even MacArthur does not totally shy away from the "i" word. Elsewhere he says,[218] *"Special grace, better called saving grace, is the **irresistible** work of God...."* [219]

---

[214] See R.C. Sproul, *Faith Alone,* p 26.

[215] MacArthur, *Saved Without a Doubt,* p 58.

[216] Ibid., p 59.

[217] MacArthur, *The Gospel According to the Apostles,* p 60.

[218] Ibid.

[219] Here MacArthur is talking about 'common' versus 'special' grace. Some predestination theologians including MacArthur invent a category called 'common grace.' This is a form of supernatural influence radiating down on all mankind that enables them to show the goodness we often see among those who are not Christians. Even in totally heathen countries one finds acts of honesty, mercy and kindness. Since predestination theology claims man is totally depraved, therefore incapable of any good deed, they find it necessary to attribute goodness among the unsaved to a special outside influence from God called common grace. Common

So MacArthur, like advocates of predestination in general, takes a more moral line than those who espouse extreme eternal security. After wading through the antinomian claims of extreme eternal security, listening to MacArthur is truly refreshing. I was so impressed by his perceptive assessment of Christian antinomianism. MacArthur acknowledges openly that antinomian heresy is promoted by Reformation Christianity disguised as spirituality. Here are two of his observations: [220]

> Most antinomians vigorously appeal for Christians to walk in a manner worthy of their calling.... Antinomians typically believe Christians *should* yield to the lordship of Christ; they just do not believe surrender is a binding requirement in the gospel call to faith. Antinomians do not necessarily despise the law of God; they simply believe it is irrelevant to saving faith.
>
> **Antinomianism makes obedience elective.** While most antinomians strongly *counsel* Christians to obey (and even urge them to obey), they do not believe obedience is a necessary consequence of true faith.

How sad that such sound teaching on morality and avoiding the deception of antinomianism, for MacArthur rests on a foundation of predestination theology. In the end, despite a refreshing breeze of spiritual truth in some aspects, lordship salvation still is enmeshed in the grave errors of predestination theology – philosophic contradiction of scripture, the immoral rejection of billions of helpless human beings, and the antinomian effects from its own unique heretical beliefs, as we saw above.

Both extreme eternal security and traditional predestination theology deceive by cloaking themselves in genuine spirituality and biblical truth.

---

grace can be resisted, they say, which explains why the unsaved are sometimes, but not always good. 'Special grace' is their name for the grace reserved for themselves, which produces regeneration and eternal life. Special grace is irresistible when applied to the chosen, yet like common grace it too does not make its recipients completely perfect.

I have never found a logical explanation for why the unsaved are imperfect because common grace can be resisted, but regenerated Christians also are imperfect even though their 'special' grace is irresistible. I also wonder: If common grace is given to all mankind, and common grace imparts spiritual qualities, then man apparently is not 'totally depraved' and should be able to respond to God without first being magically regenerated. What a tangled web we weave. Is it any wonder much of Hellenistic Christianity today has abandoned predestination?

[220] MacArthur, *The Gospel According to the Apostles,* p 95. Bold emphasis added.

Consider MacArthur himself. He argues for example that it is not lack of grace, but sin that keeps people from being reconciled to God.[221] Most Primitive Christians would heartily agree. But remember, predestination theology inevitably comes back to the fact it is not really sin that keeps people from being reconciled to God, but the fact they were arbitrarily chosen to fail. Billions of individual human beings are condemned, before they are born, to roast forever in hell fire. There is nothing they can do about it and God will not lift a finger to help them. Is that what it's all about? Is that the "good news," the gospel of the New Covenant and the gracious acts of a loving God?

---

[221] Ibid., p 66.

– 11 –

Reformation Theology
Part 3

(Conclusions)

By this time it should be obvious that Reformation theology includes a very substantial antinomian component. In this chapter we look at the surprising evidence that Gnosticism is the actual source of that antinomian theology.

First, however, we look at one of the primary traits of antinomian theology – the immorality that it licenses and tends to produce. After all, Nicolaitan Gnosticism is condemned in the book of Revelation for both its theology and the immorality it produced. Do we see that reflected in Hellenistic Christianity today? For the medieval Roman church the answer is fairly obvious. But what about the Reformation itself?

Did Reformed Spirituality Work for Its Founders?

If Reformation theology were a genuine return to the original truth of the apostolic church, one might expect it to be marked by a rejection of the horrible abuse of humanity to which medieval Roman Christianity had sunk. Sadly, this was strikingly not true for one of the two great architects of the Reformation, namely John Calvin.

Calvin lived and worked in Geneva, Switzerland, where he ruled with absolute authority. During his time, Geneva was regarded as a center of the Reformation, called by some the Rome of Protestantism. Calvin himself sometimes was referred to as the Protestant Pope of Geneva. The comparison is only too real, as the history of the early years of the Reformation unfortunately demonstrate.

Predestination apologists sometimes try to explain away what happened in Geneva by noting that many of the executions and abuse there officially were authorized by the city council. Yet Calvin was the ultimate authority in Geneva, and the historical evidence shows clearly that he took an active role.

During just five years from 1542 through 1546, there were 58 executions in Geneva, with many more banished, imprisoned and property confiscated to force obedience to Calvin's religious dictates. Burning at the stake was the traditional form of execution for heretics. In addition to the above, 20 persons were burned between 1541 and 1559 on charges of witchcraft.[222]

How was such violence justified? Calvin subscribed to the same theology first preached more than a thousand years earlier by St. Augustine. It was Augustine who first laid the theoretical foundation for the violent abuse carried out by the medieval Roman church. Like Augustine, Calvin found justification for the use of violence in the words of one of Jesus' parables:

> Then the master said to the slave, 'Go out into the roads and lanes, and compel people to come in, so that my house may be filled.' (Luke 14:23)

To 'compel' was interpreted as authorizing the use of force, including violent force up to and including burning at the stake. Armed with this saying by Jesus, Calvin unleashed a reign of terror on the territory under his control, similar to that practiced by the Roman church. Religious officials cruelly harangued those who were condemned in an attempt to elicit a confession and recant before they were executed. (The execution proceeded even when they recanted.) Thus they believed they were fulfilling Jesus' word to 'compel' even the condemned to enter the kingdom as they were being executed, doing their victims a wonderful and righteous service when they succeeded.

---

[222] See Corner, *The Believer's Conditional Security,* p 36.

The scandalous case of Michael Servetus, a Spanish physician and lay theologian, amply demonstrates Calvin's style and state of mind. Servetus was executed on charges that he rejected both the doctrine of the Trinity and the practice of infant baptism. This was a common stance taken by Reformation groups known as Anabaptists. The name means "re-baptism." It comes from their belief that the baptism of infants is not valid because they are not old enough to make a decision to follow Christ. Thus they insisted that converts to their faith be re-baptized. (The prefix *ana* means 'again.'). Anabaptists did not play a very important role in the Reformation because they were mostly peaceful and pacifist, and were soon pushed aside in the bloody competition for control of the movement.[223]

Servetus' death was the culmination of a theological feud spanning many years. Calvin and Servetus corresponded at some length, but Calvin's attempts to convert Servetus to his point of view in the end were frustratingly unsuccessful. During this time Servetus reportedly made the fatal mistake of returning some of Calvin's religious writings with insulting comments written in the margins.

The problem for Calvin was that Servetus lived and published his ideas only outside the territory controlled by Calvin. Technically Calvin had no jurisdiction and no right to move against him. However, the contest between the two had hardened to the point that Calvin openly expressed his intentions if he ever got his hands on him. In a letter to a friend in 1546, Calvin stated:

> Servetus lately wrote to me, and [attached to] his letter a long volume of his delirious fancies... I am unwilling to pledge my word for his safety; for if he shall come, **I shall never permit him to depart alive**....[224]

That was seven years before Calvin found himself in a position to fulfill his wish.

---

[223] There were many groups known as Anabaptist. A few became involved in scandalous behavior and violent resistance to their oppressors. The majority, however, were pacifist in spite of cruel persecution. A more detailed review of Anabaptism is planned for *Gnostic Christianity Reborn*, volume three of our series The World of Primitive Christianity.

[224] Corner, *The Believer's Conditional Security*, p 38, quoted from Henry C. Sheldon, *History of the Christian Church*, Vol. 3 (Hendrickson Publishers edition, Second Printing, 1994) p 159 footnote. Emphasis added.

During the Reformation those who held Anabaptist sentiments were intensely hated by both Reformation leaders and the Roman church. Servetus was convicted of heresy and imprisoned first by the Roman church. He narrowly escaped death by means of a prison break, after which he headed for Italy. For some unknown reason, on the way to Italy Servetus stopped in Geneva to hear Calvin preach. There he was recognized and arrested immediately at the end of the service.

In 1553 Servetus was chained to a stake just outside the city of Geneva for the traditional execution of a heretic. In his case a special consideration was made. Green instead of dry wood was used, and a wreath doctored with sulfur was placed on his head. Dry wood creates a tremendous blaze that kills within minutes. Green wood was used for Servetus in order to prolong the agony, to inflict one last, excruciating torture on this tragic figure. There are two accounts of the execution indicating its length. One claims it took thirty minutes for Servetus to die, the other three hours.[225]

Calvin was condemned, correctly, as a cruel tyrant by a few of his contemporaries, especially for his treatment of Servetus. Yet, to the end he maintained his actions were just, claiming that Christianity owed him a great debt of gratitude for ridding the earth of such an evil creature. Calvin responded to criticism by threatening to crush anyone who challenged his right to kill those who disagreed with him. Thus Calvin's wrote the following:

> Whosoever shall now contend that it is unjust to put heretics and blasphemers to death will knowingly and willingly incur their very guilt. This is not laid down on human authority; it is God who speaks and prescribes a perpetual rule for his church.[226]

Calvin was not someone to take lightly if you wanted to continue among the living.

Today, some Hellenistic Christians who reject predestination have the courage to print the historical facts about Calvin's sordid career as a theologian, and question whether he is qualified to teach anything about

---

[225] Corner, *The Believer's Conditional Security*, p 41.

[226] Ibid., p 55, quoting from Philip Schaff, *History of the Christian Church*, Vol. 8 (Grand Rapids, MI, Wm. B. Eerdmans Publishing Co., Reprinted 1995, reproduction of Third edition, Revised) p 791.

Christian theology because of his conduct. Here are the comments of Daniel Corner, one such brave individual:

> It should be apparent that, from Calvin himself down to us to-day, the "perseverance of the saints" doctrine (commonly known by some as "once saved always saved") has most often been a "license for immorality" taught under the banner of *grace*.[227]

At this point Corner quotes Jude 3–4 about those who turn grace into a license for sin, a passage we identified in a previous chapter as a key anti-Gnostic sermon. Corner then continues:

> As Calvin's own theology allowed for his cruel, unscriptural actions against Servetus, many in our day are sexually immoral, liars, drunkards, filled with greed, etc., while they still profess salvation. **This is a ramification of Calvin's grace message** – a teaching which has spread from a man who could openly burn another to death and for the remaining ten years and seven months of his life, never publicly repent of his crime and sin.[228]

The Arminian Crisis

After Calvin passed from the scene, a crisis in the Netherlands briefly threatened to undo Calvin's work. The city of Amsterdam was caught up in a swirl of dissension over Calvin's theology. In an attempt to stop the controversy, the city magistrate commissioned James Arminius, a staunch Calvinist, to study the issues and formulate the most effective defense of Calvin's Reformation theology. Unfortunately for the magistrate, when Arminius completed his study he concluded Calvinism is not supported by scripture.

Thus James Arminius embarked on a short and painful career of opposing Calvinism. In the end he embraced an essentially Primitive Christian view of salvation. Arminius taught that man possesses free will, that salvation is offered to all men, that man can accept or reject God's offer of salvation, and that man can lose salvation after conversion.[229]

---

[227] Corner, *The Believer's Conditional Security*, p 50.

[228] Ibid., p 51.

[229] There is some dispute over whether Arminius taught that salvation can be lost, and there is some evidence that he waffled and was uncertain on this issue. However, his followers unquestionably were certain of this

These doctrines, known as Arminianism, spread throughout the Netherlands. To stem the tide of what had now grown into a national crisis, a convention was organized to discuss and settle the questions raised by the Arminians in their dissent from classical Calvinism. This is known today as the Synod of Dort. It met in 1618–1619 in the city of Dort.

Dort began as a democratic convention of religious leaders from both sides. Both those who supported and those who opposed Calvinism were to participate as equals. Delegates were elected by districts from across the Netherlands. In the end, unfortunately, the ruling Calvinist authorities decided against taking the risk of a democratic process and converted the Synod of Dort into an inquisition that crushed the opposition by force. Elected delegates who supported Arminianism were unseated and allowed to attend only as officially designated defendants of their 'heresy.'

The man who chaired the Synod was a veteran of the vicious persecution of Anabaptists. This individual was quoted as previously urging local magistrates to *"strike down valiantly these* [Anabaptist] *monsters in the guise of men."* [230] It was not an auspicious start for the Arminians, forced to plead their case before individuals who considered religious dissenters as less than human. Indeed, the situation was reminiscent of a later period of European history and the Nazi attitude towards Jews.

After the Synod completed its work and rubber stamped Calvinism, some 200 Arminian ministers were purged and their leaders arrested. It is perhaps fortunate that Arminius died young. If he had been alive at the time, he undoubtedly would not have survived the persecution unleashed by Dort. Of the top Arminian leaders, Hugo Gratius was sentenced to life in prison. He escaped after three years with the help of his wife who smuggled him out, concealed in a book chest. Van Olden Barneveldt was less fortunate. He was beheaded at The Hague soon after the Synod ended. Arminian preaching was made a criminal offense, punishable by banishment and confiscation of property. Many Arminian ministers fled the country and many were stripped of their possessions.

Part of the work of the Synod of Dort was to systematize Calvin's theology, which they did. Today the Synod is praised by many advocates of predestination as a great spiritual accomplishment and milestone in the development of Reformation theology.

---

truth. By the time of the Synod of Dort, what was known as 'Arminianism' clearly embraced all four principles as stated here.

[230] Corner, *The Believer's Conditional Security,* p 62. Bracketed words added for clarity.

After languishing for many years, Arminianism was partially revived in England in the late 1700s through the preaching of John and Charles Wesley and George Whitefield. From their work came the Methodist church, one of the first major Protestant organizations to reject the doctrine of predestination. Today, however, the term Arminian still carries a distinctly negative connotation. Though many praise Arminius for rejecting predestination, Reformed churches in general still reject the teaching that salvation can be lost after conversion. On that basis most Primitive Christian groups today likewise would be labeled and condemned as Arminian.

Martin Luther, the Man

Luther was an entirely different person than Calvin. Both espoused predestination and eternal security, but in personal style and disposition they were in many respects opposites. Calvin was methodical and calculating, given to lengthy technical analysis of scripture by which he forced the twin foundational doctrines of the Reformation onto New Testament scripture.

By contrast, Luther was a passionate, compulsive man, driven by insecurity and inner doubts that plagued him most of his adult life. His embrace of the radical ideas of Reformation theology came as the end result of unusual anguish and a long series of emotional crises in his life. In 1505 he was knocked off a horse by a bolt of lightning. In the moments of dazed terror that followed, he swore to St. Anne he would become a monk, a vow he fulfilled. Five years later, on a pilgrimage to Rome, he was profoundly shocked by the open corruption of the clergy there, and nearly lost his faith in Christianity.

Luther was continually troubled by guilt. He was a monk, in a system that taught that monks by diligent effort could achieve perfection in conduct. The Roman church taught that the perfection of monks and nuns was an important source of merit that could be stored up in the church. Through grace (sometimes aided by the payment of money) the faithful could then draw on that storehouse of merit to achieve salvation.

Luther's instability and compulsive personality threw him into constant conflict with his mission as a monk. This caused him great anguish. For such a person, suffering from alcoholism, given to emotional outbursts and fits of anger, in poor health and suffering from fainting spells, it was painfully difficult to follow the monastic life and feel he was accomplishing what the church laid out for him as his life's work. How could he feel justified and secure in his faith, while burdened with so many personal problems that filled him with guilt and uncertainty?

It is in this context that one can understand Luther's strangely radical statement that he could murder and commit adultery a thousand times a day and still be saved. In the idea of eternal security Luther finally found solace from his personal problems, many of which continued to plague him throughout his life. Luther espoused both predestination and eternal security, but it was in eternal security that he found the spiritual solace and confidence that had so escaped him in the Roman church. So it is not surprising that Luther, shall we say specialized in the eternal security side of Reformation theology.

From one point of view, we might congratulate Luther that he did not resolve his insecurity and guilt by becoming hardened and ignoring the dictates of his own religion, as did much of the Roman clergy at that time. Luther displayed amazing courage in bucking the system in a time when doing so often ended in death. His troubled personality and difficulty in social integration may even have helped in that respect.

At the same time, it is tragic that he found the answer to his anxiety in eternal security, a grossly radical teaching at the other end of the religious spectrum. What a tragedy he did not come to understand the true doctrine of Christian security, that God demands obedience but is merciful and will forgive without limit those who turn to him in genuine repentance. Some of us are more damaged and troubled than others. Some of us have more difficulty than average with various aspects of our conduct. Yet, God is merciful. He is not a respecter of persons. He is patient and loving. He will not give up on anyone regardless of how often they fall, as long as they do not wantonly turn away or reject him. Luther, with all his problems, could have found complete acceptance and peace of mind in the true doctrine of Christian security.

Fortunately, Luther did not fall into the practice of violent oppression of his opponents to the degree practiced by Calvin. Unfortunately, however, that distinction is only a matter of degree.

When Luther finally was forced into open rebellion against the papacy, his life was in constant jeopardy. Many attempts were made to isolate him politically so he could be killed, as happened to nearly all reformers before him. The only reason Luther survived is the political alliance he forged with the princes and nobility of his German homeland. They rejected Rome's repeated calls to hand him over, and at one critical point hid Luther in a remote castle to prevent the papacy from seizing him.

Unfortunately this later led to tragic events in which many innocent people were slaughtered.

Germany, as part of the then proclaimed Holy Roman Empire, was being drained by a huge tax burden imposed by the church. German princes were only too happy to espouse a new religious ideology that legitimized their attempts to get out from under the economic burden of Rome. Now they could claim they were not greedy men wanting to keep everything for themselves, but merely acting on religious principle when refusing to pay the ruinous taxes demanded by Rome.

The general populace was equally exploited and ready to revolt. On the religious level there were the fees extracted by the church for clerical services, from baptism to funerals and everything in between, not to mention indulgences, by which Rome milked everyone within its grasp. But there was a secular, political dimension as well. Remember, this was medieval Europe where a substantial part of the common populace lived in a state of semi-slavery known as serfdom. The average person's life was quite miserable. The secular princes and nobility of Germany exercised the same ruinous exploitation of the common man long practiced by the princes of the church. It was merely a question of which set of greedy nobility should take the lion's share of the spoils, whether German or Roman, secular or religious.

The problem for Luther arose when the general populace began to apply his teaching about religious liberty to political liberty as well. Soon revolts of the common man spread across Germany amid demands for freedom from exploitation by the ruling class. And they often justified themselves by quoting from Luther's own writings about freedom from exploitation by Rome.

Luther was an astute politician. He quickly realized the seriousness of his situation. If he lost the backing of the German princes, Rome would have its way, which meant certain death. So Luther proclaimed that anyone revolting against the established political system should be killed outright and that this was sanctioned by God. In fact, Luther proclaimed, anyone participating in the slaughter of rebellious peasants was performing the Lord's work. So Luther deployed the full force of his prestige to protect the economic base of the German princes who were protecting him, and the popular political revolts were violently crushed. Luther's rhetoric in support of the nobility was so openly violent it shocked many of his contemporaries, and surprised even some of the German princes themselves.

Witchcraft and the Reformation

Unfortunately, Luther also did not escape one of the most common superstitions in his time, namely witchcraft. Both Roman and Reformation churches executed witches in the late Middle Ages. Luther openly supported the burning of witches, with the provision they first be tried and convicted.

For some people witch hunting was a lucrative business. Some of these were religious officials who specialized in going from town to town looking for situations to exploit. Poor harvests, sickness and misfortune of any kind often were blamed on the presence in the local community of persons in league with the devil.

When a town was suffering misfortune, its citizens often could be persuaded to pay large sums of money to have these specialists rid them of the cause. Meetings would be held in which the townspeople were exhorted to turn in the witches who must be in their midst. Parents would question their children if they had seen anything unusual. Sometimes the accused were social misfits, often women whom the neighborhood children hated or feared, or merely victims of personal animosity or neighborhood and family feuds.

If a trial were held, a variety of tests might be applied. One test involved stripping the woman naked in front of the court. (These were especially popular court sessions, open to the public.) It was believed Satan branded his followers with a special mark so he could recognize them. Unfortunately, birthmarks and moles of nearly any kind were accepted as Satan's mark.

It is estimated at least 100,000 adult women and teenage girls (as well as some men) were executed as witches under medieval Christianity. This occurred mostly in Europe but also in a few other parts of the world, including the American Colonies. Thirty-two Americans were executed in conservatively Protestant Salem, Massachusetts, in the famous witch trials that occurred there in 1691–92.

I have to ask the question: Why is it that Martin Luther, as well as many other supposedly Christian people, didn't know better? How do you get around this? Is it possible Martin Luther was not aware of the New Testament example of Jesus and the adulterous woman? Can anyone seriously suggest he didn't know that under the New Testament capital punishment by religious authorities has been abolished?[231] What about grace and mercy? Why did they execute them even when they recanted? Further, is it reasonable to suggest Martin Luther was so intelligent and educated that he could argue fine points of biblical criticism and write sophisticated books of commentary on the Bible, and at the same time not comprehend that the witch trials going on around him were a monstrously irrational fraud?

If we wish to explain away Luther's actions by saying he was only caught up in the culture and backward beliefs of his time, how then can we understand God's condemnation of the Israelites for sacrificing their children to Baal? Were they any less caught up in the superstitions of their time? Is the senseless murder of an innocent teenage girl in the Middle Ages any less evil than the senseless killing of a baby in ancient Israel?

Martin Luther is a great figure of history and he fought for many good ideals. On the negative side, however, are Luther's superstition and belief in witchcraft, obsession with the devil, his racist hatred of Jews, lack of self-control and unusually foul mouth even for that time and culture, his life-long habitually violent, explosive temper, and the bitter, caustic attacks he unleashed on anyone who disagreed with him, friend or foe.[232]

The leading founders of the Protestant Reformation – that is, those leaders who emerged victorious from the bitter struggle for control of the

---

[231] The famous example of Jesus and the adulterous woman – 'whosoever is without sin cast the first stone.' John 8:3–11.

[232] An excellent source for anyone wishing to obtain a balanced view of Martin Luther is also one of the most recent and widely acclaimed biographies of the man, available in English as *Luther: Man Between God and the Devil*, by Heiko Oberman. It presents a generally sympathetic view of Luther, but preaches the necessity of presenting the whole story, both positive and negative, which the author appears to do in a reasonably balanced fashion.

The picture I receive from the historical data is of a tremendously courageous and driven man who stood up to a horrible tyranny that had overtaken the world of Hellenistic Christianity, which had reached such excess it was teetering and ready to fall under its own weight. The Reformation, and the secular age of enlightenment that accompanied it, sharply reduced many forms of abuse and, as such, did much good. For Primitive Christians, however, I believe the most important issue is that though they probably would agree with Luther's rejection of the authoritarian and legalistic abuses of medieval Roman Christianity, and praise his tremendous courage and conviction, in the end it was only a reformation of Hellenistic Christianity. The end product, though much less abusive and authoritarian, was still only Hellenistic Christianity.

Reformation, a victory obtained often through persecution and murder – are far from shining lights of Christian virtue. One of them was an obsessive tyrant and unrepentant serial murderer. The other was a deeply troubled individual who found solace for extensive personal problems in the radical teachings of eternal security. When cornered he traded enthusiastic support for the violent massacre of countless peasants to secure his own personal safety. One might reasonably ask: If they both believed in irresistible grace, why didn't God irresistibly make them at least a little more Christian in their conduct?[233] In the history of the Protestant Reformation we see a repetition of the sad history of Nicolaitan Christians of the first century A.D. Religion based on antinomian theories of inner spirituality necessarily ends in failure because it is not sanctioned nor supported by God and the power of his Spirit.

Today many Hellenistic Christians themselves see the problem, condemn moral failure within the Reformation movement, and correctly attribute the problem to heretical, antinomian theology. The problem is that so many merely condemn theological positions more radical than their own, failing to recognize the very foundation of Reformation theology itself is both imbalanced and unbiblical.

How did the Reformation go so wrong? Where did these strange ideas come from? The answer to that is almost as surprising and strange as Reformation theology itself. It is to this question of origins we now turn.

The Augustine-Gnostic Connection

Where did Reformation theology come from? Both Luther and Calvin simultaneously came up with the foundational doctrines of predestination and eternal security. Calvin emphasized predestination to such a degree that the term Calvinism has become synonymous with predestination. Luther leaned more heavily on eternal security, as we see from his surprising 1521 letter in which he boasts Christians can engage in unlimited murder and fornication and still be saved. Yet both endorsed both predes-

---

[233] These are lifelong patterns of conduct, not comparable to figures such as King David who fell into egregious sin but repented and turned back to God. Indeed, Christians can experience terrible sin, both before and after conversion, but through repentance and grace are restored to a relationship with Jesus and the Father.

tination and eternal security as the doctrinal foundation of the Protestant Reformation.

Was the Reformation the miraculous work of the Holy Spirit, or is there a more prosaic explanation? Did miraculous inspiration of the Spirit cause both Luther and Calvin to simultaneously come to the same conclusions? Or, was Reformation theology an already existing ancient tradition, resurrected by both Luther and Calvin as their solution to medieval Roman legalism?

Luther and Calvin themselves give the simple answer, recognized and accepted by all historians. Both attribute their discovery of Reformation theology to one of the major theologians of the Roman church – St. Augustine, who lived in the fifth century some thousand years before the Protestant Reformation.[234]

Today many consider Augustine the most important theologian in the history of Hellenistic Christianity. Both Protestants and Catholics trace their theology to this one individual. Augustine developed the Roman theories of church authority, including both the justification for using violence to enforce the church's will, and the concept of basing theology on church tradition.

But Augustine also wrote two important treatises, *On the Predestination of the Saints,* and *On the Gift of Perseverance.*[235] In these Augustine laid out the primary ideas of predestination and eternal security, which lay largely dormant for centuries until picked up by Luther and Calvin.

Hellenistic Christians who oppose predestination make a special point of the fact that through all the approximately 1,500 years before the Protestant Reformation, Augustine was the only major Christian theologian to teach the concept of predestination and irresistible grace.[236] If these are foundational principles of religious truth, and if they were indeed taught by the apostles in the first century, how could they have become lost between the first century and Augustine, then become lost again for a thousand years only to be rediscovered by Luther and Calvin?

---

[234] E.g. Corner, *The Believer's Conditional Security,* p 23 ff.

[235] *On the Gift of Perseverance* contains Augustine's elaboration of the doctrine of eternal security. 'Perseverance' sometimes is used to refer to eternal security since, in predestination theology, eternal security is effected by God supernaturally causing the saints to endure (persevere) to the end of their lives, or to at least return to the faith before death.

[236] See Geisler, *Chosen But Free,* p 29.

That is as far as Hellenistic Christian criticism goes, because the full story is much more embarrassing. Christians actually did teach the basic tenets of Reformation theology beginning in the first century and extending right up to Augustine. Not in the Roman church, however. The first teachers of the basic tenets of Reformation theology were Gnostic Christians. As we saw in previous chapters, eternal security – salvation as a gift that cannot be lost – was a component of Gnostic Christian theology (see above, page 191). Many Gnostics also believed that a portion of humanity is predestined to be saved, and another portion predestined to be lost.

There remains a gap, however. How did an originally Gnostic Christian theology, including eternal security and predestination, get into the Roman church from whence it was handed down to Luther and Calvin? The answer is Augustine. What few today realize is that Augustine's involvement with Christianity began not with the Roman church, but with Gnostic Christianity. For nine years before he joined the Roman church, Augustine was a practicing Gnostic Christian of the Manichean sect.[237]

Augustine was a controversial figure in his day. Some Christians in his time openly accused him of introducing Gnostic teachings into the church. He was so accused because that is exactly what he was doing. For example, it was Augustine who first interpreted the fall of man with the sexual overtones that later became orthodox in the Roman church.[238] This was classic Gnostic theology, and it was accompanied in Augustine's thought by the idea of total depravity. Augustine specifically argued that after the fall in Eden man lost free will.[239] This became the basis of the extreme Reformation concept that man plays no role in salvation, which in turn underpins predestination and eternal security.

The full story of how ancient Gnostic Christian theology was adapted by Augustine, how it was resurrected and transmitted by the Protestant Reformation and evolved ultimately into the modern forms we see preached today, is a huge topic of its own and must be reserved for a separate volume. God willing, the third volume in our series, The World of Primitive Christianity, will cover this amazing story. The proposed title

---

[237] After nine years as a Gnostic Christian Augustine returned to teaching Hellenistic philosophy for several years, after which he converted to Roman Christianity. For a brief review of Manichean Gnosticism see above, pages 55 and following.

[238] See the excellent discussion by Elaine Pagels, *Adam, Eve and the Serpent*, p 99 ff.

[239] Ibid.

at the time of this writing is *Gnostic Christianity Reborn! The Strange, Untold Story Behind the Protestant Reformation.*

What is so little understood today is that there was a terrific and bloody battle for control of the Protestant Reformation. There were essentially three groups involved in the struggle. On one side was Rome, of course, and on the other were the traditional Reformers headed by Luther and Calvin, and a third group, today often referred to as the Reformation Radicals. Among the radicals were various groups, such as Arminians and some Anabaptists. Some of these rejected the doctrine of the immortal soul and were moving rapidly back toward the original apostolic teaching of the first-century church. Calvin got his start as a theologian by fighting against this, struggling successfully to preserve Hellenistic Christian doctrines such as the immortality of the soul. In the process, many groups were viciously persecuted and butchered by both Roman and Protestant authorities, including Calvin with his murderous reign of terror from Geneva, Switzerland. It is a vital part of the history of Christianity, long suppressed, that desperately needs to be told.

The end result of this process was that the movement by some to reverse the Hellenization of Christianity and return to the Jewish Christianity of the first century was aborted. In its place were substituted the resurrection of some of the key teachings of ancient Gnostic Christianity.[240]

Survival of Gnostic Theology

There are two primary doctrines of Reformation theology (predestination and eternal security) and another important underlying principle supporting both doctrines (total depravity, loss of free will). All three of these teachings appeared first in Gnostic Christianity. Is that significant? Is it significant that the basic principles of Reformation theology were first taught by an ancient religious movement roundly and repeatedly con-

---

[240] It is important to note that we are *not* talking about the survival of "Gnosticism" per se, but rather the survival of certain key doctrines of Gnostic Christianity. Gnosticism itself was a broad and diverse movement incorporating many, sometimes contradictory teachings. Reformation theology in the end picked up certain key Gnostic ideas that exaggerated the genuine Christian theme of the power of the Spirit to heal and regenerate, as well as libertarian and libertine antinomian themes, all of which were important in resolving the Reformation's philosophic concern with legalism.

demned in the New Testament as a horrible apostasy leading to spiritual failure? Is it significant that the major issue on which the New Testament condemns that ancient theology is antinomianism? Is it significant that Reformation Christianity preaches essentially that same antinomianism today?

Eternal security was a primary staple of Gnostic Christian theology. Gnostic Christians taught that salvation is a free gift and therefore cannot be taken back. Valentinian Gnostics taught that outward sin could never derail salvation as long as their inner soul was attached to the perfection of the heavenly *pleroma*. The early church fathers roundly and correctly condemned them for believing there is nothing they must do to be saved.

Predestination equally was a common feature of Gnostic Christianity. Many Gnostic sects believed there are separate classes of people, some of whom are predestined to be saved and others predestined to be lost.

Valentinians claimed that some people, whom they called *pneumatics*, were born with a spiritual soul, and this predestined them to be saved. Another class of humans, called *hylics,* were believed to be born without a spiritual soul. These unfortunates are predestined to die like animals, totally and irreversibly without hope of salvation. This early predestination theology embraced by Gnostic Christians in fact is mentioned in the New Testament. Remember, as we saw in an earlier chapter, this was the reason the Apostle Jude referred to Gnostics as irrational animals, insulting them with their own theology about a class of persons they believed are predestined to fail.[241]

In Gnostic as well as in Reformation theology, the key event of salvation is **regeneration**. Christ came to reveal the existence of the heavenly *pleroma* and reconnect mankind to it. Doing so restores the soul to a state of spiritual perfection. This was the original, Gnostic precedent for the Reformation doctrine of regeneration.

Many Gnostics also taught the concept of the **total depravity** of man after falling from an originally perfect state in heaven. This is expressed in some of the Nag Hammadi texts in mythological terms. When man was created, they say, he lay helpless on the ground, unable even to stand. Then an element of spirit was injected into them, which enabled them to function as men, giving them the ultimate hope of salvation.

---

[241] Jude 10. See above, discussion of the book of Jude, beginning on page 90.

The concept also is found in the almost universal Gnostic idea of man's ignorance of the connection of his immortal soul to the heavens. That is cured by the regenerating effect of reestablishing that knowledge. Before regeneration, cutoff from the spiritual power of the heavens, man is helpless. He is literally unable to express spirituality, hopelessly in bondage to the material world. Once the soul is reconnected to the heavens, however, the spiritual goodness of the soul awakens and reasserts itself naturally, without any effort by man. Some libertarian Gnostic sects indeed were the first Christians to preach that man plays **no role in salvation**. (Remember our discussion of Valentinian Gnosticism in which the healing of the soul – regeneration – leads to spirituality naturally, without effort. See above, pages 99 and following.)

Augustine's Sources

What are the Gnostic sources from which Augustine received the doctrines that serve as a precedent for Reformation theology?

Augustine participated in a Manichean Gnostic sect for nine years as a 'hearer,' from age 19 to 28. During that time he lived with a woman to whom he was not married, by whom he fathered a child. Though Manichean hearers were enjoined to moral conduct, they faced the same problems with immorality as the Nicolaitans, the same problems that later befell medieval Roman Christianity and the Carnal Christianity of modern Reformation Christianity. If Manicheans departed from their own standards, even willfully, all was not lost. They could look forward to rectifying their failings after death in purgatory. If they faithfully supported the ministry of their church they could depend on the blessings and ritual interventions of the clergy to speed them through the process of purification in the afterlife. In this the Manicheans anticipated the structure and theology of the medieval Roman church, while other groups such as Valentinian Gnostics reflect more of the libertarian spirit of Reformation theology.

Both Valentinian and Manichean Gnosticism taught that portions of the human population do not possess a spiritual soul, and therefore are predestined to be lost. Gnosticism in general taught that the purpose of salvation was to gather all fallen particles of Spirit, generally lodged in human souls, and return them to their true home in the heavens. In essence that means any soul containing a particle of spirit is predestined to be saved.

This of course is not exactly the same as predestination in Hellenistic Christianity today. The difference for predestination, for example, is that Reformation Christianity says it is done by God explicitly choosing individuals by name before the world began, while Gnostic Christianity generally attributed it to various cosmological circumstances through which some humans received souls with a particle of fallen spirit while others did not. In either case, however, the result is the same – some people are destined to be saved and will be saved like it or not, while others are destined to fail and there is nothing they can do about it.

The Process of Historical Transmission

Some vigorously protest that such differences prove there is no connection, and borrowing could not have occurred. That is misguided. For one thing, we are not talking about transmission of a single doctrine, but a complex of doctrines that mutually support each other. Eternal security, predestination, the concept of total depravity that underlies both of those doctrines, regeneration, mystical identification with God, salvation with no participation by man, and most importantly the antinomian concepts attached to those teachings, all took form in various ancient Gnostic Christian groups and appear again today in their most developed and complete form in Reformation Christianity.

If this is accidental coincidence, it was an accident constantly repeating itself to the point coincidence is not a credible explanation.

Wouter J. Hanegraaff is an eminent scholar in the historical transmission of Hellenistic ideas from antiquity to the present day. In writing about the survival of ancient Hellenistic theology and philosophy within modern esoteric cults in Europe and America, he explains the natural process of change and adaptation as religious beliefs are passed down through time:

> Ideas do not move through history unchanged: what "continues" is never simply "the original idea" but, rather, the original idea *as perceived through the eyes of later generations.* ... Each generation not only reinterprets ideas of the past, but also makes its own personal selection while adding innovations of its own. With

respect to the past, it generally selects what suits its purposes while simply disregarding the rest. [242]

Hellenistic scholars and ministers have no problem making comparisons between Gnostic Christianity and modern phenomena such as New Age cults. When it comes to applying the same scientific analysis to Hellenistic Christianity, however, we run into a major stumbling block. It is a very human problem. Many who believe in Hellenistic Christianity today are horrified by the idea their teachings may have come from some other source than the Bible.

Nevertheless, the evidence is very clear. If the New Testament condemns Gnostic doctrine of the first century, should we condemn those same doctrines today? For those who believe in progressive revelation, on the other hand, it may not matter at all. If the apostles Peter and Jude had only understood today's doctrine of the Carnal Christian, perhaps they wouldn't have been so hard on Gnostic Christians back in the first century. Maybe the apostles' complaints against Gnostic Christianity were all a big mistake!

In the end, this is one of the most enduring and critical issues in Christianity. Do we know better than the authors of the New Testament? Jude began his epistle by exhorting first-century Christians *"to contend for the faith that was **once for all** entrusted to the saints"* (Jude 3). Controversy over progressive revelation and replacement of the original revelation of Christianity was just as hot an issue in the apostolic church in the first century as it is today.

Is first-century apostolic Christianity the standard for all time, *once for all* as Jude expressed it? Or was there a second, more spiritual revelation of Christianity from after the earthly ministry of Christ and the writing of the New Testament? Is the Jewish Christianity of the first century what God willed for his church, or was the subsequent Hellenization of Christianity the will of God and the standard we should follow today?

---

[242] See Hanegraaf, *The New Age Movement and the Esoteric Tradition,* p 376, in **GH**.

New Testament Prophecies about the Presence of Gnostic Theology in Our Day

When considering the question of the resurgence of Gnostic theology within Protestantism, we need not rely solely on historical analysis. The Bible itself predicted this would happen.

As we saw in an earlier chapter, the first two epistles of the Apostle John were written as a rebuttal of Gnostic Christianity in the first century. In his letters John frequently refers to the Gnostics of his time as antichrists because of their heretical teachings. In the following passage, he talks about this, and then connects what was happening in the first century with the "end times."

> ...so now many antichrists have come; **therefore we know that it is the last hour.** They **went out from us**, but they were not of us; for if they had been of us, they would have continued with us; but they went out, that it might be plain that they all are not of us. (1John 2:18-19)

Here John is referring to the exodus of Gnostic Christians from the church that began late in the first century (*they went out from us*). It seems as if John thought the end times (*the last hour*) began in the first century with the rise of Gnostic Christian heresy and that mass exodus of Gnostics from the church. Of course we know now, nearly 2,000 years later, that was not the *"last hour"* as John phrased it. The timing is off by a mere two millennia. Was John mistaken?

Is the Bible wrong? Not at all. This passage from John's first epistle is entirely valid, but its complete fulfillment was not for that time. Gnostic Christianity and the turmoil it caused in the first-century church was not destined to fulfill this prophecy. Rather, the complete fulfillment of John's prophecy is meant for today. Indeed, the reappearance of Gnostic theology in our day is a fulfillment of biblical prophecy.

Mysticism and Antinomianism

Mysticism and antinomianism go hand in hand. That is true for Gnostic Christianity in the early centuries after Christ as well as for Reformation theology today. In this section we review the theme of Christian mysticism and how its development in Gnostic and Reformed theology resemble each other.

Laurence Vance, a modern Reformation theologian, summarizes for us what he and many like him today regard as the essence of Christian salvation. It is not about righteous living, he says. It is not even about persevering in the faith. Instead, he insists, it is solely about mystical union with Christ and the heavenly Father.

Vance lists numerous New Testament passages about mystical union with Jesus – *"For as in Adam all die, even so in Christ shall all be made alive"*, we are *"joined unto the Lord"*, *"members of his body, of his flesh, and of his bones"*, *"partakers of the divine nature"*, *"together in heavenly places in Christ Jesus."* [243]

Vance then argues it is in fact mystical union with Jesus that gives Christians the option to willfully disobey. His primary text is 2 Timothy 2:12–13, where Paul quotes a common Christian saying from his time:

> if we endure, we shall reign with him;
>
> if we disown him, he will disown us;
>
> if we are faithless, he remains faithful,
>
> for he cannot disown himself.

Notice in the first and second lines Paul witnesses powerfully against eternal security. He says we must endure, and if we disown Jesus then Jesus will disown us. Advocates of eternal security counter with the third and fourth lines. Here it says if we lack faith, Jesus still will be faithful on his part, because he *"cannot disown himself."* What they are saying is that the third and fourth lines override the first and second lines. (In typical fashion, Hellenistic Christianity here continues its tradition of contradiction rather than harmonizing scripture.)

Their interpretation of the third and fourth lines is that mystical identification with Jesus guarantees our acceptance regardless of any sin. In their view the third and fourth lines can be paraphrased as: "Still, regardless of what was just said, Jesus will never turn his back on you because of your conduct. He cannot disown you because, since you are mystically part of him, that would be the same as disowning himself." Therefore, they claim, the key to salvation is mystical union with Jesus and the Father. Once you achieve that, Jesus couldn't disown you if he wanted to,

---

[243] Vance, *The Other Side of Calvinism,* p 587.

because cutting you off would be the same as cutting off a piece of himself.

This is salvation exactly as it always was in a large part of Gnostic Christianity – mystically reconnecting the soul to God through Jesus and the heavenly *pleroma*.

Mystical identification with Jesus is a valid biblical concept (*it is no longer I who live, but it is Christ who lives in me* – Galatians 2:20). The problem is that both Gnostic and Reformation theology combine genuine Christian mysticism with heretical antinomian license. This is a classic example of the survival of Gnostic patterns of antinomian reasoning within Reformation theology.

How should we understand the Christian saying in 2 Timothy 2:12–13? What it really seems to be saying is something quite different. In the third and fourth lines it is talking about Jesus' nature, which is to be faithful. What Jesus cannot disown is his own nature. Because by nature he is always faithful, we need never fear that Jesus will fail us as we sometimes fail him, except for the specific situations in lines one and two where he says we must endure, and he will disown us if we disown him. This should be a powerful source of Christian comfort.

Antinomian Mysticism and the Epistles of John

The antinomian interpretation of 2 Timothy 2:12–13, based on mystical identification with Christ, is widely taught in the world of Reformation theology today. And the Epistles of John are especially important in understanding the Gnostic origin of this problem.

The Apostle John's first two letters were written to counter Gnostic Christianity. These same letters also specifically attack the antinomian doctrine of mystical union with God. We find this especially in the third chapter of John's first letter.

Keep in mind the Gnostic teachings that are the target of John's message. For Gnostic Christians, salvation was attained by knowledge of God (*gnosis*). That creates mystical union with him, magically regenerating the soul and turning it into a spiritually perfect copy of the heavens.[244] Good conduct is the byproduct of mystical union with God. But good conduct

---

[244] See above, pages 130 and following in chapter 6 "Gnostic Spirituality", also chapter 7, "Thyatira and the Deep Things of Satan."

has nothing to do with salvation itself – sin, even willful sin, can never block salvation. Salvation is guaranteed by mystical connection to the heavenly *pleroma*, which imparts its purely heavenly perfection to the soul.

What is so important is that here in 1 John 3, the Apostle is countering this very theology, shared by both Gnostic and Reformation Christianity. John is very direct. You can NOT experience mystical union with God, he insists, if you continue willfully in sin. You can neither 'know him' nor 'abide in him' nor consider yourself 'born of God':

> No one who **abides in him** sins; no one who sins has either seen him or **known him**. (1 John 3:4–6)

> Everyone who commits sin is a child of the devil; ... **Those who have been born of God do not sin**.... The children of God and the children of the devil are revealed in this way: all who do not do what is right are not from God.... (1 John 3:8–10)

What John is saying in chapter 3 is the same as in chapter 1 verse 6, *"If we say we have fellowship with him while we walk in darkness, we lie...."*

Reformation theology explains this by saying Christians indeed lose fellowship with God when they continue in wanton sin, but they never lose salvation. Sinful Christians supposedly will be barred from direct contract with Christ in heaven, so in that fashion they are punished for their sins, but still are saved. The importance of 1 John chapter three is it addresses those arguments by laying out, even more clearly, the biblical stand on this issue. John says that Christians who continue in willful sin are not born of God. It even describes them as "children of the devil." Now, is it possible to be a child of the devil, not born of God, and still be saved? Christ himself witnessed, *"Except a man be born again, he cannot see the kingdom of God"* (John 3:3, KJV).

The Apostle John's first letter condemns the basic assumptions underlying eternal security and antinomian mysticism. Why does John do this in a letter attacking Gnostic Christianity? Is this not proof that Gnosticism is the source from which these heretical teachings came? Why was eternal security and predestination first introduced to the orthodox Roman church by Augustine, a convert from a Gnostic sect? Why did Augustine's contemporaries accuse him of introducing Gnostic teachings in the church? Once again, how much clearer can it get?

Extreme Eternal Security, America, and the End-Time

Once one sets out on the slippery slope of pursuing religious truth through human wisdom, the only certainty is that the road leads downhill. How bad can it get? The tragedy of Reformation theology is most fully realized in the antinomianism of extreme eternal security. Here, anything goes. That is not an exaggeration. Literally *anything* goes! The saved are licensed to get away with anything and everything for which the unsaved are sent to hell. The only thing that matters, in the end, is mystical union with Jesus and the guaranteed ticket to heaven.

Extreme eternal security has become the dominant theology of American Evangelicalism. It was developed and flourishes primarily in America. Tragically, the nation that leads the world in the global export of immorality and violence in entertainment, also leads the world as the primary source of the most licentious, extreme antinomianism within the Reformation movement.

The error and perversity of Reformation theology has come to a head in the huge American Evangelical movement, with its more than 100 million followers. Indeed, much of the rest of the Reformation movement around the world is scandalized by what is happening here. If such a thing could be measured, America today would be considered a prominent global center of the mystery of lawlessness, both religious and secular.

This is not a frivolous intellectual exercise. In *Spirit of Antichrist,* volume two of our series The World of Primitive Christianity, we will be exploring the problem of antinomian Christianity as it relates to the end-time prophecies of Revelation. These prophecies specifically mention major antinomian movements together with the political entities in which they operate. Revelation describes one of these antinomian movements as having its power and influence terminated in a catastrophe that affects the economic stability of the entire earth. The phenomenon of extreme eternal security could have an horrific impact on all our lives in the not too distant future.

Part 3

Conclusions

What does this mean for us today? Is this just an interesting intellectual exercise, an entertaining tour through history? If these matters are to be taken seriously, if we take seriously the exhortation to *"listen to what the Spirit is saying to the churches,"* then how do we apply these sometimes-complex issues to our lives today?

In the following three chapters we attempt to summarize much of the information already covered, and outline how and why it applies to our world today.

First we examine how Gnostic Christianity fits into the larger picture of Hellenistic apostasy, and what New Testament prophecy says about Gnosticism and Hellenistic religion in the end time. Is the presence of Gnostic theology in our day a fulfillment of Bible prophecy?

Next we consider some important New Testament teachings about spiritual balance. Here we discover that New Testament prophecy is much more than just foretelling future events.

In the final chapter we summarize the biblical and historical arguments of this volume, but most importantly we review additional information about the underlying issue of this entire book – What does the New Testament demand of apostolic Christians in their relationship with Hellenistic Christianity? This is a topic of the utmost importance for Primitive Christianity today. New Testament prophecy indicates that in the final turbulent years before Christ's return we will become embroiled in one of the greatest religious crises ever experienced on earth, the time of the final and full revelation of the mysterious "man of sin" mentioned in 2 Thessalonians chapter 2. What specifically does Jesus expect from us during those critical years?

– 12 –

Hellenistic Apostasy
in
New Testament Prophecy

The story of Gnostic Christianity explains so much about how we got to where we are today. But that is only half the story. There was a second wave of Hellenistic apostasy that occurred after Gnostic Christianity had been expelled from the apostolic church. This second wave developed its own independent Hellenistic religious tradition that competed with Gnosticism for control of Christianity. New Testament prophecy foretells the survival of both of these Hellenistic apostasies into our day, where they will play important roles in tragic events of the end time.

In this chapter we will trace the history and prophecies relating to Gnosticism, the first wave of apostasy, the second wave that came after Gnosticism, and then the survival of Primitive Christianity itself. As we will see, the religious landscape of Christianity in the early centuries after Christ was remarkably similar to the present day.

Gnostic Christianity

Gnostic Christianity first formed inside the apostolic church where it flourished as proto-Gnosticism. Gnosticism is especially important because it was the first intrusion of Hellenistic apostasy into the church. As such, it laid the groundwork for everything that came after it. Because it sprang in part from Hellenistic Judaism, which already existed before Jesus was born, it got in on the ground floor. It was off and running within just a few decades after the church was founded.

Gnosticism reached a high point inside the church late in the first century. Its sudden flourishing provoked a crisis, which is reflected in the epistles of John, Jude, and 2 Peter chapters 2–3. The apostolic church was shocked by its grossly antinomian theology. This first attack by Hellenistic apostasy was successfully contained.

Beginning late in the first century there was a mass exodus in which most Gnostic Christians left the church. After several centuries their fragmented churches and sects had mostly died out. Their characteristic antinomian theology did not resurface in a major way until the Protestant Reformation, more than a thousand years later.

Classic Gnosticism's Last Hurrah

Though the classic Gnostic sects of the second and third centuries eventually died out, a few survived in the eastern Mediterranean. From there they moved up through the Balkan countries of Eastern Europe. In the 12th and 13th centuries there was a major revival as Gnostic Christian sects spread across all of southern Europe. These were known under various names, including Albigensian, Bogomil and Cathar. These indeed were classic Gnostic religions. Cathars, for example, condemned marriage and taught that the creator of the world (Yahweh) is Satan. In France there were pockets of countryside in which virtually the entire population converted to Gnostic Christianity and successfully drove out local Roman church authorities.

Gnostic Christianity championed individualism and a personal relationship with God based on the private inspiration of the Spirit. It championed freedom from authority and a process of transformation to righteousness that works magically and exclusively from inside. Therefore Gnostic Christianity was one of the first to stand up against the authoritarian abuse of the medieval Roman church and champion individualism and freedom of conscience. These early attempts at reform were crushed by bloody campaigns of the Catholic Inquisition. And so the brief medieval resurgence of classic Gnosticism in southern Europe died out.

Gnosticism has played a much larger role in shaping the religious landscape of Christianity than is commonly recognized. That is true for Catholicism as well as Protestantism. The wild antinomian excesses of Gnosticism pushed the early church to overreact with authoritarianism and legalism, both in the early centuries after Christ and in the Middle

Ages. The establishment and growth of the dreaded Inquisition was in part a reaction against the resurgence of Gnostic Christianity in the 12th and 13th centuries.

There appears to be no historical connection between the classic Gnostic churches of southern Europe in the 12th and 13th centuries and the revival of Gnostic theology shortly afterward, in the 16th century, in the Protestant Reformation. The historical evidence indicates the mode of transmission was the reworking and preservation of Gnostic teachings by Augustine, from whom both Luther and Calvin acknowledge they obtained the primary doctrines of the Protestant Reformation.

A Second Wave of Apostasy – the Roman Church

The rest of the story is what happened to the apostolic church after most Gnostic Christians had left. Though the church had fought off the radically lawless theology of Gnosticism, the Hellenization process it initiated continued, culminating in a second great Hellenistic apostasy.

This produced new forms of Hellenistic Christianity, much less radical than classic Gnosticism and much more biblically palatable. As time progressed, segments of the apostolic church continued observing Sabbath while more and more converted to Sunday. Some observed both. Passover was replaced by Easter and the Hellenistic doctrine of the immortality of the soul gained ground. All the while, the authority of the church became more concentrated in the capital of the empire, and Rome rose as the head of the church.

Rome never took on the freewheeling libertarian individualism typical of Gnosticism. Instead, Roman Christianity developed more of what one might call institutional antinomianism, an authoritarian approach to the mystery of lawlessness. Like Gnostic Christianity, Rome also believed in a second more spiritual revelation of Christianity. But it handed the power to modify the original faith to the church hierarchy. Gnostic Christianity and later, Reformation Christianity, gave the same power to the collective private inspiration of individual Christians. This difference in part reflects the distinct paths followed by ancient Roman versus Gnostic Christianity.

As the Roman church and Gnostic sects went their separate ways, Rome gravitated to other schools of Hellenistic belief, especially the philosophic-religious cult of Neoplatonism.[245] Finally, in the fourth century, the now severely wounded apostolic church experienced a fateful encounter with the Roman emperors that brought the continuing Hellenization of the church to a head, culminating in the second major Hellenistic Christian apostasy.

Imperial Rome and the Church

Pagan Hellenistic religion for centuries had claimed there is an underlying, single universal truth present in all ancient belief systems.[246] So they taught that all religions must be reinterpreted to bring out the hidden, universal truths of the immortality of the soul and its connection to the heavens.

As time progressed, that led to belief in a universal pagan religion. This came to a head in the fourth century. The Roman emperors for some time had been searching for a way to synthesize the best of Hellenistic religious belief, with the goal of uniting the empire under a single, universal religion. For certain political reasons, the emperor Constantine in the fourth century selected the Hellenistic Christianity of the Roman church as the medium for accomplishing that goal.

Roman Christianity never would have been considered by the emperors for this role unless it first had become as Hellenized as it already was. It was Gnosticism that made this possible by launching, centuries earlier, the fateful process of Hellenization.

Thereafter the Roman emperors took a direct interest in completing the Hellenization of the church. When Constantine in the fourth century offi-

---

[245] The Roman church was attracted more to Neoplatonism, Chaldean theology and theurgy, which emphasized submission to earthly manifestations of divine energies and authorities. This had a more authoritarian bent compared to the radical libertarian theories of Gnosticism. (The separate development of Hellenistic theology in the Roman church is covered in more detail in *Spirit of Antichrist,* the second volume in our series The World of Primitive Christianity.)

[246] Recall how so many of the early teachers and schools of philosophy and religion, including Orphism and Plato, taught that the truths of the great pagan reformation of religion in ancient Greece could be found in ancient pre-reformation religions, from which it could be drawn out by allegorical interpretation. The Orphic Mysteries, for example, were a more spiritual reformation of the Mysteries of Dionysus.

cially imposed Sunday as the exclusive day of worship, he talked about the "venerable day of the sun." His choice of words was no accident. He didn't say the "venerable day of Jesus" or the "Lord's Day," because he literally was not talking about that.

What Constantine was talking about was the Roman imperial cult of which he was head. The Roman imperial cult venerated the sun as the principle of immortality and a symbol of the supreme god of pagan Hellenistic religion. The rising of the sun was understood as a daily victory over darkness and death. The unchanging persistence of that celestial phenomenon gave proof to paganism of their hope of immortality. What Constantine was doing was forcibly completing the Hellenization of the church and obliterating its Hebrew roots in order to build a common ground for merging his own Hellenistic paganism with Christianity.

Scholars frequently argue about whether Constantine genuinely converted to Roman Christianity or was using it cynically for his own political ends. In fact there is truth in both views. Though Constantine ultimately did genuinely embrace Roman Christianity, he saw it as many people of his time saw it, as merely another religious expression of the ancient truths of pagan Hellenistic religion.

The Second Apostasy Was Prophesied

Because Gnosticism overlapped with the first century, when the New Testament was being written, it is mentioned frequently in scripture, as we saw above in chapter five, "Gnosticism in the Bible." The second wave of apostasy, which produced Roman Catholicism, occurred after the New Testament was written. Nevertheless, it too is mentioned in scripture. We find it in New Testament prophecy where the church's subsequent veering into a second Hellenistic apostasy, ending in the arms of the Roman emperors, is accurately described in amazing detail.

Paul talks about this in 2 Thessalonians chapter two. Here he describes the problem of apostasy in the church as something already underway, but with significant events yet to occur in the future.

Paul is writing this in the second half of the first century. At this point, he says, the mystery of lawlessness has already appeared (*for the mystery of lawlessness is **already** at work* – 2 Thess 2:7). We know from the historical evidence this refers to the appearance of proto-Gnosticism inside the first century church. From the epistles of John we also know that Gnostic Christians left the church en masse beginning late in the first century (1 John 2:18–19). Though they were responsible for what already had happened, if Gnostic Christians were leaving the church, they could not be directly responsible for what was to follow. Therefore there is a distinction to be made between Paul's description in Thessalonians of what already had taken place and what at that time was yet future.

History confirms all of this. The first wave of apostasy ended somewhat cleanly, with the exodus of those responsible. Still they left their mark. Hellenistic theology had been planted inside the church, and that served as the foundation for what was to follow. Therefore it is appropriate to characterize the Hellenistic apostasy that overwhelmed the early church as two distinct yet connected events, exactly as they are characterized in 2 Thessalonians chapter two.

By the late first century there is nothing indicating an apostate takeover of the leadership of the church. The apostolic church is still intact. So far the problem is limited to the introduction of sophisticated antinomian doctrines, collectively called the 'mystery of lawlessness.' This has taken root inside the church, but the surviving apostles are vigorously fighting back, as seen in the sharply worded anti-Gnostic sermons in Jude, 2 Peter 2, and the first two epistles of John. And the apostolic counterattack apparently is having an effect, as proto-Gnostics begin to leave the church in large numbers.

Unfortunately, however, there is worse to come. According to Paul, this initial apostate tradition will subsequently blossom, resulting in the appearance of a new church leadership headed by *"the lawless one"* (2 Thess 2:3, 7). What began as theological innovation in the first century ultimately turns political. The church will become dominated by an individual who makes great claims for himself and exercises great power and authority – *"He opposes and exalts himself...he takes his seat in the temple of God, declaring himself to be God"* (vs 4).

The new authoritarian leadership is prophesied to gather around it a following that rejects the original truth preached in the apostolic church: *"all that have not believed the truth"* (vs 12), and those who *"refused to love the truth"* (vs 10).

Consider those words in the context of the second half of the first century A.D. when it was written. Paul is complaining about something that will soon replace *"the truth"* preached in the first-century church. And that replacement is something that developed out of the Hellenistic Gnostic heresy already in the church in the first century – *'the mystery of lawlessness'* that is *'**already** at work'*. What could Paul possibly be talking about other than the rejection of Primitive Christianity and its replacement by some form of Hellenistic Christianity?

History confirms the fulfillment of Paul's prophecy. This is the second wave of apostasy, the end result of the Hellenization process begun by Gnostic Christianity, exactly as Paul described it. In the second, third and fourth centuries there was only one historical process within the church that fulfills the prophecy of 2 Thessalonians chapter 2. There is only one religious tradition, only one "truth" within the church that was rejected, and that is Primitive, "Jewish" Christianity. What replaced it was the second wave of Hellenistic religion (Neoplatonism and related Hellenistic traditions), imposed on the church by a new authoritarian leadership headed by one man in the form of the Roman emperor, whose office eventually ceded its authority to the papacy.

Further on in Thessalonians chapter 2, Paul exhorts the faithful: *"So then, brothers and sisters, stand firm and hold fast to the traditions that you were taught by us, either by word of mouth or by our letter"* (vs 15). Here Paul is directly exhorting Christians to reject Hellenistic Christianity, and return instead to the first-century Primitive Christianity taught by the apostles (*the traditions that you were taught by us*).

Today Hellenistic Christians tout Paul as the architect of their second revelation of a supposedly more spiritual, Hellenistic Christianity. Paul's reference to *'traditions...taught by us'* sometimes is used to argue for the acceptance of Hellenistic religious traditions that contradict the Bible, passed down separately from the Bible through the church leadership. Paul, however, is saying exactly the opposite. Taken in the correct historical context, Paul is talking about the contest between the original Primitive Christianity of the first century, and Hellenistic religious heresy. And he makes it clear which is true and which is to be rejected.

What could be more clear or simple? Paul's divinely inspired instruction about how we should view this, is as valid for us today as it was then.

No Longer God's Church

The end of the second wave of apostasy was not as clean as the end of the first. Gnosticism, the first wave of apostasy, was wrapped up by the exodus of those responsible. The second wave, in contrast, did not end in a clean separation of those responsible. In 2 Thessalonians chapter 2 Paul describes it as an apostasy that takes over the leadership of the church.

History again confirms these events, exactly as characterized by Paul. After the Gnostics left, Rome, and Alexandria in Egypt, became centers of the ongoing infiltration of Hellenistic apostasy. Because of its geographic position as the capital of the empire, Rome eventually became dominant. When the Roman church received the backing of the emperors, it actively forced its version of Hellenistic Christianity on the entire empire. It used its new-found power to crush Gnostic Christianity, whose unique antinomian version of Christianity lay largely dormant until the Protestant Reformation.

Rome's rise, the intervention of the Roman emperors and finally the imposition of the Papacy, is the prophesied formation of an apostate hierarchical leadership topped by the authority of one man.

That process culminated in the fourth century. When the Roman emperor Constantine embraced the church, there was a large-scale purge of Jewish church leaders, replaced by those favoring Hellenistic theology and practices. Shortly thereafter St. Augustine, sincerely convinced that Christianity was intended to carry on the ancient truths of pagan Hellenistic religion, formulated and passed on the Hellenistic theology on which both Roman and Reformation churches are founded. (For Augustine's shocking, open endorsement of Hellenistic paganism, see below, pages 322 and following.)

How does Jesus relate to the Roman church that emerged from the second wave of apostasy? Jesus is not the leader of this church. This movement is described as driven by the *"working of Satan"* (2 Thess 2:9). It is a *"powerful delusion,"* a curse sent from God that condemns those who take part in it:

> ...God sends them a powerful delusion...so that all who have not believed the truth...will be condemned" (vs 10–12).

Today some view the Roman church after Constantine as a defective yet valid episode in the history of the church headed by Jesus. Second Thessalonians chapter two suggests otherwise. Indeed, the history of the true church is not traced through Rome.

God is not the author of apostasy, but in cases of egregious evil and willful rejection of him, he sometimes gives people over to their evil ("hardens their hearts"). We saw an example of this in our earlier discussion of Romans 9 in the chapter on predestination. As in that case, God sometimes says, If you don't really love and respect me and don't treasure the truth you have been given or respect the warnings I send, then go ahead and experience for yourself the full evil of your disloyalty and rebellion.

So the fallen church that emerged from this second wave of apostasy, the medieval Roman church, fell into a mind-boggling orgy of human exploitation and oppression, murder, torture, and warfare – one of the worst violations of humanity the world has ever seen, in which tens of millions of people were killed.

Much of medieval history is a chronicle of the evil visited on Europe as the natural result of its rejection of the true religion of the first-century church, which it exchanged for the human wisdom, so-called, of Hellenistic religion. So Europe experienced the natural fruit of that human wisdom, handed down through the ages, beginning with the great pagan reformation in ancient Greece centuries before Christ. Its depravity was evident from the beginning. Recall one of its greatest proponents, the famous Greek philosopher Plato. It was he who first preached that Hellenistic religion will enlighten all mankind, but anyone who resists should be put to death (see above, pages 11 and following). And so medieval Europe was fated to prove for itself the ultimate, tragic results of this ancient tradition.

But what of the true church? From the time of the completion of the second wave of apostasy in the fourth century A.D., a remnant of the apostolic church survived as an outcast, hunted and persecuted by Rome, exactly as described in Revelation chapter 12: *"But the woman was given the two wings of the great eagle, so that she could fly from the serpent into the wilderness to her place where she is nourished for a time, and times, and half a time"* (vs 14).

The second wave of apostasy was resolved when the apostolic church was driven out by the new hierarchical leadership, exactly as described in Revelation. Thereafter the Primitive Christianity of the first century survived as an outcast, initially mostly at the margins of the Roman Empire, in Africa, and especially the British Isles.

History Repeats Itself

Understanding the distinction between two waves of apostasy is tremendously important. Both waves produced their own unique forms of apostate Christianity. And those distinct Hellenistic apostasies are reflected respectively in the two primary Hellenistic Christian movements in our world today, namely Roman Catholic and Reformation (Protestant)

Christianity. As we now discover, these two distinct branches of Christian apostasy play important roles in the prophecies of the end time.

2 Thessalonians 2:8 says the Roman church will be active in the end time, when its final leader is destroyed by Christ at his second coming. History confirms that. The Roman church has an unbroken chain of development from the early centuries after Christ until now.

As we will now see, Gnostic Christianity also is to be a major player in the end time.

Gnostic Christianity's Repeat Act

We do not rely solely on secular history to prove that Gnostic theology has survived and is destined to be a major player in the end time. New Testament prophecy tells the same story.

At one point in his first letter to the church, the Apostle John directly connects Gnostic Christianity with the end time:

> ...so now many antichrists [Gnostic Christian teachers] have come; **therefore we know that it is the last hour.** They **went out from us**, but they were not of us; for if they had been of us, they would have continued with us; but they went out, that it might be plain that they all are not of us. (1John 2:18-19)

Here John is referring to the exodus of Gnostic Christians from the church that began late in the first century (*they went out from us*). It seems as if John thought the end times began in the first century with the rise of Gnostic Christian heresy and the masses of Gnostics leaving the church. Of course we know now, nearly 2,000 years later, that was not the *"last hour,"* as John phrased it. Was John mistaken?

Is the Bible wrong? Not at all. This passage from John's first epistle is completely valid, but its complete fulfillment was not for that time. Rather, the complete fulfillment of John's prophecy today is unfolding through Evangelical Protestantism and its infiltration into Primitive Christian churches in our time.

So we see that today, just as in ancient times, the world of Hellenistic Christianity is split between two major players, both Hellenistic but bitterly opposed to each other and competing for the leadership of Christianity. What once was a splintered community of individualistic, protesting Gnostic sects, lives on as the splintered community of individualistic

Protestant denominations, competing against the same authoritarian and unified Roman church. Indeed, is there really anything new under the sun?

Primitive Christianity in the End Time

John's prophecy implies something as well about the state of Primitive Christianity in the end time. It says that Primitive Christian churches will be infiltrated by Gnostic heresy, causing many to depart from the original faith. Indeed, it is given to us as a sign that we are in the end time. But that also implies that Primitive Christianity will be flourishing in the end time as well, presenting a tempting target for Gnostic heresy, just as it did in the early centuries after Christ.

Other scriptures also predict a comeback for Primitive Christianity in the end time. What happens after the second wave of Hellenistic apostasy is complete and the faithful have been driven out? The resulting period of persecution and suppression of the remnant church is prophesied to last 1260 days (three and a half years – Rev 12:14). Based on prophetic symbolism in the Bible, some take that to signify 1260 years. Applying it to the historical events of that time, many believe it was fulfilled in the period from 538 to 1798 A.D. In 1798 the power of the authoritarian Hellenistic leadership from the second wave of apostasy was broken. The secular forces of the French revolution intervened in Italy, arrested the Pope, and the representative of that once mighty power languished and died in prison.

The office of the papacy was thought to have ended, though it was soon revived in a weakened state. This is what is meant by the beast in Revelation 13:3 who receives the deadly wound. It was the culmination of several centuries of decline for the papacy, whose final 'mortal' wound freed apostolic (Sabbatarian) Christianity. Within decades Primitive Christianity began a huge revival. Today it has a following numbering some 16 million and flourishes openly around the world.

Two Waves of Apostasy Repeated

But the prophetic scenario does not end there. There are indications the apostasy of the early centuries of Christianity is to be repeated.

In the end time the 'deadly wound' is prophesied to be healed (Rev 13:3). So the former glory and authority of the papacy will be restored. At the very end, 10 nations will make a pact with the Papacy (Rev 17:12), restoring the Roman church's civil authority to impose its Hellenistic religion by force of law. This, in effect, is a replay of the second wave of apostasy in the early church. Authoritarian rule by the man of sin, foretold in 2 Thessalonians 2:3–4, will once again prosper, until he and the institution of his office is finally and completely destroyed by Christ (*annihilating him by the manifestation of his coming* – 2 Thess 2:8).

But the end time is not limited to a repetition of the second wave of apostasy. There is much more to the story. Today, in fact, we are witnessing the beginning of a replay of the entire set of both waves of Hellenistic apostasy that attacked the early church.

Who is the Great Harlot?

New Testament prophecy clearly reflects the breadth and scope of Christian apostasy in the end time. What it lays out is a distinctly pluralistic scenario. Protestantism tends to interpret prophecy to lay all the blame on its one arch-competitor, Roman Catholicism. This surfaces especially in its interpretation of the prophecies of Revelation chapters 17 and 18.

Here we read of an apostate religious movement symbolized by a great harlot. Faithful Christians are warned: *"Come out of her, my people, so that you do not take part in her sins, and so that you do not share in her plagues"* (Rev 18:4). What this signals is that by the end time much of Primitive Christianity will exist in ecumenical union with Hellenistic Christianity. But union with which version of Hellenistic Christianity? Is this talking solely about Catholicism as Protestants claim? What does the historical evidence indicate?

Protestants believe there is an historical basis for their interpretation. They point to Revelation 18:24 (*in you was found the blood of the prophets and of saints*), and 17:2, 18:3 (*kings of the earth have committed fornication with her*). Only the historical conduct of Catholicism fulfills this description of the harlot, they argue. The reference to killing saints and prophets is understood as the mass killing of dissident Christians by the medieval Roman church. Committing fornication with the kings of the earth is interpreted politically. This is fulfilled symbolically, they believe, by the Roman church's political influence, including the practice of medieval Popes crowning European kings.

Is that an accurate assessment? Historically, that view is woefully incomplete. The true significance of Revelation's great harlot actually runs much deeper. Here we get into important evidence that unfortunately will not appear until publication of *Spirit of Antichrist,* the second volume of our series The World of Primitive Christianity. What follows is a very brief summary of that information:

In ancient Babylon there was a sacred marriage ceremony, held each year in the spring shortly after the New Year celebration. It was a typical fertility ritual in which the procreative power of nature is renewed. The centerpiece was a literal act of sexual intercourse between a goddess and a male savior figure, both roles played by human participants. The specific goddess involved in this ritual also happened to be the patroness and protector of prostitutes. One of her many titles was "Sacred Harlot." Not only that, she was also patron goddess of the city of Babylon. In other words, she was, quite literally, the "great harlot of Babylon," exactly as described in Revelation 17.

In the sacred marriage ceremony, a priestess played the role of the goddess. The role of the male figure was played by, you guessed it, the king. This ceremony was performed concurrently by various local kings in the many city-states that composed Babylonia at that time. So, indeed, in ancient Babylonia the "kings of the earth" were committing fornication with the great harlot, *literally,* exactly as described in Rev 17:2.

But here is the point as it affects us: The great harlot of Revelation 17–18 is not limited to the Catholic church nor any other single church today. She is exactly who Revelation says she is in chapter 17 verse 5. She is Babylon, the name written on her forehead. The 'mystery' of the harlot, explained in the remainder of verse 5, is that she lives on in her harlot daughters.

Babylon the city and Babylon the empire are no longer with us. But the religion of Babylon – especially the one goddess known as the Sacred Harlot and certain deities associated with her – spawned an antinomian religious tradition that spread throughout the ancient Near East. This specific antinomian tradition passed into ancient Greece and was picked up by the great pagan religious reformation there in the 7th and 6th centuries B.C. That pagan reformation, as detailed in this volume, became the foundation of Hellenistic religion, from which it passed into Christianity through Gnosticism, and survives to this day as Hellenistic Christianity.

When Revelation 17–18 talks of the prophets and saints slaughtered by the great harlot, it is speaking in the broad sense of the entire religious tradition going all the way back to Babylon. Participants in this same apostate religious tradition in all its many manifestations, stretching over thousands of years, have repeatedly slaughtered the people of God.

Remember how the Canaanite priestess Jezebel murdered hundreds of Yahweh's prophets in ancient Israel. Jezebel worshipped a Canaanite goddess (Asherah) patterned on the same great harlot goddess of Babylon. Thus even in the Old Testament God's people were being murdered in the name of one of the many harlot daughters of Babylon, exactly as described in Revelation 17–18.

Babylon has been with us through all of human history, always tempting and pulling the people of God into disobedience. As we have seen demonstrated throughout this volume, Reformation Christianity, despite much biblical truth, is solidly part of that same antinomian Hellenistic tradition, descended ultimately from ancient Babylon.

The point is that Babylon survives today through her harlot daughters, spread over multiple Hellenistic traditions.[247] Above all they are harlot daughters, ***plural***, exactly as described. [248]

The pluralism of end time apostasy is demonstrated clearly in Revelation 17. Note how the beast and harlot, though they are connected (the harlot rides the beast), at the same time are distinct and separate institutions. At the very end, the beast will turn against the harlot, attack and destroy her power, leading to a global economic depression as indicated in Revelation 18. Though this is connected to the end time, it too is a repetition of the early centuries after Christ. The Roman church and Gnosticism, though they sprang from the same Hellenistic roots, became bitter enemies as they competed for control of Christianity. When the

---

[247] As demonstrated in Appendix C, the daughters of the pan-Indo-European reformation in the 7th to 6th centuries B.C. produced a multitude of similar religious traditions that today dominate the entire world, many of them Christian but equally many non-Christian, including even Islam.

[248] The prophecies of Revelation are for all Christians throughout the entire New Covenant era. Apostate religion and rebellion against the God of the Bible extends back to the very beginning of time, and these warnings apply to the people of God through all history. At the same time, there is a special application of these prophecies to the final end time, as seen in the on-going description of the great harlot as it continues through Revelation 18 and the beginning of chapter 19.

Roman church gained the official backing of the Roman emperors, it used its power to viciously persecute and crush Gnostic Christianity.

Today the initial wave of apostasy is being repeated especially through American Evangelicalism, the epitome of the antinomian spirit of ancient Gnostic Christianity. Evangelicalism is the driving force behind extreme eternal security and dispensationalism, the modern justification for rejecting Jesus' earthly ministry.

John Gerstner is a prominent Hellenistic Christian author who decries the error of Evangelical antinomianism. He describes what he calls a "veritable explosion" of antinomian teaching within Evangelicalism beginning in the 1980s.[249] This latest surge of antinomian theology coincides with the beginning of significant acceptance of Evangelical theology among Primitive Christian churches.

Today many Primitive Christian ministers and churches openly hail Evangelical Protestantism as a model of advanced spirituality based on a personal relationship with Jesus. Some have even embraced eternal security and rejection of binding moral standards as a necessary step to achieving that higher state of spirituality. In the future, as we look back at history, I believe the 1980s and 90s will be viewed as a great historic turning point, the beginnings of what will become a great religious crisis in the end time. This is all part of a pattern replicating the first wave of Hellenistic apostasy in the early church.

A Symbiotic Relationship

Politically, Gnosticism was surprisingly gentle and benign. It focused on grace, freedom from authority, and individual, libertarian pursuit of a more advanced, inner spirituality centered on Christ and the Spirit. It incorporated much genuine religious truth from the New Testament, except it championed freedom from the law of God, rejection of all things Jewish, and replacement of Jesus' earthly ministry by a second, supposedly more spiritual revelation of Hellenistic Christianity.

In the second wave, Hellenistic Christianity morphed into an authoritarian political movement. It took control by force and aggressively pur-

---

[249] Gerstner, *Wrongly Dividing the Word of Truth,* p 293. The author, writing in his work published in 1991, refers to this explosion of antinomianism occurring "in recent years."

sued and murdered any remaining Primitive Christians it could get its hands on.

The full process of Hellenization was so clever. Start with a soft touch, promising an even deeper spirituality and love for Jesus. Only after that is in place comes the iron fist when apostolic Christianity is outlawed on pain of death. That same clever pattern appears to be unfolding again in our day.

Prophecy Covered in Volume Two

In this appendix we have very briefly touched on prophetic highlights from Revelation and elsewhere. This is a topic that appears in greater detail in *Spirit of Antichrist,* volume two of our series The World of Primitive Christianity.

Today we know so much more about these prophetic passages, and much of it comes, as we have seen throughout this volume, from better understanding the historical background involved. Today, for example, not only can we historically trace Hellenistic religion all the way back to ancient Babylon, validating the prophecies of the Babylonian origin of the harlot and beast in Revelation 17, but we also have unraveled the strange tale of the beast and the seven kings associated with him.

We know the special significance behind the mysterious statement that he *"was, and is not, and is about to ascend"* (Rev 17:8). We also know exactly who the eighth king is, and why he is the eighth but at the same time belongs to the seven (Rev 17:11). We know who the Sons of God were in Genesis 6, and the significance of their fathering a race of heros and giants. All this, from Genesis to Revelation, fits into one grand story of religious apostasy culminating in the end time.

We wish we could present that evidence here, but it requires so much additional background information it must occupy an entire separate volume.

Summary

As we enter into the end time we find a strikingly similar situation to what existed in the early centuries after Christ. We see modern representatives of the same two Hellenistic religious traditions from early Christianity – one libertarian, highly antinomian and fragmented (Protestantism), the other unified and authoritarian (Roman Catholicism).

Today Primitive Christian churches are increasingly forging ecumenical links with the modern epitome of the first wave of apostasy from the early church, Evangelical Protestantism, and adopting elements of its antinomian theology. Thus, just as in the first centuries after Christ, Primitive Christianity is being compromised theologically in preparation for something much worse to come. If the pattern of the early church is fully played out, then the ecumenical embrace with Protestantism will lay the foundation for a second stage that completes the process, sweeping both Protestant Christianity and its new Primitive Christian allies into a global ecumenical movement that ends in violent oppression.

Once again Primitive Christians are being enticed by the soft hand and promise of an even greater spiritual relationship with Jesus, through the libertarian, antinomian theology of Evangelical Protestantism. And once again, those who do not treasure the original truth of the apostolic church will suddenly find themselves in the grip of a violent authoritarian beast that demands complete capitulation.

Many today are looking for a violent, oppressive turn in religion as the main signal for the beginning of the end time. That indeed will come, but the beginning itself, just as in the first century A.D., is much more clever, much more subtle. Exactly as described in scripture it is a mystery, all the more effective by not being easily recognized for what it really is.

Understanding New Testament prophecy depends, in part, on understanding the Hellenistic backdrop to Christian apostasy and the two waves with which it attacked the primitive church. Gnosticism itself is important because, after all, that is where it all started, nearly two thousand years ago. There is no single, simple solution to the prophecies of the end time. There is no single apostasy, no single set of 'bad guys,' no single church to blame for everything that will happen. There are many roles to be played. This is a huge topic of its own, and is covered in more detail in *Spirit of Antichrist,* the second volume in our series The World of Primitive Christianity.

The Way to Safety

Even in the worst of times God always has preserved a remnant of his people. In Elijah's day, God preserved 7,000 people who rejected compromise with the worship of Baal (1 Kings 19:18). We know that God will preserve at least one (and perhaps more than one) Christian group in the end time, depicted by the first-century church at Philadelphia (Rev

3:7–13). This church is directly linked with the end time and is promised protection: *"...I will keep you from the hour of trial that is coming on the whole world to test the inhabitants of the earth"* (vs 10).[250]

In the next chapter we will examine Revelation's prophecy of the seven churches, and how Jesus identifies those he will protect in the end time.

On the following three pages is a graphic presentation of the historical flow of Hellenistic apostasy in relation to the apostolic church. Here we attempt to trace the shifting interaction through time between apostolic Christianity and both waves of Christian apostasy – **libertarian**, Gnostic-style Christianity, the first wave, and **authoritarian** Roman Christianity, the second wave. Included is the presumed full repetition of those two waves of apostasy in the end time, as suggested by recent historical events and passages in New Testament prophecy.

---

[250] All seven churches of Revelation 2–3 are presented as models of church problems and successes for the education of all Christians through all time. Philadelphia presents an extra dimension. In one of its multiple applications it presents a prophecy of a specific church or group in the end time.

Figure 1, <u>History of Apostate Christianity</u>

Time line	Apostolic Church	Hellenistic Apostasy	
		Libertarian	Authoritarian

27 BC		Roman imperial rule begins	Rome converts from Republican to Imperial rule; creates the institution on which the Antichrist is founded, later transferred to the Papacy.
3 BC	Birth of Christ		Messiah, the true Christ
30s AD	Apostolic church.		Christ crucified, resurrected, Church established.

FIRST WAVE OF APOSTASY BEGINS

50s		Proto-Gnosticism	Proto-Gnosticism makes early progress in apostolic church.
90s		Classic Gnostic sects	Growth of proto-Gnosticism ignites crisis. Gnostics begin to leave, found independent libertarian Christian groups.
2nd-4th centuries		Roman Church	Apostolic church drifts along its own path of Hellenization, splitting into Hellenistic Christianity centered at Rome, and segments remaining loyal to Primitive Christianity.

SECOND WAVE OF APOSTASY

313 AD		Constantine	Roman emperor Constantine completes Hellenization of Roman church by force.
400 AD		Augustine	Augustine openly embraces Christianity as a final refinement of Hellenistic paganism; creates theology for Roman and Reformation churches.
538 AD	Remnant church	Papacy replaces Rome	Emperor Justinian turns over authority to the Papacy, which now officially replaces beast power, Rome. Suppression of Apostolic Christianity for 1,260 years begins now.
7th century			Classic Gnosticism has mostly died out.

Figure 1, <u>History of Apostate Christianity</u>

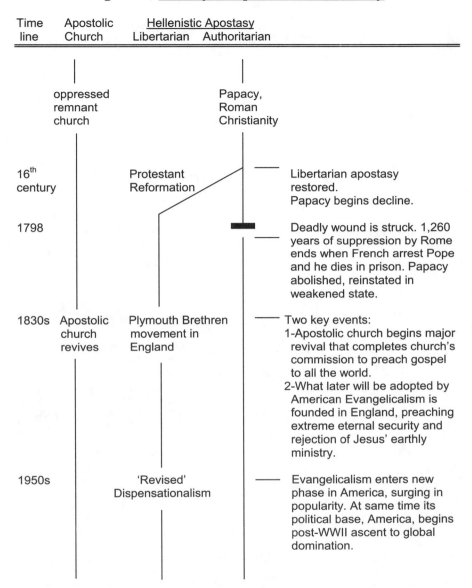

Time line	Apostolic Church	<u>Hellenistic Apostasy</u> Libertarian	Authoritarian	
	oppressed remnant church		Papacy, Roman Christianity	
16th century		Protestant Reformation		Libertarian apostasy restored. Papacy begins decline.
1798				Deadly wound is struck. 1,260 years of suppression by Rome ends when French arrest Pope and he dies in prison. Papacy abolished, reinstated in weakened state.
1830s	Apostolic church revives	Plymouth Brethren movement in England		Two key events: 1-Apostolic church begins major revival that completes church's commission to preach gospel to all the world. 2-What later will be adopted by American Evangelicalism is founded in England, preaching extreme eternal security and rejection of Jesus' earthly ministry.
1950s		'Revised' Dispensationalism		Evangelicalism enters new phase in America, surging in popularity. At same time its political base, America, begins post-WWII ascent to global domination.

Figure 1, <u>History of Apostate Christianity</u>

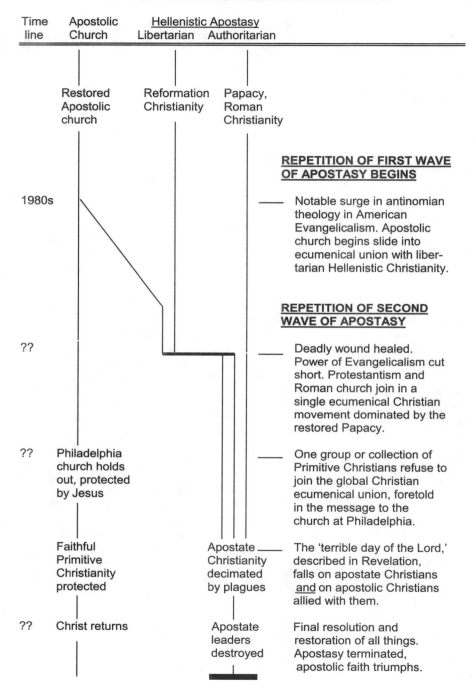

Time line	Apostolic Church	<u>Hellenistic Apostasy</u> Libertarian Authoritarian		

Restored Apostolic church   Reformation Christianity   Papacy, Roman Christianity

REPETITION OF FIRST WAVE OF APOSTASY BEGINS

1980s — Notable surge in antinomian theology in American Evangelicalism. Apostolic church begins slide into ecumenical union with libertarian Hellenistic Christianity.

REPETITION OF SECOND WAVE OF APOSTASY

?? — Deadly wound healed. Power of Evangelicalism cut short. Protestantism and Roman church join in a single ecumenical Christian movement dominated by the restored Papacy.

??   Philadelphia church holds out, protected by Jesus — One group or collection of Primitive Christians refuse to join the global Christian ecumenical union, foretold in the message to the church at Philadelphia.

Faithful Primitive Christianity protected   Apostate Christianity decimated by plagues — The 'terrible day of the Lord,' described in Revelation, falls on apostate Christians <u>and</u> on apostolic Christians allied with them.

??   Christ returns   Apostate leaders destroyed   Final resolution and restoration of all things. Apostasy terminated, apostolic faith triumphs.

280

– 13 –

Spiritual Balance
in the
The New Testament

Prophecy and the Testimony of Jesus

In the prophecies of the book of Revelation, chapters two and three, we have seen how the message to each of seven churches is followed by the statement it is intended for all Christians in all churches. These messages contain information that goes beyond the technical forecasting of what will happen to those specific churches.

In Revelation 19:10 we find an enigmatic statement about the nature of prophecy: *"Worship God! For the testimony of Jesus is the spirit of prophecy."* [251] What this is saying is that prophecy, and here specifically

---

[251] In Rev 19:10 the angel in effect argues that revealing Christ is the purpose of the prophetic revelation he is giving to John. The immediate issue is the problem occasioned by John attempting to worship the angel. The angel stops him, explaining *"You must not do that! I am a fellow servant with you and your comrades who hold the testimony of Jesus."* What the angel is saying is that he is on the same level with them, possessing the testimony of Jesus just as they do.

The latter part of the verse, then, is the angel's explanation why they are on the same level: *"For the testimony of Jesus is the spirit of prophecy."* I.e., if the prophecy the angel is giving John, namely the book of Revelation, testifies to Jesus Christ, then the angel is a minister proclaiming the message of Jesus Christ, just as John is. Therefore the angel is unworthy of being worshipped by John.

See also Rev 1:2 for the clearly stated purpose of the book, in part to reveal *"the testimony of Jesus Christ."*

the prophecies of the book of Revelation, are much more than just the revelation of historical events. Much more than that, they are revelations of Jesus Christ himself, of who he is, what he stands for, and spiritual instruction for those who worship him.

Is there a spiritual component to prophecy that we tend to overlook? Should we look to prophecy for spiritual instruction as well as knowledge of future events?

Gnostic Christianity and its mystery of lawlessness play an important role in New Testament prophecy. It is a component in three of the messages to the seven churches, as described in Revelation chapter 2. As we read how different churches successfully closed their doors to it (Ephesus), partially avoided it (Pergamum) or largely gave in to it (Thyatira), we glean important instruction from Jesus about how he expects Christians to relate to apostate Christianity.

But indeed there is more to the story. Once we understand the Gnostic backdrop to the messages of the seven churches, the entire prophetic passage comes alive with new meaning. Indeed, the messages to the seven churches, taken together, present an even more powerful message. And that message is about **spiritual balance**.

Ephesus and Thyatira

Look again at the message to Ephesus (Rev 2:1–7). Here is the church that really got it right on the issue of Hellenistic apostasy. They saw through the fancy claims of a more spiritual revelation of Christianity. They identified its teachers as false apostles. They understood the issue of antinomianism and were sickened by the immorality those teachings fostered. You couldn't fool them by claiming it was all right because it actually leads to a more spiritual relationship with Jesus. They slammed the door on Gnostic Christianity. You would think the Christians at Ephesus had it made. Or did they?

Jesus praises them for their stand against Gnostic Christianity. But then he announces: *"I will come to you and remove your lampstand from its place, unless you repent"* (vs 6). What does it mean to have your "lampstand" removed? In chapter one there are seven lampstands, each representing one of the seven churches (Rev 1:20). To be a lampstand means to be a bona fide church through whom Jesus works. To have your lampstand removed therefore means to be cut off as an organization through whom Jesus works. This is a truly serious matter. After standing up so courageously to apostate Christianity, how could Ephesus have gone so wrong?

Consider next the church at Thyatira (Rev 2:18–29). Here is the church that fell headlong into the mystical antinomianism of Gnostic Christianity. It was so bad Jesus instructs the few who remain faithful to keep their distance from the apostate leadership of their own church (vs 22). What is happening here so disturbs Jesus he says he will bring about some un-specified catastrophe to physically destroy much of the church. He will engineer their destruction as a warning to the rest of the churches (vs 23). It seems you couldn't get much lower than that.

But then look at what else Jesus says about Thyatira: *"I know your works – your love, faith, service, and patient endurance."* Not only that, this church is *growing* spiritually: *"I know that your last works are greater than the first"* (vs 19). Is this the same church he was just warn-ing to repent or he would have them killed? How do we make sense of this?

Look again at Ephesus. They locked Gnostic Christianity out of their church. At the same time, however, they had lost their passion for Christi-anity, as it says, *"you have abandoned the love you had at first"* (vs 4). That doesn't mean they quit trying, because Jesus confirms they perse-vered; they *"have not grown weary"* (vs 3). It's just that the joy and pas-sion were gone.

If we were able to go back in time and attend a church service at Ephe-sus, I think we would find the atmosphere cold and calculating. They were very serious about correct doctrine. They were intense in their de-termination to remain pure from the apostate Christianity that swirled around them. Obviously, however, Jesus expects more than just that. In contrast, attending a church service at Thyatira would have been a genu-inely warm experience as the Christians there excelled in the saintly qualities of love, patience, kindness and hospitality, stirred by the Spirit.

What is the lesson we should draw from this? Very simply, keeping free from the apostasy of Gnostic Christianity is not the only thing. On the other hand, growing in inner spirituality and expression of love are not the only thing either. What Jesus demands is ***both!*** That is the powerful message of balance we first encounter in the messages to the seven churches.

Remember the Apostle Peter's warning about antinomian teachings: *"...beware that you are not carried away with the error of the lawless and **lose your own stability**"* (2 Peter 3:17). Antinomian apostasy is char-acterized by lack of spiritual balance. But now in Revelation we see the issue of balance indeed extends to both sides of the spectrum. You can go so far to either extreme that you leave God behind.

Pergamum and Laodicea

The example of the church at Pergamum also is filled with spiritual instruction (Rev 2:12–17). Here we find a faithful church resisting pressure from the Roman imperial cult, a prominent feature of pagan religion at Pergamum. They resisted even to the point of death (vs 13). When faced with openly non-Christian, pagan religion, Pergamum knew exactly what it must do. When faced with apostasy from inside Christianity, however, this church completely missed the point.

The main body of the church did not teach or practice antinomian apostasy. But they apparently believed in Christian diversity, to the point they openly accepted and fellowshipped with Gnostic Christians in their midst. The Gnostic sect involved is identified as the Nicolaitans (vs 15), the same Gnostics the church at Ephesus successfully rejected. Ecumenical fellowship with antinomian Christians is a terrible mistake, recorded here as an example for all Christians throughout all time. The lesson is that God expects his people to reject evil whether it comes from inside or outside Christianity.

Today many Primitive Christian ministers preach the ecumenical brotherhood of all people who merely "love Jesus." I have listened to Primitive Christian ministers, the same ones who promote conversion to Evangelical Protestant theology, preach that the only thing that really matters is "being on fire for Jesus." This is the very mistake exemplified by the Pergamum church, and this error will only grow more common as we proceed into the end time.

There are other churches demonstrating the common human problem with balance. The final church, Laodicea, also had serious problems (Rev 3:14–22). This is a self-satisfied church, *"neither cold nor hot"* (vs 15). It is wealthy, and it views its material success as validation by God. It is especially proud of its growth and treats that as proof it has no faults: *"I am rich, and increased with goods, and have need of nothing"* (vs 17, KJV).

Instead, according to Jesus, Laodicea is spiritually *"wretched, pitiable, poor, blind, and naked"* (vs 17). The problem is that their material prosperity and lavish church operation have become their focus instead of Jesus. In this church message Jesus depicts himself as outside the church, knocking on the door, inviting the Laodiceans to open and enter a personal relationship with him (vs 20).

A church's evangelistic work is important. Jesus commissioned the church to go to the entire world. But as with anything, imbalanced focus on one thing can blind people to the full range of biblical teaching, the full 'testimony of Jesus.' Thus, at Laodicea we again find Jesus threatening to divorce one of his churches, saying he will "spit" this church out of his mouth.

What happens to a church when Jesus rejects it and refuses to continue working through it? Jesus says he will never leave those who do not leave him.[252] But when an organization is abandoned, Jesus no longer works through that organization, no longer granting the Holy Spirit and begetting new Christians. Over time, existing Christians leave, grow old and die, until there are no born again members remaining. The church will drift, possibly die or be swallowed back into apostate Christianity. There is a continual process of birth and death of Primitive Christian churches from the time of Christ down to the present. There are sad cases of the spiritual death of Primitive Christian churches in our time, coincident with the rise of many new groups.

Philadelphia, the Balanced Church

Philadelphia is another key church exemplifying the issue of spiritual balance (Rev 3:7–13). Most conspicuous in this message is what is missing. Jesus does not say anything terribly bad about them. We derive several important conclusions from that.

First it means this church does not suffer from failure to recognize and reject Christian apostasy as happened at Pergamum and Thyatira. And it means they did not suffer from the error of Ephesus where they had lost their passion and joy for Christianity. It also means they must have had a personal relationship with Jesus and were not blinded by pride because of rapid growth and a great work as at Laodicea. If they had suffered from any of those serious errors, surely Jesus would have mentioned it.

I think we can say Philadelphia was a spiritually balanced church. They promoted lawfulness, but recognized the central role of a personal

---

[252] E.g. Heb 13:5 *"I will never leave you or forsake you";* Phil 1:6 *"...the one who began a good work in you will bring it to completion...."*

relationship with Jesus. They taught obedience, but at the same time were devoted to Christian service and appreciated the loving grace of their savior. They also must have sought to evangelize as much as their means allowed, but they did so humbly and without pride.

In verse 8 it says, *"you have but little power, and yet you have kept my word and have not denied my name."* Here is a church that has few if any miracles or political and economic clout to validate itself, yet they are steadfast in following the "word." I think we must assume the "word" includes both the warnings against apostasy by Peter, Jude and John, as well as the repeated exhortation to Christian works of love and spirituality by Paul.

Why does it mean when it says the Philadephians have *"not denied my name"*? Immediately following in verse 9 it says *"I will make those of the synagogue of Satan...come and bow down before your feet, and they will learn that I have loved you."*

The synagogue of Satan apparently disagrees with the idea that Jesus accepts and loves Philadelphia Christians. Because of that, Jesus says he will make a great show of whom he really loves.

It appears that the Philadelphia church gets involved in some kind of confrontation with Hellenistic Christianity in the end time.[253] The synagogue of Satan disputes the Philadelphians' claim to be a true church of God (to be loved by God), and pressures them to reject their form of worship (to deny his name). What Jesus especially appreciates about this church is they don't give in. Jesus praises their *"patient endurance."*

The Philadelphians look apostate Christianity straight in the eye and don't blink. In effect they say, "Do what you want, but we won't come back to the synagogue of Satan; we won't compromise, we won't soften or modify any teaching to please you." Because of that, Jesus says he will protect them from the final horrors to fall on human society just before Christ returns (*I will keep you from the hour of trial that is coming on the whole world* – vs 10).

What is the "open door" mentioned in verse 8? That is never clearly explained. The context of the entire message suggests it may refer to the church's survival rather than its evangelizing. On the other hand, it may

---

[253] Note the specific reference to the end time in verse 10. While all the seven churches are intended primarily as examples for spiritual instruction of Christians through all time, Philadelphia contains an apparent reference to a specific fulfillment in the end time. (Some of the seven churches may fulfill multiple prophetic roles.)

indeed include the church's work in fulfilling the commission to preach the Primitive Christian gospel to the entire world. But the true greatness of Philadelphia is its balance, its dedication to the Word and its unflinching loyalty.

It gets into trouble with apostate Christianity. For some time, Philadelphian Christians live in the shadow of the beast, constantly under threat of being crushed by the synagogue of Satan. Because of their loyalty, endurance and standing up for Jesus' name and the truth of his Word, Jesus protects them. He keeps open the door for them to exist and not submit, and perhaps at the last moment rescues them from the clutches of the synagogue of Satan, just as the final great tribulation gets underway. This may be done as a special witness to the entire world. It may also be a witness to other Primitive Christian churches that have been less faithful and less balanced in their relationship with Jesus.

Conclusions Regarding Prophecy

So we see that even New Testament prophecy is filled with spiritual instruction. The book of Revelation contains information that affects our conduct – *"blessed are those who hear and who keep what is written in it"* (Rev. 1:3). If indeed we *"keep what is written in it,"* that includes taking to heart and obeying the principles Jesus reveals through the messages to the seven churches about our relationship with apostate Christianity. If we *"keep what is written in it"* we also will obey his instructions to follow balance, pursuing all of what he asks of us, both keeping separate from apostate Christianity while at the same time pursuing inner spirituality, trusting in grace and the power of the Spirit, and reaching out to all mankind in love and Christian service.

The messages to the seven churches are living prophecies. They apply to all Christians throughout the entire church age. In just recent decades we have witnessed one dramatic instance in which a flamboyantly successful Primitive Christian church has been destroyed. It boasted of its material wealth and astounding growth rate, unable to see that it was spiritually blind and naked, so in love with itself that Jesus finally spit it out of his mouth, exactly as he warned he would do to churches that fall into the error of the Laodicean church model (Rev 3:15–20).

Truly these are living prophecies, to be taken very seriously. If Jesus did not spare them, will he spare us if we likewise do not *"listen to what the Spirit is saying to the churches"*? As we proceed on into the end time, we will see many more, sometimes tragic examples of the fulfillment of these prophetic warnings.

Truth and Heresy

There are so many dimensions and aspects of spiritual balance. Religion itself seems such a fragile entity, so ripe for human exploitation, abuse, exaggeration, fanaticism and foolishness. Remember again the sage advice of Philip Lee, the Protestant critic of Gnostic tendencies within Protestantism, who said, *"...heresy involves a truth being carried to an illogical or dangerous degree."*[254] There is so much wisdom in that statement.

Both medieval Roman Christianity and the Reformation are characterized by imbalance and gross exaggeration of biblical truth. The medieval Roman church focused on authority and the individual's external responsibility to the church and to God. Through philosophical reasoning and exaggeration of those themes the church eventually was led to believe that by external works of charity and service a man could gain merit that licenses specific sins he wished to commit in the future.

The Reformation went to the other extreme. It focused on internal response to Jesus and individual experience of the Spirit. Through equally unbalanced philosophical exaggeration of those themes, Reformation theologians finally came to believe that a fleeting, momentary experience of faith is all that is necessary to license a lifetime of unlimited, unrepentant sin.

Christian apostasy almost always begins from a foundation of biblical truth. It almost always begins as an exaggerated and imbalanced approach to genuine biblical teachings. The original intent of the Roman church and the Reformation was entirely sincere. The Roman church felt that its approach was necessary to control and reform human conduct, to see that Christians did not continue willfully in sin. Likewise, the Reformation felt its approach was necessary in order to transform the inner man, to see that Christians genuinely turned to righteous conduct. Both became imbalanced and failed, however, because they became exaggerated and imbalanced through human philosophic reasoning. The challenge for Primitive

---

[254] Lee, *Against the Protestant Gnostics*, p 45.

Christians is to avoid those same mistakes that distort and pervert biblical revelation.

Therein lies a tremendous pitfall. As Primitive Christians we can react against the error of Christian apostasy so strongly that we go to the opposite extreme. Reformation Christianity grossly exaggerates and misuses the concept of inner spirituality. Do we then set the matter straight by ignoring inner spirituality? Do we condemn inner spirituality on sight, automatically assuming any mention of inner spirituality is contaminated by antinomian apostasy?

If we overreact against misuse of God's word to the point that we do not heed "every word that proceeds out of the mouth of God," then we too fall into the same trap of imbalance. If we adhere religiously to the Sabbath without responding to Jesus' call for reform of our inner nature, are we any better off than anyone else who makes use of only those parts of the New Testament revelation that appeal to them?

Here is another example. Hellenistic Christianity misuses the concept of empowerment through grace and the Spirit. They exaggerate this to the point of arguing that man plays no role in salvation and that salvation cannot be lost. Yet consider the truth of the genuine biblical concepts, as found in the preaching of Paul:

> ...that you may be strengthened in your **inner being** with **power through his Spirit** (Eph 3:16)

> ...that you may be filled with all the **fullness** [*pleroma*] of God. Now to him who **by the power at work within us** is able to accomplish abundantly far more than all we can ask or imagine.... (Eph 3:19–20)

The New Testament regularly preaches the power of God through the Spirit to transform lives. The example above is doubly striking, for it uses the word *pleroma,* translated "fullness" of God. This is one of Gnosticism's favorite words. They believed that by connecting to the heavens and drawing on the Spirit flowing down from the heavenly Paternal Depth, they established the fullness of the Father (*pleroma*) within themselves. This was the rationale for much of their antinomian theology. They claimed that because they had the power of the Spirit and the perfection of the heavenly *pleroma* planted within them, they had no need of anything external such as law or written scripture to guide them.

The New Testament nowhere condones such antinomian reasoning. Yet the teaching about Spirit and the fullness (*pleroma*) of God are entirely biblical. Will we miss out on this New Testament teaching because it has been so terribly misused by apostate Christianity? Will we be equally imbalanced, only at the opposite extreme?

Consider the doctrine of progressive revelation, by which Reformation teachers justify the antinomian Hellenization of Christianity. This is based on a fascinating biblical passage, where Jesus is speaking to his disciples shortly before he was crucified:

> I still have many things to say to you, but you cannot bear them now. **When the Spirit of truth comes, he will guide you into all the truth;** for he will not speak on his own, but will speak whatever he hears, and he will declare to you the things that are to come. He will glorify me, because he will take what is mine and declare it to you. (John 16:12–14)

Reformation theology uses this to justify its claim there was a second revelation of a more spiritual Christianity from after the resurrection, which *overturns* the earthly ministry and teachings of Jesus. That is nonsense. Nevertheless this passage is a ringing endorsement of the fact the Holy Spirit conveys truth to Christians.

It does not say Spirit will overturn the original revelation of the Christian faith by Jesus, during his earthly ministry. But it does specifically say that the Spirit will reveal truth through prophecy (*the things that are to come*), which relate to Jesus (*he will glorify me, because he will take what is mine and declare it to you*).

The continuing revelation of truth by the Spirit is the power behind the warnings of Christian apostasy in Jude and 2 Peter 2, the epistles of John, the book of Revelation, and the prophecy in 2 Thessalonians 2 about the beginning and continued growth of the mystery of lawlessness. There is no reason to interpret Jesus' words about the gift of the Spirit in an antinomian fashion. The Spirit today will not contradict what it conveyed to the authors of the New Testament in the first century. Recognizing there is nothing to fear from this, we must accept the guidance of the Spirit as a wonderful Christian truth. To ignore this biblical teaching is to fall into the same error of imbalance suffered by apostate Christianity.

Hellenistic Imbalance vs. Simplicity in Jesus

There are two traditions within Christianity that stand in stark contrast to each other. One is libertarian Hellenistic Christianity, encompassing both Gnostic Christianity and its latter day incarnation Reformation Christianity. As we have seen repeatedly in this volume, it is characterized by scriptural contradiction. That is the inevitable result of its reliance on the human wisdom of Hellenistic philosophy and religion, from which it originally sprang. The Apostle Paul saw this tradition in the same light, as we see in his advice to Timothy:

> Avoid the profane chatter and **contradictions** of what is **falsely called knowledge;** by professing it some have missed the mark as regards the faith. (1Timothy 6:20)

In sharp contrast we see the other tradition – Primitive Christianity, the religion of the apostolic church – described by Paul as simplicity itself:

> But I fear, lest somehow...your minds may be corrupted from **the simplicity that is in Christ.** (2 Corinthians 11:3, NKJV)

Paul emphasizes the simplicity theme repeatedly in his correspondence with the Corinthians. In his first letter he says:

> ...I decided to know nothing among you except Jesus Christ, and him crucified. (1 Corinthians 2:2)

This passage is misused frequently by Hellenistic Christians, including some in Primitive Christian churches who are converting to Reformation theology. Here they emphasize that Jesus' sacrifice and grace form a central core of New Testament truth. Therefore everything else, they say, is optional. Having thereby stripped Christianity down to the core ideas of grace and Christ's sacrifice, which are shared by almost all churches, on that basis they promote the ecumenical union of Primitive and Hellenistic Christianity.

When we look more closely at what was happening at Corinth, however, we see a much deeper and very different significance. Immediately preceding, in verse 1 he says, *"When I came to you, brothers and sisters, I did not come proclaiming the mystery of God to you **in lofty words or wisdom.** "*

Remember that in this ancient time there was a close connection between philosophy and religion. The early Greeks saw evidence of their religious ideas in astronomy and other natural phenomena. They believed they could use human reason and science to arrive at religious truth. As we saw in previous chapters they developed their ideas about the immortality of the soul and its escape back to heaven, in part out of their scientific observation of the heavens.

The point is that when Paul in his letters talks about *"human wisdom"* and the *"contradictions of what is falsely called knowledge,"* he is referring directly to the philosophic-religious mixture of Hellenistic religion and its characteristic reliance on human reason.

The problem at Corinth was this same Hellenistic religion based on 'human wisdom.' What Paul was saying in 1 Corinthians 2:2 is, 'Come back down to earth. Forget the fancy Hellenistic reasoning and misinterpretation of Christ.' In contrast to that, Paul was saying, 'let's get back to the historical Jesus, his sacrifice for sin, and the simplicity of Messianic salvation preached within the Jewish Christianity of the first century.'

The problem at Corinth was essentially the same problem as Paul was talking about in his letter to Timothy. Paul was not arguing for the limitation of core truth to Christ's sacrifice for the purpose of promoting ecumenical fellowship with Hellenistic Christianity. In fact, the purpose of his argument is **the exact opposite.** Paul is arguing *against* mixing Christianity with Hellenistic religion and its typically fancy, philosophic reasoning. Mixing Christianity with Hellenistic religion was a key problem at Corinth, as it increasingly was for all churches as time progressed towards the end of the first century. What was happening at Corinth is just one of the earliest records of this developing trend. [255]

It was this very rejection of reliance on human reason that frequently got the early church into hot water. Because Hellenistic religion was based in large part on scientific observation of the heavens, on astronomy, and on the technical human reasoning of philosophy, it was considered logical and rational. Primitive Christianity, in contrast, based its claims on divine revelation and faith, which Roman authorities generally considered irrational and superstitious. This frequently was used as the legal justification for persecuting the early church.

Returning to the present day, let's briefly revisit Reformation theology and specifically consider it in light of these two contrasting traditions – contradiction introduced by the human wisdom of Hellenistic religion versus the balanced simplicity of the message of the apostolic church.

The New Testament says God loves all mankind and wishes all men to come to repentance and salvation. How much simpler could that be? In contrast, Reformation theology falls into a tangle of reasoning over this

---

[255] The problem at Corinth was Hellenistic Jews who were promoting private revelation and heavenly speculation similar to that preached by Gnostic Christianity. This is treated in more detail in a later volume in our series, The World of Primitive Christianity.

because of its extreme theory about God's irresistible will. If God loves those supposedly predestined to eternal torture, then technically that implies he wants them to be saved, which means everyone would have to be saved since his will cannot be thwarted. That in turn requires extensive manipulation of scripture to prove God really doesn't love everyone, in the end piling contradiction upon contradiction.

The doctrine of eternal security is another major pitfall. The New Testament openly states many times that converted Christians can neglect or abuse their relationship with God to the point God will reject them. How much simpler could that be? Does God have the right to do that if he so chooses?

Why is that a problem? The problem, as always, is the complexity introduced by human wisdom. The New Testament says there are certain things required of man. From a strictly philosophical point of view you can argue that means man earns salvation. But, is that how God sees it? The New Testament says all men have sinned and are condemned to death unless they come under the forgiveness of Christ's sacrifice. Therefore, though there are things God requires of man, since those things don't forgive sin and don't qualify a person for salvation without Christ's grace, man does not earn salvation by doing what God demands of him.

How do we know that is true? Very simply, the Bible says both that God requires certain things from us and that we cannot earn salvation. The only way to harmonize those two ideas is to admit that God does not consider doing what he requires of us to be earning salvation.

Grace, not law, and not works, is the basis of forgiveness (Gal 5:4). Nevertheless, law and works are part of what God requires of Christians. Paul says that by faith we *"uphold the law"* (Rom 3:23). This is the same thing James talks about when he says that faith without works is dead faith (James 2:17). If works are necessary for faith to be genuine, and genuine faith is required for salvation, then works ultimately are required for salvation. They just are not the basis of salvation.

(On the other hand, one's individual attitude about grace and works is a critical ingredient. We must adjust our attitude to recognize that salvation is by grace in order to make that true in our own lives. If we do not clearly recognize it is grace that saves us, rather than what God says we must do, then we may indeed end up trusting in works for salvation.)

Though certain things are required of Christians, those things do not forgive sin and so cannot earn salvation. That is reserved solely for grace. What could be simpler than that? [256]

Consider the tangled mess that comes from philosophically dissecting these issues instead of looking to the revelation of scripture. Many Reformation theologians conclude that Christians are licensed to sin without limit and never repent. They admit that multitudes avail themselves of that license because of their teaching. What could bring anyone to such bizarre, unbalanced conclusions? This is the result of seeking truth through human reason. It is the same "philosophy and empty deceit" that drove their Gnostic Christian forefathers to the same bizarre conclusions in the first centuries after Christ.[257]

Balance in Denouncing Christian Apostasy

There are Primitive Christian churches that make rejection of Hellenistic Christianity almost the central doctrine of their faith. Some take a hard-edged approach, creating an antagonistic atmosphere within their evangelistic programs. Though the New Testament genuinely argues for keeping separate from apostate Christianity, does that mean faithful churches should engage in public programs angrily denouncing apostate Christianity in the most aggressive manner?

The New Testament in so many ways demonstrates the message of the church is a message of hope, the "good news" of salvation. It is the power of God to transform man into righteous beings who will enter the coming kingdom of God and live forever with Jesus and the Father. Keeping separate from apostate Christianity is an important part of faithfulness to Jesus. But it is neither the sole, nor central theme of the gospel of salvation.

Looking back in time we see how God frequently raised up prophets to warn against religious apostasy and foretell what God will do if man will not repent. The style of prophecy in the Old Testament frequently was 'in your face' witnessing, designed to get people's attention. Consider one

---

[256] Some Hellenistic Christians themselves understand the sound balance of faith and works, in principle, as preached by James. See John Gerstner, *Wrongly Dividing the Word of Truth*, p 250.

[257] "Philosophy and empty deceit," Paul's description of the Hellenistic theology of Gnostic Christianity in Colossians 2:8.

startling example from the prophet Isaiah. He walked naked in public for three years as a witness against Egypt (Isaiah chapter 20). I suppose if a church wanted to make a really big splash today, all its ministers could strip naked and march down Fifth Avenue in New York or around the White House in Washington D.C., screaming a warning message about Hellenistic apostasy. Surely that would attract the desired press coverage. But would it really advance the cause of the gospel?

If God decides to give an 'in your face' warning to the world, to denounce apostate Christianity in the same powerful fashion as done by Old Testament prophets, then surely he will raise up individuals to do that. In fact we know of two such persons who fill that type of role – the 'two witnesses' described in Revelation chapter 11. These two individuals both witness to Israel and openly oppose the final blossoming of Christian apostasy in the end time (the final revelation of the "man of sin" described in 2 Thessalonians chapter 2). There will be action enough – worldwide plagues, attempted assassinations and death visited suddenly by divine power.

For Primitive Christian churches, however, the primary commission is preaching the gospel of the coming kingdom of God. The story of apostate Christianity has a role in that work, mainly to educate the church itself so that it will remain separate and pure, as we see in the example of the church at Ephesus.

In Revelation 18:4 Jesus calls for all to come out of the religious apostasy symbolized by Babylon. So the story of apostate Christianity must be presented to the world as well, always in a loving fashion, as Paul counseled the church at Ephesus, *"speaking the truth in love"* (Eph 4:15). In preaching to the world at large, Primitive Christians will warn against the antinomian doctrines of Hellenistic Christianity. They will invite the world to join in balanced obedience to Jesus and his original and only revelation of genuine Christianity. The attitude should be to provide a blessing to the world by educating them about the need to come out of practices and beliefs that separate them from Jesus.

Finally, it is important to say the following: Though the knowledge about Christian apostasy presented in this book is important, and assumes increasing importance as we proceed into the difficulties of the end time, it is equally true that this knowledge is useless if we do not also have a personal, saving relationship with Jesus Christ. Understanding the story of Gnosticism never saved anyone. Coming to know the mercy, grace and power of Jesus Christ and his sacrifice, submitting to him as our master and savior, and respecting his will as revealed through his law and the Spirit, is the road to salvation.

The story of Christian apostasy does assume increasing importance in the end time. Those of us who have the fortune, or perhaps misfortune, to live in the end time, are facing terrible events to come. Primitive Christians, in the not too distant future, will be forced to make fateful, even life and death decisions. I believe it is God's will for this information to become available to us specifically in this era, to assist us through those troubled times.

– 14 –

Final Conclusions

In this final chapter we begin with a general summary of the historical and biblical arguments presented in this volume. In this we attempt to focus on what is most pertinent to our situation today.

Next we review history from a New Testament Christian perspective. How did key changes in pagan religion, centuries before Christ, setup an historic confrontation within Christianity in the first century, igniting a gigantic battle stretching over two millennia, a battle which rages yet today?

After that we review some additional key evidence for what this author considers two primary issues: 1) Is the Hellenization of Christianity sanctioned by God as a second, more spiritual revelation of the Christian faith? Is there direct, specific evidence from scripture on this matter? 2) Should Primitive Christianity join hands in ecumenical unity with Hellenistic Christianity?

And finally, we review some of the prominent features of the mystery of lawlessness. If Hellenistic Christian apostasy were infiltrating your church, would you know how to recognize it?

Summary Review

1. In the seventh to sixth centuries B.C. a great pagan religious reformation spread across the Indo-European world. In Greece this produced a new religious tradition focused on inner spirituality and connection between the heavens and an immortal soul in man.

2. At the same time, in Israel, the temple was destroyed and Hebrew prophets began to openly foretell the coming of Messiah and a New

Covenant. Thus two great religious movements were set in motion, leading to an historic collision and battle for the hearts of mankind.[258]

3.   In Greece the great pagan religious reformation first appeared in the form of Orphism and Pythagoreanism. Plato popularized it and it soon spread throughout Greek culture. Greece and then Rome spread the new religion throughout the Near East and across Europe. In Israel it produced Hellenistic forms of Judaism. Thus when Christianity appeared, its world was totally under the influence of what would become its chief adversary.

4.   In the first century A.D., pagan Hellenistic religion, Hellenistic Judaism and Christianity all combined to produce Gnostic Christianity, the first of many Hellenistic Christian movements. Gnosticism first developed inside the church in a form scholars call proto-Gnosticism. The leaders of the apostolic church fought back vigorously. Beginning late in the first century, most Gnostic Christians left the church and fragmented into multiple diverse organizations of their own.

5.   Gnostic Christianity pioneered the 'mystery of lawlessness' inside the apostolic church. This was the beginning of what historians call the Hellenization of Christianity. The mystery of lawlessness itself is a highly sophisticated, spiritual philosophy that licenses willful disobedience. It is called a 'mystery' because its lawlessness is disguised as obedience to a supposedly higher form of non-material spirituality.

6.   Second Thessalonians chapter 2 prophesies that Gnosticism's mystery of lawlessness will flourish until Jesus returns. Prophecies of the survival of Gnostic Christianity's antinomian legacy are fulfilled in two ways, as outlined in points 7 and 8:

7.   The lawless theology of Gnostic Christianity survives today in its purest form in Reformation Christianity, especially Evangelical Protestantism. Key Protestant doctrines such as predestination, eternal security and rejection of Jesus' earthly ministry, were first

---

[258]   For more historical perspective, see below, Appendix C, "The Great Pagan Reformation."

invented by Gnostic Christian heretics in the first three centuries
A.D.

8.   The Hellenization of Christianity pioneered by Gnosticism setup
the apostolic church for a second and final wave of Hellenistic
apostasy. The apostolic church built on the foundation introduced
by Gnosticism, but continued down its own unique path of Hellenization. Roman emperors forced the church's final capitulation when
they adopted the already Hellenized church as the medium for uni-
fying the empire under a single Hellenistic religion. This continues
to the present day as the Roman church.

9.   Mainstream Christianity today, in all its many forms, is called
Hellenistic Christianity because it is descended from the Hellenization of the apostolic church, pioneered in the first century by Gnosticism. The Hellenized church, from the Gnostics of the first
century to today, openly proclaims its belief system to be a second,
supposedly more spiritual revelation of the Christian religion.
Primitive Christianity, in contrast, claims to hold to the original
revelation from Jesus' earthly ministry and the preaching of the
apostles in the first century.

10.   The New Testament directly talks about the infiltration of Hellenistic religion in the church in the first century. It roundly condemns both Gnostic theology specifically, and the Hellenization of
Christianity in general. The Apostle John, in his epistles, specifically condemns Hellenization as a primary indication of Christian
apostasy.

11.   Hellenistic religious ideas were the driving force behind the conversion from Sabbath to Sunday. Eighth Day theology was first
popularized in Gnostic Christian circles and then adapted by Hellenistic factions within the primitive church. The beginning of the infiltration of these ideas into the church is reflected in the book of
Colossians.[259]

12.   The New Testament commands Christians to keep separate from
Hellenistic Christianity. Christians are instructed to reject the lawless doctrines of Hellenistic Christianity, and to avoid ecumenical

---

[259]   See below, Appendix A, "The Full Story Behind Colossians 2."

embrace and validation of Hellenistic Christianity, its organizations and ministers.

History from a New Testament Christian Point of View

The vast majority of modern Christianity accepts the Hellenization of Christianity as the will of God. This is an outgrowth of the doctrine of progressive revelation, which they believe justifies overturning various parts of the recorded teachings of Jesus and the apostles. According to this way of thinking, there was a second revelation of a more spiritual Christianity that replaces the earthly ministry of Jesus.

Many of those who embrace extreme eternal security also teach that portions or all of Jesus' earthly ministry as recorded in the four gospel books Matthew, Mark, Luke and John are legalistic and apply only to Israel. This is the teaching known as dispensationalism, supported by the majority of the more than 100 million followers of American Evangelicalism. (Dispensationalism is explained in detail in *Spirit of Antichrist,* the second volume in our series The World of Primitive Christianity.)[260]

In like fashion, Gnostic Christians claimed Jesus' earthly ministry could not be fully trusted because it was contaminated by the religion of the Old Testament.[261]

Primitive Christians generally reject both the Hellenization of Christianity and the idea that progressive revelation can overturn New Testament revelation, especially Jesus' earthly ministry. Naturally this produces a radically different view of history and Christian doctrine. We begin with a recap of religious history from a Primitive Christian point of view:

When Jesus was born, paganism had been preparing for his arrival for nearly seven centuries. Before the great religious reformation in ancient Greece, creator gods generally were respected figures of worship. Now, as a direct result of an ancient pagan religious reformation, the creator has been demoted to anything ranging from a well-intentioned but deficient

---

[260] The rationale for rejecting Jesus' earthly ministry commonly takes the form of arguing that the "gospel of the kingdom" preached by Jesus during his earthly ministry is different from and is replaced by the gospel of grace preached by Paul.

[261] See above, section "2 John," pages 107 and following.

angelic being, to a silly, deluded and proud creature. His goal is to prevent man from practicing the true spiritual worship of the heavenly Father. In general, the God of material creation has been thoroughly discredited. Now, one of the chief purposes of religion is to escape his authority and control.

By the time the church was founded it was all in place. Virtually every form of religion in the Hellenistic world had been converted to a new spiritual teaching focused on one's internal spiritual state. It was not the same, yet in many ways very similar to Jesus' emphasis on righteousness that comes from the heart. Animal sacrifice was out. Spirituality of the inner man was in. Most important, it had become universally accepted that all religions must be interpreted allegorically as expressions of the underlying Hellenistic truths of the immortality of the soul, liberation from material creation and the promise of entering heaven after death.

The pressure mounted by Hellenistic culture was universal and unrelenting. It was all right to have your own unique beliefs and a religious tradition going back to ancient times. However, to be taken seriously, to have any respect at all, you had to reinterpret your religion in Hellenistic terms. That's what everyone was doing. If you didn't you were a backward fool. You were laughing-stock.

Not only that, the Hellenistic tradition by this time came ready-mixed with biblical religion, in the form of Hellenized Jewish sects. Jewish concerns with evil and how to escape from it, and antagonism towards the official temple worship in Jerusalem, became mixed with Hellenistic aversion to material life and philosophic reasoning about the heavens and the immortal soul. It was a time bomb, and Christianity was the match that lit the fuse. Enriching the mixture with genuine Christian teachings about grace and freedom from penalty of the law, produced an outpouring of antagonism against the law-giving God of material creation. Thus Gnostic Christianity was born.

Within just a few decades of the founding of the church, the surviving apostles were fighting with their backs against the wall. That struggle is clearly reflected in New Testament scripture, such as the books of Jude, 2 Peter, and the epistles of John. Not long after the turn of the century the church was solidly on the road to joining the Hellenistic cultural mainstream.

The appearance of Jesus on earth was one of the most critical events in human history. This was true as much for pagan religion as for the people of God. It was not something paganism could afford to ignore. Viewed from a short-term perspective, it is one of the most spectacular success stories in pagan religious history. It was an ambush, prepared and set up over many centuries. When the primitive church was founded and set out to fulfill its mission, it walked right into the trap. It blew up right in its face.

Many of the patterns of opposition to Primitive Christianity established at that time continue to the present day. The savaging of the apostolic church is a process that continually repeats itself over centuries and millennia. Yet new movements always surface to carry on the same Primitive Christian tradition, some as recently as the last century and in some cases even in recent decades. Through divine intervention the gates of hell never prevail against the church, exactly as Jesus promised.

ISSUE #1 – Should Christians embrace Hellenistic Christianity as a second, more spiritual revelation of Christianity?

Faith of Our Fathers

At the very end of the Old Testament, in fact in the final verses, we read that in the end time God will send another, latter day Elijah with a warning message to God's people (Malachi 4:5–6). John the Baptist fulfilled this prophecy before Jesus' first appearance on earth (Matt 17:10–13). Yet, this seems to refer to the second appearance of Jesus on earth. Malachi says it will happen just before *"the great and terrible day of the Lord,"* which points to the final end time (see Malachi 4:5).

What is the message God sends to man just before Jesus' final return and the terrible events of the end-time? *"He will turn the hearts of the fathers to the children and the hearts of the children to their fathers. Lest I come and strike the earth with a curse"* (vs 6). This has been interpreted various ways. Because Malachi criticizes the people of his time for departing from their ancestral faith, some scholars and Primitive Christians see in it, in part, a message of the reconciliation of God's people to the spiritual fathers of their faith.

The message preached by the original Elijah, as described in 2 Kings chapter 17, emphasized this theme. Here the problem was characterized specifically as Israel's disloyalty to the religion of their ancestors. Note 2 Kings 17:13, *"Turn from your evil ways and keep my commandments...in accordance with all the law that I commanded your ancestors."* Also verse 15: *"They despised his statutes, and his covenant that he made with their ancestors....* " In place of loyalty to their ancestral faith, *"they followed the nations that were around them, concerning whom the Lord had commanded them that they should not do...."*

When Jesus first appeared on earth, the religion of the Bible had sunk to an all time low. Judaism had covered over the original faith of their fathers with a mountain of added rules and regulations. It had become an impossible burden and effectively thwarted the original spiritual purpose of the Hebrew faith. In preparation for Jesus' first coming, God sent John the Baptist to preach repentance and a return to the original spiritual and moral values of their covenant.

When Jesus comes again, will he find Christianity in any better shape? Today nearly one hundred million Christians attend churches that officially believe they are licensed to commit unlimited sin based on no more than a fleeting moment of faith, or because they were winners of a cosmic lottery in which they are irresistibly predestined to be saved. Virtually all Hellenistic Christianity claims the original, ancestral revelation of Christianity has been replaced by a supposedly more spiritual (Hellenistic) second revelation of the faith.

How did this happen? As we have seen throughout this volume, it is the end result of a long process of Hellenization beginning with Gnostic Christianity, departing from the ancestral Christian faith of the first century A.D. It is essentially the same process of apostasy experienced by Israel in the time of Elijah.

Malachi not only foretells a repetition of the Elijah message in the end time. He also witnesses to the specific antinomian heresy involved in our departure from the ancestral faith today. *"You have wearied the Lord with your words,"* he says. How? *"By saying, 'All who do evil are good in the sight of the Lord, and he delights in them.' "* (Malachi 2:17). Who today is saying that Christians are loved and eternally secure, and *"he delights in them"* despite literally any evil they do? How truly and completely Malachi's words are fulfilled in our time!

The Hellenization process has covered over the original revelation of Christianity with a mountain of pagan Greek theology and human wisdom. Hellenistic Christianity today despises the original faith Jesus gave to our Christian ancestors, the apostolic church. Hellenistic Christianity replaces the ancestral faith with a supposedly superior revelation drawn from the Hellenistic *"nations that were around them."* It is a virtually identical repetition of the events in ancient Israel.

Just as at Jesus' first coming, so the warning to man at his second coming is to return to the spirituality and morality of the original faith. For us today that is the original revelation by the apostles and by Jesus himself during his earthly ministry, all recorded for us as the New Testament. This is 'Primitive Christianity,' the original, ancestral faith embodied in the New Testament, understood as the harmonizing of the entire New Testament. It stands in sharp contrast to Hellenistic Christianity and its claim that later portions of the New Testament override earlier portions, which are overridden yet again by theology developed after the New Testament was completed.

Just as Jews in Jesus' day were called to throw off their disobedience and legalistic additions to their covenant, so today Jesus is calling on Christians to throw off their disobedience and antinomian additions, and return to the original faith of the first-century apostolic church.

Jesus condemned the perversion of the Hebrew faith in the strongest language: "*Woe to you, scribes and Pharisees, hypocrites! For you cross sea and land to make a single convert, and you make the new convert twice as much a child of hell as yourselves*" (Matt 23:15). Is Jesus any less upset with our perversion of Christianity today?

'From the Beginning'

The same Elijah message – loyalty to the ancestral faith – is found in the epistles of John. Here John repeatedly talks about the faith that was "from the beginning," meaning Jesus' earthly ministry:

> We declare to you what was **from the beginning** (1 John 1:1)

> This is **the message we have heard from him** [Jesus] and proclaim to you (1:5)

> Beloved, I am writing you no new commandment, but an old commandment that you have had **from the beginning** (2:7)

> Let what you heard **from the beginning** abide in you (2:24)

> For this is the message you have heard **from the beginning** (3:11)

> ...not as though I were writing you a new commandment, but one we have had **from the beginning**.... And this is love, that we walk according to his commandments; this is the commandment just as you have heard it **from the beginning** (2 John 5–6)

What is the basis for claiming that John's oft-repeated phrase "from the beginning" refers to Jesus' earthly ministry? The key is in the very beginning of his first epistle, chapter 1 verses 1–3. *"We declare to you what was from the beginning,"* John says, and then goes on to link that phrase to the apostles' personal contact with Jesus during his earthly ministry. He mentions how they personally heard him speak, how they observed him with their own eyes and even touched him (*"what we have heard...what we have looked at and touched with our hands"*).

We find the same thing in John's gospel book:

> When the Advocate [Holy Spirit] comes...he will testify on my be-half. **You also are to testify because you have been with me from the beginning** (John 15:26–27).

For John, the inspiration of the Holy Spirit does not override the witness of the apostles to the earthly ministry and conduct of Jesus. Both equally witness to the true Jesus and confirm the importance of his earthly minis-try for the church.

Though John's use of the phrase *"from the beginning"* points to Jesus' earthly ministry, the issue is slightly more complex than that. In John's epistles this phrase also refers to biblical teachings from before Christ. For example, 1 John 2:7–11 contains the phrase *"from the beginning"* in relationship to the commandment of love. Here it is described as some-thing both old and new. It is old because this foundational principle of the New Testament actually is very ancient, dating from the Old Testament – *"You shall love the Lord your God with all your heart"* (Deuteronomy 6:5) and *"you shall love your neighbor as yourself"* (Leviticus 19:18).

Yet, in verse 8 John explains that at the same time it is a *"new com-mandment."* Why? John explains: because in the person of Jesus this existing, ancient tradition of spirituality is more fully revealed and passed on to those who follow him. As John phrases it, this spirituality of love *"is true in him* [Jesus] *and in you, because the darkness is passing away and the true light* [of the New Covenant] *is already shining"* (1 John 2:8).

John's central point throughout is that Christian spirituality is an an-cient tradition, not something totally new that replaces the Old Testament and everything that went before, as Gnostic Christians claimed. It is this ancient spiritual tradition that has been revealed more completely and with heightened emphasis in the person and earthly ministry of Jesus Christ, and in Christians as they walk by the power of the spirit.

This is the message of 1 John 1:1–3 and 5, where it argues that what was *"from the beginning"* was revealed through Jesus at the time he walked on the earth, and therefore we should look to Jesus' earthly minis-try as the full revelation and foundation of Christian spirituality: (*We declare to you what was from the beginning, what we have heard, what we have seen...what we have...touched...*[which] *was with the Father and was revealed to us.... This is the message we have heard from him and proclaim to you....*)

Back in chapter two, John exhorts Christians to *"walk just as He* [Jesus] *walked"* (vs 6). When John says to walk as Jesus "walked" (past tense), what could he have meant except Jesus' earthly ministry?

Why is John emphasizing that Christian spirituality is an ancient tradition, that it has reached its culmination in Jesus and that we should look to his earthly ministry as the foundation of that revelation? Remember, John's epistles were aimed squarely at Gnostic Christianity. What John is doing is contrasting the apostles' source for their teaching of Christianity against that of the Gnostics. The apostles taught the original revelation that was "from the beginning," given to them personally by Jesus.

In contrast, Gnostic ministers were preaching two key heretical ideas. First, they were saying that Christian spirituality is totally divorced from the Old Testament and everything that went before. But second, and most importantly they were even saying that Jesus' earthly ministry is defective. "Trust us," they said, "Jesus' earthly ministry had serious defects and cannot be trusted. His earthly ministry was polluted by the human side of his Docetic (dual) nature. But not to worry. Since he returned to heaven he has been talking to us in dreams and visions – really! – and he gave us a second, more spiritual revelation of Christianity." Given that choice, whom would you trust?

What John is doing is demonstrating the superiority of the source of the apostolic revelation (Jesus himself), and its ancient heritage, compared to the Gnostics' private revelation of something entirely new.

Through the prophet Amos, God promises: *"Surely the Lord God does nothing, without revealing his secret to his servants the prophets"* (Amos 3:7). Many Old Testament prophets predicted the advent of Christianity. If God intended there to be a secondary revelation of Christianity that overturns the first revelation and Jesus' earthly ministry, wouldn't he also have revealed that clearly in his Word?

What is striking is that the New Testament not only does not endorse a second revelation of a supposedly more spiritual Christianity, in John's epistles it directly refers to this claim and explicitly rejects it. And it is significant that all this is done in the context of an epistle in which the Apostle John is targeting Gnostic Christianity, the very group that pioneered the heretical claim that the Hellenization of Christianity is a valid second revelation of 'spiritual' Christianity.

In this the Apostle John echoes the same themes from the prophets Malachi and Elijah about adhering to the original ancestral faith. There should be no doubt which Christianity the Bible endorses as the true faith.

ISSUE #2 – Should Primitive Christianity join hands in ecumenical unity with Hellenistic Christianity?

Once again we turn to the Apostle John, who comments directly on this matter. In his epistles John clearly identifies his target: *"I write these things to you concerning those who would deceive you"* (1 John 2:26). This refers to Gnostic Christians, who started their movement inside the first-century church. John further explains: *"They went out from us, but they did not belong to us.... But by going out they made it plain that **none of them belongs to us"** (2:19).

Here John is emphasizing the importance of recognizing the theological gulf separating the two. In John's view, Gnostic Christians leaving the church at the end of the first century, and faithful Christians who remained with the church, are two opposing camps that have nothing to do with each other (*none of them belongs to us*).

Does John's view of the separation of apostolic and apostate Christianity apply to us today, when we are faced with modern versions of the same heretical theology? Indeed, do Primitive and Hellenistic Christianity belong to the same spiritual tradition, or does '*none of them belong to us*'?

'Do Not Receive or Welcome'

Today, the vast majority of Primitive Christianity has begun to accept and teach the ecumenical unity of Primitive and Hellenistic Christianity. This, in spite of the fact we have many warnings in the New Testament against exactly that very thing.[262] Today, incredibly, the majority of

---

[262] Not least are the Ephesus church which Jesus praises for recognizing Hellenized Gnostic Christianity for what it is, calling its ministers what they really are (false apostles) and closing its door to them (Rev 2:2, 6); the Pergamum church which Jesus criticizes for allowing Hellenistic Gnostic Christians to worship in their midst (Rev 2:14–16); and the Thyatira church whose leadership adopted a Hellenistic antinomian the-

Primitive Christianity validates and embraces churches and ministers that speak biblical truth from one side of their mouth, at the same time from the other side spouting theories of a more advanced revelation of Christianity in which Christians engage willfully in unlimited sin, without repentance, without fear so long as they merely love Jesus.

In the epistles of John we are warned:

> **Do not receive** into the house **or welcome** anyone who comes to you and does not bring **this teaching**; for to welcome is to participate in the evil deeds of such a person. (2 John 10–11)

"This teaching" refers to avoiding Gnostic heresy in the first-century church. (For the significance of the phrase *"this teaching,"* see above, pages 107 and following, section "2 John.")

Therefore, does it matter that today we welcome and validate Evangelical Protestant organizations and ministers who openly teach many of the same ancient heretical doctrines first preached by Gnostic Christianity?

Consider again Jesus' warning in Revelation 18:4, calling us to separate ourselves from the 'harlot' (a symbol of religious apostasy). The reason for separation is that we *"do not take part in her sins."* Does that mean it is all right to engage in ecumenical union with heretical groups as long as they don't influence us to directly participate in their errors? What is the full implication of the phrase *"do not take part in her sins"*?

According to the Apostle John, in the passage cited above, 'participation' includes merely validating others who teach heretical doctrines: *"for to **welcome** is to **participate in the evil deeds** of such a person."* According to John, ecumenically embracing those who teach Gnostic heresy – "receiving" and "welcoming" them – is sufficient to trigger the definition of "participation" in the sins that their systems of belief wittingly or unwittingly promote.

Surely this does not contradict Jesus' teaching to show courtesy, love and kindness to every human being with whom we come in contact. What it does say, however, and very specifically, is that we must not validate or give encouragement to the work of individuals and groups that teach Hellenistic apostasy, even by "welcoming" them. By this it means 'welcoming' in the sense of ecumenically validating their ministry.

---

ology such that Jesus tells the remaining faithful to keep their distance from their own apostate leaders (Rev 2:20–25).

Ecumenical association by its very nature validates the other partner and their teachings as Christian. If licensing unlimited sin and rejecting the earthly ministry of Jesus are insignificant details, if they are mere denominational 'distinctives' as some are fond of saying, then that's fine. But if they are not, then ecumenical association with Hellenistic Christianity is a deadly game that will not end well for those who ignore these biblical warnings. If proto-Gnostics taught these doctrines in the first-century church and the New Testament condemns them, is that not a significant clue for how we should view the same thing today?

Jesus demands that we distinguish between those who merely differ in detail from our own teaching, and those who are involved in truly serious apostasy against the word of God. To understand why this is important, consider the following:

What if a minister preaches the common antinomian idea that you should be a good person, but technically you have the option to sin willfully and still be saved. Though he vigorously urges people not to take the antinomian option, someone believes him and decides to take that option. But because that is a false teaching, those who take that option are lost. Do you think God would not hold that minister and his church responsible for the loss of that person?

But now take that one step further. What if you are a leader in a Primitive Christian church. You don't preach the doctrine of the Carnal Christian. You don't teach that people have the option to sin willfully, without limit. No one could get the wrong idea from listening to you. But, you publicly praise ministers and churches that do preach the antinomian doctrines of Reformation theology. You may admit their antinomian theories are wrong. But still, you reason, it's ok because they do urge people to act righteously in many ways, they preach many other things that are perfectly right and proper, they love Jesus and in fact they do a lot of good.

However, someone listening to you believes you when you praise Reformation ministers and their churches. He therefore goes to those ministers and churches you validated as Christian, believes their antinomian teaching and chooses to take the option to sin willfully and still be saved. But because that is a false teaching, that person is lost. Do you think Jesus will not hold you as well as the persons you validated accountable for the loss of that person?

So we see that validating people who preach antinomian apostasy can have very real consequences. The excuse that "we don't teach those things ourselves, and we disapprove their error" does not change Jesus' warning that merely *"to welcome is to participate in their evil deeds,"* nor his command to *"come out of"* the great harlot and her many daughters.

Primitive Christianity's plunge into ecumenism today is the beginning of a great spiritual struggle that will determine the fate of many Primitive Christian churches in the end time.

Ecumenical Crisis in Ancient Israel

More than two thousand years ago, in ancient Israel, Elijah stood up against the same kind of ecumenical apostasy facing us today.

Ancient Israel frequently viewed Canaanite religion as entirely compatible with the worship of Yahweh. It was not difficult to assume Canaanite and Hebrew religion were branches of the same faith. One of the names of the supreme deity of Israel was Elohim. The supreme deity of Canaanite religion was El, a Semitic root word from which Elohim is derived. Israel's God Yahweh frequently was called *Adonai, the Lord.* The Canaanite savior of mankind, and son of the supreme God, was called Baal, which also meant Lord.

The problem in ancient Israel was not so much people forsaking Yahweh to worship Baal as it was worshipping both Yahweh and Baal at the same time. That is why Yahweh constantly described himself as the "jealous" God, who demands *exclusive* worship from his people.

Jeremiah records a classic example of Israel combining the worship of Yahweh and Baal, together with licentious, antinomian grace, in the following words:

> You [Israel] steal, you murder, you commit adultery...you burn sacrifices to Baal, and you run after other gods...; will you then come and stand before me in this house which bears my name [the temple of Yahweh], and say, 'We are safe'! [saved, exempt from punishment] Safe, you think, to indulge in all these abominations! (Jer 7:9–10, **REB** translation)

When Elijah faced down the priests of Baal at Mt. Carmel, he clearly defined the nature of the problem. *"How long,"* he told Israel, *"will you go limping with two different opinions? If the Lord is God, follow him; but if Baal, then follow him"* (1 Kings 18:21). Israel failed to distinguish between deities who went under almost identical names and promised many of the same things. Elijah challenged Israel to make a choice and stop straddling the fence with their ecumenical worship of both Yahweh and Baal. Indeed, ecumenical apostasy was at the center of the religious crisis in ancient Israel.

What is wrong with ecumenism? On the one hand there are people so exclusive they condemn everyone, even over tiny, technical issues. As with everything, this is an issue requiring balance. On the other hand, is it an insignificant matter to join hands with and validate the ministry and worship of churches that openly proclaim Christians are licensed to engage in unlimited sin? Does it matter that they believe they are licensed to do all the things for which the unsaved are condemned to hell, never repent and get away with it? If the New Testament condemns proto-Gnostic Christians for embracing those doctrines in the first century, does it not equally condemn those who teach the very same doctrines today? If the Apostle John told the first-century church to view departing Gnostics as having nothing to do with the true faith (*none of them belong to us*), does that not apply to us today?

The significance of Israel's problems for our time is reinforced by the promise spoken through Malachi that Elijah's message will be repeated in the end time (Malachi 4:5–6). The religious crisis of the end time is one of the greatest challenges the people of God will ever face in all of human history. The conditions of ecumenical apostasy reflected in Revelation 18:4, which mirror ancient Israel in the time of Elijah, undoubtedly will happen – indeed it has already begun!

The only question is where you and I fit into this picture. Will we be one of the foolish? Will we ignore the direct warnings of New Testament scripture, swept away by the great swelling religiosity of Hellenistic apostasy? Or will we heed the testimony of Jesus contained in New Testament prophecy, which Jesus urges us to take very seriously? *"He who has an ear listen to what the Spirit is saying to the churches."*

What then is the conclusion? Should Primitive Christians join hands in ecumenical unity with Hellenistic Christianity? The evidence is overwhelming. How can these warnings not apply to us, when we are surrounded by Hellenistic Christians preaching the same antinomian doctrines today as when those warnings were first given?

Identifying the Mystery

The New Testament says the mystery of lawlessness will survive and flourish in the end-time (2 Thess 2:1–8). If the mystery of lawlessness is with us today and is flourishing, can we accurately identify it?

What is the essence of Christian antinomianism? The church at Perga-mum was devout and faithful even to death, but they failed to fully recog-nize the antinomianism of Gnostic Christianity as apostasy. If they were fooled, could we be fooled too? On the other hand, if we don't accurately understand the essence of these warnings, can we go too far? Can we condemn true teachings of the Bible as apostasy and wrongly insult and reject our own Christian brothers and sisters?

Gnostic Christianity devoted itself to the inner guidance of the Spirit. They preached love, grace and mercy. Does that mean anyone who preaches about the Spirit, emphasizing love, grace and mercy, is an apos-tate Christian? What are the principle ideas and traits we should look for? When is it apostasy? When is it not?

1 – Antinomianism / the mystery of lawlessness

Perhaps the most critical issue is antinomianism and various associated teachings that license willful sin as a viable option for Christians. Just as in a mystery, these doctrines often are hidden beneath very beautiful teachings of obedience to a more spiritual form of Christianity.

What, then, is the essence of the mystery of lawlessness? A primary example is the Nicolaitan Gnostic sect, first mentioned in Revelation 2 in association with the church at Ephesus. Jesus is quoted as praising the Ephesian Christians, *"Yet this is to your credit: you hate the works of the Nicolaitans, which I also hate."* (vs 6). We know from history what this means. The Nicolaitans used the theology of their founder to justify ignoring material sin. Likewise the Apostle Jude warned against Gnostic teachers *"who pervert the grace of our God into licentiousness"* (Jude 3).

We know this also from the dramatic passage in John's first letter (1 John 3:4–10), where the apostle says over and over that you cannot have a relationship with God and continue willfully in sin. Remember that John's first and second epistles were written explicitly to refute Gnostic Christi-anity. This is not talking about licentious pagan beliefs. It is talking about Christians within the first-century church who believed that as Christians they had the option to willfully sin and still be saved.

So, the first biblical principle is so very simple. Systems of belief that license willful sin for Christians are apostasy. What in our present day demonstrates that very teaching? How much simpler could it be? It doesn't take a rocket scientist to figure this out. The Reformation teach-ings of eternal security, and most dramatically the theology of extreme eternal security championed by Protestant Evangelicalism, openly and proudly teach that Christians are licensed to commit unlimited sin, without repentance, and still be saved.

"But," some will object, "aren't you being terribly unkind? None of us are perfect, therefore why are you being so hard on Christians who likewise are less than perfect in their practice of Christianity"? That is a valid question. All Christians continue to experience sin throughout their lives. Development of Christ-like attitudes and conduct is a life-long process. How then do we clearly distinguish between antinomian apostasy and simple human fallibility?

Very simply, it is one thing to seek righteousness and fall short, and it is another to explicitly believe in and teach doctrines that license willful sin. It is one thing to stumble and fall, and another to say written biblical standards don't matter, so I'll just pick and choose how I want to demonstrate my spirituality.

Jude describes apostate Christians as those who "reject authority" (Jude 8). Peter describes the same Gnostic Christians as teaching doctrines that "promise freedom" and "despise authority" (2 Peter 2:19). So apostasy involves specific doctrines that claim to give blanket protection to Christians from divine authority and punishment. Peter emphasizes that such people, despite their claims of Christian liberty, will be punished just as the disobedient were punished in stories from the Old Testament (vs 5–10).

Who today preaches a theology that rejects authority and denies condemnation of the willfully evil, replacing concrete standards with a vague private revelation of the Spirit whispering in your ear?

There are many theoretical approaches to morality in Hellenistic Christianity today. Some say you can do literally anything, commit any sin, even murder and commit fornication a thousand times a day, as Martin Luther claimed, and supposedly it has no effect on salvation. (They equally urge against using their Christian license to sin; it is only an *option*.)

Others insist Christians cannot get away with totally wanton conduct. Some soften antinomian theology by saying there are minimums. There has to be at least an initial demonstration of goodness after conversion. You have to be good to at least some degree for a little while, but after that you can do anything you want.

Some say you need never repent. Others say at the end of your life Jesus will work on your heart to make you sorry and forcefully bring you back to the faith just in time to die and go to heaven. There remains this question, however – Is partial licensing any better than total licensing of immorality? Can you pick and choose some standards with which to comply, and knowingly and consciously choose to willfully ignore others?

2 – Antinomianism as a means to a more advanced, spiritual relationship with God.

Here we encounter a significant problem in identifying antinomian apostasy. Does Reformation theology *officially* promote sin? No, *technically* it doesn't.

Consider Gnostic Christianity in the first century. Did Nicolaitan Christians *officially* promote sin? Did this or any other antinomian group say that sin is a good thing? Remember the classic stories about Nicolas, founder of the Nicolaitan Gnostic sect, and how he was a very sincere and devout Christian. He led an exemplary moral life (see above, pages 40 and following). His theology in fact was designed to bring man out of sin. By divorcing your mind from the concerns of material life, he reasoned, and devoting yourself exclusively to spiritual matters, you will be lifted out of sin naturally.

Notice how Jesus praised the Ephesian Christians for being perceptive and correctly labeling Gnostic Christian ministers as false apostles: *"...you have tested those who claim to be apostles but are not, and have found them to be false"* (vs 2). The fact he singles this out implies it is something special. And indeed it is. Confusing antinomian spirituality with genuine Christianity is a common mistake. Antinomian Christians never admit they are antinomian. They always, then and now, claim they are obedient to a higher calling revealed exclusively through the Spirit.

The *mystery* of lawlessness is called a mystery because that is exactly what it is. The term *mystery* implies something hidden, and indeed the mystery of lawlessness that entered the church in the first century (2 Thess 2:3–7) has always, from that time until now, hidden its true nature under the guise of a higher spirituality.

Thereby, a primary biblical principle for identifying Christian antinomianism is that it never openly advocates sin. It only licenses it. Indeed, it vigorously encourages its followers to be good, according to one or the other natural human standard. John MacArthur, founder of the Lordship salvation movement, makes this point very forcefully and poignantly in the following words:[263]

---

[263] MacArthur, *The Gospel According to the Apostles,* p 95. Bold emphasis added.

Most antinomians vigorously appeal for Christians to walk in a manner worthy of their calling.... Antinomians typically believe Christians *should* yield to the lordship of Christ; they just do not believe surrender is a binding requirement in the gospel call to faith. **Antinomians do not necessarily despise the law of God; they simply believe it is irrelevant to saving faith.**

Antinomianism makes obedience elective. While most antinomians strongly *counsel* Christians to obey (and even urge them to obey), they do not believe obedience is a necessary consequence of true faith.

Gnostic Righteousness and Rejection of Sin

The New Testament so strongly condemns Gnostic Christianity you might get the idea Gnosticism never said or did anything good. That is a huge mistake. A prime example of this is the Valentinian Gnostic sect. This was a prominent group of Gnostic Christians condemned by the early Roman church because they believed Christians have no need to perform good works in order to be saved.[264] Does that mean they didn't teach Christian righteousness? Not at all! Consider the following passages from one of their ancient texts, *The Gospel of Philip*:

> He who has knowledge of the truth is a free man, but the free man does not sin, for "he who sins is the slave of sin."[265]

Here, the Gnostic author paraphrases the words of the Apostle Paul (Romans 6:17–22), making it clear their concept of antinomian liberty was not intended to promote sin. Unfortunately, whereas Paul says that means ceasing from sin, in both ancient Gnostic and modern Reformation theology ceasing from sin is understood much more vaguely. Paul says that Christian righteousness "upholds the law" (Rom 3:31). But in modern Evangelical theology, for example, it means that 1) righteousness is voluntary and therefore willful sin technically remains a viable option, and 2) biblical law is replaced (not expanded or 'upheld') by the private inspiration of the Spirit. Recall the antinomian teaching of the evangelical author McVey – see above pages 172 and following. Still, even antinomian

---

[264] See above, pages 52 and following.

[265] From Nag Hammadi text *The Gospel of Philip*, 77,15 – 78,12, after Desjardins, *Sin in Valentinianism*, p 96–97.

Christianity, both then and now, teaches that we *should* be 'good' in some general sense, and we *should* cease from sin, once again in some general sense.

Another Valentinian Gnostic text, the *Second Apocalypse of James,* illustrates Gnostic embrace of righteousness in a context of genuinely orthodox biblical concepts. This text claims to record the prayer of the apostle James immediately before he was executed by Jewish authorities in the first century. It talks of grace, forgiveness from and rejection of sin, and the hope of the resurrection. As always, Gnostic texts can be difficult reading, but we will explain as we go.

> My God and my Father...who **made me alive through a mystery of what he wills**.... ...your grace...is alive in me to accomplish a work of fullness! **Save me from sinful flesh,** because I trusted in you with all my strength! ... Do not give me into the hand of a judge who is severe with sin! **Forgive me all my debts**.... Because I am alive in you, **your grace is alive in me**. I have renounced everyone, but you I have confessed.[266]

Notice how James praises the heavenly Father for regenerating him through the mystery of God's sovereign will (*who made me alive through a mystery of what he wills*). This is the Gnostic precedent for the concept of regeneration and God's irresistible will in Reformation theology. Still, he admits he is not without sin. Thus James begs that he not be given over to a harsh judge. Rather, he pleads for forgiveness. Notice the beautiful, orthodox sentiment about grace, mercy and forgiveness, together with rejection of the sinfulness associated with material life (*save me from sinful flesh*).

In light of Gnostic texts such as this, is it surprising that the Pergamon church failed to recognize Gnostic Christianity for what it is?

3 – Presence of ancient Gnostic doctrines, and heretical exaggeration of genuine New Testament doctrines

Many Gnostic doctrines survive today, and in their heretical antinomian form are key markers of Christian apostasy. These include total depravity, regeneration and salvation with no participation by man, predestination, eternal security, and antinomian mystical union with God.

---

[266] From Nag Hammadi text *The Second Apocalypse of James,* 62,16–63,29, after Desjardins, *Sin in Valentinianism,* p 111–112.

4 – Substitution of 'Heavenly' for 'Jewish' Christianity – religious anti-Semitism

Here we refer to the extreme bias against all things Jewish, blanket rejection of the Old Testament, and substitution of symbols and practices oriented solely to the heavens, as in the Eighth Day theology of Sunday observance.

Biblical religion maintains that the creator of the material world has laid down standards governing human conduct within his creation. Those standards are contained in law, passed down through written scripture. Man has an obligation to obey God's will as revealed in those scriptures. Jeremiah foretold that under the New Covenant those laws would be written on our hearts (Jer 31:31-34), and Christ explained how that means expanding the law to the inner man (Matthew chapter 5).

Gnosticism took an entirely opposite approach. Gnostic Christianity was based primarily on Hellenistic philosophy and religion. In Hellenistic religion the creator is a deficient being. Creation is a materialistic trap. Therefore the religion of the creator similarly is a materialistic trap. According to Gnosticism, religious practices involving material existence simply won't work. You can't become spiritual through Hebrew religion and its creation-centered rituals. Therefore, as we saw in previous chapters, they concluded that everything in Christianity *must* be reinterpreted to point solely to the heavens.

Paul openly talked about this in his letter to the Colossians. The church there was under attack by that same theology about connecting to the heavenly *pleroma*. This required reinterpreting Jewish celebrations to point to the heavens instead of material creation. (See below, Appendix B, The Full Story behind Colossians 2," beginning on page 331.) Thereby we know that another of the primary traits of Christian apostasy is rejection of Jewish practices simply because they are Jewish, i.e. because of their association with material creation and the Old Testament. Chief among these is insistence on Sunday observance and its related Eighth Day theology. (See above, chapter 3, "The Hellenistic Sabbath," beginning on page 57.)

The Apostle Jude referred to Gnostic bias against Hebrew religion when he spoke of *"all the harsh things that ungodly sinners have spoken against him* [the Lord]*"* (Jude 15). This is a direct reference to the constant drumbeat of anti-Judaic condemnation of the Old Testament and Jewish Christianity.[267]

Irrational, bitterly rabid condemnation of Hebrew religion was a trademark of virtually all Gnostic sects. That phenomenon is with us yet today, and it too is a signal marker of Christian apostasy.

5 – Hellenistic philosophy and human wisdom

The use of human reason to override biblical revelation was a key indication of apostasy in the first century, and continues in that same role today.

The New Testament regularly contrasts the soundness of its teaching with the folly of human reason. In the Hellenistic world, philosophy and human reason were an integral part of religion. We have seen how the same tendency to philosophy and human reason continues to play a large role among Reformation theologians. To this day it still leads Christians into tortured reasoning, contradiction, sometimes almost comical interpretation of scripture, and ultimately strange and astoundingly extreme doctrines such as salvation without knowledge of Jesus (the 'saved heathen'), the doctrine of the Carnal Christian, the option to murder and commit fornication a thousand times a day and still be saved, according to Martin Luther, and many more.

As we saw in an earlier chapter, the Reformation claim of *sola scriptura* never has meant what many assume (see above, pages 177 and following). Throughout Hellenistic Christianity's long history, playing games with scripture has been the norm, not the exception, and this is another signal marker and indication of Christian apostasy.

6 – Progressive revelation

The mystery of lawlessness from the earliest times has depended on the idea of a second and more advanced revelation of Christianity that **overturns** the earthly ministry of Jesus and the original 'Jewish' Christianity of the apostolic church.

It is significant that the only direct biblical warning against progressive revelation occurs in the epistles of John. This is no accident, as John's letters were written specifically to counter Gnostic Christianity. Gnostic Christians indeed pioneered the concept of progressive revelation. There

---

[267] Verse 15 continues the theme introduced in verse 14 where the term 'Lord' is to be taken in the Old Testament context as a designation of Yahweh.

are various aspects to this issue, but all revolve around the idea of replacing the original revelation of Christianity with a later, supposedly more spiritual Christianity. For Gnostics, that second revelation just happened to be their combination of apostolic Christianity and pagan Hellenistic religion.

Using the doctrine of progressive revelation, mainstream Christianity today claims its conversion to Hellenistic religion was sanctioned by God and is not the apostasy, the great falling away to lawlessness predicted by Paul in 2 Thessalonians 2:3, *"...for that day will not come unless the rebellion comes first and the lawless one is revealed...."*

The Apostle John, however, specifically warns against this very thing:

> Be on your guard.... Everyone who does not abide in the teaching of Christ, **but goes beyond it**, does not have God. (2 John 8–9, see NRSV translation)

John's words are a direct reference to the widespread use of progressive revelation by Gnostic Christianity.[268] In an earlier chapter we demonstrated that the "teaching of Christ" beyond which John says we should not go, means both the earthly ministry of Jesus and Jesus' divinity. (Jesus' full divinity is the basis by which we know we can trust his earthly ministry – see above, section "2 John," pages 107 and following.)

Gnostic Christianity generally taught that Jesus' earthly ministry was defective because he had two natures. One half of his nature was that of a man, a Jew, whose Jewish heritage contaminated his earthly ministry with supposedly unspiritual doctrines from the Old Testament. Thus Jesus' earthly ministry had to be modified and replaced by new revelations from after the resurrection.

John is directly referring to this Gnostic teaching of progressive revelation and specifically its use in supporting antinomianism. Many modern Christian theologies use progressive revelation for the same purpose, to circumvent the lawful implications of Jesus' original, pre-crucifixion teachings as recorded in the four gospels.

The scholar John Turner, in his introductory comments to his translation of the Nag Hammadi text *The Book of Thomas the Contender,* has the

---

[268] *"Goes beyond it"* is the **NRSV** wording, not found in other translations. The original Greek is "transgresses it," referring to transgressing the teaching of Christ, which signifies rejection of or failure to follow the teaching of Christ, i.e. to "go beyond" the teaching of Christ.

following to say about the Gnostic penchant for progressive revelation. Here he comments on a certain class of Gnostic texts that promote replacement of Jesus' earthly ministry by a new revelation from Christ after his resurrection:

> These dialogues are set at a time between the resurrection and ascension, when...both he and his teaching were available to select apostles in a form unclouded by the sort of materiality which was believed to obscure the spiritual significance of his...earthly, preresurrection teaching. This special teaching might consist of enlightening commentary on his darker earthly teaching, or even new revelations to special apostles.[269]

After Christ was resurrected and especially after he ascended to heaven, having shed his material body and become fully spiritual again, supposedly he provided the Gnostic Christian elite with a second, fully spiritual revelation of Christianity.[270]

Progressive revelation is another critical marker of the survival of Gnostic Christian apostasy in our time.

7 – Hellenistic characteristics and doctrines in general

The very fact of being 'Hellenistic,' of incorporating beliefs and practices derived from ancient Greek religion and philosophy, is a primary indication of apostasy according to the Apostle John. Numerous features of modern Christianity, from Sunday observance to belief in the immortal soul, were developed in the early church under the influence of Hellenistic religion.

Today, scholars commonly refer to modern mainstream Christianity as Hellenistic Christianity. From evidence presented throughout this volume, we know that modern mainstream Christianity is a mixture of apostolic Christianity and pagan Hellenistic religion. The Hellenization of Christianity began in the first century under the influence of Gnosticism, at the

---

[269] **NHLE**, p 199.

[270] A typical example from Gnostic Christianity is the *Apochryphon of James,* which purports to come from the Apostle James (see **NHLE**, 29f). This text claims that Christ appeared to the apostles 550 days after the resurrection, at which time Jesus imparted a special, new revelation to James and Peter only. This special revelation was necessary in order to enter the kingdom of heaven. This new gospel was intended for a special class of people described as the children and sons of the Lord, who were to come after the original disciples. Of course, the Gnostics viewed themselves as those special people.

same time the New Testament was being written. So it is not surprising that the New Testament directly comments on it.

One of the most direct references to these early problems occurs in the letters of John:

> They are from the world; therefore what they say is from the world, and the world listens to them. We are from God. Whoever knows God listens to us, and whoever is not from God does not listen to us. From this we know the spirit of truth and the spirit of error. (1 John 4:5–6)

John contrasts **they** and **we**. In the context of this passage, *they* refers to Gnostic Christians. John talks about them in the immediately preceding verses (vs 1–4).[271] *"They are from the world,"* means that Gnostic Christianity is from the world of Hellenistic culture and religion, which dominated Palestine and the entire Mediterranean in the first century A.D.

What John is saying, and this applies today just as then, is that Christians who embrace the Hellenization of Christianity are by nature antagonistic towards the original faith preached by the apostles. They openly and brazenly reject the teaching of the first-century apostolic church (*does not listen to us*). Is it any surprise that in our day we find Hellenistic Christianity still caught up in that same antagonism against Primitive Christianity?

I don't know what could be more clear. The New Testament considers Hellenistic Christianity to be apostasy because of the very fact it is Hellenistic. Therefore Hellenization itself is another signal marker of Christian apostasy.

There is little dispute over the historical accuracy of our current state of knowledge of the Hellenization of Christianity. Even the early Roman church fathers such as Origen and Clement openly talked about it. In fact they were quite proud of their Hellenistic heritage.[272] Augustine, the great Roman church father and former Gnostic, who reworked and preserved Gnostic teachings and passed them on to Luther and Calvin, openly embraced pagan Hellenistic religion as a wonderful revelation of divine truth.

---

[271] In verses 1–4 John identifies Gnostic Christians by one of their common teachings, namely Docetism, which says that Christ did not truly appear on earth as a human being.

[272] See above, pages 119 and following.

Augustine came on the scene (around 400 A.D.) when the process of Christian Hellenization was already fairly advanced. From his vantage point in history, Augustine viewed Christianity as merely a final refinement of Hellenistic religion. Consider the following assessment of Augustine's thought by one of the leading scholars on the subject. He describes the sixth book of Augustine's major work, *The City of God,* as designed to:

> ...demonstrate its [Christianity's] **thorough accordance with the deepest insights of Greek philosophy.** This view of Christian theology as confirming and rounding out the truths of pre-Christian thought expresses very well **the positive side of the relations between the new religion** [Christianity] **and pagan antiquity.**[273]

> To St. Augustine it is inconceivable that any true religion should be restricted to a single nation. God is essentially universal and must be worshipped universally. ...it is in the **universalism** of Greek philosophy that St. Augustine finds its chief support.[274]

Note Augustine's open veneration of the pagan Hellenistic tradition, which in his time generally equates with the thought of Plato and Pythagoras, and its latter day incarnation as Neoplatonism. Greek philosophy was the foundation of Hellenistic religion, by which they developed their ideas about the soul, its fall and return to heaven, in part by observation of the stars and planets and working out a philosophically rational explanation for how the universe came to be and man's place in it.

And who is the person praising Hellenistic religion, the same tradition the Apostle John condemns? It is Augustine, the greatest church father of Hellenistic Christianity, hailed by both Reformation and Roman churches as the originator of their theology. Notice how Augustine saw the universal acceptance of Hellenistic religion in the pagan world as proof of its validity – *"it is in the universalism of Greek philosophy that St. Augustine finds its chief support."*

Compare that to the Apostle John who saw it as exactly the opposite. For John, the universal acceptance of Hellenistic religion in the pagan world was a sign of apostasy – *"They* [Gnostic Christians] *are from the world; therefore what they say is from the world, **and the world listens to them"** (1 John 4:5). John is explaining why the innovations of Gnostic

---

273 Jaeger, *The Theology of the Early Greek Philosophers,* p 1.
274 Ibid., p 3.

Christianity were so popular and well received by the people of his time. Because it was Hellenistic, it rang true for those raised in that culture. For Augustine that is a sign of truth. But for John it is a major sign of apostasy – *"From this we know the spirit of truth and the spirit of error"* (vs 6). Whom should we believe, the Apostle John or St. Augustine?

From a biblical point of view the term 'Hellenistic' is not a compliment. According to the Apostle John it is one of the chief markers of Christian apostasy.

Summary

What is the final conclusion? How should we understand this? Is Hellenistic apostasy one of the most obscene, vile human concoctions in all of human history? Is Reformation theology the revival of an ancient heresy roundly condemned by the New Testament?

Is Reformation theology's dark side the only basis on which it should be judged? What about its good side? Reformation theology is also filled with much biblical truth. Inspiration of the Spirit and the power of grace to transform the heart are important biblical truths. Hellenistic Christianity encourages reformation of human conduct in many positive ways. Are we justified in condemning something when there is so much good in it?

Which way do you want to spin it? Is it a vile human concoction with a thin veneer of goodness? Or is it a wonderful body of biblical truth with an unfortunate but relatively insignificant taint of apostasy?

But should we spin it at all? In the end, isn't it exactly what it is – both of the above? It is a truly vile human concoction that licenses the most horrible sin, whose license is significantly and almost universally exploited to some degree. At the same time, it also incorporates extensive biblical truth and is a huge force for good. Once you take it factually for exactly what it is, the final conclusion is quite simple. Isn't this the very definition of a **mystery**, the mystery of lawlessness in which a core of vile theological justification for disobedience and willful sin is wrapped in layers of genuine biblical truth and goodness?

When you take it for exactly what it is, you see the amazing historical accuracy of the New Testament and its choice of the phrase *"mystery of lawlessness."*

For those who regard the Bible as divinely inspired, then the key question is what God thinks about it. And clearly in the view of the New Testament, Hellenistic Christian antinomianism is a tragic error, a primary tool of deception and the epitome of Christian apostasy.

The spirituality of Hellenistic Christianity drips with sweetness and love. But it is, after all, only a mystery. In this volume we have peeled back the cover of that mystery to glimpse the imbalance and depravity hidden within. Having seen this, can anyone in good conscience join hands with and brazenly validate such evil, and then come into the house of the Lord and say, "I am safe"?

The Choice

Where does that leave mankind as we face the frightening events of the end time? The final years of human rule on earth will be a time of polarization. It will be a time for choosing sides, indeed a time when choosing will be forced on us whether we want it or not.

For those who adhere to Primitive Christianity, there will be increasing pressure to disregard the advice of the Apostle John. There will be intense pressure to make political and religious compromises, to seek acceptance by Hellenistic Christianity in the vain hope of escaping its wrath. Substantial portions of Primitive Christianity already are joined in ecumenical union with Hellenistic Christianity. Over time this will both spread and lead to increasing compromise and closer ties.

This is no small matter. When Jesus returns as an avenging judge of the entire earth, will he overlook his own church? Judgment begins at the house of God (1 Peter 4:17). Some groups, typified by the church at Thyatira, will be literally, physically destroyed because of their disloyalty. Biblical promises of protection for Christians in the end time do *not* extend to those who join hands with apostate Christianity – *"Come out of her my people...so that you do **not share in her plagues"** (Rev 18:4).

For those who are learning the historical truth about Primitive and Hellenistic Christianity for the first time, now is the day of decision. The opening moves of an end time religious crisis are already underway. If you have previously been misled to mix your faith in Christ with the apostasy of Hellenistic Christianity, now is the time to heed the advice of Malachi. Now is the time to return to the original faith of our fathers, the Primitive Christianity of the first-century church.

For those who are torn by the tempting allure of antinomian spirituality, consider the following:

Do you accept the totality of God's Word? Are you willing to submit yourself, your own religious sensibilities, biases and preferences, to the will of Jesus Christ as expressed in New Testament scripture? Do you believe the warnings in John's epistles in which he condemns progressive revelation that contradicts the original revelation of Jesus' earthly ministry?

Do you believe those passages of God's Word in which Jesus warns against the religious deception of Gnostic Christianity and the mystery of lawlessness? Do you perceive the significance of that great 'mystery,' a religious system that hides its true nature under the guise of obedience to a more advanced spirituality?

Does it matter that Reformation theology today preaches that Christians are licensed to commit unlimited sin, without repentance, and still be saved? Is this excused by the fact that technically they only license unlimited sin, while officially recommending against using that license?

Can you see through the beautiful, spiritual pronouncements of Hellenistic Christianity as the church at Ephesus did? If current standards of political correctness say we must join hands in ecumenical union with Hellenistic Christianity, and scripture says the opposite, which do you choose? Are you willing to stand with Jesus by rejecting an antinomian religious system that he condemns?

Does your Bible contain the epistles from John and Jude, and 2 Peter 2, Revelation 2 and 2 Thessalonians 2? Am I just imagining this? Am I making this up? Hear again the words of Jesus Christ concerning what awaits Christians who are beguiled by the beauty of the beast:

> Repent then. If not, I will come to you soon and make war against them with the sword of my mouth. (Rev 2:16)

> ...and I will strike her children dead. And all the churches will know that I am the one who searches minds and hearts, and I will give to each of you as your works deserve. (Rev 2:23)

The choice is given to every man. On the one hand is Jesus' original revelation of Christianity – that which is "from the beginning." On the other hand is the mystery of lawlessness, the deceptive human promise of an even greater spirituality, a latter, second revelation of Christianity steeped in Hellenistic paganism. Superficially, however, it is absolutely beautiful, layered and lavishly wrapped in biblical truth and spirituality. It is a mystery, indeed, one of the greatest mysteries of all human history.

Let anyone who has an ear listen to what the Spirit is saying to the churches. (Rev 2:7)

Figure 2, <u>THE HELLENIZATION OF CHRISTIANITY</u>

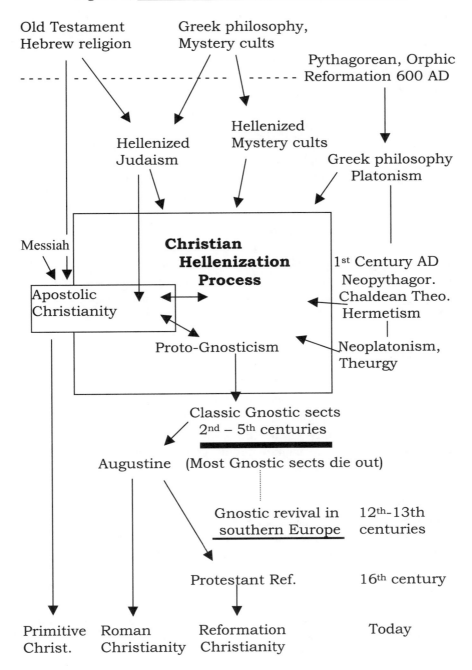

Figure 2 on the previous page is a rough approximation of the interplay of religious movements that led to the development of Gnostic and Hellenistic Christianity. To accurately represent all details of this intricate process would require so many lines, arrows and comments it would be unreadable, so this is only a very rough approximation.

Before the great pagan religious reformation (approximately 700-500 B.C.), there was Old Testament Hebrew religion in Israel, and surrounding it materialistic pagan religions frequently with mystery cults celebrating the cycle of death and rebirth in nature. The great pagan reformation affected both pagan and biblical Hebrew religion, producing Hellenistic versions of each. It invaded classical Greek philosophy as well, especially the teachings of Plato.

In the Roman world of the first century A.D., the multiple products of the pagan reformation all came together in a great collision with Christianity. This began the process known as the Hellenization of Christianity. The apostolic church was caught up in a giant melting pot, shown on the diagram as the circle labeled "Christian Hellenization Process." The Hellenized mystery cults and various schools of Greek philosophy all fed into the process. Hellenistic Judaism especially influenced the apostolic church via the flood of Jewish converts during the first decades of the church's existence.

Neoplatonism and Theurgy were latter developments in the Hellenistic philosophic tradition. They played an important role in a second wave of Hellenistic apostasy culminating in the fourth century A.D.

Apostolic Christianity of the first century split into three Christian tracks, as shown in the diagram. Some continued to follow the first-century form of what is known as Primitive Christianity, also called 'Jewish' Christianity. The Hellenization process created two other major Christian traditions.

The most radically Hellenized Christianity surfaced almost immediately. It appeared inside the church as proto-Gnostic groups, who began to leave the church late in the first century. These became the independent, classic Gnostic sects of the second and third centuries. Like all other Hellenistic Christian offshoots, they claimed to be a God-ordained replacement for the Jewish Christianity of the first century. They lost momentum, however, were persecuted by Roman authorities after Hellenistic Roman Christianity was officially sanctioned by the empire, and had mostly died out by 600 A.D.

A few Gnostic sects survived, moved up through the Balkan countries of Eastern Europe, and spread throughout southern Europe in the 12th and 13th centuries. The Roman Inquisition crushed this final revival of classic Gnostic Christianity.

After Gnostic Christians left, the Hellenization process continued unabated inside the apostolic church. Soon Rome emerged as the leader of the on-going Hellenization of the church. This produced a more moderate form of Hellenization, which evolved into Roman Catholic Christianity and formally parted with apostolic Christianity in the fourth century. The original 'Jewish' Christianity of the first century was pushed aside and survived as a progressively smaller minority at the margins of the Roman Empire, in parts of the Near East, Africa and especially in the British Isles.

In the early centuries after Christ, therefore, we find these three Christian tracks of development – Primitive Christianity, Hellenized Roman Christianity, and Hellenized Gnostic Christianity. All three claimed to be the sole genuine heir to the Christian tradition.

Primitive Christianity claimed to be a continuation of the same Christianity practiced in the first-century church. In contrast, both Roman and Gnostic Christians claimed to possess a second, more spiritual revelation of Christianity that replaces and overturns portions of the New Testament revelation. By this they openly acknowledged the Hellenization process, which they hailed as God's will.

The existence today of Primitive (Sabbatarian) Christianity, Roman Christianity, and Reformation Christianity, directly reflects the same general characteristics of the three-fold division of Christianity in the early centuries after Christ.

Gnostic Christianity went into a state of eclipse when most of the early, classic Gnostic cults died out, a process completed by around the end of the fifth century. However, various key Gnostic ideas were adapted and preserved in the writings of St. Augustine, where they lay largely neglected for more than a thousand years until resurrected by the founders of the Protestant Reformation. Thus in the Protestant Reformation much of Gnostic theology was reborn to its former glory. This is shown in the diagram as the arrows leading from "Classic Gnostic sects" to Augustine, and then from Augustine to the Protestant Reformation.

Many object to the claim there is a link between ancient Gnostic Christianity and Hellenistic Christianity today because of many individual differences between the two. Though often strikingly similar, they frequently differ in many ways. Part of the problem comes from trying to compare the independent Gnostic sects of the second and third centuries with modern Hellenistic Christianity. As we see in the diagram, however, the classic Gnostic sects were just one branch of the tree. It is more appropriate to compare modern Hellenistic Christianity to proto-Gnosticism as it developed inside the apostolic church. This is the original form of Hellenistic Christianity and the object of criticism recorded in the New Testament.

Even for Reformation theology, Gnostic doctrine was filtered and only transmitted indirectly, through Augustine. There is no reason to expect them to be identical. Nevertheless, Reformation Christianity preserves the flavor of ancient Gnosticism as well as some of its key ideas.

The importance of Gnosticism is its role in initiating the mystery of lawlessness and the process of Hellenization in the apostolic church, and supplying the basic doctrinal outline for the Protestant Reformation. The classic Gnosticism of the independent sects of the second and third centuries A.D. did not survive intact. What was prophesied to survive is the mystery of lawlessness. As we have seen amply demonstrated in this volume, that prophecy has been fulfilled dramatically and fully in our day.

Appendix A

The Full Story behind Colossians 2

The New Testament describes the appearance of proto-Gnosticism in the first century church. It even mentions one Gnostic sect by name – the Nicolaitans. Despite that, Sunday observance and Eighth Day theology are never explicitly mentioned.

We know why that is. Though Gnostic Christianity championed Sunday observance, the conversion process did not get underway inside the church until after the last books of the New Testament were written. And it was a gradual process, lasting many centuries, until Constantine imposed Sunday observance by imperial decree in the fourth century.

Wouldn't it be so much simpler if the New Testament directly told us where the apostles stood on this issue? While that is impossible because the change occurred after their time, the New Testament does provide important clues. In the first century, Hellenistic/Gnostic influence within the church already had introduced the theology that later provided the justification for converting to Sunday observance. Already in the first century there were Christians agitating for a more spiritual, heavenly reinterpretation of Hebrew religious practices. And that incipient movement, focused on heavenly spirituality, is recorded in the New Testament.

If we can more clearly define what that precursor theology was, and see what the apostles thought of that, we can with reasonable certainty judge how the apostolic fathers of Christianity would view the latter fruit of that movement. As we will see, once introduced into the primitive church, the nature of that precursor theology made conversion from Sabbath to Sunday virtually inevitable.

The case in point is the Apostle Paul and his letter to the Colossian church. Here we find Paul defending a group of Primitive Christians from critics complaining about the survival of Jewish practices in the New Testament church.

The Colossian Critics

The key to understanding Colossians is identifying the theology of the people who were criticizing this local church. Nearly all scholars recognize that Paul in chapter two is addressing the problem of some group interfering in the church at Colossae. Paul repeatedly refers to this: *"I am saying this so that no one may deceive you"* (vs 4), *"See to it that no one take you captive"* (vs 8), *"Therefore do not let anyone condemn you"* (vs 16), *"Do not let anyone disqualify you"* (vs 18).

If we knew who that group was, then we could compare their theology with Paul's words and understand more clearly what he meant. Unfortunately, there is hardly any agreement among scholars on who the critics at Colossae were. There are nearly as many theories as scholars involved. Can we ever understand what Paul meant in his letter to the Colossians? In fact we can.

The method is simplicity itself. Instead of starting with an identification of the critics and then bending Paul's words to fit that identification, we need approach it the other way around. First we identify Paul's arguments and terminology, and then identify which first-century theologies most closely fit what Paul is saying. Finally, we then determine if that makes the whole chapter come together logically as one coherent message.

The first step in this process is understanding the term *elemental spirit*. This appears in Colossians 2:8 and 2:20 as *"the elemental spirits of the universe."* See the New Revised Standard translation (NRSV), which accurately translates this as 'elemental spirits.' In the King James (KJV), it is translated as 'rudiments of the world.'

This is important because elemental spirit is a specific name for something in Hellenistic religion that has significant implications for the theology involved. Therefore we turn first to this issue.

Hellenistic Religion and Elemental Spirits

Hellenistic religion was obsessed with what are called 'elemental spirits.' These are angelic or demonic creatures who operate on a level below the gods. The sense of the term *elemental* relates to the idea of 'elementary' or 'rudimentary.' There were spirits of various elementary forces of nature, such as wind and rain, as well as spirits who govern the wide range of human pursuits such as romantic love or success in business. We encountered this idea earlier in this volume in association with the Chaldean Oracles, in which elemental spirits are mentioned frequently.[275]

The underlying idea was that all phenomena on earth, both spiritual and material, are sustained by these elemental spirits. Without them, the world as we know it would cease to exist. As such, humans can appeal to them to direct their energy for our benefit, to gain success in life, both material and spiritual.

The power by which elemental spirits sustain the world radiates down from heaven. Therefore, and this is the key concept, elemental spirits function as the point of contact between man and the heavens. This is directly expressed in one of the Chaldean Oracles, in which elemental spirits are described as spirits:

> clothed in ... [material] bodies, being **intermediate links** existing to connect the Father [God] with Matter.... (**CO** 73)

What is important for us here is to understand that at the time Paul was writing the book of Colossians, some Hellenistic religions were teaching that man can invoke elemental spirits for both material and spiritual assis-

---

[275] The connection between Paul's references to elemental spirits and pagan Hellenistic religion is fairly clear. Neoplatonism, Hermetism and some Gnostic sects commonly referred to lower level angelic beings associated with material matters as elemental. This is prominently mentioned in the Chaldean Oracles (**CO**), such as **CO** 77: *"There are certain Water Elementals whom Orpheus calls Nereides, dwelling in the more elevated exhalations of Water, such as appear in damp, cloudy Air...."*

Also **CO** 75: *"There are certain Irrational Daemons (mindless elementals), which derive their subsistence from the Aerial Rulers;"* Here they are called mindless because they are viewed as manifestations of cosmic forces that operate according to the powers of fate. Belief in the 'mindless' flow of energies into the cosmos from the heavens is associated with Hellenistic astral fatalism.

tance. Those elemental spirits provide a means to connect to the heavens and its power. Further, and very importantly, they are roughly equivalent to angels in both Gnostic and orthodox Christian belief.

Gnostic and Christian Factors

The way Gnosticism reinterpreted Christianity in terms of the elemental spirits also is important. Gnostics equated these spirits with Yahweh who created the world, and with his angels who assisted him in creation and through whom he administered the Old Covenant. Because of their radically antagonistic view of materialism, Gnostics taught that Christians must be liberated from these elemental spirits.

In Gnostic Christianity not all angels are evil, however. Some classes of angels have not fallen. These are available to help man in his battle against materialistic lust, and so be purified spiritually and ascend to heaven after death. These are the unfallen, faithful angels who still exist in the highest heaven. Many Gnostic sects referred to the highest heaven as the *pleroma*. (*Pleroma* means "fullness," in the sense of spiritual completeness or perfection.) Like the materialistic angels of rain and romantic love, these angels also are personifications of elementary forces raining down on earth, only in this case they are personifications of spiritual qualities. There were angels called Faith, Love, Church, Savior, etc.

These good spirits are the spiritual point of contact between man and the heavens. As we will see later in this appendix, there were Gnostic systems of theology that promoted using good elemental spirits (angels) to connect Christians to the heavens. Connecting to the heavens via good angels supposedly regenerates the soul, awakens its natural spirituality, and guarantees it will rise to heaven after death.

Orthodox, New Testament Christians held sometimes similar concepts about angels. In fact, it was easy for Gnostic Christianity to sell their ideas inside the New Testament church because they closely resembled certain orthodox biblical teachings about angels. Remember from our earlier discussion of Colossians in chapter 5, the authors of the New Testament frequently referred to the Old Testament as administered by angels (see above, pages 95 and following). Both Gnostic and orthodox Christians viewed angels as enforcers of the Old Covenant, meting out punishment for disobedience.

So we see that Gnostic and orthodox Christianity had somewhat similar ideas about angels and the Old Covenant. Both taught that man is or needs to be liberated from the angelic administrators of the Old Covenant. A key difference, of course, is that Gnostic Christians regarded those angels and their leader, Yahweh, as evil.

A Jewish or a Gnostic Problem?

Some biblical commentators argue that in Colossians Paul is criticizing Jewish legalism. However, the context points much more towards the Hellenistic bias against Hebrew religion. The context of the first two chapters of Colossians strongly indicates a problem coming from a Hellenistic/Gnostic theology that was antagonistic toward traditional Hebrew practices. Given that background, it would be much more reasonable to think the Colossian critics were unhappy with the traditional observance of Jewish biblical celebrations, and were arguing for reinterpreting them in a way to fit a heavenly, Gnostic point of view.

How do we know that? The answer, in addition to the prominence of Gnostic terminology in Colossians, is covered in the following six points:

1) The asceticism mentioned in 2:20–23 (*Do not handle, Do not taste, Do not touch...they are simply human commands and teachings*).

These verses, taken as a whole, suggest the severe harshness of ascetic denial rather than the ritual purity of Jewish law. Note the phrase *"severe treatment of the body."* Paul also calls them *"human commands and teachings,"* i.e. not biblical practices.

Here Paul clearly does not appear to be arguing against Jewish legalism, but rather something coming from the world of Hellenistic religion.

2) The theme of chapter 2 is introduced in verse 8 by a reference to "elemental spirits" (see NRSV translation), which Paul here explicitly associates with non-biblical philosophy and human reasoning (*through philosophy and empty deceit, according to human tradition*). By specifying philosophy and elemental spirits, Paul is going beyond saying the problem is merely a non-biblical theology. This directly implicates the philosophical religious mix known as Hellenistic religion.

Therefore, when verse 16 says *do not let anyone condemn you in matters of food and drink or of observing festivals, new moons or Sabbaths,* is it condemning the weekly Sabbath and Jewish celebrations? Or is it saying don't listen to critics from the world of Hellenistic philosophy and religion and its typically anti-Jewish bias by which they consistently criticize all such Jewish practices? If Paul here is going after Hellenistic theology, then he is telling the Colossians to not listen to people who were traditionally critical of the practices listed in verse 16.

The infiltration of anti-Jewish bias into the church via Gnosticism is historically well documented. This fits with Paul's Colossian theme of opposing Hellenistic philosophy, elemental spirits and human tradition. Remember, the Jewish practices listed in verse 16 are biblical, not the *'human tradition'* that Paul is condemning.

3) The reference in 2:18 to *"self-abasement and worship of angels."*

These were prominent features of various Hellenistic traditions, including certain Gnostic sects in which the Christian convert subjected himself to an angelic partner in a mystical heavenly marriage that supposedly healed his sinful nature. (See above, "Submission to Angels, Colossians 2:18," pages 99 and following.) As we will see shortly, these angels were the personifications of spiritual qualities raining down from heaven, in effect the 'elemental spirits' of the heavens. Once again the context points to Hellenistic apostasy.

4) The reference in 2:17 to Jewish practices as a *'shadow'* of things to come, *"but the substance belongs to Christ."* This requires a more lengthy explanation, since it relates to the very heart of the concept of heavenly spirituality in certain Hellenistic religious traditions.

Shadow and Substance

Biblical interpreters have wrestled with the terms 'shadow' and 'substance' in Colossians 2:17 for centuries. Yet, the meaning is very easily extracted by going back to the Hellenistic/Gnostic context of the entire passage. Here is the text:

> These are only a **shadow** of what is to come, but the **substance** belongs to Christ. (Col 2:17)

Shadow and substance are biblical terms.[276] But they also occur in Hellenistic theology. The Hellenistic view of these terms is the key to understanding Colossians 2, because we know that Paul is specifically going after Hellenistic apostasy derived from pagan society outside the church. His target was the Hellenistic "philosophy" and "human tradition" of his day, as he explicitly states in verse 8.

First understand the definition of the terms. Shadow simply means 'symbol.' Substance is the thing to which the symbol points. If a flag is a symbol of a country, then the flag is the *shadow* and the country is the *substance* it symbolizes.

The word translated 'substance,' in the original text is 'body.' That has led some to interpret this passage as a reference to the 'body of Christ,' meaning the church. Thereby Paul's argument is interpreted as saying we should let the apostolic church (the body of Christ) judge these matters rather than the outside critics who were bothering the church.

That makes a valid point. However, the context seems to point to something else. This passage is structured to make its argument by contrasting shadow versus the object (body) that casts the shadow. That is why some Bible versions translate body with other English words – some using 'substance,' while others translate it as 'reality.' In other words, it is contrasting shadow (which is not real) versus the real object (Christ) which casts the shadow. For example, the New International Version translates verse 17 as *"These are a shadow of the things that were to come; the reality, however, is found in Christ."* [277] As we go further into the Hellenistic background of the problem at Colossae, we will see increasingly why this is more likely the correct approach.

In verse 16 the critics of the Colossians are depicted as complaining about the observance of various Jewish practices. But what is the essential point of Paul's argument? Is Paul saying they shouldn't continue those Jewish practices under the New Covenant? Notice the language: *"But* the substance belongs to Christ." Or, in the *NIV* translation, "the reality, *however*, is found in Christ." The argument appears to be over what the shadows of biblical customs and practices really point to, whether to

---

[276] The Hebrew temple was an earthly shadow of heavenly and angelic realities, and the Hebrew sacrificial system was a shadow of future Messianic events. See Hebrews 8:5.

[277] See also Revised English Bible's similar translation using 'reality.'

Christ or to something else.[278] If Paul is insisting they point to Christ, then the Colossian critics apparently were claiming they point to something else.

In Primitive Christianity, Old Testament celebrations generally are considered shadows of Christ because they symbolized the future events of his death and resurrection. The most classic example is the interpretation of Passover and the Exodus as symbolic of Christ's sacrifice and Christians' exodus and freedom from sin. For example, in 1 Corinthians 5:7 Paul says, *"For indeed Christ, our Passover, was sacrificed for us."* (NKJV)

Paul is adamantly coming down on the side of interpreting the shadows (Jewish festivals, new moons and Sabbaths) as pointing to Christ. Therefore Paul's warning against teachings of submission to angels in the very next verse (vs 18) implies that the Colossian critics were interpreting the shadows as pointing to angels. If this is correct, we would expect to find some group or groups in the world of Hellenistic Christianity that promote those beliefs, and indeed we do. First, let's see what Gnosticism taught in regards to shadows.

Classical Greek philosophy often defined the heavenly world as real, and the material world as an imperfect copy (a shadow or image) of the heavenly world. The origin of all this was Plato and his famous Theory of Forms. According to Plato, the heavenly world is populated by idealized forms or archetypes. Everything on earth is a copy (shadow) of some archetype in heaven.[279]

To give one simple example, that means all trees in our world are based on the pattern of a single, idealized tree in the heavens. In our world trees are not identical copies of each other. But when we look at them we recognize them as members of the tree family because of their connection to the single tree archetype in heaven. Material objects in our world are

---

[278] This is further supported by analysis of the text of verses 16–17. "But the substance belongs to Christ" is an ellipsis, and a full reconstruction of the text would clearly express the idea that Christians are being exhorted to properly interpret the biblical practices named here as pointing to Christ. See the paper *"But Let Everyone Discern the Body of Christ (Colossians 2:17)"*, by Prof. Troy Martin of St. Xavier University, Chicago, in *Journal of Biblical Literature*, Vol. 114, No. 2 (1955), p 249–255, reviewed in an excellent article for the layman by Jared Olar, in the journal *Grace and Knowledge*, No. 2 (December 1998), p 25–35.

[279] See above, p 13 where Plato's belief in heavenly archetypes was first mentioned.

illusory in that they are unstable and subject to change. They suffer disease and damage. They grow old and die. Therefore things in our world are imperfect copies (shadows) of the heavenly world. But the archetypes in heaven are 'real' in that they are perfect, unchanging and eternal.

The same is true of man. We too are copies of a heavenly archetype. And like trees we too are imperfect, unstable, and subject to death. However, there is hope. If we can somehow attach ourselves to the heavenly world, we can take on the spiritual perfection of the heavens and ultimately its unchanging, immortal existence. And the medium for connecting to the heavens, as we will see, is through angels by which we are changed from imperfect to perfect copies of the heavenly reality.

One of the Gnostic sects that used this extensively in its theology is the Valentinians.[280] They were well known for their use of Pythagorean and Platonic philosophy, from which they borrowed the idea of shadow and reality.

Valentinians taught that the ultimate reality is the *pleroma*, the highest heaven. This is the abode and source of pure spirituality, existing in a state of perfection and rest.[281] Inside the *pleroma* all things are 'at rest' in the sense they are unchanging and therefore real. All things outside and below the *pleroma* are chaotic and to some degree defective, only a shadow of the reality within the *pleroma*.

When anything leaves the *pleroma* to enter our world it becomes at least in part a shadow. This was true even of Christ when he appeared on earth bringing *gnosis* and salvation to mankind. The church father Irenaeus talks about this. Speaking of the Valentinian Gnostic interpretation of Christ and his mother, Irenaeus writes:

---

[280] Many Gnostic sects incorporated the Hellenistic Theory of Forms to some degree in their theology. One example is various Nag Hammadi texts where the material world is depicted as a mirror image of things found in the heavens. Just as mirror reflections are reversed images of the real object, and otherwise vague and distorted, so the material world was interpreted as a defective image of the spiritual reality in heaven. Note that this is not limited just to strictly material objects such as trees. Everything, including the concept of Church, Grace, even Savior as it is known in our world, are only vague shadows of a fixed spiritual reality in the heavens.

[281] See above, pages 52 and following for a general description of Valentinian Gnosticism, and pages 140 and following for Valentinianism as an example of Paternal Depth theology.

...he [Christ] was brought forth by the Mother, after she had gone out of the Fullness [pleroma], with some shadow, because of her memory of better things. He, being masculine, severed the shadow from himself and entered the Fullness;[282]

Here it is saying that Christ's mother descended from heaven, and therefore she retained some knowledge of the heavenly pleroma (*because of her memory of better things*). She passed this on to her son, Christ, which made him partially reflect the spirituality of the heavens (*with some shadow*). When Christ ascended back to heaven (*the Fullness*) he lost his shadow qualities (*severed the shadow from himself*), i.e. he became fully real (spiritual) again.

The fact that Jesus only partially reflected the spirituality of the heavenly *pleroma* was a key doctrine among various Gnostic sects. The point they were making is that Jesus' earthly ministry was deficient because it was contaminated by Hebrew religion. Like everything else on earth, it was only a defective reflection of the true spirituality that exists in the heavenly world. That is how they explained away the lawfulness found in Jesus' preaching, such as when he taught the correct, spiritual observance of Sabbath (Matthew 12:12), and called himself Lord of the Sabbath (Mark 2:27–28). But when he ascended back to heaven that deficiency was repaired (*He...severed the shadow from himself*).

Gnostics generally espoused the Hellenization of Christianity as a second, more spiritual revelation of Christianity. They justified this by those same theories about shadow and the deficiency of Jesus' earthly ministry. After the resurrection or after his return to heaven when, they claimed, he had become fully spiritual again, Jesus gave his inner circle (of Gnostic Christians) a second, more spiritual revelation of Christianity, which just happened to be a combination of Christianity and pagan Hellenistic religion.

Gnostic rejection of Jesus' earthly ministry is duplicated today in Hellenistic Christianity as 'dispensationalism.' This modern doctrine, espoused by most of Protestant Evangelicalism, argues that substantial portions of Jesus' earthly ministry are materialistic and therefore not binding on Christians. Just as their Gnostic forefathers, they use this to reject the many lawful teachings of Jesus' earthly ministry. This surprising doctrine, little understood outside scholarly theological circles, is explained

---

[282]   Irenaeus, *Against Heresies,* 1.11.1 .

in detail in *Spirit of Antichrist,* the second volume in our series The World of Primitive Christianity.

Valentinian Gnostics used the supposed deficiency of Jesus' earthly ministry to justify a massive reinterpretation of his message. If Jesus' teaching was understood as defective shadows of a higher spiritual reality, then it is necessary to engage in obscure allegorical interpretation to get at the reality behind the shadow. This often involved the use of number symbolism, which they borrowed from Pythagoreanism.[283] One of their most important numbers was 30, which they believed is the number of archangels in the *pleroma.*[284]

Valentinians observed that Jesus was thirty years old before he began to preach. That, they said, symbolizes the 30 archangels of the *pleroma.* Christ's 'silence' during those thirty years before he began to preach, supposedly is a shadow pointing to the silence of the heavenly *pleroma.*[285] Silence represented the state of rest and non-material spirituality of the heavens. This was an important antinomian theme for Valentinians. Because spirituality must be non-material, they said, Hebrew religion, its God of material creation, and his law that regulates material life, are a materialistic trap that must be rejected. And all that could be inferred from the mere fact that Christ was 30 years old before he began to preach!

Valentinians applied the same symbolism to the parable of the laborers in Matthew 20:1–16. If you add the hours at which the laborers were sent into the vineyard, you arrive at 30.

Valentinians in effect spiritualized Christianity by interpreting biblical topics as shadows of the angelic spiritual reality in the heavenly *pleroma.* Speaking of the Valentinian penchant for using the concept of shadow to allegorize scripture in general, Irenaeus comments:

---

[283] Remember the Pythagorean interest in science and mathematics and its significance as a manifestation of heavenly spirituality. See above, p 32f, section *Pythagoreanism to Neopythagorianism.*

[284] The 30 chief angels in the heavenly *pleroma* function as the heavenly forms (archetypes) for various intellectual and spiritual categories on earth. Among them are Man, Church, Depth, Mind, Faith, Hope, Praise, Understanding, etc. In effect the 30 primary angels of the *pleroma* embody spiritual realities which are found in our world only as imperfect shadows.

[285] Irenaeus, Against Heresies, 1.1.3 . For the significance of silence and the Depth in the *pleroma*, see above pages 140 and following, *Thyatira and the Deep Things of Satan.*

...they claim that these are great and wonderful and unutterable mysteries.... And if...anything of the many things mentioned in the Scriptures can [be so interpreted, they]...adapt them to their fabrication.[286]

Now, keep in mind one vital piece of information. The *pleroma* is composed of angels – 30 great angels plus a multitude of others that emanated from the original 30. The *pleroma*, the highest heaven to which Christians ascend after death, is an angelic institution! Therefore when the Valentinians allegorized the contents of scripture as shadows of the *pleroma*, in effect they were saying that the substance behind shadow are the angels! Valentinian Christianity indeed was obsessed with angels, as was much of Hellenistic religion.

There are the evil angels associated with Yahweh, condemned by Gnostics for participating in creation and the administration of the Old Covenant. The purpose of the Valentinian sacraments in part was to protect and free man from these angels and their supposedly evil religious system. That is why Paul took the time to explain to the Colossian church that the angelic administrators of the Old Covenant have no power to punish faithful Christians. For those who are under grace, the authority of the angelic administrators of the Old Covenant is ended (Colossians 2:13–15). Therefore the Gnostic claim that we must *carte blanche* reject Old Testament practices is invalid, because we *already* are free from the angelic authority of the Old Covenant.

On the other hand there are the good angels of Valentinian theology. These are the "elemental spirits" of the heavens, embodying spiritual qualities such as Faith, Hope and Understanding.[287] We can appeal to these spirits for help in becoming spiritual.

If the way to attain spirituality is through identification with the *pleroma* and its good angels, then as a Valentinian Christian you would want your worship to always and exclusively symbolize the heavens. The way to accomplish that, the way to make anything spiritual, is to reinterpret it as a shadow of the heavenly *pleroma*.

Valentinians believed that even Christ while on earth was only a shadow of a great Savior archangel within the *pleroma*. That Savior angel

---

[286] Irenaeus, ibid.

[287] Remember from chapter 7, "Thyatira and the Deep Things of Satan," how the lead archangels of the Valentinian heavenly pleroma were named Paternal Depth and Silent Grace. All thirty of the lead archangels in fact were named after various spiritual qualities or entities.

produced lesser beings who are the innumerable angels to which individual Christians are married. (For marriage between Christians and angels in Gnosticism, see above, pages 99 and following.) Thus Valentinian Christians, through their angelic partners, also are bound as shadows to the reality of a great Savior archetype in heaven.

In *The Gospel of Philip*, Valentinian Christians several times are addressed as the *'image.'* [288] This is similar to saying 'shadow.' Even more telling, in the same Gnostic text and referring to the sacred marriage ceremony, we find a reference to the Christian 'image' receiving his angelic partner in the following language: *"One receives them from the mirrored bridal chamber."* [289] This is talking about the divine marriage ceremony, which some scholars believe was a sacrament literally acted out. The *'mirrored bridal chamber'* refers to the belief that through marriage to angels, Christians become a mirror image (shadow) of the heavens. Hellenistic religions often used the idea of a reflection to express the idea of an imperfect shadow, as in a reversed and hazy mirror image.

Valentinian salvation comes from the Father via Christ, but it is effected through the agency of angels who connect man to the heavens. The entire focus of Valentinian Christianity was the *pleroma* and its angels. For some Hellenistic groups, both pagan and Christian, angels were the very substance, the heavenly reality behind the spiritual shadows of our world. This is what Paul is combating in Colossians 2:17–18.

The basic idea underlying salvation in Valentinian Gnosticism is that man can regenerate his immortal soul to achieve the same state of perfection that exists in the highest heaven. They believed the regenerated soul becomes a literal copy of the heavenly *pleroma*, in the sense that it duplicates the perfection of the heavenly *pleroma*. That is what guarantees our soul will rise to the highest heaven after death. To assure the continued state of perfection in our soul, and prevent contamination from our continued material existence, we must reinforce that original regeneration with rituals and ceremonies, such as the divine marriage ceremony, that point exclusively to the heavens, and avoid any celebrations associated with the material world such as the seventh-day Sabbath.

Remember the criticism of Valentinian Gnostics by the church father Epiphanius'. He said they believed material conduct was totally unimportant, and their spirituality was maintained by *"only knowledge and the*

---

[288] *The Gospel of Philip*, **NHLE**, 145 and 149.
[289] Ibid., 149.

incantations of their rites" (see above, pages 53 and following). Their saving knowledge (*gnosis*) is the knowledge of the soul's origin from and connection to the heavens. Renewal of that knowledge ignites the regeneration of the soul. The Valentinian 'rites' to which Epiphanius refers are their divine marriage and many other rituals and ceremonies that point exclusively to the heavens and its angelic *pleroma*. Through these rituals they maintained and protected the regenerated state of the soul.

Remember the Valentinian text that says as long as Christians keep their minds focused on the heavenly *pleroma*, no damage can come to their soul (see above, page 150). Given that theology, could Gnostic Christians ever tolerate having the shadows of their celebrations point to anything else than the heavens? Is it any wonder they were the first to insist that Christians must convert to Eighth Day theology and Sunday observance?

It All Comes Together

Does Valentinian style Gnosticism explain what Paul is talking about in his letter to the Colossians? Let's go back, this time to chapter one (using the NRSV translation), and see if this identification yields coherent results. In chapter one we find Paul, point after point, directly refuting Gnostic/Hellenistic theology about the heavenly *pleroma* and its angels:

- In 1:15 Paul mentions that Christ is the 'image' of the Father. By implication, Paul is combating the Valentinian teaching that Christ is the image (shadow) not of the Father, but rather the shadow of an angelic Savior archetype in the heavenly *pleroma*.

- In 1:16 Paul emphasizes the connection between Christ and creation, both spiritual and material. All things in heaven and earth were created *"through and for him* [Christ].*"* Christ is the central focus of all creation. He is the reality behind everything.

   By contrast, in Valentinian Gnosticism it is the *pleroma* and its angels that are the primary focus, not Christ.

   Paul is also emphasizing Christ's connection to material creation to counter Gnostic rejection of the creation-centered celebrations of Hebrew religion. He is setting up his argument for chapter two verses 16–17 where he says creation-centered Jewish practices such as Sabbath should not be condemned. If Christ is the reality behind all creation both physical and spiritual, then there is no reason to condemn Hebrew religious celebrations because they are associated with creation and material life.

- In 1:19 Paul insists that the *pleroma* is contained within Christ. Valentinians argued the exact opposite. They said Christ is an angelic being contained within the *pleroma.*

- In 1:20 Paul reiterates that God reconciles everything to himself through Christ. Once again Valentinians taught the exact opposite. In their view, God reconciles everything to himself through angels and the heavenly *pleroma*, by turning everything, including Christians themselves, into shadows that point to the spiritual reality of the angelic *pleroma.*

There is substantial circumstantial evidence that Paul selected and formulated the information presented in chapter one as a calculated rebuttal to the type of angelic *pleroma* theology promoted by Valentinian Gnosticism.

Interpreting scripture as mere shadows of spiritual archetypes allowed Gnostics virtually unlimited freedom to reformulate Christianity in any way they wished. Their method was to take any custom, practice, story or doctrine, and recast it as 'spiritual' by making it a shadow of whatever they wished.

A prime example is the Gnostic reinterpretation of Sabbath rest. For Gnosticism, the Old Testament Sabbath and seventh day was a materialistic trap. So they spiritualized it by transforming it into a shadow of the heavenly *pleroma*. In Valentinian Gnosticism the 30 chief archangels were subdivided into three groups – twelve angels known as the Dodecad, ten angels called the Decad, and eight angels known as the Ogdoad (which means eight).

By recasting Sabbath rest as the Eighth Day it became a shadow of the Ogdoad, a major subdivision of the angelic *pleroma*. Thus it became spiritual, cleansed of its former involvement with the materialism and supposed evil of Hebrew religion. Remember from chapter three, "The Hellenistic Sabbath," how Eighth Day Theology was a primary force for the conversion from Sabbath to Sunday. And the point of Eighth Day

Theology was to recast biblical rest as spiritual by connecting it to the heavens.[290]

Colossians 2:18

Verse 18 is especially important for our understanding of the problem at Colossae. Unfortunately, the meaning of the original Greek in one critical portion of this verse is uncertain. Check multiple translations and you may find widely different interpretations. Here is what I regard as one of the better translations, from the Revised English Bible:

> You are not to be disqualified by the decision of people who go in for self-mortification and angel-worship and access to some visionary world. Such people...lose their hold upon the head [meaning Christ].... (Col 2:18–19, REB)

The critical, and contested, portion of verse 18 is the phrase "access to some visionary world." The Greek here is uncertain, but it seems to suggest the idea of "intrusion" or "entry" into other worlds, either "visionary" or "invisible" worlds.[291] The implication is that the Colossian critics were claiming they had the power to enter or connect to higher worlds. The means of entry into those higher worlds appears to be what is named at the beginning of verse 18 – separating oneself from the material world via ascetic practices, and the use of angelic intermediaries.

Beliefs and mystical practices of that type were common among a number of Hellenistic groups, including both Hellenistic Jews and Gnostic Christians.[292] Many of these believed in mystical ascent to heaven where they received special revelations.

---

[290] The Epistle of Barnabas, which promoted Sabbath rest as a shadow of Eighth Day rest, applied the same spiritual allegorizing process to a long list of Old Testament law and customs, all of which were reinterpreted as spiritual shadows of New Testament and Hellenistic teachings. The epistle specifically explains that this was done to prevent Christians from being deceived into literal observance of biblical law. See above, p 61, in section *The Hellenistic Sabbath.*

[291] For the translation of Colossians 2:18 and its difficulties, see Sappington, *Revelation and Redemption at Colossae,* 154 ff.

[292] There are many parallels in Colossians to heterodox Jewish religion, which is not surprising, as Gnosticism itself evolved out of heterodox Hellenistic Jewish sects in Palestine. Proto-Gnostics in the first century worshipped with the orthodox church, and therefore participated in Sabbath worship with the early church. Over time they gradually shed

What especially makes us focus on Gnosticism, in relation to verse 18, is the continuity from verses 16–17, where Paul mentions shadow and reality.[293] It is in Gnostic Christianity, especially a number of Gnostic sects such as the Valentinians, that we find shadow and reality as key ideas in how Christians access the higher worlds and connect to the spirituality of the heavens. Valentinian Christians, for example, believed they had access to the angelic world of the highest heaven, by voluntarily rejecting marriage to a human partner, opting instead for a mystical marriage to angels descended from the heavenly *pleroma*. This supposedly quenched their earthly lusts. They also believed that conversion to Christianity transformed their souls into a duplicate image or shadow of that angelic world.

The Colossian critics were arguing for reinterpreting the Hebrew religious practices that survived in the first-century church, in order to bring Christian celebrations in line with the heavenly worlds mentioned in verse 18. Remember from chapter three, "The Hellenistic Sabbath," that the theology that ultimately led to substitution of Sunday for Sabbath began as a *reinterpretation* of biblical rest as the Eighth Day, designed to make it spiritual by connecting it to the heavens and removing its connection to the material world. What we are witnessing in the book of Colossians is the beginning stages of this reinterpretation of Jewish celebrations.

The Colossian critics were preaching that those who disagreed with them would be 'disqualified,' meaning those who did not accept their heavenly theology concerning biblical celebrations. As Paul says, *"Do not let anyone disqualify you...."* (verse 18, NRSV translation). Given the Gnostic/Hellenistic background we have just reviewed, we can now better

---

their Jewish traits and gravitated towards Hellenistic theology, as their antinomian theology evolved into its distinctly antagonistic view of Hebrew religion. Some scholars regard the Colossian critics to have been a specifically Gnostic Jewish sect.

[293] Some Hellenistic Christians use the mention of asceticism in Colossians to try to connect Jewish communities with the Colossian critics, so as to caste Colossians 2 as a criticism of Jewish practices. They point to Jewish apocalypses about ascent to heaven that is mediated by angels. And they argue that the asceticism mentioned in Colossians must have been a means for purification in preparation for such ascent. However, while asceticism was common among Gnostic groups to facilitate their connection to the heavenly realms, asceticism as a mechanism to facilitate ascent is almost completely lacking in the Jewish apocalypses. See Himmelfarb, *Ascent to Heaven in Jewish and Christian Apocalypses,* 106ff. The argument for connecting Colossians to Hellenistic Jewish legalism, therefore, is very weak.

understand what that disqualification signifies. Valentinian Gnostics, for example, believed that because they had connected to the heavens and been infused with the perfection of the heavenly *pleroma*, at death they would rise directly to the eighth level of heaven to spend eternity with Christ and the heavenly Father.

Orthodox Primitive Christians, however, supposedly would rise only to the seventh level of heaven, where they spend eternity with their God, Yahweh. Valentinian Christians believed that orthodox Primitive Christians were specifically 'disqualified' from receiving their superior, heavenly salvation, because they continued to participate in the materialistic religion of the Old Testament, including the seventh-day Sabbath. Other Gnostic groups held similar views of grading the level of one's destiny in the hereafter based on the degree to which Christians had purged materialism from their religious practice and beliefs. It appears that is the type of 'disqualification' to which Paul refers in verse 18.

Already Free in Christ

In the final two points, we begin to see clearly one of Paul's primary, underlying arguments for ignoring the biased arguments of Hellenistic religion. The Hellenistic/Gnostic critics of the Colossian church were insisting that Christians must do certain things to free themselves from the creating angels of the Old Covenant and in turn submit to the spiritual angels of the heavenly *pleroma*. According to Paul, however, we *already* have been freed from the angelic administrators of the Old Covenant, and we *already* have contact with the perfection of the heavenly *pleroma*. And we receive all that by attaching ourselves to Christ, not angels. That is what Paul is explaining in chapter two, verses 9–10, where he says,

> "For in him [Christ] the whole fullness [*pleroma*] of deity dwells bodily, and you have come to fullness [*pleroma*] in him...."

5) The meaning of *"rulers and authorities"* in verse 15: *"He disarmed the rulers and authorities and made a public example of them, triumphing over them in it."*

"Rulers and authorities" appears in both verse 15 and verses 9–10. If you understand what verses 9–10 are talking about then you understand verse 15.

In verses 9 and 10 Paul associates the terms *rulers* and *authorities* with the concept of angels. Here he is talking about the angelic heavenly *pleroma*: *"...and you have come to fullness* [pleroma] *in him* [Christ], *who is the head of every ruler and authority."* The reason he makes the point that Christ is above the angels *(the head of every ruler and authority)* is that the Colossian critics were preaching the opposite, that the angels were the most important beings in achieving heavenly perfection.

Back in verse 15, *"rulers and authorities"* also refers to angels. At this point, however, Paul is addressing the other side of the angelic question. Here Paul is addressing Gnostic rejection of the angels involved with creation and administration of the Old Covenant. Gnostics insisted that Christians must free themselves from these angels and their religious system, which they regarded as evil.

Paul is pointing out that the Old Covenant ended at the cross. Therefore the angelic administrators of the Old Covenant *(rulers and authorities)* no longer have any power over us. That was accomplished by Christ on the cross. Therefore we have no need to free ourselves by modifying Hebrew celebrations to point to the heavenly *pleroma*. Angels are not the big issue that Gnostics were trying to make of them. The big issue is Christ! Therefore the Colossians should ignore their critics. That is Paul's argument throughout chapter two – who and what is the center of our faith, Christ or the heavenly *pleroma* and its angels?

To summarize Paul's argument, we have no need to free ourselves from the angelic administrators of the Old Covenant, nor subject ourselves to heavenly angels in order to become spiritual. According to Paul, everything we need already has been accomplished in Christ.

6) The reference to circumcision in 2:11 further sets the stage for Paul's arguments about materialism and ascetic denial that follow.

Paul refers to *"a spiritual circumcision, by putting off the body of flesh in the circumcision of Christ...."* This was a major issue for Gnosticism – freedom from the material world, from our material human bodies with all their material needs, lusts and temptations. Remember how Valentinian rituals and celebrations depicted connection to the heavens, which magically heals the human urge to sin.[294] Once again, however, Paul is arguing we don't need what the critics at Colossae were offering, because freedom

---

[294] See above, pages 99 and following.

from the lusts of our material existence is accomplished through Christ (*putting off the body of flesh in the circumcision of Christ*).

In view of the larger context, what Paul is saying is we don't need to practice asceticism (vs 20–23) nor reinterpret Hebrew religious practices to cleanse them from their supposedly materialistic orientation(as reflected in vs 16), in order to free ourselves from material lust (*the body of flesh*). We become free from material lust through Christ.

When they argued that as Christians we must free ourselves from bondage, Gnostic Christians in effect were saying we still are in bondage to the world. That is what Paul is talking about when he complains in verse 20:

> If with Christ you died to the elemental spirits of the universe,
> why do you live **as if you still belonged to the world?** (Col 2:20)

In contrast, Paul exhorts Christians to *"Set your minds on things that are above, not on things that are on earth, for you have died and your life is hidden with Christ in God"* (Col 3:3–4). It is the true teaching of Christ that brings us to genuinely heavenly spirituality. Sabbatarian celebrations in fact are heavenly, since they are shadows of Christ (Col 2:17). Therefore ignore those who condemn the continued observance of biblical celebrations with material feasting (Col 2:16). In Christ we are already free, and none of this can possibly hurt us.

Who Were the Colossian Critics?

The short answer is we don't know precisely who they were. What we can be sure is they were Hellenistic, they espoused asceticism, regarded angelic beings as mediators between man and the heavenly *pleroma,* and were critical of the Jewish heritage of the first-century church. They probably were Gnostic Christians who espoused teachings similar to Valentinian Gnosticism. But there are many other Hellenistic groups that could have been involved.[295]

An exact identification of the Colossian critics is not necessary. What is important is understanding the general class of Hellenistic theology

---

[295] There were many Gnostic sects with similar traits to the Valentinians, one such likely candidate being the Naassenes, who are described in volume two of our series, *Spirit of Antichrist.*

involved in the controversy, which today enables us to understand what Paul was and was not saying. The modern, Hellenistic Christian interpretation of Colossians chapter two is essentially the reverse of what Paul actually was saying. In fact, Paul was rejecting the very Judaeophobic Hellenistic theology that modern Hellenistic Christians claim he was preaching.

Could Valentinian Gnosticism itself be involved in the Colossian problem? Paul's letter to the Colossians was composed around 60 A.D. The Valentinian sect did not come into existence as an organized religious movement until the first half of the second century, some 60 to 70 years later.

However, Valentinians provide a unique insight into proto-Gnosticism within the early church. Independent Gnostic sects of the early second century, such as the Valentinians, were a product of the mass exodus of proto-Gnostics from the New Testament church that began late in the first century. Therefore they reflect the proto-Gnostic theology that had been fomenting within the church in the first century. Valentinian Gnosticism was one of the most highly Christianized of the independent Gnostic sects. It promoted a deep spirituality and profound emotional attachment to Christ and the Father. It viewed itself as an ally of the orthodox Roman church, a sort of more spiritual elder brother (a view not shared by the Roman church, of course). Its founder Valentinus had been active in the church at Rome and very nearly became its leader before leaving to found his own movement.

It is not surprising therefore that Valentinian Christianity displays striking similarities to more than one of the first-century apostasies described in the New Testament, including both the Colossian problem and the 'deep things of Satan' apostasy in the church at Thyatira.[296]

Colossians Summary

To sum up Colossians chapter two, Paul is emphasizing Jesus Christ as the heart and highest point of Christian religion.

Paul's argument with the Gnostic critics at Colossae was over their heretical view of the angelic, heavenly *pleroma* as the focus of salvation

---

[296] The apostasy of the Thyatira church is described in chapter 7, *Thyatira and 'the Deep Things of Satan.'*

instead of Christ, and their insistence on connecting to the heavens through angelic mediators. It was this very theology about freeing man from materialistic angels while submitting to heavenly angels, which led them to insist that Jewish celebrations must be reinterpreted.

Part of that argument, therefore, was over the symbolism of Old Testament practices that continued to be observed in the apostolic church. Gnosticism condemned these observances on the basis that their symbolism is materialistic and the celebrations themselves included materialistic feasting. Instead, they insisted, Christian must reject material pleasure, and the symbolism of their religious celebrations must be non-material and point exclusively to the angelic spirituality of the heavenly *pleroma*.

Against this, Paul argues that Christ is intimately connected with both material and spiritual creation (Col 1:16). Therefore there is no need to radically change or reject creation-based Jewish celebrations, which in fact point to Christ (Col 2:17).

Paul directly addresses two major Gnostic/Hellenistic doctrines. First are their radical ideas about avoiding materialism. This involved asceticism, but also extended to avoiding or spiritualizing away Jewish religious practices. Reinterpreting Jewish celebrations was necessary because of their association with material creation, the Old Covenant and the elemental spirits (angels) who administered the Old Covenant.

In response, Paul says Jesus already has taken away the power any angel or spirit had over us under the Old Covenant (vs 15). This was accomplished by Jesus' grace established at the cross (vs 14). Therefore Jewish celebrations and the feasting associated with them are no threat to us. They will not bring us back under the control of Old Covenant angelic powers, nor place us under bondage to the material world.

Second is the Gnostic/Hellenistic idea that we must submit ourselves to good elemental spirits (angels) in order to ritually connect ourselves to the heavenly *pleroma* (Col 2:18). On that basis Gnostics insisted that Jewish-Christian symbols must be changed to point exclusively to the heavenly *pleroma*. Paul is saying No, that isn't necessary. Jewish celebrations point to Christ, and through Christ we already possess the spirituality of the heavenly *pleroma* (Col 2:9–10).

The real argument at Colossae was about how to define the spiritual reality to which Christian celebrations point. From the historical evidence we know Gnostic Christianity in the early centuries after Christ was vigorously pressing this very point, condemning Primitive Christians for continuing to observe Hebrew practices and customs. The Colossian critics were, in effect, spiritualizing Christianity to rid it of its Hebrew content. They were doing the very same thing as found in the Epistle of Barnabas, whose author openly stated his intention to allegorize Old Testament scripture in order to turn Christians away from literal observance of Old Testament practices (see above, pages 61 and following).

When we identify the critics of the Colossian church as Hellenistic Christians promoting a Valentinian Gnostic style theology, all of Colossians chapter two becomes a single, coherent message. The key words are "Jesus Christ" and "already." Everything that Hellenistic/Gnostic theology promises, we already possess through Jesus Christ.

- We already are in contact with the perfection of the heavens (the *pleroma*) by our identification with Jesus (vs 10).

- It is Jesus, not angels, who separates us from material lust through a 'spiritual circumcision' (vs 11). We don't have to free ourselves by practicing asceticism. We are already free.

- We don't need to identify with and become subject to heavenly elemental spirits (angels – vs 18). We have already achieved spirituality by identification with Jesus (vs 10). We are buried with Jesus in baptism and raised with him through faith (vs 12). Jesus is our connection to spirituality.

- The angelic administrators of the Old Covenant no longer have any claim over us (vs 15). We are already free through Jesus' sacrifice for sin. Therefore we have no need to play the games prescribed by Hellenistic Christianity to free ourselves from the angelic administrators of the Old Covenant.

This logically leads to conclusions Paul implicitly lays out for us:

- Don't let yourself get bogged down in biased arguments about Jewish celebrations. Don't let anyone frighten you by saying you will be disqualified, that you will not be saved if you don't accept their Hellenistic, heavenly reinterpretation of Sabbath rest.

- Biblical celebrations point to Christ and Christ is the real issue, the true source of spirituality. Biblical celebrations, which point to Christ, cannot hurt us.

PRIMITIVE CHRISTIANITY IN CRISIS

- Reject your critics' substitute Hellenistic spirituality by which they reinterpret everything as a symbol of the heavens, subjecting you to heavenly elemental spirits (angels), and plunging you into ascetic denial of the flesh (vs 18, 20–23).

The basic message of Colossians 2 is that everything Hellenistic religion promises, *Jesus already* has given us. Old Testament celebrations including Sabbath observance are no threat and do not by nature conflict with New Testament spirituality. Just say NO to Gnostic-style, Judaeophobic, Hellenistic spiritualizing of Christianity!

Why is Colossians 2 So Misunderstood?

The problem behind misinterpretation of Colossians 2 is failure to understand the context of the entirety of chapters one and two.

Most biblical commentators isolate only four verses from chapter two (vs 14–17). They begin with the conclusion that Paul is saying the Old Covenant was abolished at the cross, and in this they are correct. However, taking just this short passage by itself, they then are misled into concluding the Colossian critics were saying the opposite, that the Old Covenant was not abolished at the cross. Therefore, they argue, in verses 16–17 it is the critics who are preaching that Christians should continue to celebrate Sabbaths, and therefore Paul is saying Christians should not celebrate Sabbaths.

Many such commentators describe the Colossian critics as some vague, unknown Hellenistic group, or sometimes make a wild guess based on one or two traits mentioned in the surrounding verses. The problem is that most such biblical commentators fail to make a detailed examination of the entire context. And, to be fair, frequently they simply lack the in-depth understanding of the historical background necessary to accurately process the extensive and detailed context found in both chapters one and two.

Looking at the context before the critical verses 14–17 we find clear statements that the problem coming from the Colossian critics was not biblical arguments, but pagan religious teachings from the Hellenistic culture of that time. By looking at the context after the critical verses 14–17 we find that these Hellenistic teachings involved submission to angels that supposedly connect Christians to the heavens. And when we synthesize all the contextual information together, it points directly to one common heretical tradition preached by a number of Gnostic Christian groups in the early centuries after Christ. It is surprising how perfectly all the context fits together when understood in this way.

In the end we discover the reason Paul explained we are free from the angelic administrators of the Old Covenant is because the Colossian critics claimed we are still in bondage to them and have to free ourselves. And since they believed that feasting and celebration of biblical Sabbaths keep us in bondage to the angelic administrators of the Old Covenant, it was the critics, not Paul, who were condemning the continued celebration of Sabbaths.

Colossians 2 and Sabbath as a Shadow

Paul's epistle to the Colossians reflects the opening salvos of the war between Hellenistic and Primitive Christianity over the continuity of Hebrew religion within Christianity. The historical material covered in chapter 3, "The Hellenistic Sabbath," documents the continuation of that same war in the contest of Jewish versus Hellenistic symbolism in the early church.

In chapter 3 we saw that one of the core ideas behind replacing Sabbath with Sunday the Eighth Day, was the idea that the Eighth Day points to the heavens, the future home of the saved. (See above, pages 57 and following.) As Origen graphically expressed it:

> The number eight, which contains the virtue of the Resurrection, is the **figure** [shadow] of the future world [the heavens].[297]

Exactly as the Colossian critics of the first century insisted that Christian celebrations must be a shadow of the heavenly *pleroma*, Origin here expresses the very same rationale behind the transfer of Sabbath to Sunday. The idea of shadow and reality indeed played an important role in the transition from Sabbath to Sunday. We see that graphically expressed, again, this time by the great Hellenistic church historian Eusebius. He praises Sunday the Eighth Day as an image (shadow) of a great Sabbath archetype, the heavenly reality and heavenly perfection to which it points:

---

[297] Origen, *Sel. Psalm;* P.G. 12, 1624B-C.

[It, the Eighth Day]...is the image of that (heavenly) Sabbath...
that perfect and blessed rest....[298]

Sabbath rest is much more than just a symbol. It provides tremendous physical, emotional, as well as spiritual benefits. It is one of God's greatest gifts to man, as Jesus described it during his earthly ministry (Mark 2:27). Nevertheless, the Hellenistic assault against Sabbath was played out primarily on theological and symbolic grounds. It was a question of its suitability as a Christian symbol, because of its association with material creation.

Rejecting Sabbath is the natural outcome of an epic struggle between Hellenistic and Primitive Christianity, the beginning of which is reflected in Paul's epistle to the Colossians. Because of its heritage of antagonism towards the material world, there is no way Hellenistic religion could accommodate Jewish religious practices. Indeed, once Hellenistic religion took root in the church, rejection of Sabbath observance was just a matter of time.

Paul's observations about the struggle between Hellenistic and Primitive Christianity in the Colossian church are as valid today as they were then. Indeed, when Hellenistic Christians today condemn Sabbatarian worship, they are troubling the primitive church in essentially the same way the critics of the Colossians were doing nearly 2,000 years ago.

---

[298] Eusebius, P.G. 23, 1168 C – 1169 A.

Appendix B

Hebrews 4
and the Sabbath

The Hellenistic Roman church insisted Christians must convert from Sabbath to Sunday because they considered the Sabbath spiritually unfit as a symbol of Christian salvation.

As we saw above in chapter 3, "The Hellenistic Sabbath," their rationale was founded substantially on pagan Hellenistic religion and philosophy. Sabbath symbolizes creation of the material world, but in Hellenistic culture that is evil, while Sunday the Eighth Day symbolizes Heaven and its unchanging stability and eternal rest. The goal of conversion to Sunday observance supposedly is to turn Christians away from materialism and refocus on the promise of a future, eternal rest with God.

Controversy over the day of worship started in the second century, so we have almost nothing about it in the New Testament. However, we see some of the ideas behind Sunday observance already forming in the Colossian church in the mid-first century.[299] Here some Hellenistic Christians already were criticizing the continued observance of Jewish customs, including the weekly Sabbath. Even at this early time, some were teaching that everything must point to the heavens (the *pleroma*), and criticizing "earthly" Jewish celebrations that involved material feasting. We can draw conclusions from the presence of such problems at the Colossian church. But wouldn't it be helpful if the New Testament directly answered our principle question:

Is Sabbath fit or unfit as a symbol of Christian salvation?

---

[299] See above, Appendix A, "The Full Story behind Colossians 2."

Is Sabbath associated *only* with Hebrew religion and the Old Covenant? Must Christians choose something else as a symbol of their New Testament hope of salvation and relationship with Jesus? That is the crux of the matter. Thankfully, the New Testament does supply an answer, albeit brief but very clear. Ironically, it comes from a passage of scripture that is used today by Hellenistic Christianity to criticize and reject Sabbath observance. That passage is the fourth chapter of Hebrews.

The significance of Hebrews 4 is hotly contested. Hellenistic Christians frequently claim it teaches a spiritual rest in Christ that replaces literal Sabbath observance. Getting at the truth of the matter, however, as we have seen so often in previous sections of this volume, involves understanding the background and context of the issue.

This appendix on Hebrews 4 is based substantially on the work of the Primitive Christian scholar Roy Marrs. Parts of what follow are a condensation from his study on Hebrews 4, contained in his book *God's Revised Will and the "Rest" of the Story,* and is done with his permission.

The Background

Sabbath is a day of rest. But what does 'rest' signify in the larger sense as a theological concept? What does it have to do with Christian salvation, if anything?

This is a key issue, because the idea of rest is linked with the 'kingdom' as a reward offered by God to his faithful followers. And we find this in both the Old and New Testaments.

The story begins in the Old Testament with the promise to the Hebrews that they will find rest in their own land (the Promised Land). From the time that God chose Abraham and decided to form a special nation from his seed, there was the promise that they would inherit their own land. As Yahweh told Abraham:

> I will establish my covenant between me and you, and your off-
> spring after you...for an everlasting covenant, to be God to you
> and to your offspring after you. And I will give to you...the land
> where you are now an alien, all the land of Canaan.... (Genesis
> 17:7–8)

Here, free from outside interference, Israel can establish a righteous society based on the worship of their God, Yahweh.

Until the Israelites obtain their own kingdom they are being harassed and abused by the foreign nations in which they are forced to live. To come into their own kingdom means rest – rest from political turmoil, social pressures and rest from the temptations of foreign cultures and foreign religious practices that plagued the early Hebrews.

For Primitive Christians today, for example, it would be the same as being able to live in a purely Sabbatarian society where there is rest from economic pressure to work on the Sabbath, and rest from the harassment of Hellenistic Christians trashing Primitive Christianity as an inferior and backward form of worship.

Israel's promise was partially fulfilled by the Exodus from Egypt and resettlement in the Promised Land, the ancient land of Canaan. But, as we next discover, Israel's kingdom was only one small part of a much larger kingdom promise.

Kingdom and Rest in the New Testament

The same twin concepts of rest and kingdom promise are found in the New Testament. Here we find Jesus repeatedly preaching the 'gospel of the kingdom.' For example:

> Then Jesus went about all the cities and villages, teaching in their synagogues, and proclaiming the **good news** [gospel] **of the kingdom**.... (Matt 9:35)

Paul preached the same gospel of the kingdom. For example, speaking to the Thessalonians he refers to:

> ...the righteous judgment of God...intended to make you worthy of **the kingdom of God**.... (2 Thess 2:5)

The Christian gospel of the kingdom was not just a temporary message to Jews. It is the same message Jesus prophesied would be preached to all nations, throughout the entire New Testament era, up to the time Jesus returns:

> And this **good news** [gospel] **of the kingdom** will be proclaimed throughout the world, as a testimony to all the nations; and then the end will come. (Matt 24:14) [300]

The hope of finding rest in a kingdom ruled by God appears in both Old and New Testaments. Indeed, the book of Hebrews claims kingdom rest in the New Testament is a continuation of the same promise found in the Old Testament:

> For indeed the good news [gospel] <u>came to us **just as to them**</u>....
> (Heb 4:2)

The author of Hebrews further argues that Israel never really received its promise of rest. If the promise was never fulfilled under the Old Covenant, he says, then it remains for Christians today:

> Since therefore it remains open for some to enter it, and those who formerly received the good news failed to enter because of disobedience.... So then a Sabbath rest still remains for the people of God (Heb 4:6,9)

Old Testament Promise Transferred

What is the connection between the kingdom promises in Old and New Testaments? Jesus explained this himself. Speaking to the Jewish leadership in the temple at Jerusalem, Jesus proclaimed:

> Therefore I tell you, the kingdom of God will be taken away from you and given to a people that produces the fruits of the kingdom. (Matt 21:43)

---

[300] Dispensationalism, espoused by the majority of Evangelical Protestantism, rejects the gospel of the kingdom, viewing it as a purely Jewish and legalistic message intended solely for Israel. This supposedly is replaced for Christians by the gospel of grace preached by Paul. Dispensationalists deflect this verse by saying the gospel of the kingdom will be preached again in the end time just before the restoration of Israel at the start of the Millennium. However, this verse says the gospel of the kingdom is to go to all nations, not just Israel, and its context casts the gospel of the kingdom as the great commission of the church – preaching the gospel of Christian salvation.

Who are the new recipients of the promise? Jesus, speaking to his follow-ers, says:

> Do not be afraid, little flock, for it is your Father's good pleasure to give you the kingdom. (Luke 12:32)

In the preaching of the Apostle Paul, the kingdom promise is depicted as no longer by physical descent, but through Christ. Yet, Paul says, it re-mains the same promise given through Abraham:

> ...not all Abraham's children are his true [physical] descendants (Romans 8:6–7)

> And if you belong to Christ, then you are Abraham's offspring, heirs according to the promise. (Gal 3:29)

Why was the kingdom promise taken from Israel? In the Promised Land they were free to worship God without interference from the world around them. But, as we saw above, the fruit they produced was not what God expected. Jesus condemned the Jewish leadership for their failure to live up to the kingdom promise, and then, worse yet, trying to block their fellow Jews from receiving the kingdom through Christ:

> But woe to you, scribes and Pharisees, hypocrites! For you lock people out of the kingdom of heaven. For you do not go in your-selves, and when others are going in, you stop them. (Matt 23:14) [301]

This is why the author of Hebrews says that Israel never achieved rest, even though they physically entered the Promised Land: *"For if Joshua had given them rest, God would not speak later about another day"* (Heb 4:8). Even though Israel finally entered Canaan under Joshua's leader-ship, they never really achieved the goal.

The foundation of Hebrews 4 is this very point. The Hebrew nation failed to create the godly society and culture that was the very purpose of the kingdom promise. Therefore, it was transferred to Christ and his fol-lowers.

In Hebrews chapters 3 and 4, the author is warning Christians to learn from Israel's problems. If they failed to fulfill their kingdom promise,

---

[301] Matthew, alone of the four gospels, interchanges kingdom of God and kingdom of heaven, both of which refer to the same thing.

likewise today we can fail if we do not through faith persevere in obedience.

Kingdom Promise Spans Old and New Testaments in Five Phases

The Old Testament nation of Israel in the land of Canaan was the first literal fulfillment of the kingdom promise. When it was transferred to Christ and his followers we find a new phase and a new literal application. What land are we promised to inherit?

The kingdom promise today is expanded globally! Christians ultimately will inherit the entire earth:

> The kingship and dominion...of the kingdoms under the whole heaven shall be given to the people of the holy ones of the Most High; their kingdom shall be an everlasting kingdom, and all dominions shall serve and obey them. (Dan 7:27)

In the very end a heavenly city, the New Jerusalem, descends to earth. This becomes the headquarters for a renewed earth where the saints live in total peace with the heavenly Father and Jesus. This is the final fulfillment of the kingdom promises, which lasts on into eternity:

> Then I saw a new heaven and a new earth.... And I saw the holy city, the New Jerusalem, coming down out of heaven from God.... See, the home of God is among mortals. He will dwell with them as their God; they will be his peoples, and God himself will be with them; (Rev 21:1–3; see also 2 Peter 3:13, and 1 Cor 15:24)

These are the literal phases of the kingdom promise. There are multiple literal fulfillments – national Israel, the Millennium, and New Jerusalem.

But there are also time periods when there is no literal kingdom. There is a huge gap between the appearance of Jesus on earth, when the kingdom promise was transferred to the saints, and its next literal fulfillment for Christians. During the New Testament church era there is no literal kingdom.

There was another substantial gap between the time God made the promise to Abraham and Israel first entered Canaan. These are time periods when a literal kingdom does not exist. Nevertheless, there still are a people who have received the promise and obey God, looking forward in faith to the future fulfillment of the promise.

That is why the New Testament sometimes speaks as though the kingdom is present with us today, though it does not literally exist. For example:

> Once Jesus was asked by the Pharisees when the kingdom of God was coming, and he answered, "The kingdom of God is not coming with things that can be observed; nor will they say, 'Look, here it is!' or 'There it is!' For in fact, the kingdom of God is among you." (Luke 17:20–21)

> For the kingdom of God is not food and drink but righteousness and peace and joy in the Holy Spirit. (Romans 14:17)

This present, spiritual kingdom is just as much a promise of rest as the literal kingdoms. That is what Jesus was talking about when he said, *"Come to me, all you who labor and are heavy laden, and I will give you rest."* (Matt 11:28, NKJV) Peace and joy in the Holy Spirit are very tangible rewards of rest we receive from the spiritual kingdom.

The church today is a 'spiritual phase' of the kingdom, in which we are being prepared spiritually and receive part of the promise of rest, but the full reward is yet in the future. Abraham was in the same situation. He lived his entire life in faithful obedience, without seeing the literal fulfillment of the promise. According to the author of Hebrews, Abraham in faith looked forward not just to the Old Covenant kingdom promise, but to New Jerusalem, the final, eternal fulfillment of the promise:

> By faith Abraham obeyed when he was called to set out for a place that he was to receive as an inheritance; and he set out, not knowing where he was going. ...For he looked forward to the city that has foundations, whose architect and builder is God. (Heb 11:8,10)

In fact, Abraham did not fully understand what was to happen. He merely trusted God, and the reward for his faith ultimately will be New Jerusalem, the city designed and built by God himself, the final, eternal kingdom.

We see, therefore, that there is one overarching promise of kingdom rest. But it is fulfilled in multiple stages spanning both Old and New Covenants, all progressing toward one final, complete fulfillment. Not only that, there is overlap among the promises. For example, the final, eternal fulfillment (New Jerusalem) has been available from the beginning, as we saw in the example of Abraham.

Marrs counts four phases of the kingdom promise (corresponding to my 2 through 5 below). I suggest inserting an initial pre-Israelite nation phase, as follows:

1 - The spiritual promise to Abraham, before the first literal phase of the kingdom is fulfilled for Israel.

2 - The Israelite kingdom in the land of Canaan.

3 - The spiritual kingdom in Christianity – the church era, before the next literal phase of the kingdom is fulfilled in the millennium.

4 - The millennial kingdom.

5 - The eternal kingdom, New Jerusalem, when the heavenly Father rules with the saints on earth. [302]

In one sense the spiritual kingdom always exists. Even when a literal kingdom is present, its participants still are called to a spiritual relationship with God.

That is why Israel failed, and why Israel is described as never having received rest. Though they received a physical kingdom, they failed to establish the spiritual relationship and godly society that was the purpose of their physical kingdom.

A spiritual relationship with God, which we have today through Christ, and the promise of Messianic salvation in the eternal kingdom of New Jerusalem, has been available to all mankind from the very beginning of the world. There is always a spiritual kingdom available to man. But until the final fulfillment in New Jerusalem, there are other literal fulfillments that are sometimes present, and sometimes not.

Background Summary

As we now proceed to an analysis of Hebrews chapter 4, we start with this background:

The Bible characterizes salvation as achieving rest in the kingdom of God. It is characterized this way in both Old and New Testaments.

---

[302] Primitive Christianity is divided on the location of the two future literal kingdom promises. Most believe the Millennium will be spent in heaven and the eternal kingdom on earth, while others believe both occur on earth.

The literal fulfillment of the kingdom for Israel and for Christians is not identical. The Old Testament literal kingdom was the land of Canaan, reserved for one nation. The New Testament promise is expanded to encompass the entire earth, all races and nations, and eternity. Nevertheless, the Christian hope of salvation is characterized as a continuation of the Old Covenant kingdom promise. Christ explicitly says the Old Covenant kingdom promise has been transferred to the church.

In the larger view of human history, then, we see multiple phases of the kingdom promise, which are individual parts of one overall plan, spanning both Old and New Covenants. Also, though literal fulfillments of the kingdom promise are sequential, the spiritual kingdom overlaps and is part of all the physical kingdom promises. The spiritual kingdom – a spiritual relationship between God and man that is the foundation of all kingdom promises – has always been available, from the very beginning of creation. And all these promises lead to a final fulfillment in the eternal kingdom described in Revelation chapter 21.

As we move on into analysis of chapter 4, we find the author of Hebrews talking about these very issues. He is very concerned with the unity between Old and New Testament kingdom promises. He also makes a special point about when God completed his plans for all these promises. This in turn has important implications for Sabbath observance under the New Covenant.

Hebrews Chapter Four

The main theme of Hebrews chapters 3 and 4 is faith that produces obedience and perseverance. The object of that faith is the kingdom promises and its rest. If we have faith that God will fulfill the kingdom promise for us, even though it has not yet appeared, then we will persevere.

The target audience of this letter is Christian Jews.[303] Of all people, they understood the kingdom promises made to ancient Israel. However, most of them did not understand the Christian concept of the phases of the kingdom, as explained above. They thought the kingdom promise would be fulfilled by an immediate restoration of an independent kingdom of Israel with a Davidic king, rather than the future millennial and eternal

---

[303] See Heb 3:1; 5:12 – 6:6 .

kingdoms prophesied by Jesus and the apostles, and even some Old Testament prophets.[304]

Even the apostles at first thought the kingdom would become a literal reality immediately after Christ's resurrection.[305] This was a huge issue for Hebrew Christians. The saints in Jerusalem initially gathered together in communal living, waiting for Christ's return, which they thought would happen any day.[306] When Christ did not immediately return to establish the kingdom, some began to doubt there was a kingdom promise for Christians. Especially for Jewish Christians, the apparent delay in Christ's return was a devastating disappointment.

This is what Hebrews 3 and 4 are about. Like the Jews wandering in the desert after the exodus from Egypt, who doubted that God really would give them victory over the Canaanites and so decided not to enter their promised rest, these Hebrew Christians also were doubting the fulfillment of the kingdom promises, which they thought should have happened already.

In chapter 3 the author reviews the problems Israel experienced on their way to the Promised Land, and how their lack of faith caused a whole generation to fail to enter their kingdom promise. Those people were very much like Christians today, not yet having received the kingdom but looking forward to it in hope. Like them, we too can fail:

> For indeed the good news [gospel] came to us just as to them; but the message they heard did not benefit them, because they were not united by faith with those who listened. For we who have believed enter that rest.... (Heb 4:2–3)

In this passage, entering that rest, expressed in the present tense, is talking about the spiritual phase of the kingdom. We spiritually enter the kingdom now, being prepared as a righteous people, cleansed by Christ's sacrifice and persevering in obedience through faith, looking forward to the resurrection and future literal fulfillments of the kingdom promise.

This is followed by puzzling statements that are frequently overlooked and misunderstood, but which are a key to understanding Hebrews 4. Here the author makes a point of explaining exactly **when** this rest was first available:

---

[304] For example Luke 19:11, Daniel 7:27 .
[305] Acts 1:6 .
[306] Acts 2:44–47.

"As in my anger I swore [God speaking], 'They [Israel] shall not enter my rest.' " though his works were finished at the_foundation of the world. For in one place it speaks about the seventh day as follows, "And God rested on the seventh day from all his works." (Heb 4:3–4)

Why is this important? As we will see, the author is setting up a key portion of his argument for why the New Covenant kingdom promise is a continuation of the Old Covenant promise.

First, he says, Gods salvation rest was complete and available from the beginning of the world (*his works were finished at the foundation of the world*). Then, he adds, this is proven by God's establishment of Sabbatarian rest at creation, as it says, *"For in one place it speaks about the seventh day as follows, and God rested on the seventh day..."*

But which rest is he talking about? Is it only the national rest promised to Israel under the Old Covenant? What is the scope of his argument? The author's argument encompasses the full scope of God's salvation rest, as it says, *"And God rested on the seventh day from all his works."* The point the author is making is embodied in the word "all." For ancient Israel that meant Canaan was already created, available whenever God decided to give it to them according to his promise. For us today, it refers to the existence of the entire earth, already created and available when the time comes that God will intervene to give it to the saints, according to his promise.

This refers equally to God's plans and promises of salvation rest. They too, all of them, were complete and in existence from the very beginning. Specifically, this means that the New Testament kingdom promise, given to the church, also was complete at creation. This is mentioned multiple times elsewhere in the New Testament. For example:

Just as he chose us in Christ **before the foundation of the world....** (Eph 1:4)

This grace was given to us in Christ Jesus **before the ages began,** but it has now been revealed through the appearing of our Savior Christ Jesus.... (2 Tim 1:9–10)

God's entire plan of salvation, in all its phases, is part of one overarching "eternal covenant" that was in place from the beginning. Remember how the author of Hebrews stresses the point that at creation God rested *"from all his works."*

The nation of Israel and Old Covenant, the New Covenant, the church, the Millennium and New Jerusalem were all planned and designed by

God from the very beginning. And what is the sign that all God's promises were in place from the beginning? Notice again how the author of Hebrews explains the assurance God has given us:

> **For** in one place it speaks of the seventh day as follows, "And God rested on the seventh day from **all** his works." (Heb 4:4).

The initial word 'For' marks this sentence as an explanation to clarify the previous statement, in verse 3, that the promises were available from the foundation of the world. What this is saying is that God rested on the seventh day of creation as a **sign** that the entire plan of salvation, kingdom rest in **all** its phases, which together form the whole salvation work of God, were complete at creation. God's seventh day creation rest is a sign that he already has done his part, and it is available and secure for those who persevere.

Verses 6 – 8

Proceeding through the next verses, 6–8, the author of Hebrews emphasizes the original idea that the kingdom promise to Israel was never completely fulfilled. He quotes from King David, pleading with Israel to not harden their hearts and submit to God in joyful love and obedience. This and other portions from Hebrews chapter 3 and 4 are quotations from David's words in Psalms 95.

The point the author of Hebrews is making is that at the time of King David, long after Joshua led Israel into their promised land where they should have received rest, God still is pleading with them to enter a spiritual relationship of love and obedience. As we said earlier, though Israel physically entered the Promised Land, they never established the spiritual relationship with God that was the very point of kingdom rest. That is the basis of the author's claim that Israel never really entered their promised rest.

Let's now recap what the author of Hebrews has set up for the clinching of his argument in what follows. So far he has said that Israel's promise of kingdom rest was symbolized and guaranteed by God's rest on the seventh day of creation. That is why in the Old Testament the Sabbath is a special sign of Israel's promise of national salvation and rest. However, though Israel technically entered the land where they were to receive rest, they never really achieved rest because they failed to establish a loving and obedient relationship with God.

Therefore, it says, this *same* promise of rest remains open for Christians today. Note that a key part of the argument is that our promise today is essentially the same kingdom promise that Israel failed to achieve. Now, from one point of view that cannot be true. From the evidence given above, we know that the kingdom promise for the church is much greater than the national kingdom promise given to Israel.

Yet, we also know, from verses 3–4 that all the kingdom promises are joined together as part of one overarching promise, all of which were complete at creation and are symbolized by God's Sabbath rest on the seventh day of creation. Therefore in the larger view, Christian salvation can be undersood as the same promise of rest, also complete and secure from the time of creation, and equally symbolized by God's rest on the seventh day of creation.

Notice, then, how the author of Hebrews uses all this background to tie the church's kingdom rest to Israel's kingdom rest, through the common denominator of God's rest at creation.

Verses 9 – 10

Here we come to the critical and controversial portion of the chapter. Now the author of Hebrews presents his conclusion, drawn from all the preceding explanation. Notice how it begins with *"So then,"* which is the same as saying *"Therefore my conclusion is:"*

> So then a Sabbath rest [*Sabbatismos*] remains for the people of God; for those who enter God's rest also cease from their labors as God did from his. (Heb 4:9–10)

The author of Hebrews says that a Sabbatarian rest "remains." Exactly what is it that 'remains'? In the leadup to this conclusion, he has been talking about Israel's kingdom rest, which was never really fulfilled and therefore remains open. Therefore, what remains must be this promise of kingdom rest. It is the promise of kingdom rest for Christians.

But here he presents the clinching argument for *why* the church's rest is the same rest offered to Israel. What is that argument? What is it about our rest today that makes it a continuation of Israel's rest? Because, he

369

says, *"those who enter God's rest"* (present tense, referring to our spiritual rest in Christ) ***"also** cease from their labors as God did from his."*

What he is saying is so very simple! He is noting the fact that those people who were entering God's spiritual rest in his day, in other words first-century apostolic Christians, were still observing the Sabbath in imitation of God's rest at creation. Israel's rest and Christian rest are linked by their common association with creation. That is his final clinching argument of why we should consider Christian salvation to be a continuation of Israel's kingdom promise. He is tying everything together through the common denominator of God's creation rest and Sabbath observance.

Hellenistic Christianity has its own, anti-Sabbatarian interpretations of verses 9–10. We will review some of those below. But first let's look at it from a Sabbatarian point of view. After all, the audience to which this letter was written were Sabbatarian Christian Jews. They were observing the weekly Sabbath when they received this letter, and they continued to observe Sabbath after that for several centuries. If there were an instruction contained in this letter that the Sabbath is fulfilled in another fashion and is no longer to be observed, they certainly missed the point.

There are three critical elements in verses 9–10:
1 - Sabbath rest (Sabbatismos)
2 - God's rest
3 – the phrase 'cease from their labors, as God did from his'

The first element is a translation of the controversial word *Sabbatismos*, over which scholars have long argued. It appears only this once in the Bible, and is the noun form of the verb *Sabbatidzo*, to observe Sabbath. Therefore our *Sabbatismos,* if taken at face value, means the act of observing Sabbath rest, sometimes translated "a keeping of the Sabbath." Whatever it is, this *Sabbatismos* is what *"remains."* Therefore, it is something that existed in the past, under the Old Covenant, and continues under the New.

First Sabbatismos Interpretation

There are two common interpretations of *Sabbatismos* in Primitive Christian theology. The first says it refers to literal Sabbath observance. This indeed is the most literal interpretation of the text. *Sabbatismos* means the act of Sabbath keeping. How would the intended audience of

Hebrews understand it? Since they were themselves observing the weekly Sabbath, and the author's choice of words is so bold, how could they understand otherwise unless the author clarified himself with additional explanation?

The objection Hellenistic Christians raise is *Why?* Why would the author mention the Sabbath at this point in his text? In the immediately preceding section (verses 6–8) he is not talking about literal Sabbath observance, but rather salvation (kingdom) rest. Therefore regardless of the literal meaning of the word *Sabbatismos*, they argue, isn't the author merely borrowing the word to continue talking about salvation rest?

Indeed, what is the point the author is trying to make in verses 9 and 10? If we understand that, then we may correctly understand why the author uses the word *Sabbatismos* and whether he intended it to be taken literally.

First, if the author is changing the topic to refer to literal Sabbath observance, notice that he is not taking an unexpected, sudden turn, as Hellenistic interpreters claim. From the very beginning of this section of text, in verses 3 and 4, he has been intertwining the topic of kingdom rest with the Sabbath, holding up God's institution of Sabbath rest at the end of creation as a symbol of the availability of kingdom rest and God's guarantee to us that his promises have always been and therefore are now available. He already has been arguing that God's Sabbath rest on the seventh day of creation is a sign that ***all*** God's plans for salvation were complete at creation (vs 3–4), thereby implicitly type-casting all phases of the kingdom promise as Sabbatarian.

Given the laying of all this groundwork, why is it surprising for the author of Hebrews to mention weekly Sabbath observance in verses 9 or 10? As we said above, if he didn't mean *Sabbatismos* in verse 9 to be taken literally, shouldn't he have explained that? And indeed he does explain himself in the following verse – verse 10:

> ***For*** those who enter God's rest ***also*** cease from their labors as God did from his."

How would a Sabbath observing Hebrew audience understand that? Verse 10 is a virtual restatement of the Sabbath command from the Ten Commandments – to observe the weekly Sabbath in imitation of God's rest at creation.

The most simple, most obvious understanding of verses 9–10 and its context, which most clearly harmonizes with the intended audience and the author's larger argument, could be paraphrased as follows:

"Do not lose faith in God's promise of kingdom rest. Do not turn back as your forefathers did. Christian salvation is a continuation of the kingdom promises first made to Israel, all of which were in place from before the world began and are symbolized by God's rest on the seventh day of creation. That is why we today, as Christians, continue to observe the weekly Sabbath (*Sabbatismos*) in imitation of God's rest at creation. Sabbath observance continues (*"remains"*) because our kingdom and its rest apply to us today (our rest in Christ) and also are yet to come (the Millennium and eternal kingdoms). If the kingdom promises and God's rest had been completely fulfilled by ancient Israel then there would be no more Sabbath observance. Therefore press forward in continued obedience and persevere in faith. As you meet together every Sabbath, be encouraged by this sign God has given us of the certainty of the coming full implementation of our promise of kingdom rest."

The author brings in Sabbath observance because it is part of his argument for why the promise of the kingdom remains. It is his final, clinching argument for why our kingdom rest is essentially the same as the rest promised to Israel. Continued observance of the weekly Sabbath by first-century Christians is a sign of the Sabbatarian nature of Christian salvation, which for him proves his point that our rest is a continuation of the same rest promised to Israel. The author is carefully crafting a chain of Sabbatarian connections, all pointing back to God's rest on the seventh day of creation.

A Second Sabbatismos Interpretation

There is an alternate interpretation, which is espoused by Marrs. This says that the word *Sabbatismos* refers specifically to "God's rest" on the seventh day of creation. God's creation rest is the archetype that ties together all the kingdom promises. Therefore, if the Christian promise of rest is Sabbatarian, then it logically can be viewed as a continuation of the Old Covenant promise of rest, both of which are manifestations of God's *Sabbatismos* rest on the seventh day of creation.

Hellenistic theologians favor this second interpretation or similar versions of it, because then they can argue that verse 10 means that by entering into God's rest (being "in Christ") Christians **symbolically** cease from their labors as God did from his. In other words, we no longer literally observe Sabbath; instead, by ceasing from our own works and leaning back in grace, we symbolically fulfill Sabbath observance.

The problem with that is it ignores the context and the very construction of the author's argument in chapter four. His essential argument is that all the kingdom promises are Sabbatarian. All were complete and in place at the time of creation, and therefore all are linked together by God's rest on the seventh day of creation.

The logic is this simple: if A = X and B = X, then A must = B. In other words, if both Old and New Covenant kingdom salvation are manifestations of God's creation rest, then indeed one is a continuation of the other. As his final argument in this chain of reasoning, in verse 10, he notes that all Christians (at the time Hebrews was written) were still observing the seventh day Sabbath.

With this second interpretation, therefore, though *Sabbatismos* in verse 9 is interpreted differently, verse 10 is understood exactly the same as in the first interpretation. He is still clinching his argument by connecting our New Covenant kingdom promise with weekly Sabbath observance. If both New and Old Covenant promises are Sabbatarian, then they are essentially the same. And that is why, he observes, that the archetype (*Sabbatismos*), on which both are based, indeed continued to survive in his time in the universal observance of Sabbath in the apostolic church.

Christian Salvation is Sabbatarian!

Therein lies a huge problem for Hellenistic Christianity. Their claim is based on the idea that *only* Israel's Old Testament kingdom promise is Sabbatarian. For them, seventh-day rest applies *only* to national Israel and its rest in a material, earthly kingdom.

Recall Clement of Alexandria's argument from chapter three, "The Hellenistic Sabbath," in which he claimed that the Sabbath is materialistic, while Christian salvation is of a completely different, spiritual nature. Therefore, he said, Christian salvation must be associated with something new, namely Eighth Day symbolism and theology, to separate it from the Old Testament promise (see above, pages 58 and following). But here, in the New Testament, the author of Hebrews forcefully and directly contradicts that sort of reasoning. Here Christian salvation is depicted as Sabbatarian, as a continuation of the same promise of rest from the Old

Testament, all linked together by the archetype of Sabbatarian rest, God's rest on the seventh day of creation.

The author of Hebrews does not set out to argue the question of weekly Sabbath observance. What he is talking about is the problem of Jewish Christians beginning to doubt that the kingdom promises were transferred to the church, and doubt that God would fulfill his promises to the church. In the process of addressing that question, however, he specifically refers to weekly Sabbath observance, which was a universal practice in the apostolic church at the time this was written. And in doing so, he lays out a solid theological foundation for why Sabbath observance continues under the New Covenant.

Perseverance and Obedience

To argue that this applies to us today only symbolically, totally misrepresents the context. This is not about grace versus works, not about ceasing from our own works in order to rest in grace. The very next verse (vs 11) says, *"Let us therefore make **every effort** to enter that rest, so that no one may fall through such **disobedience**...."* The larger passage of both chapters 3 and 4 is about persevering in obedience through faith, avoiding the disobedience of ancient Israel. Continuing in Sabbath observance naturally is part of that obedience.

Psalms 95, from which the author of Hebrews quotes, is a plea for Israel to enter a joyful relationship of love and obedience with their God. That is the same theme found in Hebrews chapter 4. Marrs' observations are especially poignant in this regard:

> If *anything at all* is clear in the book of Hebrews, particularly from chapters 3, 4, 6 and 10, it is that faithless disobedience is the cause of God's children being separated from God and being denied entrance into kingdom rest.[307]

Marrs points out that Hebrews is not a warning to unbelievers. It is specifically a warning to professing Christians about the importance of faith that leads to obedience. Marrs continues:

---

[307] Marrs, *God's Revised Will and the "Rest" of the Story,* p 276.

Faithless disobedience continues today among *believers* who claim to be children of God. Warning against believers disobeying *is the very purpose of the book of Hebrews.* [308]

Why is Hebrews 4 so misunderstood? What so often is overlooked are verses 3–5 where the author sets up the connection between kingdom rest and God's seventh day rest at creation. The author penned these verses for a specific reason. He is setting the foundation for his latter argument in verses 9 and 10. He is specifically coloring the kingdom promise as Sabbatarian, and holding up God's rest on the seventh day of creation as a sign and guarantee of the kingdom promises that continue into our day. Very importantly, he emphasizes that **all** the kingdom promises, including our promises today, **all** were completed at creation. Therefore **all** are Sabbatarian and to be treated equally in that regard.

Scholars agonize at such length over the question of why the author of Hebrews used the obscure word *Sabbatismos* in Hebrews 4. But the answer is so simple. What the author is saying is that every week when Christians observe the Sabbath, as these Primitive Christians were doing, the act of Sabbath observance itself is a comforting reminder of God's guarantee of the kingdom promises.

Just as Sabbath was a sign between God and Israel in ancient times (Exodus 31:13–17), so the author of Hebrews claims it is a continuing sign of the saving relationship between God and Christians today, a source of comfort and sign of God's guarantee that the promises will be fulfilled.

This is true whether one interprets *Sabbatismos* in verse 9 as weekly Sabbath observance or as God's rest on the seventh day of creation. In either case, verse 10 clearly says that Christians who enter a spiritual relationship with God, receiving rest in Christ, also observe the Sabbath in honor of that, exactly as God honored the completion of all his plans for salvation by resting on the seventh day of creation.

Conclusions

The interpretation of Hebrews 4 by modern Hellenistic Christianity, that Sabbath rest has been transformed into a spiritual rest we experience

---

[308] Ibid. p 279.

only in Jesus, contradicts the very essence of the context of Hebrews 4. It assumes that the author of Hebrews is instituting a change in Sabbath observance. Yet, the context clearly emphasizes the idea that essentially *nothing* has changed since creation! Sabbatarianism did not begin with the Old Covenant nor did it end with the Old Covenant. Sabbatarianism began at creation and is an integral part of God's entire, overarching plan of salvation, extending through both Old and New Covenants.

Is there any logical reason to conclude that Sabbatarian symbolism associated with the kingdom promises has been changed? Elsewhere in Hebrews the author talks about Old Covenant religious practices that were shadows of the New Covenant. These were significantly altered with the coming of the New Covenant. He talks about a better priesthood, a better sacrifice, a better mediator, and a better temple, all fulfilled in Christ. But he nowhere talks about a better Sabbath. If he meant that Sabbath observance is fulfilled in a new way, and he was able to express himself so clearly on other like issues, then why not here? Instead, in chapter 4 he talks about what has not been fulfilled and therefore "remains," in other words what has *not* passed away nor changed.[309]

Remember this vital point – If Sabbath observance symbolizes salvation, in both Old and New Covenants, and the New Covenant is a continuing process not yet complete, then is it any wonder the author of Hebrews mentions that Sabbath observance 'continues' as a sign of Christian salvation? The literal, final fulfillment of our promise of kingdom rest is New Jerusalem, the eternal kingdom described Revelation 21. If that is yet future – if our promise of rest is not yet completely fulfilled – is it any wonder that Sabbath observance is described as something that continues under the New Covenant?

Remember how some of the early church fathers used a similar argument about the New Covenant and the fact it is not yet completely fulfilled. But in their case they used it to support conversion to Sunday observance (see above pages 69 and following). They observed that Christian salvation is a new creation, and it has not yet ended. That part is true. Therefore they said, however, Christians cannot continue to use Sabbath, which points to *completion* of creation, to symbolize something

---

[309] How could there be a change in the kingdom promises if all were planned and present from the beginning? That is the underlying point of the author's argument. All God's plans of salvation were in place from the start, therefore all are Sabbatarian, and what we find in the New Testament church of his time, including Sabbath observance, is only a continuation of what always existed.

that has only just begun and is on-going. Instead, they reasoned, Christians therefore should observe a day that honors the *beginning* of creation, in other words Sunday the first day of the week.

There is a certain symbolic rationale to that argument. However, when viewed in light of Hebrews chapter 4, we see what a mistake that was. The author of Hebrews clearly is under the impression that this same reasoning – the fact that Christian salvation is a current, on-going process, begun but not yet complete, plus his argument that all God's plans of salvation are Sabbatarian – is why Sabbath observance continues under the New Covenant.

Some Hellenistic Christians suggest that the phrase *"cease from their labors"* in verse 10 signifies to cease from sin. But this verse also says that we cease from our labors *"as God did from his."* Since God does not sin, that analogy simply doesn't make sense. Others say it signifies ceasing from our own works so we can rest in Christ's works of righteousness, which he has performed for us. But there again this goes entirely against the context. In the following verse (vs 11) it continues, *"Let us therefore make every effort to enter that rest, so that no one may fall through such disobedience...."* This is talking about persevering in works of obedience in order to enter God's spiritual rest in Christ.

The problem is that today many want to read back into Hebrews 4 all the much later controversy over law and grace, Sabbath versus Sunday, that had hardly gotten started when this letter was written. The controversy at the time Hebrews 4 was written was something else entirely – the delay in the appearance of the promised kingdom. Christian Jews at the time would have understood it in the simple biblical terms the author used to express himself. If the author of Hebrews actually were talking about a different interpretation which requires terminating Sabbath as the traditional symbol of kingdom rest, then at some point he would have had to make that clear. But there is nothing in the text indicating that.

There is nothing in Hebrews 4 to suggest Christians should replace Sabbatarian symbolism with something supposedly more spiritual that points exclusively to Heaven. Sabbath observance celebrates **both** physical and spiritual creation. Indeed it celebrates Jesus, as Paul testifies, *"for in him* [Jesus] *all things in heaven and on earth were created"* (Col 1:15).

The Key Issue

The author of Hebrews apparently does not set out intentionally to address the issue of Sabbath versus Sunday. But in the process he lays out a powerful confirmation for the continuation of Sabbatarian symbolism and Sabbath observance under the New Covenant.

In the end, we find New Testament salvation itself is a Sabbatarian promise, wrapped in Sabbatarian symbolism and accompanied by Sabbatarian institutions to remind us and keep us focused on those promises.

In the end, the real question of Sabbath versus Sunday is not the spirituality of heaven versus earthly materialism, nor even the resurrection. The real issue is biblical revelation and symbolism, versus human philosophic reasoning and pagan symbolism.

When the author of Hebrews says those who enter God's spiritual rest in Christ (present tense) also participate in God's *Sabbatismos* rest by observing the weekly Sabbath, does that imply something about what Christians **should** be doing? Or, should we through human reason invent our own heavenly spirituality, which is all right as long as we wrap it in some form of spiritual sentiment and religious idealism?

When Paul was warning the church at Colossae against this very theology, which says we must change or discard Jewish practices in order to align ourselves with Heaven, he said this:

> See to it that no one takes you captive through philosophy and empty deceit, according to human tradition.... (Col 2:8)

This is the choice all Christians must make – biblical revelation versus human philosophy and tradition.

Appendix C

The Great Indo-European Pagan Reformation

The reformation of pagan religion in seventh and sixth century B.C. Greece was only one part of a much larger phenomenon extending throughout the Indo-European world. Similar phenomena occurred at about the same time in both Persia and India. The purpose of this appendix is to briefly describe this and related phenomena that lend historical perspective.

The primary subject of this volume has been the history of the pagan religious reformation in the Mediterranean world, because it was here that it coalesced into a force that derailed the Primitive Christian church. When we look at the entire phenomenon, however, stretching from Greece and Rome to as far as India, we see striking patterns of similarity in both theological reasoning and in historical timing. One of the most extraordinary coincidences is that the pagan reformation not only occurred simultaneously in different parts of the ancient world, but it also occurred simultaneously with dramatic changes in biblical religion in Israel.

The great pagan reformation occurred at approximately the same time the first temple in Jerusalem was destroyed. This was the beginning of the era of the Hebrew prophets, whose writings foretold the temple's destruction and spoke more openly of a coming reformation in biblical religion, the Messianic age. The Hebrew prophets described this future age as a time when God's Spirit would be poured out upon mankind. At that time, they said, man would worship God from the heart and the sacrifice of animals would be replaced by the sacrifice of a Messiah.

The great pagan reformation echoed some of these same biblical themes, emphasizing inner spirituality and rejection of animal sacrifice.

Though it is not commonly discussed in print, the widespread changes during this time have been noticed by some scholars, who refer to it as the Axial Period.[310] For us, however, I think the striking point is that at the very time when a transformation of biblical religion and the coming birth of Christianity began to be advertised more openly in Hebrew prophecy, throughout the pagan world we find the beginning of a dramatic religious transformation that uniquely equipped paganism to meet the coming challenge.

As the apostles said, the mystery of lawlessness was long predestined to occur.[311] By the time Jesus was born the opposition had been preparing for nearly seven centuries.

Now, on to our review of the pan-Indo-European, pagan religious reformations:

Persia [312]

The great religious reformation began in Persia with a man named Zoroaster (Greek corruption of Zarathustra). Though it sometimes is disputed, it appears he was an historical figure whose career spanned the end of the seventh century and start of the sixth centuries B.C. According to Iranian tradition he lived 258 years before Alexander, by which his life span is calculated at approximately 630–553 B.C. He began to experience visions at the age of 30 and started preaching at 40.

Before Zoroaster, Indo-Iranian religion was a polytheistic sacrificial system. The primary sacrifices were oxen and the *haoma* plant from which an intoxicating beverage was made. Ritual sacrifice, during which priests and celebrants consumed the sacred *haoma*, was believed to be vital for maintaining all forms of life.

The gods were associated with various socioeconomic groups or castes (similar to but not as strictly defined as the castes of India). The gods associated with the highest order of mankind were the *daivas* (heavenly

---

[310] The Axial Period is often described as a profound cultural shift, which some describe in psychosocial terms as a transformation from mythopoeic thought and outer-directed 'shame' consciousness, to scientific (transcendent cause) thought patterns and inner-directed guilt consciousness.

[311] For example, Jude 4, 2 Peter 2:3.

[312] See **EB**, articles "Zoroaster" and "Zoroastrianism."

ones).[313] A subgroup of these were the *asuras* (lords), who were noted for having an especially ethical character. Zoroaster rejected the worship of all the gods except for Ahura Mazda, one of the *asuras*.

Zoroaster's reforms were far-reaching. He banned the sacrifice of animals and refocused the religion on ethical issues of human conduct – honesty, loyalty, justice, etc. He taught that the world will soon end in a great cataclysm of fire to be followed by a new creation. In the meantime, at death the souls of the righteous are led to heaven to await the new creation, while the damned are sent to hell.

Over time, Zoroastrianism became starkly dualistic and various new forms evolved, such as Zurvanism in which some scholars see parallels to Gnostic Christianity.[314]

After Zoroaster's death the new religion spread southward into Afghanistan and westward through Persia. It was known and followed by many during the Persian domination of the Near East, but it did not become the state religion of Persia until after Christ. Today it survives only in India and Pakistan, among the Parsees, principally around the Indian city of Bombay.

The Greeks came into contact with Zoroastrianism during the Hellenistic period when they conquered the entire Near East including Persia. In the West, Zoroaster became a famous name. Many religious writings were apocryphally attributed to Zoroaster and circulated under his name. Some Hellenistic Greeks claimed that their great pagan reformation was inherited from Zoroaster. There were claims that Pythagoras had been taught by Zoroaster. Scholars, however, generally do not accept the claims of extremely early contact between Zoroaster and either Orphism or Pythagoreanism. Despite all the similarity and later contacts, the Persian and Greek reformations generally are believed to have been parallel but separate phenomena.

---

[313] Once again we encounter the separation of man into classes that relate to their spirituality. In later times, among Gnostic Christians, this evolved into the doctrine of predestination, i.e. certain classes of man were capable of salvation, which others were not.

[314] As it spread, Zoroastrianism picked up many of the gods, practices and teachings originally rejected by its founder. This includes Mitra, who became for some the son of Ahura Mazda. This is the Mithra of the Mithraic Mysteries, a Roman mystery religion prominently described in *Spirit of Antichrist*, volume two of our series The World of Primitive Christianity.

India [315]

Before the great pagan religious reformation, India followed a tradition known as Vedic Hinduism. This early religion is contained in religious texts called the Vedas and Brahmanas. It was a polytheistic sacrificial system similar to the original pagan religion of Iran, equally based on the sacrifice of animals and the intoxicating juice of the *haoma* plant.

In India the great reformation is not identified with any single individual. It first appeared in the form of a new body of scripture, called the Upanishads. The earliest Upanishads were written (you guessed it) at the end of the seventh and beginning of the sixth centuries B.C., and continued to be written after that for about 300 years.

The Upanishads introduce the idea of the cycle of reincarnation. Together with this comes the idea of *karma*, the ethical argument behind reincarnation. Karma refers to a type of fate which carries over from one's former life to a following life. If you were good in your previous life, you have 'good' *karma,* which leads to rebirth on a higher level and good luck and success in your next life. Likewise evil conduct leads to 'bad' karma, which brings bad experiences that punish you for your sins in the previous life. This by its very nature downplays animal sacrifice. Religious benefit now comes not from sacrifice, but from ethical conduct. Only in this way can one be reborn into higher forms of life and eventually escape from the wheel of rebirth. Sacrifice gradually fell into disfavor, replaced by personal worship of deity. This generally takes the form of prayer, offerings of food and flowers, incense and music.

In the West we often tend to laugh at the Hindu doctrine of reincarnation as backward. In doing so we fail to appreciate, regardless of whether such beliefs are true or false, that reincarnation is intimately bound up with the introduction of a new and advanced spirituality based on ethical and moral conduct.

Reincarnation is a common feature of the pagan reformation in both India and in the West. Reincarnation was taught by both Orphism and Pythagoreanism, the very groups that initiated the great pagan reformation in Greece. Here too, as well as in India, it was linked with the immortality of the soul and the soul's eventual return to God. When Gnosticism

---

[315] See **EB**, article "Hinduism."

merged Hellenistic religion with Christianity, reincarnation came along with it. Some Gnostic Christian sects continued to teach reincarnation for several centuries after Christ. The doctrine generally died out in the West after the demise of the classic Gnostic sects of the second and third centuries A.D.

Hinduism is polytheistic, but within a framework of monotheism. There is one cosmic Spirit called Brahman. Everything else – the gods, the material world – are illusions. Individual souls are one with Brahman. He is the only true reality. Everything evolved from him, and ultimately all will return to him.

Salvation means reunion with the ultimate reality – the monotheistic divinity Brahman. Return to Brahman is achieved through repeated rebirth to higher forms of life, ending in a merger with Brahman. The mechanisms for directing oneself in this upward path are meditation, acquisition of knowledge, asceticism, devotion to the gods and piety in general.

In the beginning of the Indian reformation, the doctrines of reincarnation and karma circulated among small groups of ascetics. From there they spread rapidly, till they had achieved near universal acceptance by the time of the Buddha several centuries later.

Hinduism always has been an open, ecumenical tradition that sees truth in all religions. In this pluralistic world many sects developed, some of which, notably Jainism and Buddhism, became separate religions that carried forward the religious reformation that began with the Hindu writings known as the Upanishads. We now turn to these offshoots from the Hindu reformation.

Jainism [316]

Jainism took a much more radical path in its reformation of Vedic religion than mainstream Hinduism. Jainism emphasizes love and compassion as the primary ethical standard. "Hurt no one" is the cardinal principle. This stems from a very literal interpretation of reincarnation. All living things are part of one spiritual community, as souls migrate through all life forms in the struggle to rise to higher states of existence. To cause emotional or physical hurt to any living thing is to harm the common spirit that resides in all of us.

---

[316] See **EB**, article "Jainism."

Therefore the sacrificial system of the original Vedic scriptures, to kill defenseless animals, was considered grossly evil. The sincerity of Jainism is witnessed in its programs of mercy, which include building asylums and rest facilities for old and diseased animals where they are maintained with kindness until they die.

Jains do not believe in the existence of the gods. Sometimes they are accused of atheism. However, it would appear this is more a philosophic argument over the Hindu doctrine that the world is an illusion. Hindus themselves believe the entire cosmos outside of Brahman is illusory, including even the gods.

The primary concern of Jainism is the evolution and perfection of the soul. Numerous principles and regulations are provided to assist the believer in developing love and compassion. Jainism today still claims a following of between one and two million in India.

Buddhism [317]

Buddhism also promotes a more radical reformation of Vedic religion than was carried out within Hinduism. Buddhism totally rejects the authority of their 'Old Testament' (the Vedic scriptures) as well as the Hindu caste system.

The Buddha began his career with a sermon at Benares, India, in the fifth century B.C. (Some scholars believe it may have been the fourth century.) He addressed his words to *"him who has given up the world."* He taught that neither materialism nor extreme asceticism can solve the human problem. Between those two extremes he championed 'the Middle Path,' a moderately ascetic system of psychological freedom from material life. Buddhism shows a striking resemblance to some Gnostic systems, such as those of Valentinus and Basilides, which focused on craving and emotional longing as the root of suffering.[318] For Buddhists the essential problem of human existence is craving for and attachment to material things. Because the material world is illusory, always changing and passing away, such cravings can never be permanently satisfied.

---

[317] See **EB**, article "Buddhism."

[318] See Basilides, above, p 50, and Valentinian concepts of psychological freedom from materiality and the law in section "Gnostic Theories of Non-material Spirituality," p 126 ff.

Release from the cycle of rebirth and union with the divine is Nirvana, a state in which all craving and suffering cease. The definition of Nirvana is left intentionally vague, since it is believed to be outside the world of sensory perception and human knowledge, therefore essentially unknowable. It is not clear whether individual consciousness survives after achieving Nirvana.

The spiritual path of Buddhism leads to insight, knowledge, tranquility, higher knowledge, enlightenment and finally Nirvana. On a practical level, Buddhists are encouraged to lead a simple and mildly ascetic life, avoiding emotional attachment to material things and pleasures. Morality and the social virtues of family and civic duty are emphasized.

Today there are more than 150 million followers of Buddhism around the world. Predominantly Buddhist countries include Japan, Thailand, Burma, Cambodia, Laos and Tibet. Buddhists comprise a minority in China, and only a small number still live in India.

Antinomian Buddhism

Buddhism, like Gnosticism in the West, developed its own tradition of antinomian spirituality. Antinomian ideas were preached by a number of later schools of Buddhism, and this occurred independently of the growth of similar ideas in Hellenistic Christianity in the West.

We find antinomianism expressed in various Buddhist morality tales. Typical of these is the following story. It begins with two monks who embark on a long trip. They have been walking all morning side by side, in complete silence as is their custom. Buddhism in most of its forms tends toward asceticism, and to understand the story one must keep in mind that for monks women are absolutely taboo. To as much as touch a woman is a terrible infraction. Well, to continue the story, the two monks come to a stream swollen with water. There stands a helpless old woman unable to cross. She begs them for help. The first monk, without saying a word, picks her up and carries her across.

The two monks proceed along the road as before, in total silence. Finally after several hours the second monk, seething inside and unable to contain himself any longer, blurts out: "What in Nirvana's name were you thinking? Do you know what you just did?!" The first monk, after an appropriate pause, turns to him and asks quietly, "Are you still carrying her?"

Buddhism emphasizes psychologically letting go of the material world in order to be united with God. If you carry that out to its logical conclusion it can be interpreted to mean letting go even of your own spiritual system and rules as they relate to material things. Remember the Gnostic Christian habit of teaching "indifference" to worldly matters. That was one of the principle themes of Nicolaitan Gnosticism. One must avoid negative as well as positive attachment to the material world. For many Gnostics, that meant you can indulge in sin as long as you don't become emotionally attached to it. In like fashion, the monk in this story could break the rules as long as he emotionally let go of it. In other words, as long as his heart and mind, his inner man, are fixed on the things above, and what happens on a material level does not distract him from devotion to God, then it can't hurt him. In fact, breaking the rules, as demonstrated in this story, is a sign he has achieved freedom from the material world. He has achieved true liberation.

It is no surprise some scholars refer to Buddhism as the "Gnosticism of the East."

Over time many distinct schools developed within Buddhism. One prominent branch, Tantrism, uses magical ritual, spells, sounds and gestures to attain mystical union with the divine.[319] Such union sometimes was expressed symbolically as a sexual union between certain gods and their consorts. In some forms of Tantric Buddhism, however, this was taken quite literally. Thus sexual acts were developed into spiritual exercises intended to unite worshippers with the divine. This caused great scandal, both inside Buddhism and in Indian society in general. It is believed to have been a factor in the eventual decline and near disappearance of Buddhism in its Indian homeland.

Summary

Parallels between the great pagan reformation in Greece, Persia and India are only too obvious. In addition to the unusual coincidence in timing, we have rejection of animal sacrifice, focus on ethical conduct, rejection of material life in favor of the inner life of the spirit, mystical identification of the soul with the heavens, immortality of the soul, focus

---

[319] Recall that forms of magic played an important role in some Gnostic sects, and in Neopythagoreanism and Neoplatonism.

on the fate of the soul in the afterlife, return of the soul to God, mystical union with God, and antinomianism.

What began as a pan-Indo-European, pagan phenomenon, today has spread throughout Asia in the form of Hinduism and Buddhism and throughout the world in the form of Hellenistic Christianity and Hellenistic Islam. (The Hellenistic role in Islamic religion will be covered in a future volume.) In fact, the pagan reformation from the seventh to sixth centuries B.C. now dominates the entire modern world. Thus has been fulfilled the words of the book of Revelation, speaking of the great harlot, *"...and **all nations** were deceived by your sorcery"* (Rev 18:23). Once we understand the historical background of the great pagan reformation, we see how literally that is to be understood. (Much more of the history behind these prophecies of Revelation, the great pagan reformation, and related topics, will appear in later volumes of our series, The World of Primitive Christianity.)

Why did the great pagan reformation originally occur only in the Indo-European world? This is a major topic of its own. Briefly, however, I believe the answer lies in understanding the history of the Indo-European dispersion. New evidence developed in recent decades indicates the final Indo-European dispersion began in the Near East, in eastern Anatolia (modern Turkey), at a much later date than originally thought. This occurred early in the second millennium B.C., which places it not long after the biblical Flood.

That explains certain aspects of Genesis chapters 10 and 11. These biblical passages derive many Indo-European societies from a dispersion of Noah's descendants occurring after the Flood. Note that eastern Anatolia is the region in which Noah's ark landed (the mountains of Ararat). The historical record associates an Indo-European dispersion from this area with the invention of chariot warfare. This gave certain descendants of Noah the power to suddenly expand and conquer other existing societies in the region.[320] The latest historical evidence perfectly supports this view as recorded in the Genesis account.

The point is that Greece, Rome, Persia and India were major Indo-European civilizations with roots in the Near Eastern tradition of animal sacrifice, cosmology, etc. handed down from the Genesis creation. This explains, in part, the similarities in sacrificial, ritual and other religious

---

[320] See Robert Drews, *The Coming of the Greeks: Indo-European Conquests in the Aegean and the Near East.* Princeton, Princeton U. Press, 1988.

beliefs and practices between ancient Israel and its many Near Eastern neighbors. Many of these religious orientations, including the same focus on sacrifice as found in Hebrew religion, were disseminated throughout the Indo-European world as part of the Indo-European dispersion.

If Hebrew religion were to be transformed as the prophets foretold,[321] and this new religion were to be extended to the Gentiles as the prophets also foretold,[322] then these Indo-European societies would be the primary target audiences the opposition would want to protect against the next stage in the revelation of God's plan of salvation. It is these cultures in which a revised Hebrew religion naturally would have the greatest appeal and sense of relevance.

Paganism's great reformation effectively subverted the introduction of Christianity in the Mediterranean world, specifically in the Indo-European societies of Greece and Rome. Further east, especially in India, it sought to counter the spread of Christianity by offering similarly spiritual religious options. Viewed from a short-term perspective, the great pagan reformation was a smashing success.

The great reformation was a critical issue for pagan religion essentially only in the Indo-European world. The world outside Indo-European lands was dominated by a primitive religion called Shamanism. The inner life of the spirit is nothing new to even the most primitive shamanistic cultures. Therefore the rationale for mounting a pagan reformation as a defensive action against the impending introduction of Christianity simply did not exist in the non-Indo-European world.

The non-Indo-European world and its shamanistic religious heritage do play an important role in the story of Christian apostasy, however. In volume two of our series, *Spirit of Antichrist,* we see how Shamanism infiltrated into ancient Babylonian religion, and played such a key role in the evolution of religious apostasy that it is mentioned in the Old Testament and even in the book of Revelation.

---

[321] Jer 31:31–34.

[322] For example Gen 26:4, Gal 3:8–9.

Appendix D

Balaam as a Symbol of Apostasy in the Primitive Church

The New Testament uses two human symbols to represent the apostasy that launched the mystery of lawlessness and ripped apart the primitive church. These are the reference to Jezebel in Revelation 2:20, and to Balaam in Revelation 2:14, Jude 11, and 2 Peter 2:15.[323]

Of the two by far the more interesting is Balaam, both because he is mentioned more frequently in the New Testament and because of the curious events of his life recorded in the Old Testament. This is the story of the apostasy of the Israelites as they fought their way through hostile nations on their way to entering the Promised Land. It is the story that sticks in most people's minds because of the enigmatic and almost comical story of Balaam's talking donkey.

As recorded in Numbers chapters 22–25, the story begins with a non-Israelite holy man named Balaam. He is approached by the king of Moab who is afraid of being overrun by the migrating Israelites on their way to the Holy Land. The king wants Balaam to curse Israel so he will be able to conquer them on the battlefield. Balaam flatly refuses. Some commentaries stress what they call the 'sympathetic' treatment Balaam receives in Numbers 22–24. Here he is depicted almost like one of God's own faithful prophets. He repeatedly states he will not do anything contrary to Yahweh's instructions, regardless of the consequences. In the process he

---

[323] The full story of Jezebel as a symbol of apostasy is presented in *Spirit of Antichrist,* the second volume of our series The World of Primitive Christianity.

utters four oracles, the last one of which is widely regarded as a prophecy of the coming of Messiah.

In Numbers 25 we read that the Moabites, instead of attacking Israel militarily, befriended Israel. They openly encouraged assimilation, inviting Israel to join them in their religious worship. A primary mechanism for this assimilation was the availability of sexual activity with Moabite women, which was a common feature of the pagan culture and religions of that time:

> ...the people began to have sexual relations with the women of Moab. These invited the people to the sacrifices of their gods.... Thus Israel yoked itself to the Baal of Peor, and the Lord's anger was kindled against Israel. (Num 25:1–3)

Further on, in Numbers 31:16, we get a much more negative view of Balaam. Here we are told the Moabite attempt at ecumenical union and assimilation with Israel was a conscious ploy executed on the advice of Balaam himself.

Why are the details of Balaam's interaction with ancient Israel prominently preserved in the Old Testament, and why do New Testament writers prominently mention him in connection with Christian apostasy? The story ends with Israel killing Balaam during the subsequent conquest of another tribe, the Midianites (31:8). Who really was Balaam and what does he represent? Was Balaam a faithful servant or enemy of Yahweh? Did he turn away after an initial faithfulness?

I believe the two depictions of Balaam are reconciled in the story of Balaam's donkey. The biblical account begins with Balaam on his way to meet the king of Moab. At first glance Yahweh seems rather unfair. Yahweh has appeared to Balaam and told him it is all right for him to go. However, on the way an angel blocks Balaam's passage. At first only the donkey can see the angel. Frightened, the donkey keeps turning off the path. Balaam beats the donkey to make it go forward until finally the donkey miraculously talks. Balaam then sees the angel and is told how close he came to being killed. In beating the donkey he was unwittingly driving himself towards destruction.

It would appear the whole thing was merely a setup by Yahweh to terrify Balaam. He is on his way to meet the king of Moab, who is making offers of ever-greater wealth and fame if only Balaam will defect to the other side. Now Balaam goes on to meet the king with the hair still standing up on the back of his neck and a fresh reminder he is being tracked by angels who can lift his head at a moment's notice if he goes against Yahweh. That doesn't sound like the kind of thing Yahweh would have to do to a sincerely faithful prophet. Numbers 22:32 reveals that already at that time Yahweh recognized Balaam was evil (*because your way is perverse before me*). Balaam's subsequent treachery bears that out.

What then does Balaam symbolize for Christians? Why did multiple authors of the New Testament choose Balaam as a symbol of Gnostic and Hellenistic apostasy?

- Balaam symbolizes people in the religion business. Recall that he was a traditional holy man and diviner who contacted gods and spirits for a price. We see this in Numbers 22:7, *"So the elders of Moab and the elders of Midian departed* [to meet Balaam] *with the fees for divination in their hand...."* The King of Moab's appeals to Balaam, enticing him with promises of wealth and honor, undoubtedly were based on experience and foreknowledge of Balaam's method of operation. Two of the New Testament references, Jude 11 and 2 Peter 2:15, mention Balaam's greed.

- Balaam symbolizes people who know the true God and respect and fear him to a significant degree, who even preach and prophesy in his name. The problem is they are not content to remain faithful to just one religion and the true God, and they try to play the angles.

  In spite of his knowledge of God, Balaam wanted the wealth and glory offered by the world around him, and in the end he tried to play both sides. What was Balaam thinking when he set up the plan for the Moabites to draw Israel into ecumenical apostasy? Apparently he did not think he was outright rebelling against Yahweh. Otherwise he would have just cursed Israel as he was asked to do in the first place. After the scary incident with the talking donkey, Balaam apparently was aware of the risk and so he chose another approach. He probably reasoned that technically he was not violating Yahweh's injunction against cursing Israel, so he could rationalize he was obedient and Yahweh would not come after him.

  Balaam had witnessed God's power and he could have decided then and there to become loyal to Yahweh and Yahweh alone. But that would have meant giving up his outside support and established financial base.

- Balaam symbolizes persons who even know and witness for Jesus. A passage in his final oracle reads, *"I see him, but not now; I behold him, but not near – a star shall come out of Jacob, and a scepter shall rise out of Israel...."* (Num 24:17). This was widely interpreted in the early church as a messianic prophecy.[324]

- Along with all the above, Balaam symbolizes ecumenism. Specifically he symbolizes the ambition and greed that leads to religious treachery and apostasy, mixing worship of Yahweh and the Messiah with foreign religious systems, including antinomianism and the licensing of immorality as seen in Numbers 25. Balaam's modus operandi was to go with the flow, to hire out to whomever and whatever advanced his own ambitions, to defer to whatever was popular and in demand. That is why Yahweh had to scare Balaam so severely to keep him in line. He could have become faithful to Yahweh alone. At the least he could have walked away from it after having faithfully discharged his responsibility by refusing to curse Israel. However, looking out over the huge mass of Israelites from the mountaintop, as Balaam did, anyone could see this new Yahweh religion was going to be an important part of the religious landscape of the future. It made sense to get in on the action.

Balaam was a famous religious figure who commanded respect and honor over a wide area. He served many tribes and kings and presumably various religions. Presumably he was making a good living from his ecumenical approach to religion. However, from his experience with the donkey and the angel, Balaam knew Yahweh was not to be taken lightly, not just another of the superstitions or mystical spirits or demonic powers that were part of his usual bag of tricks. Still, he was not about to give up his traditional power base and fame, and ally himself solely with Yahweh – a jealous God who places such narrow limitations on his followers plus a strict moral code to boot.

Balaam and those like him live in a world where lines are fuzzy and you leave yourself room to maneuver. The solution to Balaam's problem was ecumenism and the licensing of immorality. Apparently he thought that *technically* this fulfilled Yahweh's

---

[324] See Anchor Bible Dictionary, Article "Balaam."

command to not curse Israel. He thought he could get away with it, that it would be at least minimally acceptable to Yahweh. He thought he could have it all. But Yahweh indeed is a jealous God, and it cost Balaam his life.

Today, in the very same way, multitudes of Christians believe they are exempt from obedience and will be saved regardless of any degree of disobedience. They rationalize this by saying that *technically* they never advise people to disobey God. Instead, they only *license* disobedience, at the same time that, once again *technically*, they tell people it is better to not exercise that license. Even though they admit that multitudes of Christians avail themselves of that license, they insist, like Balaam, that *technically* they have not violated their relationship with Yahweh.

What we are talking about are people who preach and prophesy in the name of the true God and Jesus the Messiah, but are not willing to submit themselves to the limitations that necessarily involves. Their ambition leads them to compromise with foreign religions in order to extend their influence, to dream greater dreams, increase their following and hide their religious treachery under the umbrella of ecumenism and tolerance. What better description could one find for Hellenistic Christianity, both in the first century and today? Hellenistic Christians prophesy and preach in the name of Jesus. But, like Balaam they also are perverse through seeking success by incorporating the popular teachings and practices of the world around them.

The Hellenized Christianity of both Roman and Reformation churches, and its antinomianism and licensing of sin, is the Moabite religion to which we are being invited today. The ambition and dream of broadening our appeal, and embracing respectability and honor in the eyes of the world, continue the same struggle that confronted ancient Israel and first-century Christianity.

The Gnostic teacher Simon Magus, as described in the book of Acts, is a classic example of a latter day Balaam. The messages to the churches of Pergamum and Thyatira warn us this human tendency will be an ongoing problem among Primitive Christian churches, leading to ecumenical apostasy and licensing of sin just as happened in ancient Israel.

Is it any wonder Balaam became a popular symbol for Gnostic and Hellenistic apostasy among the authors of the New Testament? Is it any wonder we see the same problems repeating themselves in our midst yet today?

Bibliography

Ankenberg, John; Weldon, John, Knowing *the Truth about Eternal Security*. Eugene Oregon, Harvest House, 1997

Barnabas, *The Epistle of Barnabas*. Loeb Classical Library, Apostolic Fathers Vol. 1. Cambridge, Harvard U. Press, 1985.

Bultmann, Rudolf, *Primitive Christianity in its Contemporary Setting*. Philadelphia, Fortress Press, 1980. (translated from German, 1949)

Corner, Daniel D., *The Believer's Conditional Security*. Washington, Pennsylvania, Evangelical Outreach, 2000.

Cumont, Franz, *After Life in Roman Paganism*. New York, Dover, 1959. (originally published 1922)

_____, *Astrology and Religion among the Greeks and Romans*. New York, Dover, 1960. (originally published 1912)

Danielou, Jean, S. J., *The Bible and the Liturgy*. Notre Dame, Indiana, U. of Notre Dame Press, 1966

Desjardins, Michel R., *Sin in Valentinianism*. Atlanta, Georgia, Scholars Press, 1990.

Eliade, Mircea, *Shamanism: Archaic Techniques of Ecstasy*. Princeton, Princeton U. Press, 1964. (Bollingen Series LXXVI edition; originally published in French, 1951)

Filoramo, Gionvanni, *A History of Gnosticism*. Oxford, Blackwell, 1990.

Fowden, Garth, The Egyptian Hermes. Princeton, Princeton University Press, 1986

Franzmann, Majella, *Jesus in the Nag Hammadi Writings*. Edinburgh, T&T Clark, 1996.

Geisler, Dr. Normal, *Chosen But Free*. Minneapolis, Minnesota, Bethany House Publishers, 1999.

Gerstner, John H., *Wrongly Dividing the Word of Truth*. Morgan, Pennsylvania, Soli Deo Glorian Publications, 2000.

Grant, Robert M., *Irenaeus of Lyons.* London, Routledge, 1997.

_____, *Gnosticism & Early Christianity.* New York, Harper and Row, 1966.

Guthrie, W.K.C., *Orpheus and Greek Religion.* Princeton, Princeton U. Press, 1993. (Originally published 1952)

Himmelfarb, Martha, *Ascent to Heaven in Jewish and Christian Apocalypses,* Oxford, Oxford University Press, 1993

Hogart, R. C., *The Hymns of Orpheus.* Grand Rapids, Phanes Press, 1993.

Hultgren, Arland J. and Haggmark, Steven A., *The Earliest Christian Heretics: Readings from their Opponents.* Minneapolis, Fortress Press, 1996.

Jaeger, Werner, *The Theology of the Early Greek Philosophers.* London, Oxford University Press, 1947.

Jonas, Hans, *The Gnostic Religion.* Boston, Beacon Press, 1962.

Kelly, J.N.D., *Early Christian Doctrines.* New York, Harper and Row, 1960.

Kerenyi, Carl, *The Gods of the Greeks.* New York, Thames and Hudson, 1980.

_____, *Eleusis: Archetypal Image of Mother and Daughter.* Princeton, Princeton U. Press, Bollingen Mythos Series 65 Vol 4, 1991. (Originally in Dutch, 1960)

_____, *Dionysos: Archetypal Image of Indestructible Life.* Princeton, Princeton U. Press, Bollingen Mythos Series 65 Vol 2, 1996. (from German manuscript, copyright 1976)

Kingsley, Peter, *Ancient Philosophy, Mystery, and Magic: Empedocles and Pythagorean Tradition.* Oxford, Clarendon Press, 1995.

Layton, Bentley, *The Gnostic Scriptures.* New York, Doubleday, 1987.

Lee, Philip J., *Against the Protestant Gnostics.* New York, Oxford University Press, 1987.

Lewy, Hans, *Chaldaean Oracles and Theurgy: Mysticism, Magic and Platonism in the Later Roman Empire.* Paris, Etudes Augustiniennes, 1978.

Logan, Alastair H. B., *Gnostic Truth and Christian Heresy.* Peabody, Hendrickson Publishers, 1996.

Ludemann, Gerd, *Heretics: The Other Side of Early Christianity.* Louisville, Westminster John Knox Press, 1996. (translated from the German, published 1995)

MacArthur, John Jr., *Saved without a Doubt,* Colorado Springs, Colorado, Chariot Victor Publishing, 1992.

_____, *The Gospel According to the Apostles,* Nashville, Tennessee, World Publishing, 2000.

Marrs, Roy A., *God's Revised Will and the "Rest" of the Story.* Lodi, California, Focus on Faith, 2001.

Martin, Luther H., *Hellenistic Religions, An Introduction.* New York, Oxford U. Press, 1987.

McVey, Steve, *Grace Walk.* Eugene, Oregon, Harvest House, 1995.

Nilsson, Martin P., *Greek Piety.* New York, Norton, 1969.

Nock, Arthur Darby, *Early Gentile Christianity and its Hellenistic Background.* New York, Harper & Row, 1964.

Pagels, Elaine, *The Gnostic Paul: Gnostic Exegesis of the Pauline Letters.* Philadelphia, Trinity Press International, 1975.

_____, *Adam, Eve, and the Serpent.* New York, Vintage Books, 1989.

Paul, Pope John, II, *Dies Domini, On Keeping the Lord's Day Holy.* Boston, Pauline Books & Media, 1998.

Perkins, Pheme, *Gnosticism and the New Testament.* Minneapolis, Fortress Press, 1993.

Robinson, James M. (editor), *The Nag Hammadi Library in English,* third edition. San Francisco, Harper and Row, 1988.

Ricken, Friedo, *Philosophy of the Ancients.* London, U. of Notre Dame Press, 1991.

Rudolph, Kurt, Gnosis: *The Nature & History of Gnosticism.* San Francisco, Harper, 1987. (translated from German, copyright 1977)

Sappington, Thomas J., *Revelation and Redemption at Colossae,* Journal for the Study of the New Testament Supplement Series 53. Sheffield, England, Sheffield Academic Press, 1991.

Scott, Alan, *Origen and the Life of the Stars.* Oxford, Clarendon Press, 1994.

Stanley, Charles, *Eternal Security.* New York, Walker & Company, 1999.

Simonetti, Manlio, *Biblical Interpretation in the Early Church.* Edinburgh, T&T Clark, 1994 (translated from Italian manuscript, 1981).

Sproul, R. C., *Faith Alone,* The Evangelical Doctrine of Justification. Baker Books,1995.

Taub, Liba Chaia, Ptolemy's Universe: The Natural Philosophical and Ethical Foundations of Ptolemy's Astronomy. Chicago, Open Court, 1993.

Ulansey, David, *The Origins of the Mithraic Mysteries: Cosmology and Salvation in the Ancient World.* Oxford, Oxford U. Press, 1989.

Vance, Laurence M., *The Other Side of Calvinism.* Pensacola, Florida, Vance Publications, 1991.

Vermaseren, Maarten J., *Cybele and Attis: The Myth and the Cult.* London, Thames and Hudson, 1977.

White, James R., *The Potter's Freedom.* Amityville, New York, Calvary Press Publishing, 2000.

Williams, Michael Allen, *Rethinking "Gnosticism".* Princeton, Princeton U. Press, 1996.

Witt, R.E., *Isis in the Ancient World.* Baltimore, John's Hopkins U. Press, 1971.

Glossary

Antinomian

Literally "against the law." Signifies a wide range of religious theology that rejects biblical law or the requirement for obedience to biblical law as part of Christian salvation. Antinomianism often takes the form of encouraging people to follow righteousness, merely denying that it is a necessary part of salvation.

Canaanite

Original inhabitants of the ancient land given to Israel. They practiced a religion revolving around the god Baal, through which Babylonian religion infiltrated into Hebrew religion.

Carnal Christian

The modern Protestant doctrine that one can be converted and saved, to be 'in Christ,' while continuing in a completely unchanged, 'carnal' state. This is a common teaching within Evangelical Protestantism, associated with the doctrine of extreme eternal security.

Chaldean Theology

The survival of ancient Babylonian mystical ideas among Neoplatonists in late antiquity, closely associated with theurgy. This theology revolves around connecting man to the heavens. The gods are believed to have sown the world with magical symbols that function as gateways to the other world (the heavens). By use of these symbols man contacts the heavens and so secures spirituality and ascent to the heavens after death.

Cosmology

The science or knowledge of the structure and function of the cosmos. Advances in astronomical understanding of the cosmos (that the world is round, a more accurate concept of outer space, the patterns of the movement of planets and stars) played a critical role in the development of Hellenistic religion.

Dispensationalism
An antinomian theology promoted by American Evangelical Protestantism, marked by a unique separation of history into time periods known as dispensations. It is most remarkable for its separation of Jesus' earthly ministry into two separate dispensations, teaching that the gospel of the kingdom, all references to lawfulness, repentance and Jewish practices in his ministry are part of the Old Covenant and have nothing to do with Christians. It began as an anarchist theology of the Plymouth Brethren, in southern England, from where it spread to the United States and has now been adopted by the majority of the American Evangelicalism movement.

Docetism
An ancient belief, first promoted by Gnostic Christianity in the first century. Docetism says that Jesus had two distinct natures, one spiritual, the other purely human, and those two natures never mix. Many Gnostics claimed that came about by a spirit Christ descending and resting on the human man Jesus.

This was the foundation of the Gnostic rejection of most of Jesus' earthly ministry, claiming it was contaminated by the unspiritual, human half of his nature. Because his human half was Jewish, this also was supposed to explain the Jewish and lawful themes in Jesus' earthly ministry, which they rejected. This theology in its larger form, including both the docetic nature of Christ and rejection of his earthly ministry, is specifically condemned by the apostle John in his first and second epistles.

This theology is replicated in modern dispensational theology promoted by Evangelical Protestantism, also in the modern Protestant theory that individual Christians have a docetic nature that does not mix.

Eternal Security, extreme eternal security
The belief that Christians are 'eternally secure,' i.e. once saved they cannot lose salvation regardless of conduct. A more moderate form of this belief says that God magically imposes at least some minimum good conduct on Christians and either maintains that state of good conduct, or if it lapses will forcibly renew that conduct before a Christian dies.

Extreme eternal security says that good conduct is preferable but neither one good act nor even repentance is necessary for salvation. A person

can be converted (intellectually recognize and profess that Jesus historically lived and died for our sins) yet continue wantonly in sinful conduct, to any degree, with no change in the inner man, and still be saved.
The only thing at risk is the reward given to the saints in heaven. Some
proponents of this belief say that Christians who lead openly sinful lives
will find joy in heaven, but throughout eternity will never experience
personal contact with their savior.

Evangelicalism , Evangelical Protestantism

One of the largest, multi-denominational movements within Protestantism, including many large and small Protestant churches, together numbering over 100 million members in the United States. Paradoxically,
Evangelicalism follows a conservative moral ethic and proclaimed 'fun-
damentalist' interpretation of the Bible, while at the same time promoting several radically antinomian theologies, especially extreme eternal
security and dispensationalism, which continue key Gnostic antinomian
theories from the early church era.

Their theological heritage comes from the radically antinomian Plymouth Brethren movement in England in the 1830s. Their theology of
extreme eternal security has surged in popularity since the 1980s. Beginning at about the same time, Evangelicalism has attracted interest and
a following among some Primitive Christian churches.

Gnostic Christianity, Gnosticism

An heretical branch of Christianity that began inside the apostolic
church in the first century as proto-Gnosticism. It was the first of many
movements to combine apostolic Christianity with the dominant philosophy and religion of its day, the pagan Hellenistic religion and philosophy descended from the great pagan reformation of the seventh and
sixth centuries B.C. There was a backlash against the openly antinomian
theology of Gnosticism that caused most Gnostic Christians to leave the
church beginning late in the first century. By the sixth century the classic Gnostic sects and their radically antinomian theology had largely
died out, not to be revived for more than 1,000 years until the Protestant
Reformation.

The key function of Gnosticism in the primitive church was initiating of
the Hellenization of the apostolic church, which continued to develop
after Gnosticism's departure, culminating in a second distinct wave of
Hellenistic apostasy in the fourth century.

Hellenistic

The era of Greece's dominance of the Near East, beginning with the conquests of Alexander the Great in the fourth century B.C. Also a designation of the culture, philosophy and religion of that era, which were the product of the great pagan reformation in Greece in the seventh and sixth centuries B.C.

The name comes from Helen, a Greek goddess, and the name Hellenes, a designation for the Greeks. Hellenistic culture and religion spread throughout the Near East and Mediterranean worlds, and continued seamlessly through the transition of political dominance by Greece to that of Rome.

Hellenistic Christianity

The product of the merger of apostolic Christianity and pagan Hellenistic religion, which occurred in two waves from the first to fourth centuries A.D. Essentially equates to modern, mainstream Christianity today, Catholic and Protestant, in all its many forms.

The first wave was initiated by Gnostic Christianity in the first century, the second completed by Neoplatonism and theurgy, and the adoption of Roman Hellenistic Christianity by the Roman emperors in the fourth century.

Hermetism

A religious movement that combined Hellenistic and Egyptian religion, from as early as the first century A.D. that exhibited traits characteristic of Gnosticism, Neoplatonism and theurgy.

Indo-European

A designation of the lands that share a common Indo-European linguistic heritage, from Europe through India. These same lands are also joined by having experienced the same pagan religious reformation in the seventh to sixth centuries B.C.

Mystery cult

Ancient religious worship of a deity who personifies the seasonal ebb and flow of fertility in the world. A savior-like deity annually dies during the barren season and is reborn with the return of fertility. Originally very materialistic, after the great pagan reformation it was reinterpreted to focus on the soul, liberation from the material world and return to heaven.

Mystery of lawlessness

A term used in the New Testament to refer to the antinomianism of Gnostic Christianity in the first century. It is a theology that licenses disobedience, called "lawlessness" because it says that Christian spirituality is completely divorced from biblical law. It is also called a "mystery" because it does not officially promote sin, but instead teaches a spirituality based exclusively on the inner, private revelation of truth through the Spirit and mystical connection to God and the heavens. The sense of the term "mystery" is something hidden. This accurately describes Gnostic theology, which hides its lawlessness and licensing of sin under the cover of a beautiful theory of heavenly spirituality that lifts man out of sin naturally, without participation or effort on man's part.

Nag Hammadi

The location in Egypt of a major find in the 1940s of ancient Gnostic Christian texts. Also a name designating the texts found there.

Neoplatonism

The form of Platonic philosophy during late antiquity. It played a major role in the second wave of apostasy that completed the Hellenization of the church, culminating in the fourth century A.D. Produced by a mingling of Neopythagoreanism and Middle Platonism. Tended towards religious mysticism and theurgy.

Orphism

The earliest manifestation of the great pagan religious reformation in ancient Greece. It was a reinterpretation of the Dionysian mysteries, an originally materialistic mystery cult. Orphism reinterpreted this to portray the pagan reformation's doctrines of the immortal soul in man, bondage to the material world, and the way of escape to eternal life in the heavens.

Plymouth Brethren

The origin of extreme eternal security and rejection of Jesus' earthly ministry as taught in Evangelical Protestantism.

The Plymouth Brethren is an anarchist Protestant movement founded in southern England in the 1830s, at the same time as the remnant apostolic church began its recovery after the end of its 1260 years of suppression. Brethren theology is a continuation of European social anarchist movements that sprang up at the time of Reformation. The basic concept is a typical anarchist theory that man does not require leadership, but if left alone will by nature discover and do what is religiously and socially right. In that religious context it was argued that the Spirit is all that is needed to guide Christians. The Brethren had no ordained ministers or church hierarchy. In their meetings members spoke as they were moved by the Spirit.

Organized churches were viewed as misguided attempts to continue in the way of the Old Covenant with its legalistic attempts to impose righteousness on man by law and government. Christianity, they believed, is a spiritual dispensation totally separate from ancient Israel, from Hebrew religion and its law. Darby, one of the main Brethren theologians and ministers, preached both extreme eternal security and rejection of Jesus' earthly ministry.

Jesus' earthly ministry was divided into two messages. Everything said in support of lawfulness, authority, etc. were designated as a message for the Jewish nation. When the Jews rejected Jesus, he then supposedly preached a second message for Christians, which was their antinomian, anarchist message of total freedom, which however, they believed leads Christians into righteousness naturally, exclusively by the influence of the Spirit.

Predestination

One of the prime doctrines of the Protestant Reformation, a form of which was first preached within Christianity by Gnostic Christians. Predestination claims that before the world began, God knew the name of every individual who would be born on earth, and from that he arbitrarily selected each individual he wishes to save. Once selected you have no choice – you will be saved. Those not selected have no hope of salvation. Man has no choice and plays no role in salvation.

Primitive Christianity

The form of Christianity that is the earliest (primitive) form of Christianity, practiced in the first century before the church became Hellenized. Also sometimes called 'Jewish Christianity' because it viewed

Christianity as a continuity from Hebrew religion and continued to observe the seventh-day Sabbath.

Pythagoreanism, Neopythagoreanism

The second earliest sect to preach the new religion of the great pagan reformation. Founded by Pythagoras in the sixth century B.C. First flourished in southern Italy. Emphasized mathematics and science as a manifestation of the divine order and intelligence of the heavens. Pursued political dominance in Italy at which it failed and soon disappeared as an organized movement.

In the fourth century B.C. Pythagoreanism introduced the new religion of the pagan reformation to Plato. In the first century B.C., reappears at Rome as Neopythagoreanism, where it once again influences Platonism, resulting in Neoplatonism and theurgy.

Reformation (Great Pagan Reformation)

Not to be confused with the Protestant Reformation of the 16th century A.D. This was a great reformation of *pagan* religion in the seventh to sixth centuries B.C., which occurred simultaneously in various Indo-European lands, from Europe to India. The reformation was a transformation of pagan mystery cult religion, changing from an original focus on man's fate and success in the material world, to man's inner spiritual state and the fate of the soul in the afterlife. In Greece this was associated with dramatic advances in astronomical science, which in part prompted and helped shape this reassessment of religious belief.

In Greece, it produced pagan Hellenistic religion, which spread throughout the Mediterranean and Near Eastern worlds, collided with Christianity almost immediately after the foundation of the church, resulting in Hellenistic Christianity, the dominant form of Christianity in our world today.

Regeneration

The doctrine that God supernaturally awakens the Christian convert's consciousness of spiritual things. In Reformation theology this takes an extreme form, saying that man is totally dead to spirituality and through regeneration God awakens the immortal soul, which automatically and irresistibly leads to conversion and salvation. Many Reformation Christians claim regeneration is imposed by God without consent and cannot be resisted; man has no say and does not participate in his own salvation.

Glossary

About the Author

Alan Knight holds a BA degree in anthropology and archeology from the University of the Americas at Puebla, Mexico. He subsequently participated in a post-graduate research program at Columbia University, New York City, focusing on historical studies in religion, and engaged in research at neighboring Union Theological Seminary. He is a Sabbatarian Christian and participant in the 'Primitive Christianity' movement as defined in the text.